ArtScroll Series®

Rabbi Nosson Scherman / Rabbi Meir Zlotowitz

General Editors

The WISDOM

by
ZVI RYZMAN

Adapted by
Rabbi Yehuda Heimowitz
from the Hebrew *Ratz K'tzvi*

Published by
Me'sorah Publications, ltd

IN THE HEBREW MONTHS

THE MONTHS, THE TRIBES, AND THE NAMES OF HASHEM

FIRST EDITION
First Impression … April 2009
Second Impression … May 2010

Published and Distributed by
MESORAH PUBLICATIONS, LTD.
4401 Second Avenue / Brooklyn, N.Y 11232

Distributed in Europe by
LEHMANNS
Unit E, Viking Business Park
Rolling Mill Road
Jarow, Tyne & Wear, NE32 3DP
England

Distributed in Israel by
SIFRIATI / A. GITLER — BOOKS
6 Hayarkon Street
Bnei Brak 51127

Distributed in Australia and New Zealand
by **GOLDS WORLDS OF JUDAICA**
3-13 William Street
Balaclava, Melbourne 3183
Victoria, Australia

Distributed in South Africa by
KOLLEL BOOKSHOP
Ivy Common
105 William Road
Norwood 2192, Johannesburg, South Africa

ARTSCROLL SERIES®
THE WISDOM IN THE HEBREW MONTHS
© *Copyright 2009, by* MESORAH PUBLICATIONS, Ltd.
4401 Second Avenue / Brooklyn, N.Y. 11232 / (718) 921-9000 / www.artscroll.com

ISBN 10: 1-4226-0898-0 / ISBN 13: 978-1-4226-0898-2

Typography by CompuScribe at ArtScroll Studios, Ltd.

Printed in the United States of America by Noble Book Press Corp.
Bound by Sefercraft, Quality Bookbinders, Ltd., Brooklyn N.Y. 11232

This volume is dedicated to the memory
of my father

Rabbi Heshel Ryzman ז״ל

הרב החסיד ר' יהושע השיל רייזמן ז״ל

נלב״ע בעשרה בטבת תשס״ט

He was extraordinary — an elevated personality, an accomplished *talmid chacham* and disseminator of Torah, a firebrand plucked from the flames of an august generation, the author of many works exploring the beauty of Torah.

All his life he blended "Torah and *kemach*," epitomizing the balance between greatness in Torah — which was his primary occupation — and success in business — which was secondary in his scale of priorities.

He was like a pillar of fire, showing the way for the community of Torah Jews, through the depth and unquenchable enthusiasm of his learning.

To him, nothing was sweeter than total immersion in Torah. He was a very great man, and his memory will remain fresh and inspirational.

תנצב״ה

Zvi Ryzman
and family
Los Angeles

Table of Contents

Cycle One:
The Months and the Tribes

Cycle Two:
The Months and the name of Hashem

Publisher's Preface

I T IS A PLEASURE AND A PRIVILEGE FOR US TO PUBLISH THIS outstanding work: a pleasure because the author is a very dear friend and an unusual talmid chacham, and a privilege because this book sheds light on an almost totally neglected topic and does it lucidly and brilliantly.

Zvi Ryzman is unique. He is a *talmid chacham* of the first order, and the recent winner of the coveted Jerusalem Prize for his many volumes of *Ratz K'tzvi*. He combines an unusual breadth of knowledge and analytical skill with the ability to find new insights on a breathtaking array of topics. To that he adds a contagious love of learning. He swims in the sea of the Talmud with extraordinary enthusiasm that sweeps up everyone with whom he comes in contact.

But there is another, very rare element to his distinction. As a very successful businessman, Reb Zvika is the very epitome of the classic תּוֹרָה וּגְדוּלָה בְּמָקוֹם אֶחָד, *Torah greatness and business success in the same person*. It is unusual to find someone in the business world who fulfills both dicta of the Mishnah: that one should combine his Torah with commerce, and that Torah should remain his primary interest.

It is a privilege to publish this work because, as the author writes in his preface, the study of the uniqueness of Rosh Chodesh is so rare as to be virtually extinct. In this brilliant *sefer*, the author provides insights not only into Rosh Chodesh but into the tribes of Israel, the profundity of the Four-letter Name of Hashem, and of the many roles of every Jew in the Divine scheme of Creation.

Mr. Ryzman is the dedicator of several volumes of ArtScroll's Schottenstein Hebrew and English editions of both Talmud Bavli and Yerushalmi, of the Hebrew *Mishnah Sheviis*, and of Chief Rabbi Yisrael Meir Lau's commentary to *Pirkei Avos*. He is a generous supporter of the Mesorah Heritage Foundation and member of its Board of Governors. The Foundation's retreats have been elevated by his erudite Torah lectures, just as his adopted community of Los Angeles is enriched by his Torah teaching.

Mrs. Betty Ryzman is a classic woman of valor, who takes pride in the learning of her husband and their sons, and whose kindness and generous spirit make her one of the most beloved members of her community.

This volume is dedicated להבחל״ח in memory of **Rabbi Heshel Ryzman** ז״ל whose recent passing in Tel Aviv left a void in the world of Torah. He, like his son, was an illustrious epitome of the Jew who lives in both worlds, but whose unquenchable love of learning made all other success seem insignificant. His monuments are his many Torah works — and, most of all, the magnificent generations he left behind.

acknowledgments

RABBI YEHUDA HEIMOWITZ, AN AMERICAN *TALMID CHACHAM* WHO lives in Jerusalem, is a skilled writer and translator. He adapted this manuscript from the Hebrew *Ratz K'tzvi*, and did justice to the high scholarly and literary quality of the original. It was a pleasure to work with him and we look forward to bringing more of his work to the Jewish public as the years go by.

Rabbi Yosef Bondi read the manuscript, assisted in the editing process, and made many valuable suggestions. His dedicated participation made an excellent work even better.

The beautiful cover and page design are the product of the creative genius of **Eli Kroen**, a graphics artist of the first order. His stunning jacket captures the essence of the book and his page design makes the content as easy on the eye as it is satisfying to the mind.

Mrs. Sury Englard and **Reizy Knopfler** typed the manuscript and entered the editing revisions with patience, skill, and dedication.

Mrs. Felice Eisner proofread with a careful and critical eye, and made valuable suggestions along the way.

Shmuel Blitz represents ArtScroll/Mesorah in Jerusalem and is an indispensable member of the team, both for his guidance and as the liaison between our staff in Israel and the editorial offices here.

Mendy Herzberg coordinated all aspects of the production with the efficiency that is his hallmark. He is cooperative, thorough, and unfailingly calm whatever the situation.

Finally, we are grateful to Hashem Yisbarach Who has granted us and our colleagues the enormous privilege of bringing His word to His people, and to publish a work of the quality of *The Wisdom in the Hebrew Months.*

Rabbi Meir Zlotowitz
Nissan 5769 / April 2009

Rabbi Nosson Scherman

PREFACE

> Roshei Chodesh (New Moons) are likened to the festivals, as the verse states, וּבְיוֹם שִׂמְחַתְכֶם וּבְמוֹעֲדֵיכֶם וּבְרָאשֵׁי חָדְשֵׁכֶם, *On a day of your gladness, and on your festivals, and on your new moons* (*Bamidbar* 10:10).
>
> The prophet even compares Rosh Chodesh to Shabbos: וְהָיָה מִדֵּי־חֹדֶשׁ בְּחָדְשׁוֹ וּמִדֵּי שַׁבָּת בְּשַׁבַּתּוֹ יָבוֹא כָל־בָּשָׂר לְהִשְׁתַּחֲוֹת לְפָנַי אָמַר ה׳, *It shall be that at every New Moon and on every Sabbath, all mankind will come to prostrate themselves before Me, says Hashem* (*Yeshayah* 66:23).
>
> *Pesikta, Shabbos and Rosh Chodesh,* 1

ROSH CHODESH IS LISTED IN THE TORAH, PROPHETS, AND Writings, together with Shabbos and the festivals:

- Torah: "On a day of your gladness, and on your festivals, and on your New Moons" (*Bamidbar* 10:10).

- Prophets: "It shall be that at every New Moon and on every Sabbath, all mankind will come to prostrate themselves before Me, says Hashem" (*Yeshayah* 66:23).

- Prophets: "He said, 'Why are you going to him today? It is not a New Moon or a Sabbath?' " (*II Melachim* 4:23).

- Writings: "Behold, I am building a Temple for the Name of Hashem, my God, in which to sanctify Him, to burn incense of spices before Him, to [set] a permanent stack [of show-bread] and [to bring] burnt-offerings each morning and evening, and on Sabbaths and on New Moons and on the festivals of Hashem, our God — a permanent duty upon Israel" (*II Divrei HaYamin* 2:3).

Chazal went one step further, stating that Rosh Chodesh itself is called a festival (*Shavuos* 10a). *Pesikta* (quoted above) continues that Rosh Chodesh is equal to the festivals and Shabbos.

These comparisons are not limited to a theoretical sphere — several halachos also show us the significance of Rosh Chodesh:

1) *Mishnah Berurah* writes that one who spends money on Rosh Chodesh feasts is praiseworthy. *Pesikta* teaches that the income one will have from one Rosh Hashanah to the next is preordained, aside from money spent [honor of] Shabbos, Festivals, and Rosh Chodesh.

2) When the *Beis HaMikdash* stood, those who saw the New Moon were allowed to transgress Shabbos prohibitions in order to travel to Jerusalem and bear witness before the Sanhedrin, so that [the court] could declare Rosh Chodesh and the Rosh Chodesh offerings [could be brought in the *Beis HaMikdash*] (*Mishnah, Rosh Hashanah* 1:4).

Perhaps the greatest expression of the stature of Rosh Chodesh appears in *Rashi's* first comment on the Torah: "Rav Yitzchak said: [God] need not have begun the Torah but from, 'This month is for you [the beginning of months]'" — the commandment to sanctify the New Moon.

———•◦•———

In ancient times, Rosh Chodesh occupied a glorious position in public life. The day was declared as Rosh Chodesh in a festive manner. "The head of Beis Din would declare, 'מְקוּדָשׁ, Sanctified!,' and all present would respond, 'מְקוּדָשׁ מְקוּדָשׁ, Sanctified! Sanctified!'" (*Mishnah, Rosh Hoshanah* 3:1).

The Rosh Chodesh sacrifices were then offered in the *Beis HaMikdash,* accompanied by the sounding of horns and the song of Levites, similar to the sacrifices of the Shabbos and Festival offerings.

The festivities were not limited to *Beis Din* and the *Beis HaMikdash*. Individuals would have festive banquets, as we see in the verse, *"David said to Yonasan, "Behold, tomorrow is the New Moon, when I would usually sit with the king to eat"* (*I Samuel* 20:5).

When the *Beis HaMikdash* was destroyed, the festive nature of Rosh Chodesh celebrations became diminished, to the point that it is difficult to differentiate between Rosh Chodesh and ordinary weekdays. Today our observance of Rosh Chodesh is usually limited to *Tefillah*: the addition of *Ya'aleh Veyavo*, the recitation of *Hallel*, Torah reading, and *Mussaf*.

In a chapter of *Shulchan Aruch* that contains only one law, we are taught, "It is a mitzvah to enhance Rosh Chodesh meals." *Taamei Haminhagim* (*Inyanei Rosh Chodesh, Kuntress Acharon* 450) cites the Chozeh of Lublin that the *Shulchan Aruch* placed the mitzvah of enhancing Rosh Chodesh meals into its own chapter to signify the importance of this mitzvah. Nevertheless, nowadays few people make a concerted effort to enhance their Rosh Chodesh meals, and there are almost no public celebrations of Rosh Chodesh.

On a more general level, we note with sadness that the significance of Rosh Chodesh has been lost from the collective heart of the Jewish nation. We have ceased to reflect on the months of the year, on discovering how each month is unique, and on studying the unique way to serve Hashem in accordance with the particular nature of that month. Indeed, many works discuss the festivals, but almost none devote much attention to the individual months of the year. Only two works — *Bnei Yissaschar* and *Pri Tzaddik* — discuss the subject at length.

Sefer Chassidim (261) teaches, "Love mitzvos that are like a *mes mitzvah* [a dead person with no relatives to tend to his burial]. If you see a mitzvah that is treated with disrespect, or a portion of Torah that others do not study, [you should pay attention to that mitzvah and study that section]. For instance, if you see people studying the orders of *Moed* and *Nashim*, study the order of *Kodashim*. If people are reluctant to learn the chapter of *Moed Kattan* dealing with bereavement, you should study it, and you will be rewarded greatly, for those sections are akin to a *mes mitzvah*." It seems that Rosh Chodesh and the study of the significance of the months has become this sort of *mes mitzvah*.

———•◦•———

Soon after I married and settled in Los Angeles, I became aware of a "new world": the world of Rosh Chodesh celebrations.

My uncle, R' Yechezkel Kornwasser *z"l*, organized monthly Rosh Chodesh meals, which were celebrated on rotation in the homes of the participants. These meals were like those of any other festival — with food, drink, and singing. My father-in-law, R' Yaakov Kornwasser *z"l*, would tell stories of the *Baal Shem Tov* and his disciples, and I was honored to deliver Torah discourses that would usually focus on the month we were celebrating.

As time went on, we began to celebrate Rosh Chodesh at our shul, the Young Israel of Hancock Park. We would have a festive meal, including Torah lectures, immediately following *Shacharis*. In time, several *baalei batim* who work near my office would arrange to free a few hours of their business day each Rosh Chodesh. We would daven *Minchah* early in the afternoon and join for a Rosh Chodesh feast. Most of the essays that appear in this book are based on the talks delivered at those occasions.

In short order, Rosh Chodesh in general and the uniqueness of the individual months in particular began to take on more meaning. A window into a world of deep, beautiful expositions and ideas was opened before me. It was a world that had been slowly disappearing, but it had a glorious past, and the prophet Yechezkel (45:17) promised that it would eventually regain its position alongside Shabbos and the festivals: "Upon the prince shall be [the responsibility for] the burnt-offering, the meal-offering and the libation, on the festivals, on the New Moons, and on the Sabbaths, on all the appointed times of the House of Israel."

We eagerly look forward to the days when the *Beis HaMikdash* will be rebuilt and we will celebrate Rosh Chodesh in such grand fashion — may we merit to see it speedily, in our days. Even now, however, Rosh Chodesh can uplift us; it can refresh and inject vigor into our service of Hashem. *Chiddushei HaRim* notes that the commandment of Rosh Chodesh states, "This month is *for you* the beginning of the months" (*Shemos* 12:2). Why *for you*? Because Hashem gives every Jew the potential to renew his service of Him. "It is in our hands, in our power" writes *Chiddushei Harim*. "If we only realize the opportunity we have [on Rosh Chodesh], we would be sure not to waste even one second of the day."

The two sections of this book deal with two aspects of Rosh Chodesh:

(1) The Tur Shulchan Aruch explains that each of the months symbolizes one of the twelve tribes of Israel. We shall endeavor to elucidate the connection between the respective months and their tribes.

(2) The sacred mystical work *Sefer Yetzirah* relates each of the months to a combination of Hashem's holy Four-letter Name. We will explain these esoteric relationships.

The objective of the essays is to bring to the fore the deep concepts hidden in each month, so that we can use Rosh Chodesh as a tool with which to strengthen our service of Hashem.

———◆———

With all due respect and awe, I would like to honor the memory of my father ז״ל, who led our family through his Torah and wisdom. He was *niftar* as this work was being prepared for publication. It is dedicated to him and includes two of his essays on Rosh Chodesh, which we excerpted from his many brilliant works. His passing leaves a great void in my heart and in that of our family. He was an extraordinary *talmid chacham*, a *"chashiver Yid"* from the previous generations, who was close to the *admorim* of Gur, and who was a role model for all who knew him. Like very few others, he combined Torah, and *derech eretz* as prescribed by *Chazal* and the *Ramban*.

I would also like to thank my mother-in-law, who is renowned for her gentle, noble nature and for her constant, selfless assistance to us and to all of her children and grandchildren. The beauty and sanctity of Rosh Chodesh have been an integral part of her very essence since her youth, before the War. Her family celebrated Rosh Chodesh with a feast and she continues this marvelous tradition to this very day. May Hashem grant her many years of good health and happiness so that she can continue to honor Rosh Chodesh and enjoy *nachas* from her adoring family.

I am especially grateful to Alan Genauer and Yaakov Rechnitz, who have undertaken prime responsibility to organize, host, and conduct our Rosh Chodesh gatherings. They are dear friends and I know I speak for the entire group in thanking them for all they do.

I am indebted to the many good friends who participate in our Rosh Chodesh feast and who honor me by attending my *shiurim*. They provide the incentive to live up to the high standards they demand. Without them, this volume would not have been created.

There are no words to express my gratitude to my very dear friends Rabbi Meir Zlotowitz and Rabbi Nosson Scherman who undertook to have this work translated and published. They are certainly more than just publishers. They honored me by making it their mission to enable the world to share the splendor and profundity of Rosh Chodesh and they were totally dedicated to make this volume a thing of beauty — they have indeed succeeded. I cherish their friendship.

Acharonah acharonah chavivah, my wife Betty. As a wife, mother, and daughter she is matchless. She is modest and strong, sincere and devoted, principled and generous. Her encouragement and pride on my learning and the learning of our children and her pride in me are the keys to our accomplishments. *Sheli v'shelachem shelah*. May Hashem give us many healthy, successful years together to serve Him and enjoy generations of children and grandchildren.

Zvi Ryzman
Los Angeles
Nissan 5769 / April 2009

Rabbi Yehoshua Heshel Ryzman ז"ל

Rabbi Yehoshua Heshel Ryzman ז"ל, who passed away shortly before the publication of this volume, was a unique man, a man who seamlessly combined greatness in Torah with success in the business world. There were no compartments in his life. Breathtaking knowledge of Torah and unquenchable love of learning were his essence and permeated his every moment and his every activity. In tribute to his inspiring memory, we present two essays from his sefer on the haftaros of the year, *Iyunim B'Haftarot*. They illuminate the message of the haftarah to Parashah Bo (Yirmiah 46:13-28).

The Jewish Calendar Is Based on Lunar Months, Symbolizing Ascent and Descent

וְאַתָּה אַל־תִּירָא עַבְדִּי יַעֲקֹב וְאַל־תֵּחַת יִשְׂרָאֵל
כִּי הִנְנִי מוֹשִׁעֲךָ מֵרָחוֹק וְאֶת־זַרְעֲךָ מֵאֶרֶץ שִׁבְיָם ...
וְאוֹתְךָ לֹא אֶעֱשֶׂה־כָלָה.

*But as for you, do not be afraid, My servant Yaakov,
and do not be frightened, O Israel, for behold,
I am saving you from afar and your offspring
from the land of their captivity . . . of you I shall not
make an end*
(Yirmiyah 46:27-28).

THE PROPHET YIRMIYAH HAS PROPHESIED ABOUT THE DOWNFALL of the kingdom of Egypt. At the end of his prophecy he promises that the Jewish people will survive and be spared from the severe punishments that will be inflicted on the nations that oppressed them. This *haftarah* corresponds to the *parashah*, for both announce the downfall of Egypt and the salvation of Israel.

The Jewish people will survive and be spared from the severe punishments that will be inflicted on the nations that oppressed them.

The *parashah* states *The blood [on the Jewish doorposts] shall be a sign for you … and there shall not be a plague of destruction upon you when I strike in the land of Egypt* (*Shemos* 12:13). In the *haftarah*, Yirmiyah announces to the Jewish people that the kingdom of Egypt will fall to the kingdom of Babylonia, and King Nevuchadnetzar of Babylonia will destroy the Egyptian kingdom, as well as its Pharaoh. The prophet adds that God would destroy Israel's oppressors in all the lands where He had dispersed them. This means that the same punishment awaits all those who oppressed Israel throughout the years of exile. There is also an assurance that though the oppressor nations would be destroyed, God would not annihilate His people.

Though the oppressor nations would be destroyed, God would not annihilate His people.

However, this assurance came with a caution: וְיִסַּרְתִּיךָ לַמִּשְׁפָּט וְנַקֵּה לֹא אֲנַקֶּךָ, *I will punish you with justice, but I will not destroy you utterly* (*Yirmiyah* 46:28). No one is immune from justifiable punishment; when the nations are punished, Israel, too, will face retribution for its sins, but unlike the utter doom that will befall those who oppressed Israel, the Jewish People have a special promise that though individuals will be punished, the nation will not be destroyed. עַם יִשְׂרָאֵל חַי, *The Jewish People lives!* It will be justly punished for its sins, but it will not be utterly destroyed. Israel is guaranteed that it will survive forever.

This promise finds expression in the *parashah*, in the very first mitzvah given to the nation as a whole, the commandment to proclaim the new month. The essence of the mitzvah is the concept of renewal, as *Rashi* quotes the *Mechilta*: God showed [Moshe] the moon in its renewal and said to him, "When the moon renews itself, it will be the new month for you." The Sages explain that the moon's uniqueness is that it grows progressively smaller as the month ebbs away, as if it is totally enveloped in darkness, but immediately it renews like the Moon itself and begins to become visible again.

The Jewish people is likened to the moon. Periodically it seems to be declining — but then, before it is gone, it is already preparing to re-emerge and shine anew.

Like the Moon

THE JEWISH PEOPLE IS LIKENED TO THE MOON. PERIODICALLY IT seems to be declining, as if it is about to disappear from the stage of history — but then, before it is gone, it is already preparing to re-emerge and shine anew. Indeed, the Holy One blessed is He brings pain and suffering upon the Jewish people in punishment for our sins, but His goal is never extermination. Rather, the punishment is temporary until the people repent — and then the nation will renew itself and thrive with new life, as Scripture states in today's *haftarah*, *"I will punish you with justice, but I will not destroy you utterly."*

This is why, when we bless the moon, we proclaim the verse דָּוִד מֶלֶךְ יִשְׂרָאֵל חַי וְקַיָּם, *David, King of Israel, is alive and enduring!* The Sages instituted this recitation as an allusion to the Court's duty to proclaim the New Moon. At a time when the nations prohibited the Jewish people from sanctifying Rosh Chodesh, the Sages circumvented their decree by sending qualified judges to the town of Ein Tav, where they would accept witnesses who testified that they had seen the new moon. When the clandestine court had sanctified the new month, it informed the High Court with the code words, "David, King of Israel, is alive and enduring." By use of this device, Rabbi Yehudah the Prince, leader of the nation and descendant of King David, wished to hint to his people that the Davidic kingdom, like the moon, is always present, although it is periodically hidden. So, too, the Jewish nation. Sometimes it is concealed in the darkness of exile, but when we are deserving, the darkness will be removed and Jewish sovereignty will be revealed in its glory.

"David, King of Israel, is alive and enduring." The Davidic kingdom, like the moon, is always present, although it is periodically hidden.

THE SAGES STATE THAT MOSHE WAS PERPLEXED ABOUT THE REAPpearance of the moon: "What size must it be in order to be sanctified?" he asked. Hashem showed him the new lunar

Moshe's Difficulty

crescent and said, "When you see it like this, you may sanctify it" (*Rashi, Shemos* 12:2). Commentators have written at length to explain why Moshe was perplexed.

It may be that Moshe found it difficult to understand the purpose of the commandment. Why should Israel's calendar be based on the moon and not on the sun, like that of the other nations? Why not base our calendar on the heavenly body that always shines with full strength, rather than on the moon, which waxes and wanes, and merely reflects the light of the sun?

Sfas Emes comments on why the Jewish people use a lunar calendar. The Jewish people cannot be symbolized by natural phenomena that are constant and incapable of renewal. Israel is always destined to renew itself and rise from one level to the next. It is above the laws of nature, it lives in a sphere where renewal is constantly possible. In the spiritual sense, those whose lives are regulated by the sun would cease to exist if it were to disappear, for they lack the potential for renewal. By contrast, Israel is like the moon, which changes from day to day, but is always present even when it is not visible. It never sets completely; it is only obscured from our vision. So, too, Israel. Darkness often conceals us, but when the veil of exile is removed, we will glow again.

The Jewish people cannot be symbolized by natural phenomena that are constant and incapable of renewal.

This explains Moshe's perplexity. Because he knew that long periods of darkness would be Israel's lot, he was hesitant when he was given the commandment of renewal. How could the concept of renewal apply to Israel? God responded that this is indeed the best symbol of Israel's history. True, there *would* be darkness, but it would *end*, and Israel would merit complete redemption.

Moshe's difficulty with the concept of sanctification of the month flowed from his initial refusal to accept the mission of delivering Israel from Egypt. When he realized that the redemption from Egypt would not be an eternal redemption, but that the Jewish people would suffer additional exiles, he repeatedly expressed his reluctance to accept the mission, finally saying, "Send through whomever You will send." His reluctance did not stem from excessive humility, but from a longing that there be a complete and eternal redemption, one with no future exiles. Indeed, the Sages (*Pirkei d'Rabbi Eliezer*) interpret his refusal, "Send through whomever you will send," to mean that Moshe was appealing to God, "Send through *Mashiach*," i.e., through the one whose redemption will be permanent.

However, *Sfas Emes* (*Bo* 5658) clarifies that, contrary to Moshe's fear, Israel's dependence on the moon was for its benefit, because it conferred eternity upon the nation:

> In truth, people of this world cannot have the quality of renewal, because *there is nothing new under the sun* (*Koheles* 1:9), but the Jewish people belong to the World to Come, and therefore can always renew themselves, as the Torah says, *This renewal is yours,* and therefore the Sages included in our monthly *Kiddush Levanah* (Sanctification of the Moon): "*And to the moon He said, It should renew itself as a crown of splendor for those borne [by Him] from the womb* [i.e., the Jewish people], those who are destined to renew themselves like it. As noted above, the Jewish people belong to the World to Come. Nature, which is subject to the limitations of time and will eventually come to an end, does not have the power of renewal, but Israel, which belongs to the World to Come, always cleaves to the power of renewal.

Far from being a curse, Israel's connection to the moon is a blessing that enables it to survive all tribulations. *The Jewish people lives and endures forever.*

The Eternity of the Jewish People

וְיִסַּרְתִּיךָ לַמִּשְׁפָּט וְנַקֵּה לֹא אֲנַקֶּךָ.

*I will punish you with justice,
but I will not destroy you utterly*
(*Yirmiyah* 46:28).

THE PREVIOUS ESSAY DISCUSSED THE CONNECTION BETWEEN the *haftarah* and the *parashah* of the week, for both express the eternity of Israel. Pharaoh, Sichon, and Og, the kings of Egypt, the Emori, and Cheshbon respectively — all mighty kings — lost their thrones and kingdoms, and all nations of that era were filled with fear of Israel. In later centuries, such world powers as Kings Sancheriv of Ashur, Nevuchadnetzar of Babylonia, and Achashveirosh of Persia; and after them Alexander the Great of Macedonia, Titus of Rome; and even in modern times, Napoleon Bonaparte, the czars of Russia — all of them straddled the world, but when their time passed their kingdoms were destroyed, and they departed from the center stage of history. Their deeds had no permanence.

All of them straddled the world, but when their time passed their kingdoms were destroyed, and they departed from the center stage of history.

The Jewish people are different. They have been *punished with justice* and suffered terribly from various decrees and edicts, but despite every manner of oppression, and despite their wanderings to every part of the world, and despite their history of expulsions from the lands of their birth — despite all this they endure as a Jewish nation. They live and endure forever: נֵצַח יִשְׂרָאֵל לֹא יְשַׁקֵּר, *The Eternal One of Israel does not lie* (*I Shmuel* 15:29).

The uniqueness of Israel, expressed in the closing words of the *haftarah: I will not destroy you utterly*, is expressed in the *parashah*'s commandment to sanctify the New Moon. The significance of this mitzvah is apparent from *Rashi* at the beginning of his commentary on the Torah: "Rabbi Yitzchok said, the Torah should have begun with the commandment of Rosh Chodesh," i.e., the mitzvah to sanctify the month is the true beginning of the Torah, in the sense that it is the first commandment given to the Jewish people when it became a nation.

The mitzvah to sanctify the month is the true beginning of the Torah.

BUT WHY IS THIS MITZVAH SO IMPORTANT THAT IT IS THE FOUNDATION of the Jewish people, the first commandment in the Torah?

Why the New Moon?

Also, in the era of the Chashmonaim, in the time of the Second *Beis HaMikdash*, when the Syrian-Greeks wanted to eradicate the Torah from Israel, they specifically prohibited the observance of three commandments: Shabbos, Rosh Chodesh, and Bris Milah. The battle of the Chashmonaim for Shabbos and Milah is understandable; they are fundamental to the faith of Israel, but why was the commandment of Rosh Chodesh so basic that it was the subject of the Syrian-Greek decree and the stimulus for the Chashmonaim's rebellion?

The importance of this mitzvah expresses itself in the uniqueness of the Jewish people.

The importance of this mitzvah expresses itself in the uniqueness of the Jewish people, which is at the foundation of its existence. Israel is not simply a "member of the family of nations." It is different from them all. It has its own calendar and it advances through the year in a way intrinsically its own. Its seasons and observances are different. The differences are not merely technical; they are different in kind, not only in degree. The Jewish *weltanschauung* contradicts the heretical underpinnings of the nations. In ancient times, the nations adopted the theory that the twelve constellations and the heavenly bodies controlled nature, and therefore the nations adopted them as gods. It was logical, therefore, that their calendar centered on the sun.

By contrast, the uniqueness of Israel rests on the conviction that there is a Creator Who controls nature and guides everything in the universe, as the *Tanya* (*Shaar HaYichud v'HaEmunah*, Ch.1) writes:

The words and letters of God's command remain standing forever in the heavenly firmament.

> *Forever, Hashem, Your word stands firm in heaven* (*Tehillim* 119:89). The *Baal Shem Tov* explains that the "word" was God's command that there be a firmament (*Bereishis* 1:6). The words and letters of God's command remain standing forever in the heavenly firmament and provide the firmament [and every other part of the universe] with the power to continuously carry out their ordained function, as the prophet says *The word of our God shall stand forever* (*Yeshayah* 40:8), and His words are living and enduring forever .... If those letters were to be removed from the firmament [or the other parts of Creation] for even a moment, and return to their Godly Source, the entire heaven would turn to nothingness, as if it had never existed, and as it was before God declared that there should be a firmament.

The mitzvah of Rosh Chodesh affirms this fundamental concept. The difference between the Jewish calendar and the general calendar is not merely that one is lunar and the other is solar. The difference lies in what establishes the authority of the Jewish calendar. Everyone can see the stages of the moon, and millions of people may observe the re-emergence of its first sliver at the beginning of the month, but that does make the day Rosh Chodesh. Only if the court hears the testimony of valid witnesses who have seen the new moon, and the court consecrates the day as Rosh Chodesh, has the new month begun and the calendar become confirmed. Clearly, therefore, the calendar depends on the Jewish court, not merely on the arrival of the moon or the consensus of the nation.[1]

The Torah ordains that declaration of the court is binding, even if the court's calculations were made in error (*Rosh Hashanah* 25a). Not only are all the festivals dependent on the court's control of the calendar, even the Heavenly Court convenes on Rosh Hashanah only on the day ordained by the calendar, as formulated by the Jewish court. As the Sages put it (*Yerushalmi Rosh Hashanah* 1:3):

> If the government says that the court will convene today and the criminals say it should convene tomorrow, don't we obey the government? But the Holy One blessed is He is different. When the Jewish court declares that today is Rosh Hashanah, the Holy One Blessed is He says to the ministering angels, "Set up the platform. Let the defenders and the prosecutors take their places, for My children have declared that today is Rosh Hashanah." But if the Jewish court decides to proclaim the next day as Rosh Hashanah, the Holy One Blessed is He says to the ministering angels, "Remove the platform. Let the defenders and prosecutors step aside, for my children have decided to postpone [Rosh Hashanah] to tomorrow." Why is this? Because the verse (*Tehillim* 81:2) states, כִּי חֹק לְיִשְׂרָאֵל הוּא מִשְׁפָּט לֵאלֹקֵי יַעֲקֹב, *Because it is a decree for Israel, a judgment day for the God of Yaakov.* From this we derive that if [the day] has not been decreed by Israel, it is not a day of judgment for the God of Yaakov.

Therefore the Sages say (*Berachos* 49a), "Israel sanctifies the festivals," i.e., the holiness of the time, the sanctification of the Jewish festivals, depends on the Jewish people. By sanctifying the days of Rosh Chodesh, the Jewish court has determined not only the day

The calendar depends on the Jewish court, not merely on the arrival of the moon or the consensus of the nation.

The holiness of the time, the sanctification of the Jewish festivals, depends on the Jewish people.

---

1. The present Jewish calendar was formulated by the last functioning *Beis Din*, under Hillel II, in the year 4119/359 C.E. Hillel realized that the ravages of exile and oppression would sooner or later make it impossible for the courts to carry out their duty to accept witness and consecrate the months. Therefore, he and his colleagues calculated and consecrated our lunar calendar for centuries into the future. It is their calendar that we follow and that will be used until the coming of *Mashiach*, may it be speedily in our days.

of Rosh Chodesh, but also all the festivals throughout the course of the year. They also decree the length of the lunar year, whether it will be a simple year of twelve months or a leap year of thirteen months. This is the simple meaning of the middle blessing of *Shemoneh Esrei* of Rosh Chodesh and the festivals: מְקַדֵּשׁ יִשְׂרָאֵל וְהַזְּמַנִּים, *Who sanctifies Israel and the festivals*, i.e., first comes the sanctification of Israel; only then can the festivals be sanctified, for they achieve their status only because the Jewish court has established the calendar.

As we have explained, not only is the court's sanctification of Rosh Chodesh dependent on the orbit of the moon, but the very nature of the moon symbolizes the Jewish nation. The moon reappears every month and grows larger as the month progresses, and even though it shrinks after its fullness and disappears by the end of the month, it is not gone; its disappearance is only temporary. When the new month begins, the moon will shine and grow again. Such is the life of the Jewish people.

Jewish history is a succession of peaks and valleys. Sometimes the nation merits a period of glowing success, and other times it is exiled from its Land. After the exile it merits to return to *Eretz Yisrael* and rebuild the *Beis HaMikdash* anew and to be a sovereign nation. In the next era it is conquered by new enemies and descends once more into exile. Even the years of exile are a succession of peaks and valleys. There are times of suffering and persecution, and there are times of relative peace and tranquility. The succession of exiles, with their suffering and persecution, wrought devastation in the nation, both in quantity and quality, but when the era of defeat passed, they once again grew in strength and numbers, and with new vigor.

This is the suffering mentioned in the prophecy of Yirmiyah: *I will punish you with justice*. But the prophet also promises *I will not destroy you utterly*. Suffering, yes. Peaks and valleys, yes. But total destruction, never. Therefore we need not fear destruction, as the verse begins, *Do not fear, My servant Yaakov … for I am with you*. When all is done, the prophet's promise will be fulfilled:

> *But as for you, do not be afraid, My servant Yaakov,*
> *and do not be frightened, O Israel, for behold,*
> *I am saving you from afar and your offspring*
> *from the land of their captivity and Yaakov shall*
> *return and be tranquil and complacent, and none will make*
> *[him] afraid* (*Yirmiyah* 46:27-28).

CYCLE ONE

The Months
and the Tribes

Cycle One: Introduction

T UR[1] STATES THAT THE THREE FESTIVALS (PESACH, SHAVUOS, and Succos) correspond to our three forefathers, Avraham, Yitzchok, and Yaakov. Rosh Chodesh, which is celebrated twelve times each year,[2] corresponds to the twelve *shevatim* (tribes), with each month corresponding to one of the tribes.

Each month must share something in common with the tribe that it represents. By studying the relationship between a month and its tribe, we can understand the importance of the month and the tribe.

Obviously, each month must share something in common with the tribe that it represents. By studying the relationship between a month and its tribe, we can understand the importance of the month and the tribe, and the implicit messages of that association that are crucial to our service of Hashem.

There are two opinions on how the months correspond to the tribes.

Yaavetz[3] writes that the months, starting from Nissan, correspond to the tribes in chronological order of their birth: thus Nissan corresponds to Reuven, Iyar to Shimon, Sivan to Levi, and so on.

Arizal writes that the months, starting from Nissan, correspond to the order in which the tribes traveled in the Wildnerness: Yehudah, Yissachar, Zevulun, Reuven, Shimon, Gad, Ephraim, Menasheh, Binyomin, Dan, Asher and Naftali. There is also a midrashic source for his view. *Yalkut Shimoni* [4] states that the encampment of the Jewish nation in the Wilderness followed the "encampment" of the heavenly bodies — i.e., the constellations[5] — each of which represents a month of the year.

Each tribe had a banner in the Wilderness. The color of each tribal banner was the same color as that of the tribe's stone in the *Choshen* (Breastplate) worn by the *Kohen Gadol* (High Priest), and each tribe had a rendering on its flag that symbolized the tribe.[6]

---

1. *Orach Chaim* 417, quoting his brother Rav Yehudah.
2. With the exception of a leap year, in which there are thirteen months.
3. *Siddur Yaavetz.*
4. *Remez* 418.
5. The constellations are configurations of stars in specific shapes. Each month has a constellation associated with it, which will be noted in the course of the following essays.
6. For instance, Reuven's stone in the *Choshen* was *odem* (a red stone), so his flag was colored red, with a rendering of *dudaim* (see *Bereishis* 30:14-15). Shimon's stone was the green *pitda*; his flag was green, with a rendering of the city Shechem

Following the order of correspondence set forth by *Arizal, Bnei Yissaschar* presents profound essays on the months of the year, in which he explains the confluence of each month, its constellation, and tribe (including the banner) associated with the month.

The essays in this section are based primarily on the essays of the *Bnei Yissaschar*, and we will follow his method of analyzing the relationship between the tribes and their months to gain an understanding of what each month teaches.

(see *Bereishis* 34:25). See *Bamidbar Rabbah* (2:7) for a full list of the colors and renderings.

TISHREI

הַחֹדֶשׁ הזה על פי סדר הדגלים מיחס לאפרים
שהוא שביעי בנסיעת הדגלים כידוע.

(בני יששכר, מאמרי חדש תשרי מאמר א, אות א)

Tishrei corresponds to Ephraim,
the seventh tribe to travel.

(Bnei Yissaschar, Maamarei Chodesh Tishrei 1:1)

Rosh Hashanah, Not Rosh Chodesh

DESPITE CHODESH TISHREI'S PROMINENCE AS THE FIRST MONTH of each *calendar* year[1] — or perhaps *because* of its prominence — we find that the first of Tishrei is treated differently from all other months of the year in several ways:

Why is the first of Tishrei called only Rosh Hashanah, and not Rosh Chodesh?

1) Unlike the first day of all the other months, we do not consider the first day of Tishrei as a Rosh Chodesh, only as Rosh Hashanah. This is quite surprising, considering that even Nissan — the first of the months[2] — is given no special distinction over the other months. The first of Nissan is considered Rosh Chodesh, like the first day of every other month. Why is the first of Tishrei called only Rosh Hashanah, and not Rosh Chodesh?

2) Rosh Hashanah is celebrated as a two-day festival even in Eretz Yisrael, but clearly not because it is considered a month with two days of Rosh Chodesh. On the contrary, it is quite clear that Rosh Hashanah is different from Rosh Chodesh. When we celebrate two days of Rosh Chodesh, the first day is actually the last day of the old month, and the second day of Rosh Chodesh is the first day of the new month. Both days of Rosh Hashanah, on the other hand, are celebrated entirely in Tishrei — a clear indication that Rosh Hashanah differs from Rosh Chodesh.

We herald the arrival of each new month by blessing the month with a special prayer — except Tishrei.

3) We herald the arrival of each new month by blessing the month with a special prayer called *Bircas HaChodesh* on the Shabbos preceding Rosh Chodesh of each month of the year — except Tishrei, for which *Bircas HaChodesh* is not recited. Several explanations are given for its exclusion:

A) *Magen Avraham* sources its exclusion to the verse תִּקְעוּ

---

1. As noted in the Introduction, Arizal writes that the twelve tribes are associated with the twelve months, respectively, in the order of their encampment around the Mishkan in the Wilderness. Thus, Yehudah, the first tribe, corresponds to Nissan, the first month, and Ephraim, the seventh tribe, corresponds to Tishrei, the seventh month.

2. Hashem commanded us to begin counting our months from Nissan, which is therefore considered the first month (*Shemos* 12:2). Nevertheless, the yearly calendar begins in Tishrei, because the first of Tishrei was the day that humans were created and the world began to function.

בַּחֹדֶשׁ שׁוֹפָר בַּכֶּסֶה לְיוֹם חַגֵּנוּ, *Blow the shofar at the moon's renewal, at the time appointed for our festive day* (*Tehillim* 81:4). The word בַּכֶּסֶה — the appointed time — can also be associated with the word מְכֻסֶּה, *covered*. We can deduce, therefore, that the first of a month in which we blow *shofar* — i.e., Rosh Hashanah — should remain "covered," unannounced by *Bircas HaChodesh*.

B) *Mishnah Berurah* writes that *Magen Avraham's* explanation is homiletic. The simple reason for excluding *Bircas HaChodesh* for Tishrei is because Rosh Chodesh is not the outstanding characteristic of the first of Tishrei — it is overshadowed by the fact that it is Rosh Hashanah. It is totally unnecessary, therefore, to herald the arrival of Rosh Chodesh Tishrei through *Bircas HaChodesh*.

C) *Likkutei Mahariach* cites from *Hagahos Minhagim* that Rosh Hashanah does not need a special blessing on the Shabbos prior to its arrival, because it is already blessed.

4) In the times of the *Beis HaMikdash*, the Kohanim would sacrifice special offerings, called *Mussafim,* on festivals. We commemorate those offerings nowadays by praying a *Mussaf Shemoneh Esrei* on each festival, which includes the recitation of the verses in the Torah that command us to offer the specific *mussaf* offerings for that festival.

Interestingly, although the Rosh Chodesh *Mussaf* was offered in the *Beis HaMikdash* on Rosh Hashanah, *Shulchan Aruch*[3] rules that in the *Mussaf Shemoneh Esrei* of Rosh Hashanah, the Rosh Chodesh verses are omitted. We merely *allude* to the Rosh Chodesh offerings with the words וְאֶת מוּסְפֵי יוֹם הַזִּכָּרוֹן הַזֶּה, *and the Mussafim of this day of remembrance.*[4] *Rema*[5] concurs, stating clearly that we should not recite verses of the *Mussaf* of Rosh Chodesh on Rosh Hashanah.

Mishnah Berurah[6] adds that not only do we not mention the Rosh Chodesh verses, we also exclude those verses when reciting *Karbanos* prior to *davening.*[7] *Mishnah Berurah* explains

Rosh Chodesh is not the outstanding characteristic of the first of Tishrei — it is overshadowed by Rosh Hashanah.

Rema states that we should not recite verses of the Mussaf of Rosh Chodesh on Rosh Hashanah.

---

3. *Orach Chaim* 591:3

4. The plural form "*Mussafim*" alludes to the fact that aside from the Rosh Hashanah *Mussaf* sacrifice, there was also another *Mussaf* for *Rosh Chodesh*.

5. Ibid. 591:2

6. Ibid. 591:3

7. It is customary to recite the portions of the Torah discussing the various offerings sacrificed in the *Beis HaMikdash* each morning (*Shulchan Aruch* 1:5-9).

that if the Rosh Chodesh verses were to be recited, some may mistakenly deduce from the recitation that the second day of Rosh Hashanah is primary and the first day is secondary, just like a two-day Rosh Chodesh.[8]

Furthermore, concludes *Mishnah Berurah*, we do not want people to consider the first day of Tishrei as special simply because it is Rosh Chodesh. On the contary, there is a greater aspect to this day — it is Rosh Hashanah.

Mishnah Berurah notes that since we derive from בַּכֶּסֶה that Rosh Chodesh Tishrei is supposed to be hidden, we do not make open mention of Rosh Chodesh on Rosh Hashanah. Nevertheless, referring to Rosh Hashanah as "*Yom HaZikaron* (the Day of Remembrance)" is an implicit mention of Rosh Chodesh, because Rosh Chodesh is also a day of remembrance.

When we consider various aspects of Rosh Hashanah and Rosh Chodesh, we find that there are many differences between the two.

Clearly, Rosh Chodesh Tishrei is not an ordinary Rosh Chodesh. We make a concerted effort to "hide" the fact that the first of Tishrei is Rosh Chodesh. Why?

When we consider various aspects of Rosh Hashanah and Rosh Chodesh, we find that there are many differences between the two. By examining those differences, we can come to a better understanding of why we hide the Rosh Chodesh aspect of the first of Tishrei — and we can also understand the association between the tribe of Ephraim and the hidden Rosh Chodesh of Tishrei.

I. Nesinah vs. Kaballah[9]

THE KEY TO UNDERSTANDING WHY ROSH HASHANAH IS NOT considered a Rosh Chodesh, like the first days of the other

---

8. As mentioned, when we celebrate two days of Rosh Chodesh, the first day of Rosh Chodesh is the thirtieth day of the previous month and the second day of Rosh Chodesh is the first of the new month, so it is the primary day of Rosh Chodesh. Since there are *never* thirty days in *Elul*, the first day of *Rosh Hashanah* is the first day of the new month and is therefore the primary day of *Rosh Chodesh*.

9. The terms *nesinah* and *kaballah* appear often in *mussar* and *machshavah* works. Roughly translated, *nesinah* means "to give", and *kaballah* means "to take or accept." However, the English translations are not workable definitions for the broader concepts that these terms represent.

Michtav MeEliyahu points out that a person can often take something from someone and still be giving of himself. For instance, if Reuven did Shimon a big favor, and Shimon wants to give Reuven a gift to express his appreciation, by *taking* the gift Reuven is actually *giving* Shimon the opportunity to divest himself of the debt he feels he owes for that favor. Similarly, if we delve into the depths of any given situation, we

months, is that there is an intrinsic difference between Rosh Hashanah and the other Rosh Chodesh days.

Rosh Hashanah — Nesinah

The Talmud[10] records a disagreement between Rabbi Yose and Rabbi Yehudah as to which verses are recited as *Malchiyos*.[11] One of the verses in dispute is שְׁמַע יִשְׂרָאֵל ה׳ אֱלֹקֵינוּ ה׳ אֶחָד, *Hear O Israel, Hashem is our God, Hashem, the One and Only* (*Devarim* 6:4). According to Rabbi Yose, *Shema Yisrael* is an expression of kingship. Rabbi Yehudah disagrees.

Michtav MeEliyahu[12] explains the reasoning behind this dispute:

> There are two possible motives for citizens to serve their king: some serve him out of fear, and some out of love. Those who serve out of fear can be divided into two types. Some citizens submit to the king's rule because they are afraid to do otherwise, but not because they are ready to embrace his rule wholeheartedly — on the contrary, deep in their hearts they bear a burning desire to pursue their personal goals, and they constantly long for an opportunity to do so. Another group of citizens will realize that they will never be able to follow their personal interests against the will of the sovereign. Instead they learn to exercise such powerful self-control that they eradicate any desire to disobey the king. Even in this form of obedient service, however, there is still a small element of coercion, because such citizens abandon the pursuits that run contrary to the king's will only out of fear of retribution.
>
> Truly devoted citizens — those who serve the king out of love — do not need to remove any personal desires from their hearts. They serve the king because they love him intensely, and that love makes them *want* to follow his rules. Such citizens do not feel coerced into the king's service. They consider it a privilege to follow his laws, and they have no interest in engaging in any activities other than those sanctioned by the king.

They consider it a privilege to follow his laws, and they have no interest in engaging in any activities other than those sanctioned by the king.

might find that someone who is *giving* in a physical sense is actually *receiving* in an emotional or spiritual sense, because the giver derives pleasure from the fact that he is discharging a moral or emotional obligation.

10. *Rosh Hashanah* 32b.

11. As part of the *Mussaf* prayer on Rosh Hashanah, we recite three sets of ten verses, and conclude each set with a blessing. The three sets of verses are called *Malchiyos* (Kingship), *Zichronos* (Remembrance), and *Shofaros* (Shofar-Blasts). In *Malchiyos* we focus on Hashem as the King over the universe, reciting verses that mention His sovereignty.

12. Vol. II, p. 71.

The same concept applies to our service of Hashem. Some refrain from sin because they fear Divine retribution, but they still desire to sin. Others manage to banish the desire to sin from their hearts, but only because they realize that sinning angers Hashem. The most devout Jews, however, have no interest in sinning, because they love Hashem so much that they would not *dream* of doing something that runs contrary to His will.

The most devout Jews, however, have no interest in sinning, because they love Hashem so much that they would not dream of doing something that runs contrary to His will.

Since the latter group recognizes Hashem's sole sovereignty to the extent that they have no interest in engaging in, or even contemplating, any activity other than serving Him, they have reached the ultimate level of *Yichud Hashem* (the recognition of Hashem's sole control of the world).

When we recite the verses of *Malchiyos* on Rosh Hashanah, we accept Hashem's Kingship over us. Rabbi Yehudah and Rabbi Yosi's dispute revolves around *how* we are to go about accepting Hashem's Kingship upon ourselves.

According to Rabbi Yehudah, we accept Hashem as King by demonstrating our willingness to nullify our own interests and submit to His Will. When we show our subservience to Hashem, we are serving Him out of fear.

Rabbi Yose — whose opinion we follow — maintains that we should focus on accepting Hashem as King and serving Him out of love. Since those who love Hashem are at the highest level of recognizing *Yichud Hashem*, the most appropriate culmination of our expression of *Malchiyos* is the verse with which we express our faith in *Yichud Hashem* twice daily: *Shema Yisrael, Hashem Elokeinu, Hashem Echad.*

Rosh Hashanah is a day of nesinah: by totally and unreservedly accepting Hashem's will and completely eliminating any personal desire to do otherwise, we "give" ourselves to Him.

We can deduce from *Michtav MeEliyahu* that Rosh Hashanah is a day of *nesinah*: by totally and unreservedly accepting Hashem's will and completely eliminating any personal desire to do otherwise, we "give" ourselves to Him, withholding nothing for ourselves. By demonstrating our subservience to Hashem and nullifying our will in favor of His, we "give" to Him.

Conversely, Rosh Chodesh, which marks the birth of the new moon, is clearly focused on *kaballah*. The moon is the paradigm "acceptor." It cannot produce any light of its own. It can only reflect the light it receives from the sun. Thus, Rosh Chodesh portrays the usual relationship between Hashem and the world, because the entire universe receives constantly from Hashem's largess.

It seems, then, that Rosh Hashanah and Rosh Chodesh are actually opposites. Rosh Hashanah is a day of *nesinah*, and Rosh Chodesh is a day of *kaballah*.

THE HISTORY OF EPHRAIM SHOWS THAT THIS TRIBE IS A PARADIGM *mekabel*, a recipient, and is therefore closely related to Rosh Chodesh:

Ephraim — A Mekabel

- When Moshe Rabbeinu blessed the tribes shortly before his death, he did not address Ephraim directly. Rather, he addressed his blessing to Yosef (*Devarim* 33:13), and mentioned Ephraim only in passing, in the very last verse of his blessing: וְהֵם רִבְבוֹת אֶפְרָיִם, *they are the myriads of Ephraim* (ibid. 33:17). Thus, Ephraim received his blessing only through his father, Yosef, just as the moon receives its light only from the sun.

- The first — and foremost — leader of *Klal Yisrael* who came from Ephraim was Yehoshua bin Nun, Moshe Rabbeinu's closest disciple.[13] Yehoshua was clearly a *mekabel*. *Chazal*[14] point out that he received only some, but not all, of Moshe's majesty, because Hashem told Moshe, "וְנָתַתָּה מֵהוֹדְךָ עָלָיו, *You shall place some of your majesty upon him*" (*Bamidbar* 27:20). *Chazal* explain that Moshe's countenance was like the sun, and Yehoshua's was like the moon. Yehoshua did not produce light of his own; he only reflected what he received from Moshe.

  Furthermore, when it came time for Moshe to transfer the leadership to Yehoshua, Hashem commanded Moshe, "קְרָא אֶת יְהוֹשֻׁעַ וְהִתְיַצְּבוּ בְּאֹהֶל מוֹעֵד וַאֲצַוֶּנּוּ, *Summon Yehoshua, and both of you shall stand in the Tent of Meeting, and I shall instruct him*" (*Devarim* 31:14). *Rashi* explains that the word *va'atzavenu* (I shall instruct him) connotes that Hashem would encourage Yehoshua to accept the role of leadership.

  Alshich asks why it was necessary to conduct a ceremony to instruct Yehoshua to lead the Jewish people. They already knew that he was going to be the next leader, so why the need for Hashem to summon and encourage him? Based on our understanding of Yehoshua as the prototype *mekabel*, we can understand why he would have to be instructed to accept this role. As leader of *Klal Yisrael*, Yehoshua would now have to impart Torah law and leadership to others, which is *nesinah*. Since *nesinah* would not come naturally to Yehoshua, Hashem had to urge him to do so.

  Netziv explains this concept a bit further. He questions *Chazal's* statement that Yehoshua only reflected light from

Moshe's countenance was like the sun, and Yehoshua's was like the moon. Yehoshua did not produce light of his own; he only reflected what he received from Moshe.

---

13. The attributes of a tribe can usually be determined by the examining a leader who represented that tribe at some point in history.

14. *Bava Basra* 75a.

Moshe. Yehoshua was a prophet in his own right. He communicated directly with Hashem. If so, why do *Chazal* consider Yehoshua like the moon?

Chazal's statement actually is not referring to Yehoshua's prophetic ability, explains *Netziv*. *Chazal* were referring to Moshe's and Yehoshua's respective abilities to transmit Torah knowledge. Moshe's primary focus was on teaching *Torah Shebichsav* (the Written Torah). Yehoshua was the first person to excel in transmitting *Torah Sheb'al Peh* (the Oral Law of Torah), which he received from his teacher. In referring to Moshe as the sun and Yehoshua as the moon, *Chazal* teach that Yehoshua served as a "prism," taking the bright light of *Torah Shebichsav* shining forth from Moshe, and reflecting it into the vast, diverse rays of *Torah Sheb'al Peh*.[15]

Given that Yehoshua was a reflection of Moshe — that Moshe was the "sun" and Yehoshua the "moon" — *Netziv* explains that Yehoshua could not attain the status of teacher in Moshe's lifetime, just as the powerful light of the daytime sun makes it impossible to see the moon. We begin to notice the light reflected by the moon only when the sun is setting.

This explains the continuum in the verse describing the transfer of power from Moshe to Yehoshua: "Behold, your days are drawing near to die; summon Yehoshua, and both of you shall stand in the Tent of Meeting, and I shall instruct him" (ibid.). Like the moon, Yehoshua's light could not begin to shine forth until Moshe was about to pass away.

Thus, comments *Netziv*, Yehoshua was so similar to the paradigm *mekabel* — the moon — that his light could not shine forth until Moshe was about to pass away.

- When Yaakov blessed Ephraim and Menashe, he said, "And now, your two sons who were born to you in the land of Egypt before my coming to you in Egypt shall be mine; Ephraim and Menashe shall be mine like Reuven and Shimon" (*Bereishis* 48:5). Why did Yaakov deem it necessary to bless only the children who were born in Egypt prior to his arrival and not those born afterward?

---

15. We find an instance in the Talmud (*Chullin* 124a) in which one sage exclaims his strong disagreement with the opinion of another sage, saying, "Even if I heard this ruling from Yehoshua bin Nun, I would not follow it." Why did the sage choose Yehoshua to express his vehemence? *Netziv* explains that he was saying that even if Yehoshua — the "father" of *Torah Shebe'al Peh* — transmitted the ruling directly to him, he still could not accept it.

Emes L'Yaakov[16] explains that since Ephraim and Menasheh grew up in the spiritual wasteland of Egypt without the benefit of the uplifted environment of Yaakov's household, they had been at considerable risk of intermingling with their Egyptian neighbors and eventually straying from Judaism. Yaakov strengthened their connection to Judaism by recognizing them as equals of his own children, Reuven and Shimon.

It would seem, adds *Emes L'Yaakov*, that Ephraim needed this special recognition more than Menasheh, because Menasheh was *somewhat* connected to Yaakov's household even prior to this blessing, and Ephraim was not:

1) In explaining why he chose to name his firstborn son Menasheh, Yosef included a mention of Yaakov's household. Yosef said, "God has helped me forget [*nashani*] all my hardship and all my father's household" (*Bereishis* 41:51). The very fact that, despite his astounding rise to power, Yosef still thought of his origins showed that the connection still existed.

   By the time Ephraim was born, however, Yosef considered himself a citizen of Egypt. The name Ephraim was in appreciation of his success in Egypt: "God has made me fruitful in the land of my suffering" (ibid. 41:52).

2) Ephraim's name appears to fit with typical Egyptian naming patterns. The letters *feh*, *resh*, and *ayin* were common in Egyptian names: Pharaoh, Potiphar, Tzaphnas, Pane'ach, Shifra, and Puah. By basing his second son's name on two of those Egyptian-sounding letters, Yosef showed that he had come under Egyptian influence to some degree.

3) Whereas Menasheh served as his father's assistant, Ephraim was constantly studying Torah with Yaakov[17] — perhaps to strengthen his connection with Judaism. Such study was less needed by Menasheh, who spoke *Lashon Kodesh* even prior to Yaakov's arrival.[18]

We can now understand the need to "hide" the Rosh Chodesh aspect of Tishrei. Ephraim, as the paradigm *mekabel*, is strongly associated with Rosh Chodesh. Since Rosh Chodesh — and especially the Rosh Chodesh associated with Ephraim — is a day for

Ephraim and Menasheh had been at considerable risk of intermingling with their Egyptian neighbors and eventually straying from Judaism.

We can now understand the need to "hide" the Rosh Chodesh aspect of Tishrei.

16. By Rabbi Yaakov Kamenetsky *zt"l*.
17. *Rashi, Bereishis* 48:1.
18. Ibid. 42:23.

kaballah, and Rosh Hashanah is a time to focus on *nesinah*, it would be inappropriate to celebrate Rosh Chodesh on Rosh Hashanah.

II. Community vs. Individual

ANOTHER DIFFERENCE BETWEEN ROSH HASHANAH AND Rosh Chodesh is that on Rosh Hashanah the focus is on each *individual*, whereas Rosh Chodesh is a day of public celebration.

- The very first individual in history, Adam Harishon, was created on Rosh Hashanah. This foreshadows the theme of the day.

Each individual is judged on Rosh Hashanah according to his or her deeds

- Each individual is judged on Rosh Hashanah according to his or her deeds, as *Chazal* teach[19]: "When are an individual's [prayers accepted]? During the ten days from Rosh Hashanah through Yom Kippur.

In *Unsaneh Tokef* — one of the emotional highlights of the Rosh Hashanah *tefillah* — we state, "All mankind will pass before You like *Bnei Maron*.[20] Like a shepherd pasturing his flock, making his sheep pass under his staff, so shall You cause to pass, count, calculate, and consider *the soul of all the living*, and You shall apportion the fixed needs of all Your creatures and inscribe their verdict.

Rambam[21] also stresses the individualistic nature of the Ten Days of Repentance, which begin on Rosh Hashanah:

Although teshuvah and crying out [to Hashem] are always beneficial, they are extremely beneficial during the ten days between Rosh Hashanah and Yom Kippur.

Although *teshuvah* (repentance) and crying out [to Hashem] are always beneficial, they are extremely beneficial during the ten days between Rosh Hashanah and Yom Kippur. [During this time period] they are accepted immediately, as the verse states, "Seek Hashem when He can be found" (*Yeshayah* 25:6). This is true, however, only for an individual, but a community can have its repentance and

---

19. *Rosh Hashanah* 16a, 18a; *Yevamos* 49b.

20. The Talmud (*Rosh Hashanah* 18a) records a dispute regarding the elucidation of *Bnei Maron*.

   Reish Lakish explains that there was a precipitous path through a mountain called Maron, with deep valleys on either side of the path. The path was wide enough for only one person to walk. Just as the *Bnei Maron* — i.e., those climbing the mountain Maron — could walk only in single file, when we pass before Hashem on Rosh Hashanah, we do so one at a time. Rabbi Yehudah taught in the name of Shmuel that *Bnei Maron* refers to the soldiers who fought in King David's army, who were counted one by one on their way out to battle.

21. *Hilchos Teshuvah* 2:6.

prayers answered at any time, as the verse states, "… as is Hashem, our God, whenever we call to Him" (*Devarim* 4:7).

Although the entire world and all of its nations are judged as a whole on Rosh Hashanah, each individual in *Klal Yisrael* is judged on his own, as *Netziv* writes, "When one individual in *Klal Yisrael* is struck by great difficulty and illness he realizes that his sins brought this punishment upon him. So too, when a large group of Jews suffers from the difficulties of exile, *each individual had been judged on the basis of his own merit, as an individual* [i.e., no one is punished for the sins of others].Consequently when the Attribute of Justice renders strict judgment in a time of Heavenly anger, all those worthy of punishment are punished together, but individuals who are righteous enough not to be worthy of punishment would be spared."

ROSH CHODESH IS CELEBRATED ON A NATIONAL LEVEL.

Rosh Chodesh — Public Celebration

In the *Mussaf* prayer recited on Rosh Chodesh we say, "רָאשֵׁי חֲדָשִׁים לְעַמְּךָ נָתַתָּ, *Rosh Chodesh have you given to your nation.*"

In *Bircas HaChodesh*, we stress the idea of national unity by saying, "חֲבֵרִים כָּל יִשְׂרָאֵל, *all of Klal Yisrael are comrades.*"

- When the *Beis HaMikdash* stood, Rosh Chodesh was designated by *Beis Din*,[22] not by an individual.

- *Ramban*[23] comments that the mitzvah to consider Nissan the beginning of the months should have been given to the entire Jewish nation, but Moshe and Aharon represented them in receiving this mitzvah. Therefore, when Hashem told Moshe and Aharon, "הַחֹדֶשׁ הַזֶּה לָכֶם רֹאשׁ חֳדָשִׁים, *This month shall be for you the beginning of the months*" (*Shemos* 12:2), he was addressing not only Moshe and Aharon; He was addressing the Jewish nation for all generations to come. *Ramban* obviously considers Rosh Chodesh a concept of *national* significance

It stands to reason, therefore, that Rosh Hashanah — when the spotlight is on each individual — cannot be celebrated as Rosh Chodesh, which is celebrated on a national level.

The mitzvah to consider Nissan the beginning of the months should have been given to the entire Jewish nation, but Moshe and Aharon represented them in receiving this mitzvah.

---

22. When the *Beis HaMikdash* stood, each month the central rabbinical court would wait for two valid witnesses to testify that they had sighted the new moon. If the court determined that the testimony was reliable, it would declare that day Rosh Chodesh.

23. *Shemos* 12:2.

III. Rosh Chodesh: Exclusive to Klal Yisrael

Rosh Chodesh is celebrated exclusively by Klal Yisrael, but the judgment of Rosh Hashanah affects all nations of the world.

A THIRD DIFFERENCE BETWEEN ROSH CHODESH AND ROSH Hashanah is that Rosh Chodesh is celebrated exclusively by *Klal Yisrael*, but the judgment of Rosh Hashanah affects *all* nations of the world.

The word לָכֶם, *for you,* in the verse "הַחֹדֶשׁ הַזֶּה לָכֶם רֹאשׁ חֳדָשִׁים, *This month shall be for you the beginning of the months*" (*Shemos* 12:2) limits the mitzvah of Rosh Chodesh to the Jewish nation. In fact, *Ramban* notes that Nissan is not *actually* the first month of the year,[24] but we consider it the first month, in order to commemorate the great miracles that occurred in Nissan in the process of our redemption from Egypt. Obviously, then, this mitzvah applies only to the nation that was redeemed from Egypt.

Furthermore, Rosh Chodesh celebrates the renewal of the moon, and the Jewish people are compared to the moon: The moon appears very small at the beginning of the month; at the middle of the month it attains its full size, only to diminish toward the end of the month. So, too, the Jewish people are constantly rising and falling. We go through periods of national growth and success, and then through difficult times when we suffer at the hands of the other nations. No matter how difficult life is during such times, however, we are guaranteed that there will again be a process of renewed, vigorous growth, just as the moon has.

No matter how difficult life is during such times, however, we are guaranteed that there will again be a process of renewed, vigorous growth, just like the moon.

ROSH HASHANAH, ON THE OTHER HAND, IS A DAY OF JUDGMENT FOR all who walk the earth[25]:

Rosh Hashanah: For All Nations

1) The Talmud[26] states that Rosh Hashanah is not only a day of judgment for the Jewish nation — as we might deduce from the verse כִּי חֹק לְיִשְׂרָאֵל הוּא, *Because it is a decree for Israel (Tehillim* 81:5)[27] — but for the entire world, as can be

---

24. We follow the opinion that holds that the world was not created in Nissan, but in Tishrei.

25. See excerpt quoted above from *Unesaneh Tokef*.

26. *Rosh Hashanah* 8a

27. As explained by the Talmud and various Midrashim, Psalm 81 is devoted primarily to Rosh Hashanah.

understood from the second half of the verse: מִשְׁפָּט לֵאלֹקֵי יַעֲקֹב, *a judgment day for the God of Jacob* (ibid.), which implies that its significance is not limited to Israel. Since Hashem's sovereignty is universal, so His judgment embraces everyone.

2) Chanah praised Hashem for granting her a child on the day when "Hashem judges to the ends of the earth" (*I Shmuel* 2:10). "When does Hashem judge to the ends of earth?" asks the Midrash.[28] "On Rosh Hashanah."

3) In *Mussaf* of Rosh Hashanah we say, "And of the countries, it is said [on Rosh Hashanah] which is for the sword, and which will have peace, which is for starvation, and which will have plenty? And the creations are remembered for life and for death. *Who is not remembered on this day*?"

It is quite logical, in fact, that Rosh Hashanah should be a day of judgment for all who walk the earth, since Adam HaRishon — from whom all humans descend — was created on Rosh Hashanah. But it would be inappropriate to celebrate Rosh Chodesh — a festival which is exclusive to Jews — on the first of Tishrei, which is a day of judgment for *all* people.

IV. A Microcosm vs. A New Beginning

A FOURTH DIFFERENCE BETWEEN ROSH CHODESH AND ROSH Hashanah can explain not only why we hide Rosh Chodesh of the month of Tishrei, but also why it is celebrated on the first and the second of Tishrei, not on the last day of Elul and the first of Tishrei, as is the common practice of Rosh Chodesh.

Rabbi Moshe Avigdor Amiel writes:

> Rosh Hashanah is the "head" of the year, not just the beginning of the year. The head is the nerve center of the body, giving life to the entire body. So too, Rosh Hashanah is the "nerve center" of the year, from which we draw life for the entire year.
>
> The idea that Rosh Hashanah sets the standards for the year to come is also apparent in *Chazal's* teaching[29] — which

The head is the nerve center of the body, giving life to the entire body. So too, Rosh Hashanah is the "nerve center" of the year, from which we draw life for the entire year.

---

28. *Pesikta Rabbasi* 40:1.
29. *Horayos* 12a; *Kereisos* 6a.

has become accepted practice — to eat special foods on Rosh Hashanah to provide an auspicious start for the year to come.[30] Since Rosh Hashanah represents all the days of the coming year, it must be celebrated entirely in the new year, so the first day of Rosh Hashanah cannot be on the last day of Elul.

Rabbi Amiel continues:

> Whereas we would hope that every day of the year will follow the auspicious omens we ate on Rosh Hashanah, the moon does not — and should not — remain the same throughout the month. It gets larger and larger, until it reaches its fullest in the middle of the month and then begins to diminish. Obviously, then, Rosh Chodesh is not a microcosm of the entire month to come, but rather the beginning of a new month and a new cycle of growth and reduction. Since it is impossible to have two beginnings to the month, if there are two days of Rosh Chodesh, one is celebrated on the last day of the previous month.

The first of Tishrei is more than just a new beginning, it is a harbinger of what is to come.

Based on Rabbi Amiel's brilliant observation that Rosh Hashanah is a microcosm of the year, not simply a start of the new year, it stands to reason that *Chazal* considered it important to celebrate the first of Tishrei *only* as Rosh Hashanah, and not as Rosh Chodesh, to make it clear that the first of Tishrei is more than just a new beginning, it is a harbinger of what is to come.

---

30. The accepted custom in *Klal Yisrael* is to eat symbolic foods on the first night of Rosh Hashanah (some repeat this custom on the second night as well) and recite prayers alluding to those foods. For instance, we dip challah and apple into honey and pray that we should have a sweet year, and we eat *tamar* (date) and pray "*sheyitamu son'einu* — may our enemies be consumed" (the word *tamar* is similar to the fragment *tamu* in the word *sheyitamu*).

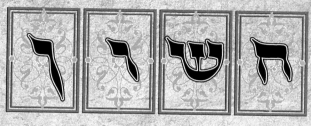

chesbvan

עַל פִּי סֵדֶר הַדְּגָלִים הֲלֹא הֵם מִתְיַחֲסִים
תִּשְׁרֵי לְאֶפְרַיִם, מַרְחֶשְׁוָן לִמְנַשֶּׁה ....

(בני יששכר, מאמרי חדש תשרי מאמר א, אות ב)

According to the order of the encampments,
Tishrei corresponds to Ephraim,
and Marcheshvan to Menasheh ....

(*Bnei Yissaschar, Maamarei Chodesh Tishrei 1:2*)

Rosh Chodesh: A Blend of Festival and Weekday

I N ORDER TO UNDERSTAND THE CONNECTION BETWEEN THE month of Cheshvan and the tribe of Menasheh, we must first analyze the nature of Rosh Chodesh.

In examining the *halachos* of Rosh Chodesh, we find laws that are seemingly contradictory. In some ways, Rosh Chodesh is considered an ordinary weekday, but in other ways it has the status of Yom Tov (festival).

Since the Torah brackets Rosh Chodesh with the festivals, it has the status of a festival in Torah law.

1) The Torah links Rosh Chodesh with the festivals: וּבְיוֹם שִׂמְחַתְכֶם וּבְמוֹעֲדֵיכֶם וּבְרָאשֵׁי חָדְשֵׁיכֶם, *On a day of your gladness, and on your festivals, and on your new moons* (*Bamidbar* 10:10). The *Tur*[1] rules that it is permissible to fast on any day, except for Shabbos, Yom Tov, Rosh Chodesh, and Chol HaMoed. *Perishah* explains that the ruling is based on *Yerushalmi*[2]; he infers that since the Torah brackets Rosh Chodesh with the festivals, it has the status of a festival in Torah law and therefore one who vowed to fast on Rosh Chodesh may not keep his vow. Talmud Bavli also refers to Rosh Chodesh as a Yom Tov,[3] stating clearly that it is considered a Yom Tov of Biblical origin.[4]

Nevertheless, despite Rosh Chodesh's status as a Yom Tov, work is permitted as if it were a weekday.

Hashem rewarded women with the privilege of observing the sanctity of Rosh Chodesh more than men do.

Conversely, *Yerushalmi*[5] records a custom that women refrain from working on Rosh Chodesh. *Pirkei D'Rabbi Eliezer*[6] explains that Hashem rewarded women with the privilege of observing the sanctity of Rosh Chodesh more than men do in return for their refusal to willingly contribute their jewelry for the

1. *Orach Chaim* 418.
2. *Taanis* 2:12.
3. *Taanis* 17b.
4. *Rashi* (ibid.) sources this to the verse "He [Hashem] proclaimed a festival against me" (*Eichah* 1:15), explaining that the festival referred to in this verse is Rosh Chodesh Av.
5. *Taanis* 1:6.
6. 44.

creation of the Golden Calf. *Tur*[7] states that is a "good custom" that women refrain from work on Rosh Chodesh.

We must seek to understand this dichotomy. On one hand Rosh Chodesh is considered a festival. On the other hand, men are allowed to work — but women should not!

2) The Torah commands us to be glad on festivals, but there is no explicit commandment to be joyous on Rosh Chodesh. Some authorities maintain that there is a mitzvah to be joyous on Rosh Chodesh. *Ramban's*[8] stance is somewhere between the two, stating that there is a mitzvah to rejoice on Rosh Chodesh with song and music in the *Beis HaMikdash*, when the special *Mussaf* offering of the day was brought. Outside the Temple, however, although Rosh Chodesh is a day of gladness, they minimized such overt expressions of celebration as song, because Rosh Chodesh is not sanctified as a festival.[9]

Even if there is no *commandment* of joy on Rosh Chodesh, it is considered a day of happiness. *Tur* quotes the ruling of *R' Yitzchak ibn Gias* that one should not recite *Tzidduk Hadin* (Acceptance of Judgment) for the dead on Rosh Chodesh, because it is considered a day of gladness.[10]

On one hand Rosh Chodesh is considered a festival. On the other hand, men are allowed to work – but women should not!

3) There is a mitzvah to observe the festivals through כָּבוֹד וְעוֹנֶג, honoring and enjoying them (through food and drink), but on Rosh Chodesh we find no such obligation. We are also obligated to eat two proper meals on festivals, but on Rosh Chodesh, although it is commendable to have larger meals than usual,[11] there is no specific obligation to do so.

4) We find several contradictory indicators in the *tefillos* of Rosh Chodesh, as well.

  (a) We recite *Mussaf* on Rosh Chodesh, which indicates that it is a festival. On festivals, however, we recite only seven

---

7. *Orach Chaim* 417.

8. Notes to *Rambam's Sefer HaMitzvos, Shoresh* 1.

9. *Ramban* explains that this might be part of the general rule to sing while offering sacrifices, and one could sing only with joy. Since there is no mitzvah to sing outside the *Beis HaMikdash*, the obligation to be joyous does not apply.

10. *Ritz Gias* cites proof that Rosh Chodesh is a day of gladness from the aforementioned verse (*Bamidbar* 10:10) that includes Rosh Chodesh with festivals and days of gladness, and from the words of *Hallel* recited on Rosh Chodesh: "This is the day Hashem has made; *let us rejoice and be glad on it*" (*Tehillim* 118:24).

11. *Tur* and *Shulchan Aruch* 419.

blessings in every *Shemoneh Esrei*,[12] whereas on Rosh Chodesh we recite the ordinary weekday *Shemoneh Esrei* (with the inclusion of *Ya'aleh Ve'yavo*), except for the *Mussaf*.

(b) If one forgets to recite *Yaaleh Veyavo* in the *Maariv Amidah* of a festival, he must repeat the *Amidah*, whereas on Rosh Chodesh he does not.[13]

(c) Similarly, if a person forgets *Yaaleh Veyavo* in *Bircas HaMazon* (Blessing After Meals) on a festival, he must recite *Bircas HaMazon* again, but on Rosh Chodesh he does not.

Krias HaTorah on Rosh Chodesh is also a "compromise" between Yom Tov and weekday.

(d) *Krias HaTorah* on Rosh Chodesh is also a "compromise" between Yom Tov and weekday. On a regular weekday, three people are called to the Torah, and on Yom Tov there are five *olim*. On Rosh Chodesh — the blend of Yom Tov and weekday — there are four *olim*.[14]

(e) We do not read a *Haftarah* (portion of *Navi* related to the Torah reading) on Rosh Chodesh — a clear indication that it is a weekday.

(f) We recite *Hallel* on Rosh Chodesh, as we do on festivals, but we omit the first sections of the two middle psalms, in order to show that this *Hallel* is of a lower status than that of the festivals. Furthermore, some authorities maintain that we should not recite a blessing on *Hallel* on Rosh Chodesh. The Talmud[15] records an incident in which Rav, one of the leading Talmudic sages, determined that the recitation of *Hallel* on Rosh Chodesh is actually a *custom*, not obligatory as it is on festivals.

---

12. *Amidah* (lit., standing prayer) is commonly referred to as *Shemoneh Esrei* even on Shabbos and festivals. Technically, however, this is a misnomer because *Shemoneh Esrei* means eighteen — the number of blessings the weekday *Amidah* originally comprised, whereas there are only seven blessings in the Shabbos and festival *Amidah*.

13. Since *Beis Din* could not declare the beginning of Rosh Chodesh at night, it was not known at night whether that day would be consecrated as Rosh Chodesh (*Berachos* 30a).

14. *Mishnah Megillah* 4:2. Appropriately, on Chol HaMoed — which resembles Rosh Chodesh as a blend of Yom Tov and *chol* — there are also four *olim*.

15. *Taanis* 28b.

1. A Day of Remembrance

CONTRARY TO ALL THESE INDICATORS THAT ROSH CHODESH IS not as holy as Yom Tov, we do find one quality in which Rosh Chodesh is superior to the festivals: Rosh Chodesh is a *Yom HaZikaron*, a Day of Remembrance. In the *Al Hamichyah* blessing, the phrase added on Rosh Chodesh prays that God "remember" us for good. In fact, the Talmud[16] explains that we are not required to make specific mention of Rosh Chodesh on Rosh Hashanah[17] (even though it is the first day of the month); the term "*Yom Hazikaron*," with which we describe Rosh Hashanah, applies to Rosh Chodesh as well. The Sabbath and festivals, on the other hand, are not considered days of remembrance.

By examining all of the facts we have gathered regarding Rosh Chodesh — its seemingly contradictory status as a semi-festival–semi-weekday on one hand, and its prominence as a *Yom Ha-Zikaron* on the other hand — we can come to a valid understanding of the association of Rosh Chodesh Cheshvan with the tribe of Menasheh.

IN *DIVREI HAGUS VEHA'ARACHAH*,[18] RABBI YOSEF DOV SOLOVEITCHIK discusses the dual nature of Rosh Chodesh. Although some of his

Concealed Holiness vs. Revealed Holiness

points have been mentioned above, we summarize his thesis in full, in order not to detract from the beauty and eloquence of his presentation:

The holiness of Shabbos and the festivals is overt: we are prohibited from performing labor.

There is a fundamental difference between the holiness of Shabbos and festivals, and the holiness of Rosh Chodesh. The holiness of Shabbos and the festivals is overt: we are prohibited from performing thirty-nine forms of labor (save for certain forms that are permitted on Yom Tov for food preparation); we are obligated to rejoice, to render honor to Shabbos or the festival, and to have personal pleasure on those days.

The holiness of Shabbos and Yom Tov manifests itself in a basic, all-encompassing transformation. The mundane feeling we have on weekdays departs, and an aura of holiness descends

The holiness of Shabbos and Yom Tov manifests itself in a basic, all-encompassing transformation.

---

16. *Eruvin* 40a.

17. I.e., although Rosh Hashanah is on the first of Tishrei, we do not mention Rosh Chodesh in *tefillah* or *Bircas HaMazon* (see previous essay on Chodesh Tishrei).

18. Page 163, essay entitled "*Baseser Uvagaluy.*"

upon the world. On Shabbos or Yom Tov we read from the Torah to seven, six, or five *olim*; and we read a *haftarah* that captures the essence of the holiness of the day. Our schedule outside the *Beis Midrash* is also different: we do not work, the worries of the weekdays disappear, and a special interest in the holiness of the day bursts forth.

The holiness of Rosh Chodesh manifests itself in a thoroughly different manner. We do not celebrate Rosh Chodesh in an outward fashion or in concrete actions. At most, we witness the uniqueness of Rosh Chodesh when we recite *Hallel* and *Mussaf* and in *Krias HaTorah*, and when we recite *Yaaleh Veyavo* in *Shemoneh Esrei* and *Bircas HaMazon*.

Otherwise, Rosh Chodesh appears to be an ordinary weekday: we do not refrain from work, and there is no mitzvah to rejoice, honor, or seek pleasure on Rosh Chodesh. We dress in ordinary clothing and carry with us the trouble and burden of seeking a livelihood. We are immersed in the dullness and secularity of daily life, constrained by our jobs. We pour out our prayers to our Master with the same words that we use on an ordinary weekday. In fact, prayers often start earlier than usual on Rosh Chodesh, so that people can rush off to open their stores or come on time to the office. The world continues to run in an ordinary fashion, unwilling to slow its pace to allow the holiness of the day to take hold.

Nevertheless, Rosh Chodesh is laden with great, powerful holiness. There is no halachic difference between a person who forgets to recite *Yaaleh Veyavo* on Rosh Chodesh (in *Shacharis* and *Minchah*) and one who forgets to recite the correct prayers on Yom Kippur (i.e., they must both repeat the *Amidah*).

Still, the holiness of Rosh Chodesh is not visible. It does not appear on the person's mental landscape in its full glory; it does not grab hold of a person's feelings and present him with a refreshed perspective. It is very shy; it distances itself from the world outside. But the modesty of Rosh Chodesh does not diminish the value of its inner holiness. Rosh Chodesh carries more significance than an average weekday. The holiness of Rosh Chodesh manifests itself in offering a special *Mussaf* offering in the *Beis HaMikdash* and in several other ways, and these manifestations raise Rosh Chodesh above the ordinariness of the weekdays and give it the status of a holy day.

Rosh Chodesh is so holy, in fact, that we find its holiness equated with that of Shabbos and Yom Tov:

- The *Mussaf* offering of Rosh Chodesh is listed in *Parashas Pinchas* along with — and with equal prominence to — the *Mussafim* of Shabbos and festivals.

- The husband of the Shunamis[19] asked her, "Why are you going to [the prophet Elisha]? It is not a [Rosh] Chodesh or Shabbos!" (*II Melachim* 4:23), thereby equating Rosh Chodesh and Shabbos.

We even find the modest and secretive Rosh Chodesh referred to as a *Yom HaZikaron*, a status that Yom Tov and Shabbos do not have.

Rabbi Soloveitchik goes on to explain why Rosh Chodesh was celebrated in a more visible fashion in the *Beis HaMikdash*:[20]

In the *Beis HaMikdash*, where the Divine Presence dwelled, hidden holiness was just as meaningful as open holiness. In the Sanctuary, internal and external holiness function at the same time — in fact, contrary to its lack of prominence in the world outside, the holiness concealed in Rosh Chodesh was very prominent in the Temple. The Levites sang as the *Mussaf* was offered on Rosh Chodesh just as they did for the *Mussaf* of Shabbos and Yom Tov; the song of the Rosh Chodesh *Mussaf* was accompanied with the same instruments that were used to accompany the song of *Nissuch Hamayim*[21] and the song of the *Mussaf* offerings on festivals.

Outside the *Beis HaMikdash*, external signs affect the inner feelings. In our mundane lives we must rely on external stimuli to inspire inner joy. Since such signs are absent on Rosh Chodesh, true joy does not exist.

In our mundane lives we must rely on external stimuli to inspire inner joy. Since such signs are absent on Rosh Chodesh, true joy does not exist.

RABBI SOLOVEITCHIK GOES ON TO DESCRIBE A TYPE OF PERSON TO whom he refers as an *Ish Rosh Chodesh* — a person who is the

---

Yosef HaTzaddik, Ish Rosh Chodesh

embodiment of Rosh Chodesh, someone who knows how to combine holiness, especially hidden holiness, with outward mundanity, just as we find them combined on

---

Rosh Chodesh. He notes that the first person who embodied this synthesis was Yosef HaTzaddik:

---

19. See *II Melachim* 4:8-37.

20. See above quotation from *Ramban*.

21. The most joyous occasion of the Jewish year was the festivity accompanying *Nissuch Hamayim*, the pouring of water on the Altar in the *Beis HaMikdash* on Chol HaMoed Succos.

Just as Rosh Chodesh has innate, hidden holiness that does not manifest itself outwardly, Yosef hid his holiness within himself. Only perceptive individuals realized that under the disguise of superficiality hid an extremely righteous and spiritually uplifted soul, which radiated brilliant rays all around it and to the entire world. And just as Rosh Chodesh is part-weekday, part festival — a blend of holiness and mundanity — Yosef, too, synthesized the two. He was the ruler of Egypt, and he was imbued with Torah and holiness.

Just as Rosh Chodesh — a blend of holiness and mundanity — Yosef, he ruler of Egypt, and he was imbued with Torah and holiness.

When Yosef was still a youth in his father's home, Yaakov Avinu tried to hide Yosef's holiness. He made Yosef a *kesones passim* (a fine woolen tunic) so people would focus on his external features rather than on his inner holiness.

Only Yosef, who knew how to hide his holiness and righteousness so well that even the rays that shone forth went unnoticed, could undergo the difficult tests he did and remain righteous. Only Yosef could be the ruler of Egypt — second in command to Pharaoh — and remain the same "Yosef HaTzaddik — Yosef the Righteous" as he was when he left his father.

When Yosef sent *agalos* (wagons) to Yaakov as a symbol of *eglah arufah* (axed heifer), the last subject they had studied together before they were separated, Yaakov immediately understood the implication. He realized that Yosef had remained the same tzaddik he had been when he had been sold into slavery in Egypt, with no blemishes on his record.

Despite ascending to the noble position of viceroy of Egypt, Yosef was able to remain steeped in Torah study. Yosef's astounding beauty — Egyptian girls would clamber onto high walls just to get a glimpse of him[22] — did not prevent him from being a pious and holy person. On the contrary, his beauty served as another mask, another layer of disguise with which to hide his piety.

There is no difference between spiritual and worldly pursuits — they must both be performed for the one purpose only: to fulfill Hashem's Will.

It appears from Rabbi Soloveitchik's beautiful dissertation that Yosef originated a new concept: Judaism *separates* holiness from mundanity, but does not *sever* them from one another. In truth, there is no difference between spiritual and worldly pursuits — they must *both* be performed for the one purpose only: to fulfill Hashem's Will.

Yosef's tactic in life was to imbue worldly matters with holiness, so that spirituality would be present in each and every action that was cloaked in a guise of worldliness, with the outer layer of worldliness overpowered by the inner spirituality.

---

22. *Bereishis* 49:22.

II. Who Deserves the Right Hand?

WHEN YAAKOV AVINU WAS ABOUT TO PASS AWAY, HE blessed Yosef's two sons, Menasheh and Ephraim. An interesting dispute transpired between Yaakov and Yosef while Yaakov was blessing them. Yosef stationed Menasheh at Yaakov's right side, and Ephraim at Yaakov's left, because, as the firstborn, Menasheh was entitled to the greater blessing.[23]

Yaakov disagreed with Yosef's assessment, however. The Torah states, "But Yisrael[24] extended his right hand and laid it on Ephraim's head though he was the younger and his left hand on Menasheh's head. He maneuvered his hands, for Menasheh was the firstborn" (*Bereishis* 48:14).

We may ask a very practical question: If Yaakov felt that Ephraim deserved to be blessed with his right hand, why did he have to maneuver his hands in order to do so? Why didn't he simply instruct Menasheh and Ephraim to switch places?

NETZIV[25] EXPLAINS YAAKOV'S SUPRISING ACTIONS:

Yaakov's Choice

Although Yaakov gave Ephraim more prominence by placing his right hand on him — a prominence that eventually extended to Ephraim leading his encampment in the Wilderness, with Menasheh following him — it did not last forever. When Moshe counted *Klal Yisrael* in *Parashas Pinchas*, Menasheh is listed before Ephraim.

Moreover, even in *Parashas Bamidbar*, when the order of the encampments was established, Ephraim's superiority over Menasheh was less pronounced than that of the heads of the other three groups of tribes. In listing the encampments, the Torah lists each leader first, and then the two tribes that followed. The tribes following the leader were usually introduced with the prefatory phrase וְהַחֹנִים עָלָיו, *Those encamping near him* (*Bamidbar* 2:5,12, 27). In saying that Menasheh followed Ephraim, however, the Torah says וְעָלָיו מַטֵּה מְנַשֶּׁה, literally, *And over him, was the tribe of Menasheh* (ibid. 2:20), which implies

Although Yaakov gave Ephraim more prominence by placing his right hand on him, it did not last forever.

---

23. The right hand has greater significance in all matters of spirituality.

24. Yisrael was the name conferred on Yaakov when he defeated Esav's angel in battle (See *Bereishis* 32:29). The name Yisrael represented Yaakov's new and higher degree of spiritual attainment.

25. *Ha'aemek Davar, Bereishis* 48:14.

that, although it was secondary to Ephraim in terms of their encampment, Menasheh was superior in another regard.

The Torah deliberately preferred Ephraim in some places and Menasheh in others to show us that Ephraim was more prominent than Menasheh only in spiritual matters, but in worldly matters, Menasheh was greater than Ephraim.

The first time Moshe counted the Jewish people was when they were traveling through the Wilderness with the Divine Presence constantly upon them — a journey that clearly transcended nature. In such times, Ephraim was more prominent, so he was listed first. When *Klal Yisrael* was counted in *Parashas Pinchas*, however, they were on the verge of entering Eretz Yisrael, where they would live under more natural circumstances. In such times, Menasheh was more prominent, so he was listed first.

Even in the Wilderness, although Ephraim was the leader of the encampment, Menasheh guided him in worldly matters, because as a firstborn, he was more capable in worldly matters.[26]

Netziv points out that Yaakov had other exemplary grandchildren, such as Peretz and Zarach, the sons of Yehudah, but only Ephraim and Menasheh merited their own blessing. Why? Ephraim and Menasheh each had a unique characteristic that made him a leader: Ephraim was a Torah giant who spent his days cleaving to Hashem, and Menasheh tended to the worldly, communal matters of *Klal Yisrael*.[27]

Netziv[28] uses this concept to explain a puzzling elucidation from *Targum Yonasan*. Yaakov told Ephraim and Menasheh, "בְּךָ יְבָרֵךְ יִשְׂרָאֵל לֵאמֹר יְשִׂמְךָ אֱלֹהִים כְּאֶפְרַיִם וְכִמְנַשֶּׁה, *By you shall [Klal] Yisrael bless, saying, 'May God make you like Ephraim and Menasheh'*" (*Bereishis* 48:20). In elucidating this verse, *Targum Yonasan* writes, "Through you, Yosef, my son, shall *Klal Yisrael* bless their infants *on the day of their Bris Milah*, saying, 'May Hashem make you like Ephraim and like Menasheh.'"

This blessing is somewhat of an oxymoron, notes *Netziv*. If we bless a child to grow up to be like Ephraim, we bless him with success in Torah study. If we bless him to be like Menasheh, we wish him success in worldly matters. It is inappropriate to bless someone who will not study Torah to be like Ephraim, or to bless someone who will

Ephraim was more prominent than Menasheh only in spiritual matters, but in worldly matters, Menasheh was greater than Ephraim.

Ephraim was a Torah giant who spent his days cleaving to Hashem, and Menasheh tended to the worldly, communal matters of Klal Yisrael.

---

26. See *Ha'amek Davar, Bereishis* 27:19.

27. Further proof of Menasheh's status as a lay leader can be seen from *Rashi* to *Bereishis* 42:23.

28. In *Herchav Davar*, his footnotes to *Ha'amek Davar*.

spend his time exclusively studying Torah to be like Menasheh! What does *Targum Yonasan* mean?

The answer lies in the timing of this blessing. At a child's *Bris Milah*, we have no idea how he will grow up, so we give him both blessings. We pray that if the child ends up devoting his time to Torah study, he should excel and be like Ephraim, and if he ends up tending to worldly matters, let him succeed as Menasheh did.

NETZIV'S ASSESSMENT OF MENASHEH AS BEING FOCUSED EXCLUsively on worldly matters, however, is in direct contradiction to an idea he expresses in *Sefer Devarim*, regarding the

Menasheh: Yosef's Heir

reason part of the tribe of Menasheh received its portion on the east bank of Jordan. In *Parashas Mattos* we read that two tribes — Reuven and Gad — asked Moshe to allow them to receive their portion of the Land east of the River Jordan, rather than in *Eretz Yisrael* proper. But Moshe decided to station half of Menasheh there as well. (*Bamidbar* 32:33; *Devarim* 3:13). Why did Moshe place them there if they did not request it?

Netziv (to *Devarim* 3:13) explains that Moshe was concerned that there would not be enough Torah authority on the eastern side of the Jordan, where Gad and Reuven had chosen to live. That is why he stationed half of Menasheh there, because it was important that the tribes of Gad and Reuven be exposed to neighbors who were superior Torah scholars.[29]

According to *Netziv's* explanation of Yaakov's blessings to Ephraim and Menasheh, however, Menasheh was the leader in worldly matters, not a Torah leader! If Moshe was trying to bolster the level of Torah scholarship in the areas across the Jordan, why didn't he station members of Ephraim there?

Perhaps the resolution to this apparent contradiction is that Ephraim's abilities were devoted *exclusively* to Torah study; he did not involve himself in worldly matters at all. Menasheh, on the other hand, was a Torah scholar who did not shun all connection the physical world — on the contrary, his Torah scholarship worked hand in hand with his ability to lead his fellow Jews in the this-worldly circumstances of settling the Land.

Apparently, then, Menasheh inherited Yosef's title of *Ish Rosh*

If Moshe was trying to bolster the level of Torah scholarship in the areas across the Jordan, why didn't he station members of Ephraim there?

---

29. *Netziv* proves that Menasheh's descendants were Torah leaders from the verse מִנִּי מָכִיר יָרְדוּ מְחֹקְקִים, *From Machir descended lawgivers* (*Shoftim* 5:14). The Talmud (*Sanhedrin* 5a) teaches that the word מְחֹקֵק refers to those who teach Torah.

Chodesh; he was able to blend holiness and worldliness, and in this respect he was greater than Ephraim. Perhaps this is why the name מְנַשֶּׁה is comprised of the same letters as the word נְשָׁמָה, *soul*. Just as the soul, the spiritual aspect of a person, is hidden inside a physical body, so too Menasheh's spirituality and Torah scholarship were hidden under his guise of worldliness. This made Menasheh uniquely qualified to elevate the quality of Jewish life in provinces that were far from the spiritual core of the nation.

> *Just as the soul, the spiritual aspect of a person, is hidden inside a physical body, so too Menasheh's spirituality and Torah scholarship were hidden under his guise of worldliness.*

We can now understand why Yosef felt that Menasheh deserved to be blessed with Yaakov's right hand, and although Yaakov disagreed regarding the use of his right hand, the Patriarch wanted Menasheh to *stand* at his right during the blessing.

Yosef saw Menasheh as his heir apparent, the child who inherited his ability to mesh holiness with worldliness, and therefore considered him worthy of receiving the blessing from Yaakov's right hand.

Yaakov Avinu realized that the quality possessed by Yosef and Menasheh is extremely rare. Only select individuals can successfully combine holiness and worldliness and use them both to serve Hashem. Most people must choose: either they are like Ephraim, devoting themselves exclusively to Torah study, or they devote themselves primarily to worldly matters, without becoming great Torah scholars.

Yaakov felt that it was important to apply the greater blessing to Ephraim, who represented the overwhelming majority of people who can succeed only in one aspect of service of Hashem. Nevertheless, Menasheh deserved to stand at Yaakov's right because of his rare ability to blend both forms of service to perfection.

> *Menasheh deserved to stand at Yaakov's right because of his rare ability to blend both forms of service to perfection.*

We can also reach a more meaningful understanding as to why Menasheh was listed first in the census recorded in *Parashas Pinchas*. In order to succeed in Eretz Yisrael, where *Klal Yisrael* would no longer experience miracles on a constant basis as they did in the Wilderness, they would need leaders of Menasheh's stature: leaders who could cope with the natural, worldly events that they would experience — both in *Eretz Yisrael*, and, as *Netziv* notes, across the Jordan as well.

The First Rosh Chodesh for the Ish Rosh Chodesh

NOW THAT WE HAVE DETERMINED THAT *MENASHEH* INHERITED Yosef's ability to mesh holiness and worldliness — to be an *Ish Rosh Chodesh*, to quote Rabbi Soloveitchik — the association between Menasheh and Rosh Chodesh Cheshvan is quite logical. As we noted in the essay on Tishrei, Cheshvan is the first month of the calendar year in which we celebrate Rosh Chodesh; Rosh Chodesh Tishrei is celebrated only as Rosh Hashanah. No tribe would correspond more appropriately to the first Rosh Chodesh of the calendar year than Menasheh, the *Ish Rosh Chodesh*.

CHASSIDIC MASTERS TAUGHT THAT THE NAME MARCHESHVAN IS AN acronym for *Merachshin Sifvasah* — the lips keep moving. The major-

Mar Cheshvan — The Lips Keep Moving

ity of Tishrei is devoted to prayer and service of Hashem, and when Cheshvan begins we are so accustomed to praying that it is as if our lips keep praying of their own accord. The rest of our limbs have already returned to ordinary, worldly matters, but the lips continue to serve Hashem.

This idea perfectly captures the essence of Menasheh — an *Ish Rosh Chodesh*. Such a person can live a dual life without contradiction. His body can perform mundane, worldly tasks, while at the same time his lips utter words of Torah and he infuses his entire body and surroundings with *kedushah*.

kislev

עַל פִּי סֵדֶר הַדְּגָלִים הֲלֹא הֵם מִתְיַחֲסִים תִּשְׁרֵי לְאֶפְרַיִם,
מַרְחֶשְׁוָן לִמְנַשֶּׁה, כִּסְלֵו לְבִנְיָמִין.
(בני יששכר, מאמרי חדש תשרי מאמר א, אות ב)

According to the order of the encampments,
Tishrei corresponds to Ephraim,
Marcheshvan to Menasheh,
and kislev to Binyamin.

(Bnei Yissaschar, Maamarei Chodesh Tishrei 1:2)

Binyamin — Mesirus Nefesh

L ET US EXAMINE SEVERAL FACTORS TO HELP US UNDERSTAND the correlation between the tribe of Binyamin and the month of Kislev.

Yaakov Avinu blessed his sons in the order of their birth. Moshe Rabbeinu, however, changed the sequence when he blessed them.

1) When Yaakov Avinu blessed his sons before he died, he addressed them in the order of their birth: Reuven, Shimon, Levi, Yehudah, Yissachar, and so on. Moshe Rabbeinu, however, changed the sequence when he blessed them. As the firstborn, Reuven was still first, but he was followed by Yehudah, Levi, Binyamin, and then Yosef and the other tribes.[1] Why did Moshe choose such a seemingly peculiar order?

Rashi[2] explains that Moshe placed Binyamin after Levi because the *Beis HaMikdash*, in which the tribe of Levi served, was built in Binyamin's portion of *Eretz Yisrael*. Moshe then blessed Yosef, because the *Mishkan* (Tabernacle), which stood in Shilo for 369 years, was in Yosef's portion; but since the *Beis HaMikdash* was more beloved than the *Mishkan* in Shilo, Moshe blessed Binyamin before Yosef. *Rashi's* explanation notwithstanding, it is still a bit strange that Moshe Rabbeinu gave precedence to Binyamin in spite of two chronological factors – Yosef was older than Binyamin, and the *Mishkan* preceded the *Beis HaMikdash* by 425 years.

In his classic commentary on Moshe's blessings of the tribes, Rabbi Samson Rafael Hirsch writes that Binyamin merited having the *Beis HaMikdash* in his portion for three reasons: he was the only one of Yaakov's sons who was born in *Eretz Yisrael*, he was the only one who did not take part in the sale of Yosef, and he cared for Yaakov Avinu in his old age. Since Binyamin had these three virtues — the holiness of birth in the Holy Land, not being tarnished by his brothers' sin, and being the one who cared for Yaakov — he more than the other tribal ancestors displayed the positive character traits that the *Beis HaMikdash* represented. Thus, it was most appropriate that it be built in his territory.

Binyamin merited having the Beis HaMikdash in his portion for three reasons.

---

1. See *Devarim* 33 for the complete account.
2. Ibid. 33:12.

Two parts of Rav Hirsch's thesis are difficult to understand. A person deserves to be rewarded for being faced with a strong temptation to do wrong and for using his free will to do the right thing. Why, therefore, should Binyamin be rewarded for being born in *Eretz Yisrael* and for not taking part in the sale of Yosef? He did not exercise his free will in those instances; he had no choice in the matter! He did not choose where to be born and he was not present when his brothers sold Yosef.

2) Binyamin had two additional names: Ben Oni (Son of my Mourning), and Yedid Hashem (Hashem's Beloved).

   (a) Ben Oni: Binyamin's mother Rachel died in childbirth. The Torah tells us, "As her [Rachel's] soul was departing — for she died — she called his name Ben Oni, but his father called him Binyamin" (*Bereishis* 35:18).

   (b) Yedid: The Talmud[3] states that the *Beis HaMikdash* was built in the portion of "*Yedid*," a reference to Binyamin, as found in Moshe Rabbeinu's blessing: לְבִנְיָמִן אָמַר יְדִיד ה' יִשְׁכֹּן לָבֶטַח עָלָיו, *Of Binyamin he said: May Hashem's beloved dwell securely* (*Devarim* 33:12).

Why is Binyamin referred to as Hashem's beloved? When we understand all of the above, we will understand the relationship between Binyamin and the month of Kislev.

I. Yehudah, Levi, and Binyamin — Partners in the Beis HaMikdash

AFTER BLESSING REUVEN, THE FIRSTBORN, MOSHE RABBEINU gave priority to the three tribes that are closely associated with the *Beis HaMikdash*. The *Beis HaMikdash* was only partially situated in Binyamin's portion of *Eretz Yisrael*; the rest of it was on a strip of land that belonged to Yehudah and extended into Binyamin's territory.[4] These two tribes had a third partner, of course. The Kohanim and the Levites, who performed the holy service in the *Beis HaMikdash*, were from the tribe of Levi. *Targum Onkelos* highlights the partnership between Binyamin and Levi in an uncharacteristically homiletic elucidation of Yaakov's blessing to Binyamin:

The Beis HaMikdash was only partially situated in Binyamin's portion of Eretz Yisrael; the rest of it was on a strip of land that belonged to Yehudah.

3. *Menachos* 53b.
4. *Zevachim* 53b.

Binyamin — in his land shall the Divine Presence dwell, and in his inheritance shall the *Beis HaMikdash* stand, [in which] the Kohanim will bring offerings in the morning and afternoon, and they will divide the remainder of the meat of the offerings in the evening (*Bereishis* 49:27).

Why were these tribes — Binyamin, Yehudah, and Levi — chosen to be partners in the Beis HaMikdash? What trait did they share that justified this august choice?

Why were these tribes — Binyamin, Yehudah, and Levi — chosen to be partners in the *Beis HaMikdash*? What trait did they share that justified this august choice?

LEVI, BINYAMIN, AND YEHUDAH ALL DISPLAYED REMARKABLE *MESIRUS nefesh* (selfless devotion, to the extent that one is willing to give his or her life to sanctify Hashem's Name).

Three Tribes With Mesirus Nefesh

• Levi — When Yaakov gathered his sons to bless them, he rebuked Shimon and Levi for killing all the inhabitants of Shechem.[5] While Yaakov Avinu considered this act irresponsible, Shimon and Levi had demonstrated incredible *mesirus nefesh* to protect the honor and sanctity of their sister.

Levi's descendants inherited his zealousness. When Moshe descended from Mount Sinai and saw the Jewish people worshipping the Golden Calf, he called out, "Whoever is for Hashem, join me!" (*Shemos* 32:26). The tribe of Levi immediately stepped forward. Moshe instructed them to execute those who had worshiped the idol, saying, "So said Hashem the God of Israel, 'Every man, put his sword on his thigh and pass back and forth from gate to gate in the camp. Let every man kill his brother, every man his fellow, and every man his dear one" (ibid. 32:27).

We can barely imagine how heartrending it was for the Levites to carry out Moshe's order — but they did it.

We can barely imagine how heartrending it was for the Levites to carry out Moshe's order — but they did it. This was *mesirus nefesh* of the highest order.

In his blessing to them forty years later, Moshe lauded them for their selfless actions: "The one who said of his father and mother, 'I have not favored him'; his brothers he did not give recognition, and his children he did not know,[6] for they [the Levites] have observed Your word and Your covenant they preserved" (*Devarim* 33:9).

---

5. Yaakov said, "Shimon and Levi are comrades, their weaponry is a stolen craft." *Rashi* explains that the craft of using weaponry to kill people was the defining characteristic of Eisav, but the brothers "stole" it from him and used it against the city of Shechem.

6. I.e., if a Levite found one of his own relatives guilty of worshiping the Golden Calf, he did not favor him — he killed him along with the others who worshiped the idol.

Pinchas, a Levite, carried this selfless zealotry to the next generation. When a prince of the tribe of Shimon committed a particularly vile act of public immorality, Pinchas killed him in the act, thereby avenging Hashem's honor and ending a Heavenly plague. Hashem rewarded him as for his zealotry by making him a Kohen, thus giving him and his offspring the everlasting right to serve in the *Beis HaMikdash*: "It shall be for him and his offspring after him a covenant of eternal priesthood, because he took vengeance for his God" (*Bamidbar* 25:13).

- Binyamin — According to Rabbi Meir,[7] when *Klal Yisrael* reached the Sea of Reeds and Hashem ordered them to go forward, each of the tribes wanted the honor of being the first to plunge into the water. While they were debating, Binyamin stepped forward and jumped in. Binyamin was rewarded for his *mesirus nefesh* by becoming the host of the Divine Presence, concludes the Talmud, as we see in the verse, "וּבֵין כְּתֵפָיו שָׁכֵן *and [Hashem's] Presence] rests between [Binyamin's] shoulders*" (*Devarim* 33:12), i.e., the hills of Jerusalem are likened to shoulders, and the Temple Mount is nestled among them.

- Yehudah — Yehudah's *mesirus nefesh* was first displayed when he admitted his own wrongdoing during Tamar's trial.[8] He bravely sacrificed his own dignity and exposed himself to ridicule for Hashem's sake, for he would not permit an innocent woman to be put to death to protect his reputation. His selfless devotion was perpetuated by Nachshon ben Aminadav, his descendant, who, according to Rabbi Yehudah, was actually the first person to step into the Sea of Reeds. While others debated who should be the first to show such bravery, Nachshon plunged into the sea.

He bravely sacrificed his own dignity and exposed himself to ridicule for Hashem's sake, for he would not permit an innocent woman to be put to death to protect his reputation.

ALTHOUGH RABBI MEIR AND RABBI YEHUDAH SEEM TO HOLD CONFLICT-ing opinions — *either* Binyamin *or* Nachshon ben Aminadav was the

Both Tribes Are Rewarded

first to enter the Sea of Reeds — *Tosafos*[9] cites a *beraisa*[10] to reconcile the dispute by means of a parable:

What actually transpired at the Sea of Reeds is akin to a king who had two sons. He told his younger son to

---

7. *Sotah* 36a-37b.
8. See *Bereishis* 38:1-26.
9. *Sotah* 37a, s.v. *Vehayu*.
10. *Beraisos* are texts that were composed at the same time as the Mishnah, but Rabbi Yehudah HaNassi did not include them in the Mishnah.

awaken him at daybreak, and he instructed his older son to awaken him three hours into the day.

When the younger son came to awaken the king at daybreak, his older brother prevented him from doing so, insisting that the king wanted to sleep until the third hour. The younger son was adamant that his father wanted to wake up at daybreak. Hearing the commotion in the room, the king woke up. "My children," he told them, "both of you intended to honor me with your actions, so I will reward both of you."

What were their respective rewards? Binyamin, who actually descended into the sea first, according to the *beraisa*, hosted the Divine Presence in their territory, and Yehudah merited the kingship, i.e., the Davidic dynasty.

Both Binyamin and Yehudah intended only to honor Hashem at the Sea of Reeds, but they differed regarding what was the best way to do it.

It is clear from the Sages' parable that both Binyamin and Yehudah intended only to honor Hashem at the Sea of Reeds, but they differed regarding what was the best way to do it. Binyamin wanted to hasten the miracle by plunging into the sea immediately, while Yehudah, like the older son in the parable, wanted to wait until later. So convinced were the people of Yehudah that a delay was necessary that they actually pelted their Binyaminite cousins with stones to prevent them from entering the sea, according to Rabbi Meir, cited above. It remains for us to understand what philosophies motivated the two tribes.

II. Binyamin's Mesirus Nefesh Transcends Nature

Yehudah's mesirus nefesh remained within the confines of nature; Binyamin held that the glory of Hashem is best displayed through open miracles.

NETZIV[11] EXPLAINS THAT THERE ARE TWO FORMS OF *MESIRUS nefesh*. Yehudah's *mesirus nefesh* remained within the confines of nature; the tribe held that it is preferable not to rely on open, unprecedented miracles, as will be explained below. The people of Binyamin held that the glory of Hashem is best displayed through open miracles. Therefore they were ready to advance into the sea, thereby requiring an unprecedented miracle to save their lives.

Kerias Yam Suf (the Splitting of the Sea of Reeds) could occur in one of two ways. It could happen through a hidden miracle, relying on "natural" occurrences, or it could happen through an

_____
11. *Herchav Davar* 33:12.

open miracle. Hashem "moved the sea with a strong eastern wind the entire night" (*Shemos* 14:21), and the wind swept the water away to dry up the land underneath, slowly but surely. This semi-natural occurrence could have disguised the miracle as a series of extreme weather changes. The other option was for a more phenomenal miracle to occur. Hashem could split the sea in one fell swoop, and no one could claim that it was caused by weather-related events.

Hashem allowed *Klal Yisrael* to choose the form of miracle that would take place. If they wanted to wait until the seabed was dry, Hashem would make it happen through a natural process and disguise the miracle through the strong wind. If, however, people would show their faith in Hashem by plunging into the sea, then He would perform an open miracle and split the sea at once.

The dispute between Yehudah and Binyamin at the sea focused on whether Hashem derives greater glory through open miracles or through hidden miracles. Yehudah felt that Hashem derives more honor when we do all we can to minimize the miraculous nature of events, because such "hidden" miracles show that Hashem controls everything — even nature. As we say in the *Modim* blessing of *Shemoneh Esrei*, we thank Hashem for the constant, ceaseless, everyday miracles. The Jew recognizes that life and nature are no less miraculous than the splitting of the sea. That we have become so accustomed to them that we take them for granted does not make them any less miraculous. The leaders of Yehudah deemed it inappropriate, therefore, to plunge into the sea and bring about a phenomenal, open miracle. They wanted to wait until the wind swept away the water, and only then would they lead the way into the sea.

The Jew recognizes that life and nature are no less miraculous than the splitting of the sea.

Binyamin felt that Hashem's glory is more apparent through open miracles, so they did not want to wait until the sea dried. The amazing phenomenon of a sea stopping its flow and walls of water standing erect would demonstrate conclusively that Hashem is not bound by the laws of nature, that nature is His tool, not His master. Since Yehudah did not want to take the lead, Binyamin plunged forward, straight into the sea.

Hashem is not bound by the laws of nature; nature is His tool, not His master.

Thus, both Yehudah and Binyamin were ready for self-sacrifice by plunging into the sea; Yehudah wanted to do so under natural circumstances, while Binyamin preferred to do so under miraculous circumstances.

Netziv concludes by explaining the parable cited by *Tosafos*:

The king in the parable commanded his older son to awaken him at the third hour, which is the hour when kings typically arise. Similarly, Yehudah, who was older and the most populous tribe, wanted to bring about the miracle of *Kerias Yam Suf* under normal circumstances, to show that Hashem is above nature and controls it.

Binyamin, the younger son and one of the smallest tribes, wanted to "awaken the king at daybreak" — i.e., to bring about an extremely unusual and miraculous phenomenon that would wipe away the myth called nature and show that all events are truly under Hashem's sole control.

Hashem rewarded each tribe as appropriate for its specific action. Yehudah was rewarded with the kingship. Binyamin was rewarded with the Beis HaMikdash.

Hashem rewarded each tribe as appropriate for its specific action. Yehudah was rewarded with the kingship. A king must guide the nation in its normal, everyday life, a life without miracles. Binyamin was rewarded with the *Beis HaMikdash* — where countless open miracles occurred constantly.

We might add that Yehudah and Binyamin's respective levels of *mesirus nefesh* are mentioned implicitly in Yaakov's blessings to them. Yaakov compared Yehudah to a lion and Binyamin to a wolf. While lions and wolves are both predators that attack and devour their prey, there is a very basic difference between the two. A lion is powerful and fearless; it attacks with the confidence that it has a natural advantage over its prey. After attacking, a lion eats at its leisure. *Netziv*[12] adds that even if a lion refrains from attacking a flock of sheep, it is not because it is *afraid* of the shepherd, but because it senses the image of Hashem inscribed on the shepherd.

A wolf is different. It has a natural fear of the shepherd and of other animals, but it goes against its nature and attacks a sheep, eats hastily, and runs away.

The highest level of Kiddush Hashem is when it is done in public.

Binyamin's Mesirus Nefesh Eclipses Yehudah's

THE TALMUD (*SANHEDRIN* 74B) STATES THAT THE HIGHEST LEVEL OF *Kiddush Hashem* (sanctifying Hashem's Name) is when it is done in public. But, the Talmud asks, "How many people need to be present to be considered a public?" The Talmud answers that there must be ten Jews, as the verse states "I should be sanctified among the Jewish people" (*Vayikra* 22:32).[13] Consequently, the law

---

12. *Herchav Davar* (*Bereishis* 49:9).
13. See *Rambam, Hilchos Yesodei HaTorah* 5:1-2, who rules accordingly.

is that if a gentile threatens a Jew with death unless he sins, if fewer than ten Jews are present, he should sin to save his life. But if ten or more Jews will witness the desecration of Hashem's Name, the victim must choose martyrdom.

We may suggest, therefore, that since bringing glory to Hashem by sanctifying His Name is more meaningful when it is done publicly, then Binyamin was correct: Hashem derives greater glory from miracles that are so undeniable that all people recognize His control of the universe.

Perhaps we can now explain Rav Hirsch's opinion that Binyamin merited having the *Beis HaMikdash* in his territory because he did not take part in the sale of Yosef. We wondered why he should receive a reward when he was not even present when the act was committed. It is understandable that his birth in *Eretz Yisrael* was an important factor in his favor. The holiness of the Holy Land is no small thing. The Torah and Talmud are filled with laws and virtues that apply only in the Land. One of those virtues, as Rav Hirsch sets forth, is that the only one of Yaakov's sons who was born in *Eretz Yisrael* should have merit over his brothers because of that. But why should he have been reward for his absence at the sale?

Now that we have ascertained that Binyamin's outstanding characteristic was his willingness to endanger himself for Hashem's Will, we can assume that if he had been present when his brothers conspired against Yosef, he would have made a stand against them and prevented the sale. The reward was not for Binyamin's coincidental absence then, but because he possessed a quality that would have made him prevent the sale had he been there.

If he had been present when his brothers conspired against Yosef, he would have made a stand against them and prevented the sale.

Now we can understand why Moshe gave priority to Yehudah, Levi, and Binyamin. They deserved precedence because they had the quality of *mesirus nefesh*. Because of this, even Binyamin, the youngest of the tribes, preceded the others, including his older brother, the great and righteous Yosef.

BINYAMIN'S WILLINGNESS TO BE *MOSER NEFESH* ALSO EARNED HIM THE title *Yedid Hashem, Hashem's Beloved.* The Talmud (*Menachos 53b*)

One Who Is Moser Nefesh Is Hashem's Beloved

states cryptically, "Let a *Yedid*, the son of a *Yedid*, come, and build a *Yedid* for his *Yedid*, in the portion of a *Yedid*, and atone for *Yedidim* in it."

Binyamin's willingness to be moser nefesh also earned him the title "Yedid Hashem, Hashem's Beloved."

The Talmud explains that "*Yedid* son of a *Yedid*" refers to Shlomo HaMelech, a descendant of Avrohom Avinu, both of whom merited the title "Hashem's Beloved."[14] Shlomo built a *Yedid*, the beloved *Beis HaMikdash*,[15] in the portion of Binyamin the *Yedid*, and there will be brought the offerings that will atone for the sins of Hashem's beloved nation.

What is *yedidus*? The word יְדִיד comprises the repetitive word יַד, *hand*. *Yedidim*, people who cherish each other, show their devotion by lending their hands to one another. They are willing to give יַד לְיַד, generously, with an open hand, even surpassing their normal capability to give. In other words, they help one another with *mesirus nefesh*.

Avraham demonstrated such devotion for the sake of Hashem. *Rambam*[16] tells us that when Avraham recognized Hashem's omnipresence and omnipotence, he went to Charan and began to convince others to have faith in the one and only God, and that only He should be worshiped. Then he went from city to city, and from country to country, selflessly spreading Hashem's glory. He was not content to serve Hashem privately. Once he recognized the existence and greatness of the Creator, he felt obligated to bring the message to an unreceptive, often antagonistic, world.

Klal Yisrael merited the title *Yedidim* by displaying similar *mesirus nefesh* throughout the generations, willingly subjecting themselves to torture and slaughter to sanctify Hashem's Name. The Midrash (*Shemos Rabbah* 42:9) states that dogs are the most impudent animals, roosters are the most impudent birds, and the Jews are the most impudent nation. The Midrash explains that this statement is not meant disparagingly — on the contrary, it is a compliment. When faced with the challenge of choosing between conversion and execution, Jews are audacious enough to choose execution.

Finally, although all three tribes — Levi, Yehudah, and Binyamin — exemplified *mesirus nefesh*, it was Binyamin, the paradigm of public dedication to Hashem, who merited being the host of the *Beis HaMikdash*.

Indeed, we might suggest that the *Beis HaMikdash* is called *Yedid* because of the *mesirus nefesh* displayed by the three partners who share it, and Shlomo shares this title because he was a descendant of Yehudah.

---

14. Shlomo in *II Shmuel* 12:25; Avraham in *Yirmiyahu* 11:15.
15. See *Tehillim* 84:2.
16. *Hilchos Avodah Zarah* 1:3.

KISLEV IS BEST KNOWN FOR THE MIRACLE OF CHANUKAH THAT TOOK place toward the end of the month. The miracle came about because

Binyamin and the Chanukah Miracle

six people — Mattisyahu and his five sons — waged a twofold battle: a physical war against the mighty Syrian-Greek army and a spiritual war against Hellenistic Jews, who wanted to adopt Greek culture and force it upon their fellow Jews.

The audacity of waging war against such powerful opponents must have seemed ludicrous. Against impossible odds, their battle against a powerful empire certainly appeared to be more of an attempt at suicide than a realistic war. But Hashem took note of their extraordinary *mesirus nefesh*, and enabled them defeated the Syrian-Greek army, restore and purify the *Beis HaMikdash*, and reinstate the Temple service.

Since no tribe embodies the spirit of *mesirus nefesh* as much as Binyamin, it is only appropriate that Binyamin corresponds to Kislev, the month in which we celebrate a miracle that occurred as a result of extraordinary *mesirus nefesh*.

Teves

הנה, אתחלתא דפורענותא היה בחודש הזה דייקא,
ולא לחינם הוא. והנראה דהנה החודש הזה
מיוחס לשבט דן, אשר בהם היה התחלת עבודה זרה,
פסל מיכה, כידוע.

(בני יששכר, מאמרי חדש כסלו–טבת מאמר יד, אות ב)

Behold, that the retribution [in the era of the first Beis HaMikdash, when Jerusalem was besieged, leading to its destruction] began in this month, was surely for a reason. It seems to me that this was because [Teves] corresponds to the tribe of Dan, who were the first people to worship an idol, namely, the graven image of Michah, as is known.

(Bnei Yissaschar, Maamarei Chodesh Kislev-Teves 14:2)

Dan and Chanukah — Corresponding to Retribution

*B*NEI YISSASCHAR TEACHES THAT THE RETRIBUTION THAT LED TO the destruction of the first *Beis HaMikdash*[1] started in Teves because members of the tribe of Dan, to whom Teves corresponds, were the first Jews in *Eretz Yisrael* to worship idols.

We may reach a satisfactory understanding of why Rosh Chodesh Teves is celebrated during Chanukah.

Surely it is no mere coincidence that the latter days of Chanukah occur during the beginning of Teves. By examining the characteristics of the tribe of Dan and what it represented, we may understand the relationship between Dan and Chanukah, reach a satisfactory understanding of why Rosh Chodesh Teves is celebrated during Chanukah, and see how the festival influences the rest of the month.

1. Dan's Blessing — To an Individual, or the Entire Tribe?

*Y*AAKOV AVINU'S BLESSING TO DAN PROVIDES US WITH A perspective into the traits of the tribe of Dan:

Yaakov Avinu's blessing to Dan provides us with a perspective into the traits of the tribe of Dan.

דָּן יָדִין עַמּוֹ כְּאַחַד שִׁבְטֵי יִשְׂרָאֵל. יְהִי דָן נָחָשׁ עֲלֵי דֶרֶךְ שְׁפִיפֹן עֲלֵי אֹרַח הַנּשֵׁךְ עִקְּבֵי סוּס וַיִּפֹּל רֹכְבוֹ אָחוֹר. לִישׁוּעָתְךָ קִוִּיתִי ה', *Dan will avenge his people, the tribes of Israel will be united as one. Dan will be a serpent on the highway, a viper by the path, that bites a horse's heels so its rider falls backward. For Your salvation do I long, O Hashem!* (*Bereishis* 49:16-18).

There is a fundamental dispute among *Rishonim* whether Yaakov was referring to a specific descendant of Dan, or to the tribe as a

---

1. As we will explain at length later in this essay, on the tenth of Teves King Nevuchadnetzar of Babylon began the siege of Jerusalem, which led to the fall of the city and the destruction of the *Beis HaMikdash*. We commemorate the troubles of that event by fasting on the Tenth of Teves, and praying that the *Beis HaMikdash* be rebuilt.

whole. According to *Rashi* and *Ramban,* following what seems to be *Chazal's* opinion, Yaakov was referring only to Shimshon, the most renowned descendant of Dan. *Rashbam,* however, maintains that Yaakov referred to the entire tribe, foretelling events that would occur in an era when the tribe of Dan would be crucial for *Klal Yisrael's* survival — the era that began with the Exodus and continued through their entry into *Eretz Yisrael.*

RASHI EXPLAINS DAN'S BLESSING AS FOLLOWS:

דָּן יָדִין עַמּוֹ — Dan (through Shimshon) will avenge his people by taking vengeance on the Philistines.

Only Shimshon

כְּאַחַד שִׁבְטֵי יִשְׂרָאֵל — The entire nation will unite under his rule, and he will lead them all.

יְהִי דָן נָחָשׁ עֲלֵי דֶרֶךְ שְׁפִיפֹן עֲלֵי אֹרַח הַנֹּשֵׁךְ עִקְּבֵי סוּס וַיִּפֹּל רֹכְבוֹ אָחוֹר — Dan is compared to a snake; just as a snake attacks the rider without actually touching him, but by biting his horse, so, too, Shimshon killed Philistines without actually touching them.[2]

לִישׁוּעָתְךָ קִוִּיתִי ה' — Yaakov foresaw that the Philistines would capture Shimshon and that Shimshon would ask Hashem to return his strength so that he could take vengeance on them. Yaakov prayed that Shimshon should receive the salvation that he would request.

The Talmud (*Sotah* 10a) expounds that Shimshon ruled *Klal Yisrael* as righteously as Hashem, as we derive from the verse, דָּן יָדִין עַמּוֹ, *Dan shall judge his people,* כְּאַחַד *like the One and only.* This implies that *Chazal,* too, interpret Yaakov's blessing as applying primarily to Shimshon.

Yaakov foresaw that the Philistines would capture Shimshon and that Shimshon would ask Hashem to return his strength so that he could take vengeance on them.

---

2. Shimshon's supernatural strength left him when his treacherous wife Delilah, a Philistine convert acting as their agent, cut off the hair that he grew as a *Nazir.* That allowed the Philistines to capture him. They gouged out his eyes and forced him to grind grain in prison. They then decided to celebrate his capture by feasting in the temple of Dagan, their idol. As they became merry at the celebration, they decided to bring Shimshon from prison and be entertained by the humiliation of their archenemy. They placed him between two pillars. He asked the boy who was leading him to allow him to lean on the pillars of the temple, and he prayed fervently that Hashem should return his strength to him. Shimshon then leaned on the pillars with such force that the entire building collapsed, killing himself along with all the governors of Philistinia — and another three thousand people who had been watching the spectacle from the roof of the temple.

See *Shoftim* Chapters 13-17 for more details of Shimshon's life and death.

RASHBAM TAKES ISSUE WITH THE OPINION OF *RASHI* AND *RAMBAN*, sharply rejecting the possibility that Yaakov would confine his bless-

ing to only one member of a tribe. He contends:

Klal Yisrael Those who elucidate these verses to refer exclusively to Shimshon do not know the depth of the plain meaning of Scripture. Did Yaakov mean to prophesy about one person who would fall prey to the Philistines who would gouge out his eyes, and who would end up dying under tragic circumstances? Heaven forbid! Rather, he prophesied about the *entire tribe of Dan*, who served as the מְאַסֵּף לְכָל הַמַּחֲנֹת, *rear guard of all the camps* (*Bamidbar* 10:25) when the Jews traveled through the Wilderness. Dan continued serving in this capacity under Yehoshua bin Nun's leadership as well, as we see in the verse וְהַמְאַסֵּף הֹלֵךְ אַחֲרֵי הָאָרוֹן, *and the rear guard went after the Ark* (*Yehoshua* 6:9).

The people of Dan, who were very powerful, had to battle the nations who attempted to attack the stragglers who fell behind in their travels, and to wreak vengeance on the nations who attacked *Klal Yisrael* from the rear. Since they defended and protected all the tribes, Yaakov blessed them דָּן יָדִין עַמּוֹ כְּאַחַד שִׁבְטֵי יִשְׂרָאֵל, *May Dan rule his people, unifying all the tribes of Israel.*[3]

Rashbam explains the rest of Yaakov's blessing along the same lines:

יְהִי דָן נָחָשׁ עֲלֵי דֶרֶךְ — May [the tribe] of Dan be like a snake upon the path, and have the power to kill the nations (who attack them).

וַיִּפֹּל רֹכְבוֹ אָחוֹר — May enemies fall before [the tribe of Dan].

לִישׁוּעָתְךָ קִוִּיתִי ה' — I [Yaakov] hope that Hashem will save you [Dan] and fortify you against the nations.

Both of these approaches need further clarification, however.

According to *Rashi* and *Ramban*, we must wonder why Yaakov mentioned specifically the tribe, without even alluding to the individual he meant.

The people of Dan, who were very powerful, had to battle the nations who attempted to attack the stragglers who fell behind in their travels, and to wreak vengeance on the nations who attacked Klal Yisrael from the rear.

---

3. We find that "judging" *Klal Yisrael* means that God takes revenge against their foes. In *Parashas Haazinu*, the Torah states, כִּי יָדִין ה' עַמּוֹ, *When Hashem will have judged His people* (*Devarim* 32:36), and then a few verses later we read, כִּי דַם עֲבָדָיו יִקּוֹם וְנָקָם יָשִׁיב לְצָרָיו, *For He will avenge the blood of His servants; He will bring retribution upon his foes* (ibid. 42). We also find the two ideas equated in the verse יָדִין בַּגּוֹיִם מָלֵא גְוִיּוֹת מָחַץ רֹאשׁ עַל אֶרֶץ רַבָּה, *He will judge the corpse-filled nations, He will crush the leader of the mighty land* (*Tehillim* 110:6).

The last verse of the blessing, לִישׁוּעָתְךָ קִוִּיתִי ה׳, is difficult to understand according to either elucidation, especially according to *Rashbam*, who maintains that it applies to the entire tribe of Dan. Why would only one tribe need salvation and fortification? Why was Dan singled out for this blessing more than the other eleven tribes?

II. The Partnership Between Dan and Yehudah

RASHI ADDS A MIDRASHIC EXPLANATION OF DAN'S BLESSING: דָּן יָדִין עַמּוֹ כְּאַחַד שִׁבְטֵי יִשְׂרָאֵל, *Dan will judge his people like the unique one* [4] *of Israel.*

The Midrash explains that the "unique one" refers to King David, who was a descendant of Yehudah. This Midrash apparently finds some sort of bond between Dan and Yehudah. How are these two tribes connected to each other, and why did Yaakov Avinu feel a need to link Dan to Yehudah?

Before we resolve these questions, let us examine several other instances in which Dan and Yehudah are associated with each other:

1) Both tribes were mighty. Yehudah's strength first became apparent when he threatened the viceroy of Egypt — who turned out to be his brother Yosef — that he would kill him together with Pharaoh. Moshe blessed *Dan* as follows: דָּן גּוּר אַרְיֵה יְזַנֵּק מִן הַבָּשָׁן, *Dan is a lion cub, leaping forth from the Bashan. Yalkut Shimoni* [5] explains that Dan resided at the border of *Eretz Yisrael*, and those who live at the border are compared to lions.

2) Yehudah and Dan were two most populous tribes. *Yerushalmi* [6] states, in fact, that Dan was selected to travel last because of its size (see *Bamidbar* 1:27). Dan's proliferation continued when the Jewish nation was in *Eretz Yisrael* as well: וַיֵּצֵא גְבוּל בְּנֵי דָן מֵהֶם וַיַּעֲלוּ בְנֵי דָן וַיִּלָּחֲמוּ עִם לֶשֶׁם וַיִּלְכְּדוּ אוֹתָהּ, *The boundary of the children of Dan was not sufficient for them, so the children of Dan ascended and battled with Leshem, and conquered it*

Dan resided at the border of Eretz Yisrael, and those who live at the border are compared to lions.

---

4. The Midrash expounds the word כְּאַחַד to mean הַמְיוּחָד, the unique, or special, leader of *Klal Yisrael.*

5. 962.

6. *Eruvin* 5:1; cited in *Rashi, Bamidbar* 10:25.

(*Yehoshua* 19:47). *Radak* explains that the territory allotted to them was not sufficient because they were so populous.

3) Members of Yehudah and Dan took the lead in building the Mishkan:

וַיֹּאמֶר מֹשֶׁה אֶל בְּנֵי יִשְׂרָאֵל רְאוּ קָרָא ה' בְּשֵׁם בְּצַלְאֵל בֶּן אוּרִי בֶן חוּר לְמַטֵּה יְהוּדָה, *Moshe said to the Children of Israel, "See, Hashem has proclaimed by name, Betzalel, son of Uri son of Chur, **of the tribe of Yehudah** (Shemos 35:30).* וּלְהוֹרֹת נָתַן בְּלִבּוֹ הוּא וְאָהֳלִיאָב בֶּן אֲחִיסָמָךְ לְמַטֵּה דָן, *He [Hashem] gave him [Betzalel] the ability to teach, [to] him and Oholiav, son of Achisamach, **of the tribe of Dan** (ibid. 34).*

Rashi comments, "Oholiav came from Dan, one of the more lowly tribes, because Dan was a son of Bilhah, one of the maids whom Jacob married, yet Hashem compared him to Betzalel, who came from one of the greatest tribes, in fulfillment of the verse וְלֹא נִכַּר שׁוֹעַ לִפְנֵי דָל', *nor [does Hashem] let a noble be given recognition over a pauper'* (*Iyov* 34:19). Thus, despite his lineage, Oholiav was equated with the aristocratic Betzalel as a builder of the Mishkan.[7]

> *Oholiav came from Dan, one of the more lowly tribes, yet Hashem compared him to Betzalel, who came from one of the greatest tribes.*

KLI YAKAR EXPLAINS THE NEED FOR COLLABORATION BETWEEN DAN and Yehudah.

The Quintessential Leaders of Klal Yisrael

Although Yehudah traveled first in the encampments and Dan traveled last, they are truly comparable to one another. Dan's reign over his fellow tribes was equal to Yehudah's, for Shimshon ruled *Klal Yisrael* in his generation as David did in his. Additionally, *Mashiach*, who will descend from Yehudah, "will strike [the wicked of] the world *with the rod of his mouth, and with the breath of his lips he will slay the wicked*" (*Yeshayah* 11:4), meaning that his curse will bring an end to evil people. Similarly, Dan eliminated the wicked members of *Klal Yisrael* by pronouncing judgment against them with his mouth, just as a snake uses its mouth to kill its enemies.[8]

> *Dan eliminated the wicked members of Klal Yisrael by pronouncing judgment against them with his mouth, just as a snake uses its mouth to kill its enemies.*

---

7. Interestingly, Dan's involvement in building the physical dwellings for the Divine Presence did not end with the Mishkan. The person whom Shlomo HaMelech chose to build the *Beis HaMikdash* was "the son of a woman of the daughters of Dan" (*II Divrei Hayamim* 2:13). The Midrash explains that the people of Dan were experts in carving and weaving, artistries they passed down from one generation the next.

8. This idea is implicit in the combination of the two clauses, "Dan will *judge* his people," and "Dan will be like a serpent."

It was imperative that Yehudah be at the head of all the encampments and that Dan should take up the rear. Yehudah is compared to a lion, whose strength lies primarily in its tail [perhaps because it is the king of the jungle and others animals are struck with fear even when they see it from behind], and when *Klal Yisrael* traveled behind Yehudah, it was figuratively as if they saw the tribe's "tail," so that the nation would not dare to rebel and be punished by Yehudah. Dan, on the other hand, is compared to a snake, whose power lies in its mouth. When *Klal Yisrael* turned around, they saw Dan's "mouth," with which he exerted control over them.

Since judges will always suffer from detractors, Yaakov prayed, לִישׁוּעָתְךָ קִוִּיתִי ה׳, a prayer that Dan should be protected from such opponents. Some commentators derive from this blessing that Dan did not show favoritism toward his own tribe. He would judge *his* people, i.e., his own tribe, not as a clan that deserved special favored treatment, but he would treat them כְּאַחַד שִׁבְטֵי יִשְׂרָאֵל, *like one of the tribes of Israel,* i.e., no differently than any other tribe.

Moshe's blessing, which compared Dan to a lion, does not contradict Yaakov's blessing comparing him to a serpent, for every judge faces enemies from the fore and from the rear, and he must be able to defend himself from both directions. Yaakov's blessing enabled Dan to fight off or ignore frontal, verbal attacks, and Moshe's blessing enabled him to fend off those who attack from the rear, and ignore comments that were made behind his back.

Thus, *Kli Yakar* teaches that the tribal formation, which had Yehudah leading the people and Dan bringing up the rear, allowed for the most comprehensive, powerful leadership.

Interestingly, Shimshon, Dan's leading son, was also a product of a union between Dan and Yehudah, for his father, Manoach, was from Dan, and his mother was from Yehudah. The Midrash[9] tells us, in fact, that Dan merited to put forth a leader of *Klal Yisrael* (Shimshon) only *because* Manoach married a woman from Yehudah,[10] since Yehudah was the historic leader of the nation.

Yalkut Shimoni[11] teaches that *Mashiach*, as well, will descend

Shimshon, Dan's leading son, was also a product of a union between Dan and Yehudah, for his father, Manoach, was from Dan, and his mother was from Yehudah.

---

9. *Bereishis Rabbah* 98:13.

10. A different Midrash (*Bamidbar Rabbah* 10:5) states that this is implicit in Yaakov's comparison of Dan to the מְיֻחָד שֶׁבַּשְּׁבָטִים, *the unique one among the tribes,* Yehudah.

11. *Parashas Vayechi* 160.

from a union between Dan and Yehudah, both of whom were compared to a lion.

IF WE EXAMINE THE *RASHBAM* CITED EARLIER, WE FIND THAT YAAkov alluded to Dan's important

לִישׁוּעָתְךָ קִוִּיתִי ה׳ —
Awaiting the Redemption

role in *Ikvesa D'Meshicha*, the period leading to *Mashiach*'s arrival. *Rashbam* linked Yaakov's words, דָּן יָדִין עַמּוֹ, to a verse in *Parashas Haazinu* that discusses *Ikvesa D'Meshicha*: כִּי יָדִין ה׳ עַמּוֹ, *When Hashem will have judged His people* (*Devarim* 32:36).

Chazal tell us that *Ikvesa D'Meshicha* will be a particularly difficult time for the Jewish people; we will be embroiled in one war after another, in which the nations of the world will attempt to eliminate us from the world. Yaakov felt that in such times we would need the special power of Dan, the "serpent on the highway," and we would also need our forefather's fervent prayer for Dan: לִישׁוּעָתְךָ קִוִּיתִי ה׳, *For Your salvation do I long, O Hashem!*

> *Ikvesa D'Meshicha will be a particularly difficult time for the Jewish people; we will be embroiled in one war after another, in which the nations of the world will attempt to eliminate us from the world.*

If we look back in history, we find that we have constantly been under attack from the nations. The very first battle was fought in the time of Yaakov, who presented Yosef with the city of Shechem, which, "I took from the hand of the Amorite with my sword and with my bow" (*Bereishis* 48:22). *Rashi* explains that after Shimon and Levi wiped out the inhabitants of Shechem, the surrounding Canaanites gathered to do battle. Yaakov armed himself, went to war, and defeated them.

The battle has been fought constantly ever since, and will continue to be fought until *Mashiach* ultimately redeems us from exile. Only the combined qualities of Dan and Yehudah can save us from annihilation. Yehudah provides the spiritual power to succeed in battle. The Mishnah tells us that the Jewish king — who must be a descendant of Yehudah — must write a special Sefer Torah to carry with him wherever he goes, including to a battlefront. This quality is best symbolized by King David, the first king from Yehudah and the ancestor of *Mashiach*.

> *David was a great warrior, but his paramount role in Jewish history is as the author of Tehillim, and the very embodiment of prayer.*

David was a great warrior, but his paramount role in Jewish history is as the author of *Tehillim*, and the very embodiment of prayer. Dan is the quintessential "rear guard" of *Klal Yisrael*, protecting us from attackers and avenging any attacks. As noted above quoting *Kli Yakar*, these are the two essential roles of the protectors of Israel.

Perhaps we can suggest that even *Rashi* and *Ramban* — who explain Yaakov's blessing in the context of Shimshon and the Philistines — do not mean that Yaakov's blessing pertains *exclusively* to Shimshon. His battles with the Philistines are simply a representative sample of the history of *Klal Yisrael*. Each generation has its Philistines who wage war against *Klal Yisrael*, and Hashem provides each generation with a Shimshon to save us from our persecutors. Therefore, the blessing of לִישׁוּעָתְךָ קִוִּיתִי ה׳, *For Your salvation I hope, O Hashem!* applies equally to all generations. [12]

III. Teves: A Difficult Month

WE CAN NOW UNDERSTAND WHY DAN IS ASSOCIATED WITH Teves. Teves is one of the most difficult months of the year. Tragedy struck three times in Teves, as described in the *Selichos* we recite on *Asarah b'Teves*:

אֶזְכְּרָה מָצוֹק אֲשֶׁר קְרָאַנִי, בִּשְׁלשָׁה מַכּוֹת בְּחוֹדֶשׁ הַזֶּה הִכַּנִי, גְּדָעַנִי הֲנִיאַנִי הִכְאַנִי, אַךְ עַתָּה הֶלְאַנִי, *I recall the distress that befell me, with three blows He struck me in this month* — He cut me down, He pushed me away, He caused me pain, but by now He has exhausted me.

Tragedy struck three times in Teves. The most familiar of the three calamities is the siege on Yerushalayim.

The most familiar of the three calamities is the siege on Yerushalayim, as we find recorded in *Navi*: "The word of Hashem came to me in the ninth year, in the tenth month, on the tenth of the month, saying, 'Son of Man, write for yourself the name of this day — this very day; the king of Babylonia has reached Jerusalem on this very day" (*Yechezkel* 24:1).

We commemorate the misfortune we experienced on the Tenth of Teves by fasting each year. In a sense, it is the most stringent of all the Rabbinically ordained fast days since, theoretically at least, if it could fall on Shabbos, we would fast on that holy day. It is the only fast (besides Yom Kippur) that we would observe on Shabbos[13];

---

12. It is interesting to note that there is evidence that the tribe of Dan made the blessing of לִישׁוּעָתְךָ קִוִּיתִי ה׳ their "mantra," feeling that this blessing was given to them more than to any other tribe. Eldad HaDani, a 9th-century traveler who claimed to descend from the tribe of Dan, writes about an Ethiopian community of Danites. On their *amud* (chazzan's lectern), in addition to the verse שִׁוִּיתִי ה׳ לְנֶגְדִּי תָמִיד, *I place Hashem before me constantly* (*Tehillim* 16:8) imprinted on a plaque, the common custom in Ethiopian shuls was to add the letters ל, ק, and ה to the plaque — the initials of the words לִישׁוּעָתְךָ קִוִּיתִי ה׳.

13. *Beis Yosef, Orach Chaim* 580. This law is theoretical because in our calendar system, the Tenth of Teves never actually falls on Shabbos. However, it is the only fast that can fall on Friday, and when that happens we actually fast until we recite Kiddush

all other fasts that fall on a Shabbos are postponed until Sunday or observed on Thursday.[14]

The other two calamities referred to in *Selichos* happened on the two days preceding the Tenth of Teves, and those days were set as "fast days of the righteous."[15] *Shulchan Aruch*[16] states that the eighth of Teves was the day that the Torah was translated into Greek on the orders of the Egyptian King Ptolemy, and the world was plunged into spiritual darkness for three days.

The eighth of Teves was the day that the Torah was translated into Greek on the orders of the Egyptian King Ptolemy.

Regarding the ninth of Teves, *Shulchan Aruch* writes that the calamity that fell on that day is unknown. *Ba'er Heitev* cites *Magen Avraham* and *Taz* that the tragedy of the ninth of Teves is mentioned in the *Selichos*:

זוּעַמְתִּי בְּתִשְׁעָה בּוֹ בִּכְלִמָּה וָחֵפֶר, חָשַׁךְ מֵעָלַי מְעִיל הוֹד וְצֶפֶר, טָרוֹף טוֹרַף בּוֹ הַנּוֹתֵן אִמְרֵי שֶׁפֶר, הוּא עֶזְרָא הַסּוֹפֵר, *I was reproached on the ninth [of this month] with humiliation and disgrace, removed from me was the mantle of majesty and my diadem, on his day was torn away the giver of beautiful works, Ezra the Scribe.*

Kaf HaChaim[17] adds that several *Rishonim*[18] write that Ezra HaSofer's colleague, Nechemiah ben Chachalyah, also died on the ninth of Teves.[19]

Other tragedies occurred in Teves as well, although no fast days were established to commemorate them. At the end of the *piyut*, the composer of the *Selichos* hints to the numerous tragedies that befell our nation in this month:

In the month of Teves I was exceedingly smitten, and its normal course was altered to my detriment.

יֶרַח טֵבֵת מְאֹד לָקִיתִי בוֹ וְנִשְׁתַּנּוּ עָלַי סְדָרֵי נְתִיבוֹ, סָדַרְתִּי פְּשָׁעַתִּי יִגָּלֶה לִי טוּבוֹ, הָאוֹמֵר לַיָּם עַד פֹּה תָבֹא, *In the month of Teves I was exceedingly smitten, and its normal course was altered to my detriment. I*

_____

on Friday night, after Shabbos has begun.

14. *Beis Yosef* sources this halachah to the aforementioned verse, which stresses that the hardship fell "*on this very day.*" That term implies that the fast may never be postponed.

15. There are many days in the year in which we experienced extreme hardship in the history of our nation. *Chazal* did not require the general population to fast on *all* of those days, because it would be too difficult, but righteous people impose voluntary restrictions upon themselves on such days.

16. *Orach Chaim* 580:2.

17. Ibid. 20.

18. *Orchos Chaim, Kolbo, BaHaG*; also cited by *Ya'avetz* in his *Siddur Amudei Shamayim.*

19. Ezra HaSofer and Nechemiah were responsible for building the Second *Beis HaMikdash*, and reinstating the Jewish settlement in *Eretz Yisrael* after the Babylonian exile.

strayed, I rebelled; may He reveal to me His goodness — the One Who told the sea, 'This far may you come!'

Among other hardships that befell us in Teves over the years: Shortly before the destruction of the First Temple, King Yechanyah went into exile, taking the Sages with him, and much later, in 5256 (1496), Portuguese Jews were given one year to leave the country unless they agreed to be baptized. This expulsion was especially painful for the multitudes who had immigrated to Portugal after being expelled from Spain just four years before.

IV. Chanukah Injects Light Into the Darkness of Teves

THE DAYS OF CHANUKAH, DURING WHICH WE CELEBRATE ROSH Chodesh Teves, are a perfect way to overcome the dark days of Teves, as explained by *Sfas Emes:*[20]

Rosh Chodesh Teves certainly receives the rays of the Chanukah candles. This causes light to spread to the entire month, because the entire month depends on Rosh Chodesh. Perhaps the reason we light 36 candles is to illuminate the 36 days from the beginning of Chanukah until the end of Teves. I heard from my Rebbi [the *Chiddushei HaRim*] that Teves comes from the same root as הַטָבַת הַנֵּרוֹת, *preparing the candles.* The holy *sefarim* state that Teves is a time of *hester* (a time when the Divine Presence "hides" from us), and therefore Hashem prepared the cure before the illness, so that the kindling of the Chanukah lights will illuminate not only the eight days of the festival, but it will illuminate all the dark days of Teves. As the Torah says of the first day of Creation, "the light is good."

> *Hashem prepared the cure before the illness, so that the kindling of the Chanukah lights will illuminate not only the eight days of the festival, but it will illuminate all the dark days of Teves.*

BNEI YISSASCHAR[21] EXPLAINS THE CONNECTION BETWEEN CHANUKAH and Rosh Chodesh Teves:

Mountaintops

Two mitzvos are performed through ראִי, *sight,* on Rosh Chodesh Teves. When a qualified *Beis Din* was in existence, the court would sanctify the

---

20. *Chanukah 5650.*
21. *Maamarei Kislev Teves, 2:26.*

month upon the testimony of two witnesses who sighted the new moon. And we light the Chanukah candles, upon which we say, וְאֵין לָנוּ רְשׁוּת לְהִשְׁתַּמֵּשׁ בָּהֶם אֶלָּא לִרְאוֹתָם בִּלְבָד, *We are not permitted to use them, only to see them.*[22]

Through a Scriptural allusion, *Bnei Yissaschar* goes on to encapsulate the opportunity we are presented with on Rosh Chodesh Teves. When the flood waters receded in the time of Noach while he was still in the Ark, he longed for the day when dry land would become visible again, and he, his family and the animals on the Ark could once again populate the barren earth. Finally the day came: בָּעֲשִׂירִי בְּאֶחָד לַחֹדֶשׁ נִרְאוּ רָאשֵׁי הֶהָרִים, *In the tenth month, on the first of the month, the tops of the mountains became visible* (Bereishis 8:5). That day was Rosh Chodesh Teves.

Bnei Yissaschar elucidates the verse homiletically to read, "Through the mitzvos we perform on the first day of the tenth month, we can hope to 'see the tops of the mountains'" — i.e., by performing the two mitzvos of the day — Rosh Chodesh and Chanukah — the "mountaintops" will become visible. The mitzvos we perform on that day through what we see — the new moon and the Chanukah menorah — will enable us to look forward to a brighter future, a future when darkness will give way to a vision of great heights — of רָאשֵׁי הֶהָרִים, *the tops of mountains.*

> The mitzvos we perform on that day through what we see — the new moon and the Chanukah menorah — will enable us to look forward to a brighter future.

Chanukah, the "Festival of Lights," symbolizes the triumph against all odds, of light over darkness, of the Jewish people over its enemies, when the many are delivered into the hands of the few, the strong into the hands of the weak, the impure into the hands of the pure, the wicked into the hands of the righteous, and the wanton into the hands of the diligent students of the Torah.

This phenomenon was instilled through blessings of Yaakov and Moshe to the tribe of Dan, which endowed the tribe with the qualities that would help all of Israel to prevail through all the trying times of our history, and that will endure through the time of *Ikvesa D'Meshicha* until the Final Redemption.

> When Israel emerged from Egyptian slavery and accepted the Torah, it needed a Mishkan.

When Israel emerged from Egyptian slavery and accepted the Torah, it needed a *Mishkan*, a place where God's holiness could rest among the nation. The *Mishkan* was built through the partnership of Yehudah and Dan — Betzalel and Oholiav — and Israel's march through the Wilderness to *Eretz Yisrael* required Yehudah at its head and Dan at its rear. The construction of the *Mishkan* required perfection, "wise-hearted people, whom I [God] have invested with a spirit

---

22. Seeing pertains to the mitzvah of Chanukah candles, since one who did not light candles may make a blessing upon seeing them.

of wisdom" (*Shemos* 28:3). Only a combination of the powers of Yehudah and Dan could attain the necessary perfection; as we saw from *Kli Yakar*, only a partnership of Yehudah, whose strength came from his tail, and Dan, whose strength came from his mouth, could lead *Klal Yisrael* properly.

Thus, the quality of Dan, which protects and supports *Klal Yisrael* through its most difficult periods of retribution, and the sanctity of Chanukah, which represents the power of light to dispel darkness, are blended precisely on Rosh Chodesh Teves, so that the Jewish nation can illuminate and overcome the darkness that is inherent in the month of Teves.

shevat

הֶחֹדֶשׁ הַזֶּה עַל פִּי סֵדֶר הַדְּגָלִים, הִנֵּה הוּא מְיֻחָס לְשֵׁבֶט אָשֵׁר, וּמַזַּל הַחֹדֶשׁ הוּא דְּלִי.

(בני יששכר, מאמרי חדש שבט מאמר א, אות ח)

Based on the order of the encampments, [Shevat] corresponds to the tribe of Asher, and the astrological sign of this month is Aquarius.

(Bnei Yissaschar, Maamarei Chodesh Shevat 1:8)

WATER AND OIL: TORAH AND WISDOM

WE FIND A SEEMINGLY DIVERSE — OR EVEN SOMEWHAT contradictory — array of factors associated with the month of Shevat:

- Following the order of the encampments, Shevat corresponds to the tribe of Asher. Yaakov blessed Asher, "מֵאָשֵׁר שְׁמֵנָה לַחְמוֹ וְהוּא יִתֵּן מַעֲדַנֵּי מֶלֶךְ, *From Asher — his bread will have richness, and he will provide the kingly delicacies*" (*Bereishis* 49:20). *Rashi* explains that the food that comes from Asher's land will be very rich. Because an abundance of olives will grow in his territory, the oil will flow as if from a spring.

    Moshe Rabbeinu took Yaakov's blessing a step further, stating, "וְטֹבֵל בַּשֶּׁמֶן רַגְלוֹ, *[Asher] will dip his feet in oil*" (*Devarim* 33:24), implying an even greater abundance of olive groves. The Talmud[1] records an incident illustrating how amply these blessings were fulfilled: Asher's land was so full of olives that one member of the tribe was able to provide an astounding amount of oil to a gentile purchaser.

- The constellation that functions as Hashem's conduit to earth during the month of Shevat is דְּלִי, *Aquarius*. A דְּלִי, literally a *bucket*, is generally used to draw water from a well, as the constellation's name implies. *Aqua* is water in Latin; in English the constellation is called Water Bearer.

Asher's land was so full of olives that one member of the tribe was able to provide an astounding amount of oil to a gentile purchaser.

These two factors are somewhat contradictory. Water tends to mix freely with other liquids. On the other hand, oil, Asher's commodity, does not mix with other liquids at all. The oil always floats to the top.[2] If so, how are we to understand that Shevat is characterized by two contradictory qualities?

Before explaining how Shevat can correspond to seemingly opposite factors, let us examine a historic event associated with Shevat.

---

1. *Menachos* 85b.
2. See *Shemos Rabbah* 36:1.

ROSH CHODESH SHEVAT WAS A SEMINAL DATE IN JEWISH HISTORY. THE Torah tells us that on that day, five weeks before his death, Moshe gathered the Jewish people for his final teaching:

A Seminal Date

וַיְהִי בְּאַרְבָּעִים שָׁנָה בְּעַשְׁתֵּי עָשָׂר חֹדֶשׁ בְּאֶחָד לַחֹדֶשׁ ... בְּעֵבֶר הַיַּרְדֵּן בְּאֶרֶץ מוֹאָב הוֹאִיל מֹשֶׁה בֵּאֵר אֶת הַתּוֹרָה הַזֹּאת לֵאמֹר, *It was in the fortieth year, in the eleventh month, on the first of the month ... Moshe began explaining this Torah* (*Devarim* 1:3,5).

The chassidic masters consider Rosh Chodesh Shevat to be a time of "*Mattan Torah*," tantamount to the day the Torah was given at Sinai, because on that day Moshe began explaining the Torah to the entire congregation of Israel for the last time.[3] That final teaching, given in Moshe's own words, became *Sefer Devarim* — which is known as *Mishneh Torah*, literally "Repetition (or Review) of the Torah," and which contains many previously unmentioned laws. For this reason, R' Tzaddok HaCohen (*Pri Tzaddik, Chodesh Shevat #6*) refers to *Devarim* as the beginning of *Torah Shebe'al Peh*, the Oral Law, which explains the Written Torah and which includes the process through which the Sages of Israel interpret the Written Torah.

To quote *Chiddushei HaRim*[4] on the Divine gift of understanding that was granted to Moshe on this day, and that is renewed every year on its anniversary:

> Since the wellsprings of Torah begin to flow on Rosh Chodesh Shevat [when Moshe began teaching *Mishneh Torah*], the ability to reach for great depths of understanding *Torah Shebe'al Peh* [the Oral Torah] is aroused. [One who has great powers of perception] can tell the difference between *Chiddushei Torah* [novel explanations of Torah subjects] developed before the first of Shevat and those developed afterward ....

The *Chiddushei HaRim's* disciples quoted him as saying, "All the *Chiddushei Torah* that a person is going to develop in the course of the entire year are presented to him from Heaven during Shevat."

[One who has great powers of perception] can tell the difference between Chiddushei Torah [novel explanations of Torah subjects] developed before the first of Shevat and those developed afterward ....

3. *Torah Shebiksav*, the Written Torah, was transmitted to Moshe at Sinai over a forty-day period, and Moshe taught it to Israel over the course of forty years in the Wilderness. Nevertheless, we celebrate *Mattan Torah* only on Shavuos, because all the teachings of subsequent days and years are based on the Torah that Hashem gave us on Shavuos. It would seem, then, that Rosh Chodesh Shevat is like a second *Mattan Torah*, because it was then that Israel began to receive *Mishneh Torah*, the basis of *Torah Shebe'al Peh*.

4. *Sefer HaZechus LeTu B'Shvat, pg. 24.*

- Moshe's gift of *Torah Shebe'al Peh* had an aspect of historic significance. Rashi[5] cites a midrash that while teaching *Sefer Devarim*, Moshe explained the Torah to *Klal Yisrael* in all seventy languages. It seems from this midrash that this was a positive initiative on Moshe's part to make the Torah available to people no matter what language they spoke.

- Conversely, we find *Chazal* reacting unfavorably to another attempt to translate the Torah. When King Ptolemy ordered the Sages to translate the Torah into Greek,[6] the "world went dark for three days,"[7] and the Sages subsequently declared that day a fast day for the righteous.[8]

- Why was Moshe's translation of the Torah considered positive, while that of the Sages in Ptolemy's time was negative?

Let us see if we can find a common thread that runs through all the above events and factors associated with Shevat .

1. Torah and Water: Wisdom and Oil

*B*NEI YISSASCHAR[9] TEACHES US THAT דְּלִי, *AQUARIUS*, IS associated not only with Shevat , but that it is also *Klal Yisrael's* constellation.

A דְּלִי is a pail used to draw water from a well; its purpose is to serve the water. We see this same concept expressed in another instance in which we find the use of the root word דְּלִי. *Chazal* teach us that Eliezer, Avraham Avinu's servant, was "דּוֹלֶה וּמַשְׁקֶה מִתּוֹרַת רַבּוֹ לַאֲחֵרִים, *He drew from his master's Torah and served it to others*."

A loyal servant like Eliezer does not choose his own course in life; he fulfills his master's will faithfully and obediently, like a water bucket that exists solely to serve its owner. Eliezer "drew" Avrohom's teachings and conveyed them to the world at large, just as a bucket is used to draw water from a well and distribute it as its owner designates.

---

5. To *Devarim* 1:5.
6. *Megillah* 9a.; *Maseches Sofrim* 1.
7. *Shulchan Aruch Orach Chaim* 580:2
8. *Tur* ibid., quoting *BaHaG*.
9. *Maamar* 1:2.

Similar to the constellation דְּלִי, *Klal Yisrael* does not chart its own course. Torah is referred to as "water,"[10] and the entire purpose of *Klal Yisrael* is to be the vessel that loyally serves the Giver of the Torah.

Bnei Yissaschar goes on to explain the correspondence between Shevat, water, and Asher. We find oil — and specifically olive oil — associated with wisdom.

The prophet tells us that when Yoav wished to reconcile King David with his errant son Avshalom, the king's general summoned a wise women from Takoah to carry out his plan. The Talmud[11] explains that regular use of olive oil made the people of Takoah wise.

Shevat is governed by דְּלִי, *Klal Yisrael's* constellation. In order to serve as a vessel for the Torah, we must be able to understand its wisdom. This is why Shevat , the month of a second giving of the Law, is associated with Asher, the tribe that was blessed with an abundance of oil, the commodity that is associated with wisdom.

TORAH AND WISDOM DO NOT NECESSARY GO HAND-IN-HAND. *CHAZAL*[12] state, "If someone tells you that there is wisdom among the nations,

Are Torah and Wisdom Synonymous?

believe him; but if he tells you that there is Torah among the nations, do not believe him."

Nevertheless, we obviously need wisdom to succeed in Torah study. *Chazal*[13] teach that one who sees olive oil in a dream can expect to experience *Meor HaTorah* — the "light of the Torah." Apparently, then, wisdom is a prerequisite for those who would like to experience *Meor HaTorah*. Why?

We can understand why wisdom is so essential for experiencing the *Meor HaTorah* by studying *Chazal's* teachings regarding Shlomo HaMelech. Shlomo's wisdom was legendary. The Navi states, "וַיִּֽרְאוּ מִפְּנֵי הַמֶּלֶךְ כִּי רָאוּ כִּי חָכְמַת אֱלֹהִים בְּקִרְבּוֹ לַעֲשׂוֹת מִשְׁפָּט, *They [all of Klal Yisrael] were in awe of the king, for they saw that the wisdom of God was within him, to do justice*" (*I Melachim* 3:28).

The Talmud[14] states that one who sees Shlomo HaMelech in a dream can expect to become wise. The Sages point out that Shlo-

Chazal teach that one who sees olive oil in a dream can expect to experience Meor HaTorah — the "light of the Torah."

---

10. The Talmud (*Bava Kamma* 17a) derives this concept from *Yeshayah* 35:1.
11. *Menachos* 85b.
12. *Eichah Rabbah* 2:13.
13. *Berachos* 57a.
14. Ibid.

mo's wisdom was not devoted exclusively to Torah; he used his wisdom to study all that occurs under the sun.[15]

Despite his wisdom, however, his success in Torah was not a given. The Talmud[16] tells us that when Shlomo instituted the concepts of *eruvin*[17] and *netilas yadayim*,[18] a Heavenly voice rang out, saying, "My child, when your heart becomes wise, then my heart, too, will rejoice" (*Mishlei* 23:15), and, "Grow wise, my child, and gladden my heart; then I will have an answer for those who humiliate me" (ibid. 27:11).

Shlomo was declared wise by this Heavenly voice only once he had proved that his wisdom extended to Torah matters as well.[19]

When Shlomo instituted the concepts of eruvin and netilas yadayim, a Heavenly voice rang out, saying, "My child, when your heart becomes wise, then my heart, too, will rejoice."

WHAT WAS SO BRILLIANT ABOUT THE TWO HALACHOS ESTABLISHED by Shlomo?

True Wisdom: A Blend of Oil and Water

The Kotzker Rebbe explains that the word *eruv* means to *mix together* or *combine* two or more things. *Netilas yadayim* causes a person to be *separated* from *tumah* (spiritual impurity). On the surface, these two concepts would seem to be contradictory, but they are not. A successful life must maintain a balance between extraversion and introversion. As the wisest of men, Shlomo realized that a person needs to incorporate the concepts of both *eruv* and *netilas yadayim* into his life. On one hand, one should "live among his people," mingling with them and understanding their challenges, but on the other hand, one must be sure to maintain his distance from impure or harmful influences.

As the wisest of men, Shlomo realized that a person needs to incorporate the concepts of both eruv and netilas yadayim into his life.

The message is that a truly wise person must recognize the importance of having both properties — oil and water — mingling with ordinary people freely, but ensuring that socializing with the

---

15. *Shir HaShirim Rabbah* 1:7.

16. *Shabbos* 14b-15a.

17. There are several types of *eruvin*. The one referred to in this passage is an *eruv* used to combine two private domains, to allow transferring objects from one to the other on Shabbos.

18. Shlomo instituted that people must wash their hands before touching sacred food.

19. The Talmud (*Megillah* 9a) teaches that the Torah may not be translated into any language other than Greek. The Sages source the primacy of Greek to Noach's blessing of his son Yefes: יַפְתְּ אֱלֹקִים לְיֶפֶת וְיִשְׁכֹּן בְּאָהֳלֵי שֵׁם, *May God extend Yefes, but he will dwell in the tents of Shem* (*Bereishis* 9:27), which the Sages expound to teach: "May the beauty of Yefes — i.e, its language — dwell in the tents of Shem, the study halls of Torah." We may suggest that the "beauty of Yefes" that is needed in the Tents of Shem is a reference to the wisdom necessary to understand the Torah.

masses does not cause him to be corrupted by the materialism of the world.

It is clear from Moshe's blessing that Asher possessed both of these qualities. On one hand, Asher "shall be pleasing to his brothers" (*Devarim* 33:24). Just as water — represented by the water bucket of Chodesh Shevat — mixes with other substances, Asher mingles freely with his brethren. At the same time, however, Asher also has the property of oil; he is able to maintain his spiritual stature regardless of the nature of the people with whom he socializes.

II. Explaining the Torah: Why Shevat ?

BNEI YISSASCHAR WRITES THAT MOSHE CHOSE ROSH CHODESH Shevat as the ideal date to begin explaining the Torah because Aquarius serves as the *mazal* of both Shevat and *Klal Yisrael*. By beginning to explain the Torah on the day of Aquarius, Moshe showed that that the true water we are to draw is the water of Torah, and as long as we observe the Torah, we are not subject to the natural forces associated with the constellation.

Based on a passage in *Osiyos D'Rabbi Akiva, Pri Tzaddik*[20] states that because Moshe humbly referred to himself as כְּבַד פֶּה, *heavy of mouth*, he was able to attain the highest possible level in *Torah Shebe'al **Peh*** (the Oral Law). Because he, in his unparalleled humility, negated his power of speech, Hashem gave him the gift of the Oral Torah, so that his "heavy mouth" became the conduit for the Divine teaching.

Because he, in his unparalleled humility, negated his power of speech, Hashem gave him the gift of the Oral Torah, so that his "heavy mouth" became the conduit for the Divine teaching.

Moshe developed some laws through *Torah Shebeal Peh*, and presented them without providing the reasoning behind them. These laws are referred to as *Halachah L'Moshe MiSinai*. One can understand the reasoning behind these *halachos* only through *Ruach HaKodesh*, i.e., Divine Inspiration. Our main objective in *Shevat* is to use *Torah Shebe'al Peh* to repair all the blemishes and destruction wrought by the serpent [which enticed Adam and Chva to eat from the Tree of Knowledge, the sin that plunged them from their pinnacle of spiritual greatness]. In the month of Shevat we endeavor to elevate ourselves to become a "chariot" — i.e., to embody the holiness of the *Tzaddik Yesod Olam* — the Righteous One Who is the foundation

---

20. By Rav Tzaddok HaKohen of Lublin, *Maamarim L'Rosh Chodesh Shevat* 6.

of the universe — and thereby to be a "chariot" that can be a host of Hashem's holiness.

Based on our understanding that Shevat corresponds to oil and water, we can suggest another reason why Moshe considered Rosh Chodesh Shevat the most auspicious date to begin explaining the Torah.

Based on our understanding that Shevat corresponds to oil and water — and the spiritual concepts they represent — we can suggest another reason why Moshe considered Rosh Chodesh Shevat the most auspicious date to begin explaining the Torah. As we have seen from Shlomo HaMelech, in order to be considered successful in Torah study, a person must master the dual characteristics associated with Shevat — the ability to mingle with the masses yet maintain his spiritual purity. No month could be more appropriate for the second *Mattan Torah* than Shevat.

WE CAN NOW UNDERSTAND WHY MOSHE EXPLAINED THE TORAH IN all seventy languages.

Making the Torah Available to All

Levush Orah writes that Moshe was afraid that after over 200 years in Egypt, some of the people might not understand *Lashon HaKodesh*. In a nation that contained more than 600,000 adult males, there were probably Jews who spoke languages other *Lashon HaKodesh*. The only way Moshe could be certain that *each and every Jew* without exception would understand the Torah was to teach it in all seventy languages. In other words, Moshe felt that the Torah should be like the דְלִי of Chodesh Shevat. Just as water mixes freely, the Torah should be available to all — learned scholars and simple Jews; those who understand *Lashon Kodesh* and those who speak other languages. Moshe made the Torah accessible to all.

Another explanation for Moshe teaching the Torah in seventy languages is given by *Sfas Emes*. Moshe was preparing the way for future exiles, when the Jewish people would be dispersed among many nations, speaking many languages. By translating the Torah into every known language, Moshe made it possible for Torah study to thrive wherever Jews find themselves.

Moshe was preparing the way for future exiles, when the Jewish people would be dispersed among many nations, speaking many languages.

But if Moshe's explanation of the Torah in other languages was considered positive, why was King Ptolemy's command to do the same so devastating in the eyes of *Chazal?*

Our understanding of Chodesh Shevat explains the difference between these two attempts. Moshe Rabbeinu wanted to make the Torah available to all, so that the average man could be spiritually uplifted by the Torah and acquire his share of the Divine wisdom. Moshe wanted the Torah to simultaneously have the qualities of water, available to all, while remaining above the mundane world, like oil floating to the top of a mixture.

Ptolemy's intention was exactly the opposite. He wanted to bring the Torah down to the level of the street, Heaven forbid, so that people could study it casually like any other subject, without recognition of its Source or its holiness. He wanted the Torah to be "literature" instead of the Word of Hashem. This caused darkness to descend and eclipse the powerful light of Torah.

THE TALMUD[21] STATES, "ONE SHOULD BE CAREFUL TO DAVEN *MINCHAH* properly, for Eliyahu HaNavi was answered only through the *Minchah* prayer."[22] *Minchah* is so important, in

Minchah — Lighting Up the Darkness

fact, that *Tur Shulchan Aruch*— which is a halachic work and very seldom cites aggadic accounts — records this passage about Eliyahu in the introduction to the laws of *Tefillas Minchah*.

As humans, our mission is to create a bridge from the light to the darkness; to illuminate the dark, mundane world with the bright, spiritual light of the Torah, but without letting the darkness affect us, following the model we have developed through our study of Chodesh Shevat.

As humans, our mission is to create a bridge from the light to the darkness; to illuminate the dark, mundane world with the bright, spiritual light of the Torah, but without letting the darkness affect us.

We can apply this concept at *Minchah* more than at any other time of the day. We pray *Minchah* as the day wanes and the darkness of night is approaching. *Minchah* provides an opportunity to preserve the brightness and purity of morning and use it to illuminate the approaching darkness and morbidity of night.

---

21. *Berachos* 6b.
22. See *I Melachim* 18:36 and the preceding verses for the full story.

ADAR I

חֹדֶשׁ אֲדָר כְּנֶגֶד שֵׁבֶט נַפְתָּלִי.

(פרי צדיק, ראש חדש אדר מאמר ו, בשם שערי אורה)

*The month of Adar corresponds to
the tribe of Naftali.*

(Pri Tzaddik, Rosh Chodesh Adar 6, quoting Shaarei Orah)

NAFTALI:
The "Connected" Tribe

WHAT IS THE CONNECTION BETWEEN NAFTALI AND THE month of Adar?

To find the answer, we must analyze the name Naftali and the unique characteristics of the tribe.

When Rachel's maidservant Bilhah gave birth to her second child, Rachel named him Naftali (*Bereishis* 30:8). The commentators offer several explanations for her choice of the name. Although the explanations seem to differ from one another, we will find that they all have something in common. After defining this quality, we will understand the correlation between Naftali and Chodesh Adar.

RASHI RECORDS THREE POSSIBLE EXPLANATIONS FOR THE NAME:

1) *Menachem ibn Saruk*[1] associates the letter combination of פ, ת, ל, with the same letter combination found in the word פָּתִיל, *fastening*.[2] Naftali's birth made the once-barren Rachel feel that she was finally "fastened" or "connected" to her sister Leah, in the sense that she, like Leah, had given children to Yaakov. Therefore, Rachel had joined her sister as a matriarch of the Jewish people.

The Name

Naftali's birth made the once-barren Rachel feel that she was finally "fastened" or "connected" to her sister Leah.

2) *Rashi* himself suggests that this word is similar to the word וּפְתַלְתֹּל *twisted*.[3] Rachel stated that she merited to bring Naftali into the world because she persistently beseeched, "twisted," constantly turned to Hashem to beg Him for the privilege of bringing tribal ancestors into the world, as her sister did.

---

1. Menachem ibn Saruk was a tenth-century Spanish scholar and the author of *Machberes*, a work on *Lashon Kodesh* often quoted by Rashi, who usually refers to him only by his personal name, Menachem.

2. As found in the verse, וְכֹל כְּלִי פָתוּחַ אֲשֶׁר אֵין צָמִיד פָּתִיל עָלָיו טָמֵא הוּא, *Any open vessel that has no cover fastened to it is contaminated* (Bamidbar 19:15).

3. As in the verse, שִׁחֵת לוֹ לֹא בָּנָיו מוּמָם דּוֹר עִקֵּשׁ וּפְתַלְתֹּל, *Corruption is not His — the blemish is His chldren's, a perverse and twisted nation* (Devarim 32:5).

3) *Onkelos*, as Rashi explains, associates the words נַפְתּוּלֵי and נַפְתַּלְתִּי with similar words in the Torah that mean "to fall before Hashem in prayer."[4] According to *Onkelos*, Rachel threw herself down and begged Hashem that Bilhah should bear some of Yaakov's children.

These three explanations of the name seem to vary greatly, yet we will find that there is a common denominator.

Likkutei Moharan[5] associates the name נַפְתָּלִי with תְּפִילִין, tefillin (phylacteries), noting that the two words are comprised of the same letters, albeit in a different order.

1. The Blessings

IN ADDITION TO THE FACTORS ASSOCIATED WITH NAFTALI'S NAME, the blessings he received from Yaakov Avinu and Moshe Rabbeinu indicate a variety of Naftali's spiritual and material traits.

Yaakov Avinu's Blessing
Yaakov Avinu described him as, "נַפְתָּלִי אַיָּלָה שְׁלֻחָה הַנֹּתֵן אִמְרֵי שָׁפֶר, *Naftali is a hind*[6] *let loose, who delivers beautiful sayings*" (*Bereishis* 49:21).

The Midrash expounds the word שָׁפֶר, stating that it alludes to the word מְשַׁפֵּר, *to perfect* and to the word shofar. Thus, the tribe of Naftali would "perfect," i.e., teach and clarify, the Torah that was given at Sinai with the sound of a shofar.[7]

The tribe of Naftali would "perfect," i.e., teach and clarify, the Torah that was given at Sinai with the sound of a shofar.

From this verse, commentators derive several character traits of Naftali:

- *Rashi* states that Naftali possessed the trait of *zerizus* (alacrity). This refers to his portion of *Eretz Yisrael*, which was extremely fertile and produced fruit so quickly that the Torah compares it to a swift hind that has been sent off to run freely. Alternatively,

---

4. In retelling the events of the Golden Calf, Moshe Rabbeinu remembered the fervent supplications he prayed to gain Hashem's forgiveness as follows: וָאֶתְנַפַּל לִפְנֵי ה׳ אֵת אַרְבָּעִים הַיּוֹם וְאֶת אַרְבָּעִים הַלַּיְלָה אֲשֶׁר הִתְנַפָּלְתִּי כִּי אָמַר ה׳ לְהַשְׁמִיד אֶתְכֶם. וָאֶתְפַּלֵּל אֶל ה׳ ..., *I threw myself down before Hashem for the forty days and the forty nights that I threw myself down, for Hashem had intended to destroy you. I prayed to Hashem ...* (*Devarim* 9:25-26).

5. *Mahadura Kamma* 47.

6. A hind is a female deer.

7. The sounds of the shofar were heard repeatedly before and after Hashem presented the Torah to the Jews at Sinai.

continues *Rashi*, it refers to the *people* of Naftali, led by Barak ben Avinoam, who joined the prophetess Deborah and fought with alacrity to defeat Sisera and his mighty army (see *Shoftim* 4:10).

- *Ramban* adds that the kings of *Eretz Yisrael's* northern kingdom would send hinds to their friendly counterparts in the south, and when a king of the south had to send a message to his colleague in the north, he would tie a note between a hind's horns and set it free. The hind would speed back to its natural habitat. Thus, a hind was often the one to bring glad tidings to people. Similarly, Naftali's land often heralded good times for the people of *Eretz Yisrael,* concludes *Ramban,* because his land was the first to produce fruit, and that would be good news to the rest of the nation.

Naftali's land often heralded good times for the people of Eretz Yisrael, because his land was the first to produce fruit,

- *Avi Ezer* writes that the end of the verse, הַנֹּתֵן אִמְרֵי שָׁפֶר, *who delivers beautiful sayings,* compares Naftali to a person who gives gifts frequently. Just as a frequent gift-giver becomes beloved to others, so too Naftali was beloved to all.

- *Kli Yakar* notes that אִמְרֵי שָׁפֶר, *beautiful sayings,* is most likely a reference to the Torah. He adds that the first part of the verse, which compares Naftali to a hind, also refers to the Torah, because *Mishlei* (5:19) compares the Torah to אַיֶּלֶת אֲהָבִים, *a beloved hind.* The Talmud[8] ponders this peculiar comparison, and answers that just as a hind always remains beloved to her mate, so too the Torah remains beloved to those who study it.

Naftali finds the words of Torah particularly sweet, and they remain tasty to him forever.

- Alternatively, *Kli Yakar* notes *Chazal's*[9] teaching that the name נַפְתָּלִי is an acronym for נוֹפֶת לִי, *it is sweet to me,* a reference to the Torah, as we find in the verse וּמְתוּקִים מִדְּבַשׁ וְנֹפֶת צוּפִים, *[Torah] is sweeter than honey, and drippings from the combs (Tehillim* 19:11). Apparently, Naftali finds the words of Torah particularly sweet, and they remain tasty to him forever.

MOSHE BLESSED NAFTALI: נַפְתָּלִי שְׂבַע רָצוֹן וּמָלֵא בִּרְכַּת ה' יָם וְדָרוֹם יְרָשָׁה, *Naftali, satiated with favor, and filled with Hashem's blessing; go possess the sea and its south shore (Devarim* 33:23). His blessing reveals yet another insight into Naftali's personality. *Rashi* states that Naftali's land satisfied the

Moshe Rabbeinu's Blessing

---

8. *Eruvin* 54b.
9. *Bamidbar Rabbah* 14.

needs of its inhabitants. This idea is echoed by *Targum Yonasan ben Uziel* and *Sifri*, who state that the people of Naftali were satisfied with their lot, enjoying their land's olives, fish, and other commodities.

Although this implies that Naftali's satisfaction flowed from the mundane, physical riches of his land, *Sforno* points out that its natural richness provided a spiritual benefit. We have already seen that *Eretz Yisrael's* first fruit each year grew in Naftali's land, which meant that the people of Naftali were the first to be able to perform the mitzvah of *Bikkurim*.[10] Thus, the verses' material blessings were primarily for a spiritual purpose.

A similar theme is found in *Ramban*, who cites a Kabbalistic Midrash[11] that Moshe told the tribe of Naftali that if they fulfilled Hashem's decrees, they would merit portions in both this world and the next.

BEFORE WE ATTEMPT TO FIND THE COMMON THREAD CONNECTING all of these factors, we note an apparent contradiction in the descrip-

Swift, but Last?

tions of Naftali. As noted above, *Rashi* taught that Naftali possessed the trait of *zerizus* (alacrity). In most places where Scripture mentions the tribes, Naftali appears last. It is the last tribe mentioned in the order of encampments in *Parashas Bamidbar*, the leader of Naftali was the last to bring his offering when the Mishkan was inaugurated,[12] and he is last on the list of leaders who took part in the division of *Eretz Yisrael*.[13] Furthermore, Adar, Naftali's month, is the twelfth and last month of each year, because we start counting the months from Nissan.

How do we reconcile Naftali's trait of alacrity with his constant appearance as the last tribe?

We have compiled a long list of factors associated with Naftali. Let us find the element that connects them.

How do we reconcile Naftali's trait of alacrity with his constant appearance as the last tribe?

---

10. *Bikkurim* are the first-grown fruit of the seven species that *Eretz Yisrael* was blessed with. These fruits are taken to the *Beis HaMikdash* and presented to a *Kohen*.

11. *Sefer Habahir* 7.

12. See *Bamidbar* 7:12-83.

13. Ibid. 34:16-28.

II. Tefillah —
Connecting to Hashem

IF WE EXAMINE THE FIRST THREE ITEMS ON OUR LIST — THE THREE explanations of the name Naftali cited by *Rashi* — we find that they are closely related to one another. Menachem associates Naftali with "connection," *Rashi* opines that it connotes persistent "twisting" to become closer to Hashem, and *Onkelos* takes it to mean prayer. When a person prays, persistently "twisting" himself toward Hashem, he "connects" with Him, so to speak. In fact, the very word *tefillah* connotes connection to Hashem. Let us explain.

When a person prays, persistently "twisting" himself toward Hashem, he "connects" with Him, so to speak. In fact, the very word "tefillah" connotes connection to Hashem.

The Midrash[14] contrasts Hashem's reaction to our prayers with the reaction we would expect from mere mortals. Humans tend to brush off paupers who come to talk to them, but when a rich man calls, they listen carefully to his every word. Hashem, however, treats all people alike. King David uses the very same word to describe Moshe Rabbeinu's supplication to Hashem — *Tefillah l'Moshe* — that he uses to describe the prayer of a pauper: *Tefillah l'ani*.[15] Thus, concludes the Midrash, David informs us that when it comes to prayer all people are equal before Hashem.

Shem MiShmuel[16] poses a difficult question. Several verses in *Tanach* state clearly that the prayers of righteous people are more worthy than those of others. A case in point is the verse in *Mishlei* (15:29) that states, "Hashem is far from the wicked, but He hears the prayer of the righteous." The Talmud[17] goes so far as to say that there is no comparison between the prayers of righteous people who descend from righteous people, and the prayers of righteous people who descend from the wicked. More specifically, the Midrash compares Moshe's prayer to a sword that can pierce all the firmaments! How, then, asks *Shem MiShmuel*, can the Midrash suggest that a pauper's prayers are equal to those of Moshe?

How can the Midrash suggest that a pauper's prayers are equal to those of Moshe?

To explain, *Shem MiShmuel* refers to the definition found in many sacred works, stating that the word *tefillah* is related to the word פָּתִיל, *fastened* or *connected*, since both words contain the same letters (although the order of the first two letters is reversed) for when we pray, we "connect" to Hashem.

---

14. *Shemos Rabbah* 21:4.
15. *Psalms* 91 and 102, respectively.
16. *Beshalach* 5676, s.v. *BiMidrash Rabbah*.
17. *Yevamos* 64a.

BUT HOW CAN A MERE FLESH-AND-BLOOD MORTAL BE CONNECTED to Hashem, Who is entirely spiritual? *Shem MiShmuel* explains that

The Jews' Essence

the essence of every Jew is a *chelek Elokah miMa'al* (a portion of God from above), and that the spiritual portion buried deep in a human being can reconnect to Hashem. But this potential for connection is impeded by the grossness of the urges and weakness of the body and its material surroundings in ths material world, all of which militate against spirituality. In order to penetrate this barrier, a person must cleanse and purify himself to bring spirituality to the body, so that its material nature will not block its Divine essence from connecting to Hashem through *tefillah*. The purer a person makes himself, by making his soul overpower the body's urges, the purer and stronger the connection, and the purer the soul itself becomes.

The soul of a righteous person, and especially one whose ancestors were also righteous,[18] is naturally purer than that of the average person, and is therefore more easily able to connect to Hashem. But even an ordinary person can purify his soul, and if he is successful he can connect to Hashem. If he can break his material impediments to such a degree that he penetrates to his very essence, his prayer will be on the very same level as that of Moshe Rabbeinu and all other righteous people, concludes *Shem MiShmuel*.[19]

This is why King David says that God is close to all who call upon him בֶּאֱמֶת, *sincerely* — literally, *with truth*. God's essential attribute is truth, so it is natural that He treasures the prayers of truthful, sincere people. By definition, this means that such a person removes himself from every earthly consideration and aspires to closeness to Hashem. Thereby his intelligence develops a constantly stronger attachment to the Supreme Light (*Orchos Tzaddikim, Shaar HaEmes*).

God's essential attribute is truth, so it is natural that He treasures the prayers of truthful, sincere people.

---

18. The holiness of righteous people has an effect on their children, who therefore have a greater potential for their spiritual side to become primary and their physical aspect secondary.

19. *Ramchal* (*Derech Hashem*, Section IV, 5:1) writes that the entire objective of *tefillah* is to enable us to come close to Hashem. He writes that mortal man would not be able to attain such closeness if not for Hashem's kindness in allowing us to break away — albeit temporarily — from the physicality of this world, and rise up and stand close to Him in prayer.

The source for this concept is in *Tehillim*: קָרוֹב ה׳ לְכָל קֹרְאָיו לְכֹל אֲשֶׁר יִקְרָאֻהוּ בֶאֱמֶת, *Hashem is close to all who call upon Him, to all who call upon him sincerely* (145:18). *Orchos Tzaddikim* explains that "calling upon Hashem *sincerely*" entails clearing foreign thoughts from our hearts and minds, and focusing *solely* on our prayer, so that we can cling to Hashem.

Rabbi Tzaddok HaKohen of Lublin[20] writes that the reason we recite *Shemoneh Esrei* quietly is because we are bonding with Hashem, and bonding is intimate; it is intrinsically a private matter.

III. Naftali, the Quintessential Connector

FROM ALL THE ABOVE IT IS CLEAR THAT THE ULTIMATE "connection" with God is achieved through prayer, and since the word *tefillah* means to connect to Hashem, then Naftali is the model of this concept.

Degel Machaneh Ephraim quotes his grandfather, the *Baal Shem Tov*, to explain Yaakov's blessing to Naftali:

נַפְתָּלִי — The tzaddik, who is called *Naftali*, because he connects and clings to Hashem;[21] אַיָּלָה שְׁלֻחָה is *a swift messenger*. In Kabbalistic terminology, the Divine Presence is referred to as אַיֶּלֶת הַשַּׁחַר, literally, a *radiant hind*, of one of the Temples' musical instruments (see *Tehillim* 22:1). Thus Naftali is a messenger of the *Shechinah*, God's Presence.

הַנֹּתֵן אִמְרֵי שָׁפֶר — [The tzaddik] provides *"sayings," for the Shechinah*,[22] i.e., he prays to the *Shechinah*, which is called *shefer*, beautiful. Alternatively, we pray that the *Shechinah*, which is called *Tiferes Yisrael*, the Splendor of Israel, be elevated in the perception of the Jewish people.

Toldos Yaakov Yosef of Polno'ah, also writes that the name Naftali connotes the connection he forges with Hashem. Naftali epitomizes the concept that a tzaddik can attach himself to the Creator, as it were, by means of prayer.

HAVING ESTABLISHED THE DEEPER SYMBOLISM OF THE NAME NAFtali, we can understand why the Midrash sees a correlation between Naftali and the shofar. The Mishnah (*Rosh Hashanah* 26b) cites an opinion that shofar of Rosh Hashanah should be a straight (not bent) horn of a mountain goat. Although the accepted halachah is that the

Naftali and the Shofar

---

20. *Likkutei Maamarim* IV:191.

21. Based on *Menachem ibn Saruk's* association of Naftali with the word פָּתִיל.

22. *Degel Machaneh Ephraim* explains that the *Shechinah* (Divine Presence) is called *Shefer* in *Kabbalistic* literature.

shofar should be a bent ram's horn, this opinion illustrates the underlying spiritual quality of the shofar, about which there is no dispute. The Talmud explains that a straight horn symbolizes that we must pray straightforwardly, without ulterior motives. Thus the character of Naftali and the message of the shofar are parallel to each other, for the shofar is an integral part of the prayers on Rosh Hashanah; it is a key component in our quest to create a bond with Hashem.

TEFILLIN, TOO, ARE A MEANS TO CONNECT WITH HASHEM; THE KNOTS on the tefillin signify a bond between the Jewish people and Hashem.

Tefillin — The Bond Between Man and Hashem

Shem MiShmuel[23] quotes his father, the *Avnei Nezer*, that the word tefillin connotes thought, as we find its root in the verse in which Yaakov tells Yosef רְאֹה פָנֶיךָ לֹא פִלָּלְתִּי, *I dared not accept the **thought** that I would see your face* (Bereishis 48:11). Thus the knot on the tefillin symbolizes the effort to connect our thoughts to Hashem. It is forbidden to let one's mind wander while wearing tefillin, and therefore Moshe Rabbeinu — whose attachment to Hashem was uninterrupted — merited to see "the knot of Hashem's tefillin," as it were. When we bind tefillin on our arms, we connect ourselves to the upper worlds, and our actions influence the upper worlds, for good or for ill.

Sfas Emes[24] explains this concept similarly: The Torah states that the mitzvah of tefillin is "(a) a sign on your arm; and (b) a reminder between your eyes; (c) so that Hashem's Torah may be in your mouth" (*Shemos* 13:9). By performing the mitzvah of tefillin properly, we can perfect three aspects of our lives: (a) our actions; (b) our thoughts; (c) our speech. By commanding us to wear tefillin, Hashem gave us an opportunity to perfect our character traits and actions, to isolate them from the mundane physical world, and to bind (devote) them to Hashem's Torah.

Chazal[25] take the concept of the "bond" of tefillin one step further. Not only do *we* attempt to connect to Hashem via tefillin, Hashem connects to the Jewish people through tefillin. Hashem "wears tefillin," which contain verses that praise *Klal Yisrael*, such as the verse "Who is like Your people Israel, one nation on earth" (*II Shmuel* 17:23).

Not only do we attempt to connect to Hashem via tefillin, Hashem connects to the Jewish people through tefillin. Hashem "wears tefillin," which contain verses that praise Klal Yisrael.

---

23. *Ki Sisa* 5679, s.v. *v'inyan.*
24. *Naso* 5646 s.v. *Bemitzvos.*
25. *Berachos* 6a.

Accordingly, *Shem MiShmuel*[26] explains, Hashem's tefillin symbolize that He clings to *Klal Yisrael*, and just as the halachah requires that one concentrate on tefillin without interruption, so, too, Hashem remains committed to *Klal Yisrael* and does not forsake His people under any circumstances.

We have ascertained that the name Naftali connotes connection to Hashem. Now that we know that tefillin are an ideal way to bind ourselves to Hashem, we can understand why Naftali is associated with tefillin, and why, as *Likkutei Moharan* notes, the two words, Naftali and tefillin, are comprised of the very same letters.

Now that we know that tefillin are an ideal way to bind ourselves to Hashem, we can understand why Naftali is associated with tefillin

NAFTALI'S CHARACTERISTIC OF CONNECTING AND FORMING RELAtionships extends to other people, as well as to Hashem. There are

Naftali and the Connection With Other People

many instances in which Naftali forged unique, loyal relationships with fellow humans, and cared for the needs of both the public at large and individual members of *Klal Yisrael,* as well.

We find that Naftali was Yaakov's trusted messenger, as hinted in his blessing, נַפְתָּלִי אַיָּלָה שְׁלֻחָה, *Naftali is a hind let loose.*[27] Thus, when Yaakov sent an unnamed messenger on a mission — וַיִּשְׁלַח יַעֲקֹב וַיִּקְרָא לְרָחֵל וּלְלֵאָה הַשָּׂדֶה אֶל צֹאנוֹ, *Yaakov sent and summoned Rachel and Leah to the field, to his flock (Bereishis 31:4)* — *Targum Yonasan ben Uziel* comments that the messenger was Naftali, who was a "swift messenger." Commenting on this Targum, Rav Tzaddok HaKohen[28] explains that since the word שְׁלֻחָה is associated with the root שָׁלִיחַ, *a messenger,* it stands to reason that whenever we find Yaakov sending an anonymous messenger on a mission, we assume that he sent Naftali.

Rav Tzaddok HaKohen explains that it stands to reason that whenever we find Yaakov sending an anonymous messenger on a mission, we assume that he sent Naftali.

The source of this idea is the Midrash[29] that states, "Naftali honored his father to an exceptional degree; his father would choose him whenever he needed a messenger, and he would do his bidding with alacrity .... Yaakov blessed Naftali with the words אַיָּלָה שְׁלֻחָה because he would run as swiftly as a deer to do Yaakov's bidding." *Targum Yonasan*[30] states that Naftali was also the one who informed Yaakov that Yosef was alive.[31]

---

26. In the essay cited above, *Ki Sisa* 5679.

27. See the explanation cited earlier (6) from *Ramban*.

28. *Igra D'Kallah*, pg. 139.

29. *Bamidbar Rabbah* 14:10.

30. *Bereishis* 49:21.

31. *Yalkut Reuveni (Parashas Vayigash)* states that when Yaakov saw Naftali from a distance, he said, "Behold, Naftali is coming; a good man who bears peaceful tidings."

Midrash HaGadol states that Naftali was also ready and willing to run off on any mission for his brothers. He is credited with saving Yosef's life, for when the brothers wanted to kill him, Naftali ran to tell Yehudah, who saved Yosef from imminent death.[32]

Naftali's role as the messenger of Yaakov's household — and the eagerness and swiftness with which he carried out his missions — teach that he was imbued with a deep-seated will to help others. This trait undoubtedly won him the love of his fellows, and enabled him to develop strong bonds with all those whom he graciously assisted. This fits perfectly with *Avnei Nezer*, who depicts Naftali as a person who is beloved by all.

Naftali and the Hind as Spiritual Messengers

INTERESTINGLY, THE HIND, TO WHICH NAFTALI IS COMPARED, AND ITS male counterpart, the deer, symbolize messengers in a spiritual manner.

Divrei Yisrael[33] writes that the hind is the *shaliach tzibbur*,[34] the devout prayer leader of the animal kingdom, as it were, which begs Hashem to provide food and drink to all animals. The hind is the most merciful animal, for when it begs for food it thinks not of its own needs, but represents the needs of all other animals. When it sees other animals eating, it feels satisfied, as if it has eaten more than they. When Hashem hears a hind call out, He is filled with mercy, as the Sages[35] expound on the verse כְּאַיָּל תַּעֲרֹג עַל אֲפִיקֵי מָיִם, *As the deer longs for the brooks of water* (*Tehillim* 42:2).

Similarly, continues *Divrei Yisrael*, Naftali served as the *shaliach tzibbur* in Yaakov's household. Yaakov compared him to an אַיָּלָה שְׁלֻחָה because, just as a hind focuses on other animals' needs, not on its own, Naftali devoted his prayers to the needs of his brethren, rather than focusing on himself. It follows that Yaakov described him as הַנֹּתֵן אִמְרֵי שָׁפֶר, *who delivers beautiful sayings*, because his *tefillos* on behalf of others ascended Heavenward and were accepted by Hashem.

Naftali's trait of graciously helping all those in need was inherited by his descendants. When the mighty general, Sisera, attacked *Klal Yisrael*, an army of ten thousand men from the tribes of Naftali

Naftali devoted his prayers to the needs of his brethren, rather than focusing on himself. His tefillos on behalf of others ascended Heavenward and were accepted by Hashem.

---

32. *Midrash Aggadah* 49:21.

33. *Parashas Vayechi*, s.v. *Naftali Ayalah Sheluchah*.

34. A *shaliach tzibbur* is a person who leads the prayers in shul. He is considered a messenger of the congregation, beseeching for Heavenly mercy on their behalf.

35. *Divrei Yisrael* cites *Zohar, Parashas Pinchas*, and the *Yalkut*.

and Zevulun, led by Barak ben Avinoam, from Naftali, defeated the enemy and saved *Klal Yisrael* from doom.[36]

Why did the salvation come through these two tribes, Naftali and Zevulun? Naftali served Yaakov, and Zevulun served Yissachar.

Why did the salvation come through these two tribes, Naftali and Zevulun? *Tanna D'vei Eliyahu*[37] states they earned this merit by serving others; Naftali served Yaakov, and Zevulun served Yissachar,[38] since Zevulun's merchants supported Yissachar's Torah scholars of.

We have seen the Midrashic teaching that Naftali excelled in the mitzvah of honoring his father, Yaakov. The Midrash[39] teaches that this trait was inherited by Naftali's offspring. At the dedication of the Mishkan, the prince of Naftali dedicated his [inaugural] offering in honor of the Patriarchs and Matriarchs. Why? Since Naftali served his father with such alacrity — and also brought him great satisfaction through his beautiful expressions — his descendant, the prince of the tribe, preserved that devotion by dedicating his offering in honor of Naftali's forefathers.

Naftali's devotion to Yaakov was another manifestation of his innate desire to bond with others.

IV. Happy With His Lot

IN HIS BLESSING, MOSHE DESCRIBED NAFTALI AS שְׂבַע רָצוֹן, *SATIATED with favor.* Literally understood — as explained by *Sifri*[40] — this means that Naftali was always happy with his lot. *Netziv*[41] points out that Naftali was actually blessed with עוֹשֶׁר, *wealth,* in both senses: he had material wealth, in the words of the verse, וּמָלֵא בִּרְכַּת ה׳, *filled with Hashem's blessing.* He also had wealth as defined by the Mishnah, "Who is rich? He who is happy with his lot" (*Avos* 4:1).

Naftali had material wealth. He also had wealth as defined by the Mishnah, "Who is rich? He who is happy with his lot."

Abarbanel takes a different approach to the blessing of שְׂבַע רָצוֹן:

There are humans whose goal in life is to please others and fulfill the desire of their fellow men .... Moshe Rabbeinu praised Naftali for being שְׂבַע רָצוֹן because he derives שׂוֹבַע, *satisfaction,* by fulfilling other people's רָצוֹן, *desire.* A person with this nature will give to others with an open hand.

---

36. See *Shoftim* 4.
37. Ch. 9.
38. Zevulun, a merchant tribe, provided for the tribe of Yissachar so that they could study Torah unencumbered by the burden of earning a livelihood.
39. *Bamidbar* 14:11.
40. *Devarim* 33:23.
41. *Ha'emak Davar,* ibid.

Abarbanel offers another explanation:

> Some people are rich and are happy with their lot, which is the best combination. Others are rich and are not happy with their lot. Another group of people is not rich, but is happy with its lot. Then there are people who are not rich, and are unhappy with their lot, which is the worst combination possible. Moshe's blessing was that Naftali would belong to the first group; he would be מְלֵא בִּרְכַּת ה', *filled with Hashem's blessing*, and he would also be שְׂבַע רָצוֹן, *satisfied with his lot*. *Sifri* states that Naftali's prosperity would derive from travels to various places, thus Moshe's blessing corresponds to that of Yaakov, who described Naftali as a swift messenger.

Abarbanel teaches that Naftali's predilection to be satisfied with his lot is connected to his trait of being a friendly person who develops strong relationships with his fellows. Indeed, being satisfied with one's lot is a sound basis upon which to be accepted and loved by all.[42]

We wondered how Naftali's trait of alacrity could be reconciled with the fact that he and his tribe are so often listed after all the others. Now that we understand Naftali's overwhelming desire to make others happy, the answer is obvious. Naftali's alacrity and self-effacement are of a piece. He hastened when he was needed to serve others and make their lot easier. For the same reason, he would always step aside and allow others to go before him to make them happy.

He hastened when he was needed to serve others and make their lot easier. For the same reason, he would always step aside and allow others to go before him to make them happy.

Shevo and Achlamah — The Connection Between Both Worlds

WE FIND CONTRADICTORY MIDRASHIM REGARDING WHICH STONE IN the *Choshen* had Naftali's name on it. *Shemos Rabbah*[43] states that the *shevo* was Naftali's stone, and the *achlamah* was Gad's. *Bamidbar Rabbah*[44] states that Naftali's stone was the *achlamah*, which was a translucent, reddish stone, similar to the color of

---

42. Perhaps the reason Naftali received Lake Kinneret in his portion is because it correlates to his own natural predisposition. Naftali builds relationships, which can only be accomplished by giving to others and receiving from them. Similarly, the Kinneret receives water from the northern streams and springs that flow into it, and it passes the water on to other places, as opposed to Yam Hamelach, the Dead Sea, which receives the water of the River Jordan, but does not feed into other bodies of water. A well-known aphorism states that Yam Hamelach earned the title "Dead Sea," because one who only takes but lacks the capacity to give is not truly alive.

43. 38:9.

44. 2:7.

wine. While we cannot reconcile the contradiction between the Midrashim, considering the concepts we have developed regarding Naftali, we can understand why either of these two stones can correlate to his character traits.

Mei HaShiloach [45] explains the correlation between Naftali and *shevo*:

> *Shevo* contains the root שב, *return*. Naftali's pursuit of a livelihood required him to be occupied with the mundane realities of the world, not with lofty, spiritual matters. Nevertheless, his heart actually *turns* to Hashem at all times, for he infuses all his pursuits with his desire to serve Hashem. The name of the leader of Naftali in the Wilderness, אֲחִירַע בֶּן עֵינָן, Achira ben Einan, alludes to this concept. Although it seems as if he turns away from Hashem — אֲחִירַע comes from same root as אָחוֹרַיִים, *back* — in reality, עֵינָן *his eyes*, focus constantly on Hashem.

Mei Shiloach implies that Naftali, our quintessential connector, doesn't focus only on relationships with others, he also connects *Olam Hazeh* (the physical, lower world) with *Olam Haba* (the World to Come). Even while engaging in mundane tasks, Naftali is connected to the lofty, heavenly world. The word *shevo* symbolizes Naftali's ability to "return" and connect to his Maker, even while he engages in mundane activities. [46] As noted above, Naftali's blessing contained both spiritual and mundane gifts, another indication that Naftali earthly pursuits did not contradict his spiritual striving.

We may also suggest the word שְׁבוֹ comes from the same root as תְּשׁוּבָה, *an answer*. In his quest to make others happy, Naftali will always take the time to discuss people's issues with them and provide answers to their questions.

The *achlamah* stone, with a color reminiscent of wine, fits perfectly with Naftali's reputation as a person who builds strong relationships with others. As the Talmud [47] says, "Great is a drink [of wine], for it brings hearts together." Wine is so instrumental in causing people to relate to one another, in fact, that *Chazal* forbade us from drinking the wine of non-Jews, for fear that the closeness it engenders could lead to intermarriage. Thus Naftali's ability to build appropriate rela-

Naftali's pursuit of a livelihood required him to be occupied with the mundane realities of the world. Nevertheless, he infuses all his pursuits with his desire to serve Hashem.

Naftali's blessing contained both spiritual and mundane gifts, another indication that Naftali earthly pursuits did not contradict his spiritual striving.

---

45. Written by Rabbi Mordechai Yosef of Izhbitzah, *Parashas Beshalach*, s.v. *Umileisah bo.*

46. As we deduced earlier from *Sforno*, Naftali's blessings contained both physical and spiritual benefits, which is another testimonial to the tribe's ability to connect the two worlds.

47. *Sanhedrin* 103b.

tionships corresponds to a stone in the color of wine, which creates relationships.

V. Adar:
Connecting Through Joy

W E HAVE SEEN THE QUALITIES OF NAFTALI: ATTACHMENT to Hashem through prayer, and the alacrity and contentment that enables him to connect to his fellows. These numerous qualities can be attributed to a common source: *simchah* (joy) — and this is the source of the correlation between Naftali and Adar, the month characterized by an outpouring of joy.

- שְׂבַע רָצוֹן, *Satisfied with Favor* — *Rav Tzaddok HaKohen*[48] quotes from *Ravad's* writings on *Sefer Yetzirah's* list of the twelve mannerisms associated with the various tribes. Naftali, the tribe of Adar, corresponds to שְׂחוֹק, *laughter*, which comes naturally to someone who is satisfied and content, for someone who lacks contentment tends to anger. Adar is a month of joy and laughter, continues Rav Tzaddok.[49] The custom to indulge in merriment and pranks on Purim, like all Jewish customs, has its source in Scripture. In discussing the downfall of wicked people, King David writes, "יוֹשֵׁב בַּשָּׁמַיִם יִשְׂחָק אֲדֹנָי יִלְעַג לָמוֹ, *He Who sits in heaven will laugh, the Lord will mock them*" (*Tehillim* 2:4). When Hashem intervenes and makes wicked people's plans fail — as occurred on Purim with the downfall of Haman — it is cause for laughter and celebration.

The custom to indulge in merriment and pranks on Purim, like all Jewish customs, has its source in Scripture.

Naftali's attribute of "satisfied with favor" is an indication of his joy, because one who is naturally joyous is satisfied with what he has; one who is naturally despondent will always complain no matter how much he has.

- זְרִיזוּת, *Alacrity* — The Talmud[50] teaches that Hashem knew that Haman would eventually attempt to purchase the rights to wipe out the Jews for 10,000 talents of silver, so He preempted Haman's plot by commanding the Jewish people to contribute

---

48. *Likkutei Amarim* 16.
49. Rav Tzaddok cites several deep reasons for the joy and happiness of Adar, which are beyond the scope of this work.
50. *Megillah* 13b.

silver shekalim for the construction of the Mishkan, and every year thereafter to contribute toward the purchase of communal offerings for the Temple service. The date when these annual contributions began was Rosh Chodesh Adar, a day that *precedes* the date on which Haman planned to wipe us out. Although the shekalim weren't needed in the *Beis HaMikdash* until the first of Nissan, *Klal Yisrael* began to donate them on the first of Adar, two weeks before the designated date of Haman's planned genocide.

Although the shekalim weren't needed in the Beis HaMikdash until the first of Nissan, Klal Yisrael began to donate them on the first of Adar, two weeks before the designated date of Haman's planned genocide.

Since the miracle of Purim occurred only because of the alacrity of the entire *Klal Yisrael* in donating their shekalim, it is appropriate that Adar corresponds to Naftali, whose alacrity Yaakov likened to that of a hind, the animal that symbolizes prayer and devotion to others.

Interestingly, *Sfas Emes* [51] connects Naftali's two traits — joy and alacrity — to each other. He observes that alacrity is found in those who are filled with joy because they realize that their actions can influence the highest heavens.

Connecting to Hashem through tefillah is another of Naftali's qualities that emanate from joy. The Talmud [52] teaches, "One should not rise to pray, unless he does so out of joy associated with a mitzvah."

Sefer Chassidim [53] writes that the root of prayer is in happiness, as the verse states, "הִתְהַלְלוּ בְּשֵׁם קָדְשׁוֹ יִשְׂמַח לֵב מְבַקְשֵׁי ה׳, *Glory yourselves in His holy Name, be glad of heart, you who seek Hashem*" (*I Divrei Hayamim* 16:10). King David used to play on his harp when he prayed, and he sang the praises of Hashem, in order to fill his heart with joy and the love of Hashem.

King David used to play on his harp when he prayed, and he sang the praises of Hashem, in order to fill his heart with joy and the love of Hashem.

Since all the traits associated with Naftali are rooted in *simchah*, it is only appropriate that Naftali should correspond to the month when we maximize our joy and happiness.

Naftali and Esther

ANOTHER CORRELATION BETWEEN ADAR AND NAFTALI CAN BE found in the Purim story. The Talmud [54] states that Queen Esther composed the Psalm לַמְנַצֵּחַ עַל אַיֶּלֶת הַשַּׁחַר, *For the conductor, on the ayeles hashachar* (*Tehillim* 22) when she was on her way to the chamber of King Achashveirosh, risking her life to save the Jews from extinction. Naftali and Esther have much in common, which explains

---

51. *Parashas Tetzaveh, Zachor* 5633.
52. *Berachos* 31a.
53. 18.
54. *Yoma* 29a.

why both are compared to the hind (*ayeles* and *ayalah* are synonymous).

1) Just as Naftali was filled with love for his brethren and selflessly gave of himself for their benefit, Esther endangered her life on behalf of her people.

2) Both excelled in raising heartfelt prayers to the Heavens.

We have shown that prayer served as Naftali's mode of connection to Hashem. In Psalm 22, Esther sensed that the Divine Presence was leaving her as she passed the room housing Achashveirosh's idols. Emotionally, she prayed that Hashem should remain with her, crying out, "קֵלִי קֵלִי לָמָה עֲזַבְתָּנִי, *My God, my God, why have your forsaken me*" (*Tehillim* 22:2).

3) Esther and Naftali both brought unity among a nation that has a history of being fractious.

Esther requested of Mordechai, "Go, assemble all the Jews" (*Esther* 4:16), which means that she recognized that she could succeed in saving her people — at the risk of her life — only if her people were united in prayer. Naftali, too, brought unity to the nation. *Emunah u'Bitachon*[55] — a work attributed to *Ramban* — states that Naftali merited a name that means "to connect" because of his ability to unite all the other tribes.

Naftali merited a name that means "to connect" because of his ability to unite all the other tribes.

May this month of joy bring the ultimate joy in the merit of people like Naftali and Esther, who set aside their own desires for the sake of *Klal Yisrael* — or, better said, whose *only* personal desire is the benefit of their people.

---

55. Chapter 25.

ADAR II

MERGING BEIN ADAM L'MAKOM WITH BEIN ADAM L'CHAVEIRO

W E HAVE BEEN FOLLOWING *BNEI YISSASCHAR'S* SYSTEM OF linking each month of the year with a corresponding tribe. His system applies only to an ordinary year, however, in which the twelve months correspond to the twelve tribes. In a Jewish leap year, there are two months of Adar, and this thirteenth month seemingly has no corresponding tribe.

In a Jewish leap year, there are two months of Adar, and this thirteenth month seemingly has no corresponding tribe.

Nor is there a *mazal* corresponding to Adar II. Indeed, *Chida*[1] writes that the extra month has no *mazal*, since it was added to the twelve months and there are only twelve *mazalos*. However, the Lubavitcher Rebbe[2] writes that it is improbable to have a month with no *mazal*.

Latter-day chassidic masters discussed this matter at length, and postulated that Adar II does have a tribal correspondence. Before we discuss their opinions, let us raise some questions regarding events associated with Adar.

1) The Mishnah[3] teaches that two events occurred each year on the first of Adar: people began to donate their half-shekalim toward the purchase of the public offerings in the *Beis HaMikdash*, and *Beis Din* began to deal with people who were growing *kila'im* (forbidden mixtures of crops). This was obviously no mere coincidence — if the same day was chosen for these two events, they must be linked to each another. How?

The half-shekels were collected so that each person would be a partner in the daily and festival public offerings.

2) The concept of *machatzis hashekel* (half-shekel) is difficult in its own right. The half-shekels were collected from every member of *Klal Yisrael* so that each person would be a partner in the daily and festival public offerings. We know, however, that the animals offered in the *Beis HaMikdash* may not have any sort of

---

1. In *Devash L'fi*, citing from Rabbeinu Ephraim's writings on the Torah.
2. Cited in *Shaarei Moadim, Chodesh Adar* 30.
3. *Shekalim* 1:1.

blemish; they must be perfect and complete. But if the offerings must be whole and perfect, why did Hashem command us to donate a *half*-shekel to the cause, not a complete shekel?

3) *Rambam*[4] rules that one may not donate his half-shekel in small increments; he must donate the entire half-shekel at one time. Why?

4) *Chazal*[5] relate that Rabbi Shimon ben Yochai's students asked him why the Jews of Mordechai and Esther's time were worthy of extinction.[6] When Rabbi Shimon asked them what they thought, they suggested that it was because the Jews partook of the feast of the wicked King Achashveirosh. It seems of this passage that the Jews of the time were nearly annihilated because of a sin of *bein adam l'Makom,* a sin against Hashem.[7] Why, then, did *Chazal* choose to commemorate the miracle of Purim through mitzvos that are clearly *bein adam l'chaveiro,* between man and his fellow, such as sending food packages to friends and distributing charity to the poor?

I. Aðar II anð Levi

OURING A VISIT OF THE *PNEI MENACHEM* (THE REBBE OF Gur) to the Lubavitcher Rebbe, the two chassidic leaders discussed the subject of Adar II. The *Pnei Menachem* suggested that the additional month corresponds to all the configurations of Divine Names[8] and to all twelve tribes — or in other words, the entire *Klal Yisrael.* The Lubavitcher Rebbe doubted the validity of this novel

The Jews of the time were nearly annihilated because of a sin of bein adam l'Makom, a sin against Hashem.

---

4. *Hilchos Shekalim* 1:1.

5. *Megillah* 12a.

6. Although it seems from *Megillas Esther* that Haman devised his sinister plot of his own accord, it is axiomatic that no plan devised by man can be carried out without Divine consent. Haman could not have come so close to wiping out the entire Jewish nation *en masse* unless Hashem deemed the Jews of that time to be guilty of a grievous sin.

7. The 613 mitzvos can be categorized into *bein adam l'Makom* (between man and God), mitzvos that do not affect other human beings, and *bein adam l'chaveiro* (between man and his fellow), mitvos that primarily affect another person. Typical examples of mitzvos *bein adam l'Makom* are keeping kosher, honoring the Shabbos, and wearing tefillin. The category of *bein adam l'chaveiro* includes giving charity, engaging in proper business practices, and performing acts of kindness.

8. See the introduction to Cycle Two for an explanation of the idea of *Tzirufei Sheimos* (letter configurations of the Divine Name).

suggestion. He said that the *Tzemach Tzedek*[9] wrote that Adar II corresponds to the tribe of Levi, which does not correspond to any of the twelve months of an ordinary year.

To understand the *Tzemach Tzedek's* correlation between Levi and Adar II, we must examine the blessings Levi received from Yaakov Avinu and Moshe Rabbeinu. Interestingly, Yaakov did not speak to Levi as an individual; he addressed him together with Shimon: שִׁמְעוֹן וְלֵוִי אַחִים, *Shimon and Levi are brothers* (*Bereishis* 49:5), admonishing the two of them for their hot-headed resort to violence.

Moshe, on the other hand, addressed Levi directly and blessed him effusively: *Of Levi he said: Your Tumim and Your Urim befit Your devout one* (*Devarim* 33:8). As *Ramban* comments, Moshe summoned each tribe toward him and gave each its individual blessing.

Rabbi Samson Raphael Hirsch notes an oddity in the order of Moshe Rabbeinu's words. The *Urim V'Tumim* is the parchment with the Ineffable, secret name of Hashem, which was inserted into the Kohen Gadol's *Choshen*. This parchment made it possible for letters on the *Choshen* to be illuminated, thus revealing Hashem's will to the people.

Throughout Scripture, the *Urim V'Tumim* is written in that order, *Urim* before *Tumim*. Why did Moshe reverse the order, placing *Tumim* before *Urim*?

If we are to examine the tribe of Levi, we must ask the most obvious question regarding this tribe: Why did Levi — of which the Kohanim are a branch — merit to serve Hashem in the *Mishkan* and the *Beis HaMikdash*? As *Pirkei d'Rabbi Eliezar*[10] puts it, Levi was considered the "tithe" of the tribes, the portion of the whole that was selected for special sanctification. When Yaakov chose Levi as his tithe, the angel Michael brought Levi to Hashem, as is were, and said, "Master of the universe, this tribe is Your lot and Your title." Hashem stretched out His right hand, as it were, and blessed him.

Which begs the question: What was Levi's unique *personal* quality that rendered him most worthy for the task of serving Hashem?

9. The *Tzemach Tzedek* was the third rebbe in the dynasty of Chabad-Lubavitch.
10. Chapter 37.

LEVI'S SPECIAL CHARACTER IS SPELLED OUT CLEARLY IN MOSHE RABbeinu's blessing.

Levi — Perfection in Bein Adam l'Makom and Bein Adam l'Chaveiro

The one who said of his father and mother, "I have not favored him"; to his brothers he did not give recognition and his children he did not know: for they [the Levites] have observed Your word and Your covenant they preserved (*Devarim* 33:9).

Rashi explains that Moshe meant to say, "When *Klal Yisrael* sinned with the Golden Calf, and I said, 'מִי לַה' אֵלָי, *whoever is for Hashem, [let him come] to me,*' only the tribe of Levi came forward, and I commanded them to kill those who had worshiped the Golden Calf, even their Israelite relatives through marriage, *for not a single Levi was guilty of idol worship!*"

Daas Zekeinim mi'Ba'alei Tosafos states that the Levites did not sin with the Golden Calf out of loyalty to their relative, Moshe Rabbeinu, who was a fellow Levi. Their kinship with him prevented them from swapping him for an alternative leader.[11] *Daas Zekeinim* continues that there were three groups in *Klal Yisrael* at that time: one group accepted the calf not as a god, but as their leader and intermediary to God. Three thousand people worshiped the calf as a god — these were the 3,000 subsequently put to death by the Levites. The third was the Tribe of Levi, every member of which clung to Hashem.

The inherent greatness of the Levites that earned them distinction, according to *Daas Zekeinim*, was that Levi excelled in blending two aspects of service of Hashem that are seldom combined to perfection: *bein adam l'Makom* and *bein adam l'chaveiro*. The Levites were loyal and reliable relatives, unwilling to betray their affiliation with Moshe; but they also bucked the trend followed by most of the nation, because they chose to cling to Hashem fiercely while the others strayed or had doubts.

The inherent greatness of the Levites was that Levi excelled in blending bein adam l'Makom and bein adam l'chaveiro.

The Levites' ability to blend these two aspects of service of Hashem without compromise is what earned them the privilege of serving in the *Beis HaMikdash*. It also explains Levi's own conduct in the incident of Shechem, when he and his brother Shimon avenged the abduction and defilement of their sister Dinah by wiping out the entire city. Levi's sense of justice was revolted by a crime that vio-

---

11. *Rambam* writes that Avraham transmitted the heritage of the Torah to Yitzchak, who transmitted it to Yaakov. Yaakov transmitted it to Levi.

lated *both* principles that he was so devoted to; Shechem committed a sin that was both *bein adam l'Makom* **and** *bein adam l'chaveiro*.[12] Levi could not remain silent in the face of a crime that ran contrary to all that was near and dear to him.

Levi could not remain silent in the face of a crime that ran contrary to all that was near and dear to him.

Rabbi Samson Raphael Hirsch reaches a similar conclusion regarding Levi. As we noted above, in Moshe's blessing of Levi, he reversed the universal order, by placing *"Your Tumim"* before *"Your Urim."* In doing so, Moshe alluded to the high moral stature of the tribe of Levi that earned its special status as the servants of God. The word *tumim* — from *tamim*, [moral] wholeness — connotes high moral perfection. The word *urim* connotes intellectual perfection. Moshe chose his words carefully. Moral perfection is the road to spiritual greatness.

Moshe chose his words carefully. Moral perfection is the road to spiritual greatness.

Moshe continued by calling Levi *"Your devout one."* Rav Hirsch explains that because the tribe of Levi was devout it earned the Tumim and Urim — which enabled its bearer to convey Hashem's Word to *Klal Yisrael.* "This is unique to Judaism," he writes. "In Judaism, reaching heights in spiritual matters does not absolve a person from perfecting his personal character traits … maintaining perfection in matters of personal conduct is considered a prerequisite for reaching spiritual greatness."

Once again, we see that Levi epitomizes a perfect blend of good character traits with which to relate to other humans, while reaching for the highest possible spiritual plateau.

They were called Urim because they shed light on the questions and Tumim because their response to questions will completely be fulfilled.

What Are the Urim V'Tumim?

CHAZAL SPOKE ABOUT THE INCALCULABLY IMPORTANT FUNCTION of the *Urim V'Tumim* — stating that they were called *Urim* because they shed light on the questions posed to them,[13] and *Tumim* because their response to questions will completely be fulfilled,[14] but the Sages did not tell us what the physical *Urim V'Tumim* were. This is the subject of a dispute between *Rashi* and the *Rambam.*

Rashi[15] states that the *Urim V'Tumim* was a Divine Name of Hashem written on a parchment and inserted between the folds of the *Choshen* that the Kohen Gadol wore on his chest. Set into the

---

12. *Arvei Nachal* (*Parashas Va'eschanan*, page 60) explains that engaging in illicit relations is considered a sin both against God and against people.

13. The root of the word אורים is אור, *light.*

14. *Yoma* 73b.

15. *Shemos* 28:30; *Yoma* 73a s.v. *Klapei Shechinah.*

Breastplate were twelve precious stones on which were engraved the names of the tribes and the Patriarchs. When the Kohen Gadol asked a question of the *Urim V'Tumim*, some of the letters would light up (*Urim*) and he would form those letters into words that answered the question perfectly and completely (*Tumim*).

Rambam, too, writes that questions were asked directly to the *Choshen*, and the Kohen Gadol would be imbued with Divine Spirit that enabled him to gaze at the *Choshen* and decipher the answers to the questions.[16] Surprisingly, *Rambam* makes no mention of the *Urim V'Tumim*.

HaKsav V'haKabbalah suggests that *Rambam* is of the opinion that the twelve stones containing the names of the tribes *were* actually the *Urim V'Tumim* — not the Divine Name on a parchment. Since *Rambam* had previously mentioned that the twelve stones were set into the *Choshen*, he did not need to mention "*Urim V'Tumim*," since the very same twelve stones were the *Urim V'Tumim*.

We might take the dispute between *Rashi* and *Rambam* one step further and suggest that according to *Rashi*, the *Urim V'Tumim* was the Ineffable Divine Name that was unique to the Kohen Gadol and his tribe of Levi. *Rambam* maintains that the *Urim V'Tumim* were made up of the twelve stones of the twelve tribes of *Klal Yisrael*. Although they were inserted into the Kohen Gadol's vestments, the stones represented the entire nation, because the names of all the tribes were inscribed on them.

We can now go back to the dispute regarding Adar II. *Tzemech Tzeddek* wrote that Adar II corresponds to *Shevet Levi*, and the *Pnei Menachem* suggested that Adar II corresponds to all twelve tribes. Perhaps the views of these chassidic leaders correspond to those of *Rashi* and *Rambam*, several hundred years before. According to *Rashi*, the *Urim V'Tumim* is uniquely related to Levi, so we may suggest that Adar II is also limited to Levi.[17] According to *Rambam*, however, the *Urim V'Tumim* is composed of the stones of the entire *Klal Yisrael*. Therefore the month of Adar II also corresponds to all twelve tribes, even though only the Kohen Gadol had the exclusive spiritual power to interpret the message of the *Choshen*.

According to Rashi, the Urim V'Tumim is uniquely related to Levi, so we may suggest that Adar II is also limited to Levi. According to Rambam, however, the Urim V'Tumim is composed of the stones of the entire Klal Yisrael. Therefore the month of Adar II also corresponds to all twelve tribes,

---

16. *Rambam* gives the example of the Kohen Gadol asking whether *Klal Yisrael* should go to war. When he gazed at the *Choshen* with the Divine Spirit upon him, the appropriate letters were aglow, either forming the word עֲלֵה, *go forth [to war]* or לֹא תַעֲלֶה, *do not go forth.* The Kohen would then read the answer to the questioner.

17. As we have seen, Levi's primary merit is his ability to excel in both matters of *bein adam l'Makom* and *bein adam l'chaveiro*. Both areas of service are included in the Divine Name found on the *Urim V'Tumim*, because the name was Divine and it had an influence on the stones of all the tribes.

We find support for our findings in *Torah Temimah's* elucidation of the passage in *Talmud Yerushalmi*[18] stating that the *Urim* "shed light for *Klal Yisrael*" and the *Tumim* "perfected them," for only as long as *Klal Yisrael* was perfect, would the *Urim V'Tumim* guide it. *Torah Temimah* explains that the *Urim V'Tumim* taught the Jewish people to perfect *their ways and their characters*, for otherwise they would not receive clear guidance from it.

In order to gain from the intrinsic powers of the *Urim V'Tumim*, *Klal Yisrael* had to perfect its ways — i.e., its observance of the Torah and *mitzvos*, and the way it interacts with other human beings. Since this unique blend of *bein adam l'Makom* and *bein adam l'chaveiro* was held by the tribe of Levi, it is only appropriate that a member of the tribe merited to carry the *Urim V'Tumim*.

In order to gain from the intrinsic powers of the Urim V'Tumim, Klal Yisrael had to perfect its ways — i.e., its observance of the Torah and mitzvos, and the way it interacts with other human beings.

II. Machatzis haShekel — Perfection Through Unity

WE CAN NOW UNDERSTAND WHY HASHEM COMMANDED us to give *half*-shekels and not full shekels. The underlying message implied by the commandment to offer public sacrifices is that we cannot attain perfection as individuals. Everyone has flaws that can be perfected through interacting with, and learning from, others who can help us improve ourselves. We give half of a shekel to remind ourselves that unless we unite with others, we will remain flawed.

The importance of this message is highlighted by its implicit inclusion in the verse commanding the nation to donate half-shekalim. The verse states, "This shall they give — everyone who passes through the census — *a half shekel of the sacred shekel, the shekel is twenty geras* — half a shekel as a portion to Hashem" (*Shemos* 30:13).

Since a shekel is twenty *geras*, it would have been logical for the verse to say simply that one must contribute "a half-shekel, which is ten *geras*." Instead the Torah's command gives the value of a *full* shekel: donate "a half of the sacred shekel [which is valued at] twenty *geras*." Why?

Our donation of half a shekel is not considered complete until it is joined by half a shekel donated by another Jew.

By placing emphasis on the value of the full shekel, the Torah teaches that our donation of half a shekel is not considered complete — and cannot be considered complete — until it is joined by

---

18. *Yoma* 7:3.

half a shekel donated by another Jew, to reach a full value of twenty *geras*.

This lesson of the half-shekel — should shape our attitude even toward an offering someone brings to atone for personal sin — and, indeed, our understanding of our performance of all commandments. Perhaps the Torah wants to teach us that even mitzvos that seem to epitomize the relationship *bein adam l'Makom*, between us and Hashem — such as the communal offerings — must be done in partnership with our fellow Jews. This is a lesson we should bring into our private lives as well. No Jew is complete unto himself. We cannot feel satisfied that we have achieved a perfect relationship with Hashem unless we are equally at peace with our fellow Jews. Even when a person brings an offering in order to please Hashem and to beg forgiveness for his sins, he cannot be whole unless he is part of the nation. Only when Jews join together can each of them hope to reach perfection.

We can also understand why *Rambam* rules that one cannot donate his half-shekel piecemeal. The half-shekel donation is meant to teach us that each Jew is only half of a whole, and that we must combine with others to become complete. Allowing someone to donate incrementally would endanger the clarity of this important lesson, making it impossible to attain the perfection caused by merging *bein adam l'chaveiro* into our *bein adam l'Makom* partnership in the commanded offerings.

No Jew is complete unto himself. We cannot feel satisfied that we have achieved a perfect relationship with Hashem unless we are equally at peace with our fellow Jews.

The significance of beginning the donation of half-shekalim in Adar is now understandable according to both opinions about the tribal identity of Adar II. If the month corresponds to all twelve months, the reason is obvious. If Adar II corresponds to Levi, that tribe is the one that is most expert in merging the *mitzvos* of *bein adam l'chaveiro* and *bein adam l'Makom*. Since that blend is the primary message of donating *half*-shekalim, it is only appropriate that we donate them in Levi's month.

Indeed, following the model of Levi and Adar II we have developed, all the issues we raised can now be clarified:

WE QUESTIONED THE ASSOCIATION OF TWO SEEMINGLY DIVERGENT *mitzvos*: *Shekalim* and *kila'im*, regarding which the *Beis Din* makes its announcements on Rosh Chodesh Adar.

Shekalim, Kila'im, and Purim

Perhaps the association of these mitzvos is precisely *because* of the vast difference between them. We have shown that the half-shekel epitomizes *bein adam l'chaveiro*. *Kila'im* is the polar opposite of *shekalim*. By planting forbidden mixtures of crops, a person sins *only* against Hashem.[19] Such planting does not harm another human being. By joining these mitzvos on the first of Adar, *Chazal* teach us that we should be careful to treat *all* the mitzvos — *bein adam l'Makom* **and** *bein adam l'chaveiro* — with the same gravity.

In establishing the mitzvos of Purim, *Chazal* followed the same pattern. *Klal Yisrael* sinned toward Hashem by partaking of Achashveirosh's feast, but we commemorate the miracle that emerged from the Purim story by sending food packages to our friends and distributing charity — both clearly mitzvos that are *bein adam l'chaveiro* — because *bein adam l'chaveiro* and *bein adam l'Makom* are not mutually exclusive; they are equal parts of the whole of Torah and mitzvos.

> *Bein adam l'chaveiro and bein adam l'Makom are not mutually exclusive; they are equal parts of the whole of Torah and mitzvos.*

WE WONDERED WHY YAAKOV AVINU DID NOT BLESS LEVI, BUT MOSHE Rabbeinu did.

Yaakov Saw Potential; Moshe Saw Results

Yaakov was apprehensive that the zealotry of Shimon and Levi when they wiped out the entire city of Shechem stemmed from placing significance *only* on the *mitzvos bein adam l'Makom*. In truth, their battle cry, "Should he treat our sister like a harlot" (*Bereishis* 34:31), may imply that they were indignant only because of the sin of harlotry, not because Shechem imposed pain, suffering, and humiliation on Dinah. Their anger suggested a zealotry that lacks a human element. Yaakov was concerned that they may have been deficient in their relationship with others, so he tried to squelch their anger by admonishing them, *Accursed is their rage for it is intense* (*Bereishis* 49:7). Yaakov did not wish to bless tribes that did not understand the equal status of *bein adam l'Makom* and *bein adam l'chaveiro*.

> *Yaakov was concerned that they may have been deficient in their relationship with others, so he tried to squelch their anger by admonishing them. Moshe, on the other hand, saw the results of Levi's righteous devotion.*

Moshe, on the other hand, saw the results of Levi's righteous devotion. He saw that Levi's sense of right and wrong was focused on his interpersonal relationships as well as on his relationship with Hashem. He saw an entire tribe that maintained its stalwart loyalty to Moshe, one of their brethren, whom most of the Jewish nation had already replaced with a Golden Calf. It became clear that the Levite's devotion to *bein adam l'chaveiro* shielded them from idolatry, the most grievous sin of *bein adam l'Makom*, thereby making the Levites worthy of the unique blessing they received from Moshe.

---

19. *Sfas Emes* (*Likutim*; quoting from *Zohar*) writes that the word *Kila'im* comes from the same root as בֵּית כְּלָא, a *jailhouse*. During Adar, a person can free himself from negative goals or desires which he is imprisoned.

MOSHE GAVE THE TRIBE OF LEVI A DUAL BLESSING, WISHING THEM success in both Torah study and financial matters. Aside from the

Levi — Torah and Prosperity Combined

effusive spiritual blessing of יוֹרוּ מִשְׁפָּטֶיךָ לְיַעֲקֹב וְתוֹרָתְךָ לְיִשְׂרָאֵל, *They shall teach Your ordinances to Yaakov and Your Torah to Israel* (*Devarim* 33:10), they also received the blessing בָּרֵךְ ה׳ חֵילוֹ וּפֹעַל יָדָיו תִּרְצֶה, *Bless, O Hashem, his resources, and favor the work of his hands* (*ibid.* 33:11). Onkelos translates, "May Hashem bless [Levi's] possessions, and willingly accept his offerings." Since the previous verse refers to the incense offering, which could be performed only by Kohanim, *Sifri* (cited by *Ramban*) derives from this verse that most Kohanim were wealthy (see *Yoma* 26a). *Ramban* adds Abba Doresh's teaching that the verse נַעַר הָיִיתִי גַּם זָקַנְתִּי וְלֹא רָאִיתִי צַדִּיק נֶעֱזָב וְזַרְעוֹ מְבַקֶּשׁ לָחֶם, *I have been a youth and also aged; but I have not seen a righteous man forsaken, nor his children begging for bread* (*Tehillim* 37:25) refers to the descendants of Aharon.

Sforno explains that these two blessings were not meant to be exclusive of one another; the blessing of wealth was to help the tribe of Levi in its quest for spirituality. As long as Levites could gain prosperity with minimal investment of time, they would be free to study and to teach Torah to *Klal Yisrael*.

Levi also lived longer than any of the other tribal ancestors. Of all the tribes, the Torah mentions the lifespan of only one: Levi, who lived to the age of 137. *Chazal* explain that as long as any of Yosef's brothers were alive, Pharaoh didn't subjugate their descendants. Since Levi was the last to die, the persecution began only upon his death. The Torah records his lifespan to teach us exactly how many years the slavery lasted.

Why was Levi fortunate enough to merit success in all aspects of life: Torah study, financial matters, and long life? Perhaps because a person who can appreciate the value of both categories of mitzvos — *bein adam l'Makom* and *bein adam l'chaveiro* — merits both spiritual and material success, and is granted a long life to enjoy those blessings.

As long as Levites could gain prosperity with minimal investment of time, they would be free to study and to teach Torah to Klal Yisrael.

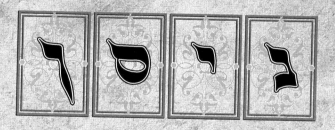

NISSAN

הִנֵּה בְּרֵאשִׁית אוֹמֵר לְךָ לִהְיוֹת הַחֹדֶשׁ הַזֶּה הוּא מֶלֶךְ
לֶחֳדָשִׁים, הַחֹדֶשׁ הַזֶּה לָכֶם (מֶלֶךְ) רֹאשׁ חֳדָשִׁים,
עַל כֵּן הוּא רֹאשׁ הַשָּׁנָה לַמְּלָכִים. וְעַל פִּי סֵדֶר הַדְּגָלִים הַחֹדֶשׁ
הַזֶּה מֻשְׁךְ שַׁיָּךְ לִיהוּדָה, שֶׁמִּמֶּנּוּ הוּא חוֹטֵר הַמַּלְכוּת.

(בני יששכר, מאמרי חדש ניסן מאמר א, אות ד)

At the outset I will tell you that [Nissan] is the "king of the months." As the Torah states, "הַחֹדֶשׁ הַזֶּה לָכֶם רֹאשׁ חֳדָשִׁים, This month shall be for you the first of the months" (Shemos 12:2), and the letters of the word לָכֶם, for you, can be rearranged to form the word מֶלֶךְ, king. This is why Nissan is considered the "New Year" of Jewish kings, who would count a new year of their reign each Nissan.[1]

In the order of encampments, [Nissan] corresponds to the tribe of Yehudah, from whom "the stump of Jewish royalty" will emerge.

(Bnei Yissaschar, Ma'amarei Chodesh Nissan 1:4)

---

1. If a king ascended to the throne just before Rosh Chodesh Nissan, the remaining days until Rosh Chodesh Nissan would be considered the first year of his kingship, and the following day, Rosh Chodesh Nissan, would be considered the beginning of his second year.

Yehudah, Yehudi, and Mesirus Nefesh

SIMPLY UNDERSTOOD, *BNEI YISSASCHAR* TEACHES THAT NISSAN corresponds to Yehudah because it is the first month, and is therefore, so to speak, "king" over all the other months, just as Yehudah was the tribe that was chosen for royalty. *Bnei Yissaschar* finds this correlation to be indicated by the interchangeable letters of the words לָכֶם and מֶלֶךְ. It seems to us, however, that there must be a much deeper significance in the relationship between the month and the tribe than the mere fact that they are comprised of the same letters and that each is a leader, one of the months and the other of the tribes.

1. Why Are All Jews Yehudim?

His name eventually became synonymous with the Jewish nation. We are all referred to as "Yehudim." How and when did Yehudah earn this distinction?

THE FIRST — AND MOST OBVIOUS — OBSERVATION WE CAN MAKE regarding Yehudah is that his name eventually became synonymous with the Jewish nation. We are all referred to as "Yehudim." How and when did Yehudah earn this distinction?

Yaakov Avinu's first words in his blessing of Yehudah are: יְהוּדָה אַתָּה יוֹדוּךָ אַחֶיךָ, *Yehudah, you, your brothers shall acknowledge* (*Bereishis* 49:8). Targum Onkelos translates interpretively that the reason for this laudatory acceptance by his brothers was because Yehudah admitted without hesitation his culpability in the matter of Tamar (*Bereishis* 38:25-26). Because of that demonstration of moral courage, his brothers would acknowledge his superiority. *Targum Yonasan* goes further and comments that because of Yehudah's admission of guilt, all the tribes will call themselves "Yehudim" based on his name.

The Midrash[1] expands on this point:

> In the last days of his life, Yaakov Avinu gathered his sons to bless them, but then he proceeded to admonish his three eldest,

---

1. *Bereishis Rabbah* 98:5-6.

Reuven, Shimon, and Levi. When the rest of the tribes saw Yaakov speaking so harshly, they began to shy away. When Yaakov saw them shrinking into the corners, he summoned each one back to him by name, beginning with Yehudah. "Yehudah, you, your brothers shall acknowledge."

Rabbi Shimon bar Yochai explains that Yaakov told Yehudah that all his brothers would be referred to by his name. No one would introduce himself as a Reuvenite or a Shimonite — they would all refer to themselves as Yehudim. Rav Yehuda bar Simon compares this to a king who had twelve sons, one of whom he loved more than the rest. In addition to his own share [of the inheritance], he gave this son an additional portion for himself.

What was so special about Yehudah's admission of guilt in the incident with Tamar that made him worthy of having all Yehudim called by his name?

LET US EXAMINE ONE OF THE MOST FAMOUS HISTORICAL APPLICA-tions of the term Yehudi. Mordechai HaTzaddik, one of the two chief protagonists of the Purim story, is referred to in *Megillas Esther* as a Yehudi: אִישׁ יְהוּדִי הָיָה בְּשׁוּשַׁן הַבִּירָה וּשְׁמוֹ מָרְדֳּכַי, *There was a Yehudi man in Shushan the capital whose name was Mordechai* (*Esther* 2:5).

Mordechai HaYehudi

Rashi explains that Mordechai is described as a Yehudi (although he was from the tribe of Binyamin) simply because he was exiled from *Eretz Yisrael* with the tribe of Yehudah, and the gentiles called everyone exiled with the Judean kings a Yehudi, no matter what tribe he was from. At first glance, *Rashi* seems to be saying that the name "Yehudi" derived from the historical fact that the tribe of Yehudah was the last to be exiled, so the Jewish people as we know it nowadays is comprised primarily of members of Yehudah. There is a much deeper concept expressed in Rashi's words, however.

The Talmud[2] states that Mordechai was called a Yehudi because he rejected idolatry, and anyone who repudiates idol worship is called a Yehudi. This is derived from the narrative in the *Book of Daniel*, where the Babylonians, speaking of three Jews who defied the royal decree to worship idols, describe them as, *there are Yehudi men*[3] (*Daniel* 3:12).

The Talmud states that Mordechai was called a Yehudi because he rejected idolatry, and anyone who repudiates idol worship is called a Yehudi.

2. *Megillah* 13a.

3. This verse refers to Chananyah, Mishael, and Azzariyah who chose to be thrown into fire rather than bow to an idol of Nevuchadnezar. Hashem performed a miracle and the fire did not burn them.

We can deduce from Chazal's words that the title Yehudi describes those who are willing to proclaim their faith in Hashem with mesirus nefesh.

A midrash[4] adds that a person who rejects idol worship proclaims Hashem's Unity to the world, so he is called a "Yehudi," a word that is similar to *Yechidi*, the firm conviction that Hashem is the One and Only. We can deduce from *Chazal's* words that the title Yehudi describes those who are willing to proclaim their faith in Hashem with *mesirus nefesh*, and to repudiate idolatry even when such defiance will cost them their lives.

II. Mesirus Nefesh Is Worthy of Miracles

THE TALMUD[5] RELATES THAT RAV PAPPA ONCE ASKED ABAYE WHY earlier generations merited to have miracles performed for them, and their own generation did not. It was surely not because the earlier generations were greater in scholarship, Rav Pappa contended, for in Rav Yehudah's generation the *amoraim* studied only *Seder Nezikin*,[6] while the generation of Rav Pappa and Abaye would study all six orders of the Talmud. Furthermore, Rav Yehudah had difficulty dealing with topics related to *Maseches Uktzin*,[7] and their generation could explain the very same concepts in thirteen different ways!

What merit, wondered Rav Pappa, did the earlier generations possess that did not exist in the later generations? "The earlier generations sanctified Hashem's Name with mesirus nefesh," responded Abaye.

However, Rav Pappa observed, despite the apparent superiority of his own generation, when a drought struck in Rav Yehudah's days and the people were assembled to pray for rain, all he had to do was remove his shoe[8] to prepare for the prayers — and the rain would begin to fall! But the scholars of his own generation would cry out in fervent prayer and their prayers were not answered. What merit, wondered Rav Pappa, did the earlier generations possess that did not exist in the later generations?

"The earlier generations sanctified Hashem's Name with *mesirus nefesh*," responded Abaye. "Ours does not." Obviously, Abaye considered those who displayed *mesirus nefesh* worthy of having miracles performed on their behalf. Interestingly, according to this passage, a person who endangers his life in order to sanctify Hashem's

---

4. 6:2.

5. *Berachos* 20a.

6. The Order of the Talmud dealing with monetary law.

7. One of the tractates in *Seder Taharos*, the order of Mishnayos dealing with the laws of spiritual purity.

8. As a sign of mourning, similar to our removing our shoes on Tishah b'Av.

Name is deserving of a miracle not only to save him from immediate, personal danger, as happened in the case of Chananya, Mishael, and Azzarya,[9] who let themselves be thrown into a blazing furnace rather than bow to an idol. As in the case of Rav Yehudah, Hashem also performs unrelated miracles for those who are *moser nefesh,* even when their *mesirus nefesh* does not put them in mortal danger.

THE SIGNIFICANCE OF *MESIRUS NEFESH* IS ALSO APPARENT IN THE fact that we still mention *Akeidas Yitzchak*[10] (the binding of Yitzchak

An Everlasting Zechus

on the altar) in our prayers to this very day, asking Hashem to apply the merit of our forefathers Avraham and Yitzchok to us. Avraham's readiness to slaughter his only son, and Yitzchak's readiness to be slaughtered if such was Hashem's will, remain a source of merit for their descendants to this day.

Rabbi Yosef Dov Soloveitchik suggests that this *mesirus nefesh* of Avraham and Yitzchak at the *Akeidah* explains why Har HaMoriah (the mountain upon which *Akeidas Yitzchak* took place) retained its holiness, eventually becoming the site of the *Batei Mikdash.* Mount Sinai, on the other hand, did not retain its holiness once the Divine Presence departed from it. At the giving of the Torah, the nation was passive; Hashem took the initiative to give the Torah to the Jewish people. They accepted it willingly, but no lives were in danger when the nation gathered around the mountain. Clearly, the merit of *mesirus nefesh,* like that displayed at the *Akeidah,* is so great that it endures for thousands of years.

It was appropriate, therefore, that the *Beis HaMikdash* was built in Yehudah's portion of *Eretz Yisrael.* A tribe epitomized by *mesirus nefesh* is the most suitable host for the Divine Presence that rested in the *Beis HaMikdash.*

A tribe epitomized by mesirus nefesh is the most suitable host for the Divine Presence that rested in the Beis HaMikdash.

WE CAN NOW APPRECIATE THE DEEPER SIGNIFICANCE OF THE NAME Yehudim. Yehudah's willingness to admit his guilt in the incident with

Yehudah, Model of Mesirus Nefesh

Tamar came with phenomenal *mesirus nefesh* and strength of character. Many people find it easier to give their lives rather than suffer humiliation and ongoing ridicule. To Yehudah, none of this mattered. To save the life of Tamar he stepped

Many people find it easier to give their lives rather than suffer humiliation and ongoing ridicule.

---

9. See footnote 5.

10. Lit., the Binding of Yitzchak; see *Bereishis* 22.

forward and admitted that he, not she, had erred; he was ready to be the butt of snickers and taunts, rather than be responsible for the death of an innocent person. No one else in the world would know that Tamar had been put to death illegally, but *he* would, so he would not permit it to happen. It is entirely fitting, therefore, that the Jewish people, who show that same strength of character from one generation the next — standing strong for Hashem's honor at all costs — are aptly named Yehudim after him.

No one else in the world would know that Tamar had been put to death illegally, but he would, so he would not permit it to happen.

Rashi's explanation of Mordechai's title "Yehudi" is far from superficial. The nation did not earn the title Yehudim simply because the remaining Jews of Israel were exiled with Judean kings, but because we *chose to emulate* Yehudah by clinging to Hashem with fierce loyalty, and accepting the consequences of our faith in Him with *mesirus nefesh.*

A Lion Cub

YEHUDAH'S *MESIRUS NEFESH* WAS NOT LIMITED TO THE INCIDENT with Tamar. *Chazal*[11] teach that Yaakov told Yehudah, "It was always known to the Holy One, Blessed is He, that you saved Yosef's life; if not for you, Shimon and Levi would have killed him. Now your brothers will also acknowledge and thank you for stepping in to save your brother's life, thus saving them from the *Gehinnom* that they would have suffered for their part in his death. You will also be rewarded in *Olam Haba* by having all Jews called by your name, 'Yehudim.'"

Yaakov's blessing to Yehudah does not seem to correspond to the action that earned him reward. Yehudah saved Yosef from *physical* death — why was he given the *spiritual* reward of having all Jews called by his name in *Olam Haba*?

Yehudah agreed with his brothers that Yosef was guilty, but he contended "What will we gain if we execute him and thus foreclose his possibility to repent and gain atonement?"

When the tribes found Yosef guilty of crimes that made him worthy of execution, Yehudah stepped in and said, "מַה בֶּצַע כִּי נַהֲרֹג אֶת אָחִינוּ וְכִסִּינוּ אֶת דָּמוֹ, *What gain will there be if we kill our brother and cover up his blood?*" (*Bereishis* 37:26).

Baal HaTurim notes — in his usual pithy style — that the word בֶּצַע appears in only one other place in Scripture: מַה בֶּצַע בְּדָמִי, *What gain is there in my death?* (*Tehillim* 30:10), implying that the words have something in common. The students of the *Chozeh* of Lublin explained the common denominator. Yehudah agreed with his brothers that Yosef was guilty, but he contended "What will we gain if we execute him and thus foreclose his possibility to repent and gain atonement? There is no repentance in the World to Come. Only in

11. *Yalkut Shimoni, Parashas Vayechi* 159.

this life can one repent, and therefore we should let him live and have the opportunity to atone for his sins."

Baal HaTurim notes that the very same idea was expressed by Yehudah's descendant, David Hamelech, generations later: "What gain is there in my death, in my descent to the pit? *Will the dust acknowledge You? Will it declare Your truth?*" (ibid.) Both Yehudah and David noted that only as long as a person is alive can he achieve atonement. Once he is dead, he can no longer do so.

Thus, Yosef's *physical* longevity was not Yehudah's primary concern; his earnest desire was for Yosef to atone for his *spiritual* shortcomings and to sanctify Hashem's Name in this world. That is what motivated Yehudah to save Yosef's life. Indeed, Yehudah's hopes were realized when Yosef sanctified Hashem's Name in Egypt, as the Talmud[12] teaches: Yosef sanctified Hashem's Name in a concealed manner, so he merited to have one letter of Hashem's Name added to his own, in the verse עֵדוּת בִּיהוֹסֵף שָׂמוֹ בְּצֵאתוֹ עַל אֶרֶץ מִצְרָיִם, *He appointed it as a testimony for Yehosef when he went out over the land of Egypt* (*Tehillim* 81:6).[13]

Since Yehudah displayed *mesirus nefesh* in order to ensure Yosef's spiritual wellbeing, and Yosef vindicated Yehudah's confidence when, as viceroy of Egypt, he displayed *mesirus nefesh* to sanctify Hashem's Name, it is appropriate that Yehudah was rewarded spiritually, and specifically, that those who display the *mesirus nefesh* he exemplified should be called Yehudim.

it is appropriate that those who display the mesirus nefesh he exemplified should be called Yehudim.

III. Mesirus Nefesh Led to the Miracles of Nissan

THE HERITAGE OF *MESIRUS NEFESH* REMAINED WITH THE TRIBE of Yehudah throughout the generations. The Talmud[14] teaches that since Yehudah sanctified Hashem's Name publicly, he merited that the four letters of Hashem's Name are included in the name Yehudah. Yehudah's great public sanctification of the Name came at the Sea of Reeds, when (according to Rabbi Yehudah) Nachshon ben Aminadav, the leader of Yehudah, plunged into the Sea while the

Since Yehudah sanctified Hashem's Name publicly, he merited that the four letters of Hashem's Name are included in the name Yehudah.

---

12. *Sotah* 36b.

13. The name Yosef is generally spelled יוסף. In this verse it appears with an extra ה', one of the letters of Hashem's Name — בִּיהוֹסֵף.

14. *Sotah* 36b.

water was still raging. This act of *mesirus nefesh* caused the Sea to split. Clearly the sea would split only when a member of *Klal Yisrael* would display *mesirus nefesh*. Who could be relied upon to show such *mesirus nefesh*? A leader of the tribe of Yehudah.

It is now clear why the month of Nissan is associated with Yehudah. Nissan is an auspicious time for miracles. Indeed, the very name of the month comes from the word נס, *miracle*. *Bnei Yissaschar* describes the month as follows:

> It is called Nissan, because it is a month of open miracles that transcend nature and the scope of human comprehension. Nissan was predestined — going back to the Six Days of Creation — for miracles. [The night of the fifteenth of Nissan] is called *Leil Shimurim* — a night of anticipation — because Hashem anticipated taking the Jewish People out of Egypt on that night, and He will bring about the final redemption on this night as well. Indeed, "Nissan" is a suitable name for this month, considering all the *nissim* [miracles] that took place in it.

And if Nissan is so called because of the miracles that took place during the month, then it is only appropriate that it should correspond to Yehudah, whose *mesirus nefesh* caused the momentous miracle that took place when the Jews left Egypt during Nissan, the miracle that caused the nation to have unprecedented faith in Hashem and His servant Moshe.

Mesirus Nefesh Causes the Exodus

UPON FURTHER EXAMINATION, WE FIND THAT THE ENTIRE PESACH festival — from the beginning of the Exodus process until the end — was precipitated by *mesirus nefesh*. On Rosh Chodesh Nissan, Hashem commanded Moshe to instruct the Jewish people to set aside a sheep that would be slaughtered as a *Korban Pesach* (Pesach Offering).[15] The Midrash[16] relates that Moshe protested, "How can I ask the Jews to do such a thing? Do You not know that sheep are the deity of Egypt? If the Jews dare to slaughter their god, the Egyptians will stone them!" Hashem answered, "By your life, they will not leave Egypt unless they slaughter sheep before the eyes of the Egyptians, thus proving that the gentiles' idols are powerless." We can only imagine the astounding *mesirus nefesh* required of a people who had so recently

15. See *Shemos* 12:1-13.
16. *Shemos Rabbah* 8:22.

been subservient to the Egyptians, and now had to audaciously slaughter the gods of their former masters.

This *mesirus nefesh* is so significant, in fact, that *Tur*[17] writes that Shabbos Hagadol earned the name "the *Great* Shabbos" because of the miracle that occurred on that day. In the year of the Exodus, Shabbos Hagadol fell on the tenth of Nissan, and each Jew took a sheep, led it into his house, and tied it to his bedpost. When the Egyptians asked them what they were planning to do with the sheep, they explained that they were going to slaughter them as Hashem commanded. The Egyptians were enraged by the plan for "deicide," but they could do nothing to stop it. This open miracle that occurred on that Shabbos entitled that day "Shabbos Hagadol" for all time. The Jews were asked to do something that normally would have subjected them to a pogrom of epic proportions — but they had complete faith in Hashem and Moshe, and this earned them safety and redemption.

Thus, *mesirus nefesh* in Egypt began the climactic process of redemption, to be culminated by the faith and courage of Nachshon, of the tribe of Yehudah, that heralded the final salvation at the Yam Suf.

The name Yehudim is eminently suitable for a nation that was born through the phenomenal *mesirus nefesh* that heralded the beginning of their redemption, and the equally astounding *mesirus nefesh* of a leader of Yehudah that finalized their salvation. That dedication enabled them to go free to produce generation upon generation of descendants who were willing to sacrifice everything for the sanctity of Hashem's Name. The trait most prominently associated with the tribe of Yehudah, from Yehudah himself through his descendants, became imbedded in the spiritual DNA of the nation, so much so that we all proudly carry the title Yehudim.

That dedication enabled them to go free to produce generation upon generation of descendants who were willing to sacrifice everything for the sanctity of Hashem's Name.

IV. Chanukah and Purim: The Common Denominator

ESIRUS NEFESH IS NOT ONLY THE KEY FACTOR THAT brought about the redemption that we celebrate through the various festivals mandated by the Torah, it is also the element that brought about the two festivals established by the Sages, Chanukah and Purim.

---

17. *Orach Chaim* 430.

Sfas Emes[18] aptly notes that the Jewish people are described in *Megillas Esther* only by the name Yehudim. He explains:

THIS NAME ALWAYS APPLIES TO ISRAEL, FOR EVEN IN ITS LOWLY generations it repudiates idolatry and acknowledges the truth.

Yehudah's Name

This is the characteristic of Yehudah, after whom Israel is called, as the Midrash sets forth in *Vayechi*, and his name is granted to those who defiantly oppose foreign gods and stand true to Hashem. This is also the deeper meaning of the verse, וְהִשְׁאַרְתִּי בְּקִרְבֵּךְ עַם עָנִי וָדָל וְחָסוּ בְּשֵׁם ה׳, *And I will leave in your midst a humble and destitute people, and they will take shelter in the Name of Hashem* (*Tzephaniah* 3:12). This Four-letter Name of Hashem appears in the name of Yehudah. The added letter ד (dalet) — when it is spelled out דָּלֶת — means "poverty," and alludes to a downtrodden status. Yehudah [and all Jews] merit the four letters of Hashem's Name because they consider themselves lowly and unworthy, and because of this, they merited [lofty insights into Divine concepts]. This very modesty is what propelled the people to eternally high levels of spiritual attainment.

The verse in *Megillas Esther* (8:16) states that the *Yehudim* had אוֹרָה וְשִׂמְחָה וְשָׂשׂוֹן וִיקָר, *light, gladness, joy, and honor. Chazal* interpret that these four words allude to Torah, tefillin, *milah* and yom tov.[19] These four attributes emanate from the great spiritual merit of the Patriarchs. Nevertheless, the Jews in the time of the Megillah were granted this high spiritual level even though they were only Yehudim, meaning, as noted above, that they were of a "downtrodden status." Even such Jews are worthy of sublime gifts.

Above we cited Rashi who explained that Mordechai was called a Yehudi because he, like the other Jews remaining in Jerusalem, was exiled together with Yehudah, which was the predominant tribe. We suggested that the deeper message conveyed by Rashi is that the name Yehudi represents *Klal Yisrael's* willingness to be accept any sacrifice to sanctify Hashem's Name, and that that willingness has given Israel the strength to survive every bitter exile.

Yehudah [and all Jews] merit the four letters of Hashem's Name because they consider themselves lowly and unworthy. This very modesty is what propelled the people to eternally high levels of spiritual attainment.

---

18. *Purim* 5663.
19. *Megillah* 16b.

THE MIRACLE OF PURIM WAS DUE TO THE *MESIRUS NEFESH* OF Mordechai, a quintessential Yehudi. *Chazal* teach that he was called

Earning Miracles

a Yehudi because he repudiated idolatry, no matter what the danger to himself. Indeed, Mordechai's refusal to bow to Haman so enraged the highest official of the land that he plotted the extermination of all the Jews. Thanks to Mordechai's courageous loyalty to Hashem, he provided the merit that brought about the miracle of Purim. The Jewish people were on the verge of destruction because they had sinned in obscenely enjoying the food and drink at the lavish feast of King Avhashveirosh. Thanks to Mordechai and Esther, the nation renewed its determination to assert the uniqueness of the *Klal Yisrael* and its unswerving loyalty to Hashem.

The miracle of Chanukah, too, was brought about by great *mesirus nefesh*. *Shem MiShmuel*[20] comments that the Syrian-Greeks were permitted to defile all the oil in the *Beis HaMikdash* because oil represents wisdom and the mind. Since many Jews of the time contaminated themselves [by marrying gentile women], the enemy was empowered to defile the oil, which represents wisdom, according to Kabballah. The amazing *mesirus nefesh* of the Chashmonaim — who were hopelessly outnumbered, yet fought for the cause of the Torah and its commandments — made them worthy of the miracles that enabled them to prevail over the Syrian-Greeks. The enemy had defiled the oil that represents wisdom and the mind, but, *mesirus nefesh* is meta-rational; it transcends the mind, and therefore brought victory over the forces of contamination. To prove how much Hashem valued their loyalty, He allowed the Chashmonaim to find the one jug of oil that had not been defiled.

To prove how much Hashem valued their loyalty, He allowed the Chashmonaim to find the one jug of oil that had not been defiled.

That a single jug of oil remained pure signifies that no force on earth can completely eradicate the *mesirus nefesh* that is the legacy of Yehudah. The brave and loyal Chashmonaim had overcome the contamination caused by those who had intermarried.

We have found that the miracles commemorated by all the festivals we celebrate during the year came as a result of *mesirus nefesh*, starting with the original redemption from Egypt and spanning all the way to the very last miracle that occurred on Chanukah.

It is that *mesirus nefesh* that earned us the title Yehudim, and has enabled us to remain true to Hashem until this very day.

---

20. *Mikeitz* 5673.

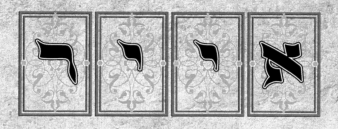

IYAR

עַל פִּי סֵדֶר הַדְּגָלִים הַחוֹדֶשׁ הַזֶּה מְיֻוחָס לְשֵׁבֶט יִשָּׂשׂכָר.

(בני יששכר, מאמרי חדש אייר מאמר א, אות ט)

According to the order of the encampments,
[Iyar] corresponds to the tribe of Yissachar.

(Bnei Yissaschar, Maamarei Chodesh Iyar 1:9)

CDonth of Counting and Connnection

Iyar connects Nissan to Sivan, bridging the gap between two phenomena: the redemption from Egypt, and our designation as the Chosen People when we received the Torah.

THE ENTIRE MONTH OF IYAR FALLS WITHIN THE PERIOD OF *SEFIRAS Ha'Omer* (Counting of the *Omer*). Iyar connects Nissan to Sivan, bridging the gap between two phenomena: the birth of our nation during Nissan with the redemption from Egypt, and our designation as the Chosen People when we received the Torah upon the conclusion of *Sefiras Ha'Omer*.

We can point to a variety of seemingly unrelated factors associated with Iyar, which, when properly developed, all center on the concept of connecting one thing to another.

We will also address an interesting question discussed by the *Rishonim*. Aside from the counting of the *Omer*, there are two other commandments that involve counting: (a) a man or woman who becomes impure through *zivah* (forms of bodily emissions) must count seven days of purity before immersing in a *mikveh*; and (b) we are commanded to count forty-nine years leading up to a *Yovel* (Biblical Jubilee year celebrated every 50 years).

Interestingly, we find that *Chazal* established a *berachah* on the counting of the *Omer* (and perhaps on the counting of the years to *Yovel* as well[1]), but not on the counting of the days of purity of *zivus*. Why?

We must also wonder why we do not recite Shehechayanu the first time we count the Omer each year, as is the common practice with all other mitzvos that occur periodically.

Once on the subject of *berachos*, we must also wonder why we do not recite *Shehechayanu* the first time we count the *Omer* each year, as is the common practice with all other mitzvos that occur periodically.

Another unusual practice associated with the *Omer* is the widespread recitation of *Lesheim Yichud* prior to each day's counting. [*Lesheim Yichud* is a kabbalistic formula that combines our intent to perform the commandment properly with a prayer that the mitzvah serve to bring "completion," as it were, to the Divine Name.] Although many authorities oppose the recitation of *Lesheim Yichud* prior to fulfilling other mitzvos, most communities *do* recite it before

---

1. The *Rishonim* discuss whether or not *Beis Din* recited a *berachah* when counting the years up to *Yovel* — see *Tosafos, Menachos* 65b s.v. *U'sfartem, Kesubos* 72a s.v. *Vesafrah*, and *Teshuvos Rabbi Akiva Eiger, Mahadura Kamma* 29.

Sefiras Ha'Omer, even those who usually do not recite it before performing other commandments. Why is the *Omer* an exception?

Other events and factors associated with Iyar:

- The month of Iyar is considered an auspicious time for those who need healing. During Iyar, shortly after the redemption from Egypt, Hashem pledged, "If you hearken diligently to the voice of Hashem, your God, and do what is just in His eyes, give ear to His commandments and observe all His decrees, then any of the diseases that I placed on Egypt, I will not bring upon you, for I am Hashem, your Healer" (*Shemos* 15:26).

  The first letters of the last three words of this verse, אֲנִי יְ־הֹ־וֹ־ה רֹפְאֶךָ, *I am Hashem, your Healer,* are an acronym for *Iyar*. In the course of our discussion, we will address the special power of healing that exists in this month.

- Two historical events occurred during Iyar on the way from Egypt to Sinai: (1) The manna first began to fall for the Jews,[2] and (2) the nation of Amalek attacked us.

Let us examine how all these factors and events relate to Iyar's common theme of connecting Nissan with Sivan.

1. Preparation as a Mitzvah

THE FIRST STEP TOWARD UNDERSTANDING THE MONTH OF IYAR lies in the answer to why we recite a *berachah* when we count the *Omer*, while a *zav* and *zavah* do not do so when they count their days of purity.

Chinuch[3] notes that there is no actual mitzvah for a *zav* or *zavah* to count the days verbally; they are simply commanded to keep track of the days of purity to ensure that they immerse in the *mikveh* on the correct day, whereas the actual counting of the *Omer* (and possibly the years toward *Yovel*) is a mitzvah in its own right.[4]

Paradoxically, while counting the *Omer* is itself a mitzvah — an end in itself — it is also a *means* to prepare ourselves to accept the Torah on Shavuos.

Paradoxically, while counting the Omer is itself a mitzvah — an end in itself — it is also a means to prepare ourselves to accept the Torah on Shavuos.

---

2. See *Shemos* 16:1-4.

3. *Mitzvah* 430.

4. This idea is expressed with more clarity in *Teshuvos Noda BiYehudah, Mahadura Tinyana, Yoreh Deah* 123, quoting *Ridvaz*.

In truth, however, this paradox answers the question we raised regarding *Shehechayanu. Radvaz*[5] points out that whenever we have a mitzvah that requires some sort of preparation, we recite *Shehechayanu* only when performing the mitzvah itself, not when preparing for it.[6] Since *Sefiras Ha'Omer* is actually a preparation for Shavuos, the *berachah* of *Shehechayanu* that we recite on Shavuos suffices.

We might suggest that *Sefiras Ha'Omer* teaches us the importance of *preparing* for a mitzvah. *Sfas Emes* offers two explanations for why the preparation for a commandment is especially important.

The actual time spent performing the mitzvah is usually far less than the amount of time spent preparing for it, so the preparation requires us to spend more time in spiritual activity.

First of all, the actual time spent performing the mitzvah is usually far less than the amount of time spent preparing for it, so the preparation requires us to spend more time in spiritual activity. This preparation time occupies a person's thoughts and leaves a permanent positive effect. Furthermore, we are usually unable to perform a mitzvah with the exact intentions and meaning with which we should, because the depth of Hashem's wisdom is beyond human capacity — but even if we lack the special *kavannos* (intentions) while preparing for a mitzvah, the very fact that we spend time preparing for it shows that we want to follow Hashem's commandments in the most meaningful way we can.[7] In addition, the time and effort one expends in preparing for the mitzvah have an ongoing effect on a person, whereas the performance of the mitzvah usually comes and goes quickly.

Perhaps we can now understand why people who usually do not recite the prefatory statement of *Lesheim Yichud* prior to performing other mitzvos do so before counting the *Omer*. Since the essence of *Sefiras Ha'Omer* is to teach us the importance of preparing for mitzvos, it is appropriate that we recite *Lesheim Yichud* before *Sefiras Ha'Omer*.

---

5. Vol. IV, 256.

6. A typical case in point is *succah*. Rather than recite *Shehechayanu* when building the *succah*, we recite *Shehechayanu* only when we perform the mitzvah of actually eating in the *succah*.

Teshuvos HaRashba (126) offers another reason for not reciting the blessing for *Sefiras Ha'Omer. Shehecheyanu* implies that one feels joy at being alive to perform the commandment. In this case, however, there is a sense of pain in that the Torah speaks of the counting as being done in anticipation of the Temple offering of Shavuos; therefore, since we do not have the *Beis HaMikdash* and cannot bring the offering, the blessing is not appropriate.

7. Similarly, it is said in the name of the *Chiddushei HaRim* that the reason why *Simchas Beis Hashoevah* was celebrated with such unparalleled joy is because it was actually a preparation for the mitzvah of *Nissuch Hamayim*, and the joy of preparation for a mitzvah is even greater than the joy of doing the mitzvah itself.

WE NOW HAVE A DEEPER UNDERSTANDING OF THE IMPORTANCE OF Iyar. As the month that connects the Exodus to the giving of the Torah, it is a time of preparation — and the significance of preparation is that it connects the aspiration toward a goal to its successful achievement. When we prepare for an event, we connect the days of preparation to the event itself.

Connecting Pesach to Shavuos

Pri Tzaddik[8] cites *Sefer Yetzirah* (according to the text of the *Geonim*):

> In Nissan [Hashem] coronated the letter *hei* through *re'iyah* (sight); and in Iyar He coronated the letter *vav* through *shemiah* (hearing).

Pri Tzaddik explains:

> In Nissan we merited a revelation of Hashem only through Divine Kindness [not because we deserved it]. The revelation appeared temporarily on the night of the Exodus, and then left us until we witnessed it once again through *re'iyah* during the Splitting of the Sea, when, "a maidservant at the sea saw [a degree of prophecy] what [even the prophet] Yechezkel ben Buzi did not. But then the vision left them."[9]

Rabbi Bunam of P'shis'cha taught that the reason Hashem showed those brief flashes of prophetic vision to every member of the nation was to show the people the spiritual heights they could attain if they would exert sufficient effort. In Sivan, when we accepted the Torah at Mount Sinai, the revelation of the Divine Glory became a permanent acquisition.

The reason Hashem showed those brief flashes of prophetic vision to every member of the nation was to show the people the spiritual heights they could attain if they would exert sufficient effort.

Iyar was coronated with the letter *vav*. Rav Hai Gaon explains that the letter *vav* symbolizes connection. As a prefix, it connects two words or clauses to one another. *Vav* is also a word, meaning a *hook*, something that connects two objects, as we see in the verse, וָוֵי הָעַמֻּדִים, *the hooks of the pillars* (*Shemos* 27:10), where the word *vav* refers to the hooks that attached the curtains of the Tabernacle Courtyard to their supporting beams.

Similarly, Iyar — the month of connection — connects Nissan to Sivan, and provides the means to *acquire* in Sivan what we *saw* in Nissan.[10]

---

8. *Rosh Chodesh Iyar* 5.

9. *Mechilta Shirasa* 3.

10. The concept that Iyar, or more accurately, all the days of *Sefirah* between Pesach and Shavuos, connects the two festivals to each other is most clearly expressed in a famous statement from *Ramban* comparing the days of *Sefirah* to Chol HaMoed. The

In stating that Iyar [was coronated] through *shemiah*, *Sefer Yetzirah* is not referring to the sense of hearing *per se*, but to *accepting* the idea or concept that was heard. We find this usage of *shemiah* in the Talmud,[11] when one Sage tells another, "*lo shemiah li*," literally, "I did not hear," but in that context it means "*I do not accept this idea*." This is what the *Sefer Yetzirah* means when it states that in Iyar, Hashem coronated *vav* through hearing. It means that Israel *heard*, i.e., accepted the concept that it would strive forever to earn the spiritual exaltation it had experienced momentarily during the Nissan of the Exodus.

Pri Tzaddik is teaching that during the Exodus and *Kerias Yam Suf*, the Jewish nation was granted a high level of revelation of Hashem's Glory, but Hashem allowed them only a "glimpse" of that exalted level so that they would be inspired to reach it on their own by purifying themselves during the days of *Sefiras Ha'Omer*. Indeed, by rising from one level to the next during *Sefiras Ha'Omer*, they were able to elevate their spiritual vision, so that by the time they stood at Mount Sinai, they could earn that high level of revelation.

Iyar was given the letter *vav* because it is the month that connects the temporary revelation of Nissan with the enduring revelation that was acquired when we accepted the Torah in *Sivan*.

Shemiyah/hearing, more than *re'iyah*/seeing, is the sense that connects people with others. Sight is unilateral; we do not need the cooperation of other people in order to see them. Listening, on the other hand, implies that we hear what someone else is saying; there is a speaker and a listener. Seeing is entirely passive; we see something that exists, but there is no communication between the seer and the person or thing that he sees. Hearing, on the other hand, involves connection, because when there is silence there is no communication.

We now reach a more satisfactory understanding of why the counting of the Omer, unlike the counting of *zivah*, is an independent mitzvah. Since the preparation period of *Sefirah* connects Nissan with Sivan and brings us to the level at which we can accept the Torah, it is appropriate that those preparations should be considered a mitzvah in their own right.

Israel heard, i.e., accepted the concept that it would strive forever to earn the spiritual exaltation it had experienced momentarily during the Nissan of the Exodus.

Seeing is entirely passive; we see something that exists, but there is no communication. Hearing, on the other hand, involves connection, because when there is silence there is no communication.

---

festival of Pesach serves as the first days of Yom Tov; all the days following Pesach serves as Chol HaMoed, and Shavuos serves as the last day of Yom Tov. Thus, Pesach and Shavuos relate to one another, and *Sefiras Ha'Omer* connects them.

11. *Eruvin* 102b.

11. I Am Hashem, Your Healer

DATING BACK TO THE YEAR OF THE EXODUS AND SINAI, IYAR is traditionally a month of healing. During that Iyar, the physical ailments and blemishes of the Jewish people were healed so that they could stand at Mount Sinai in perfect physical and spiritual health. This concept is also mentioned in the Talmud, which states,[12] "All drinks that heal [work well] between Pesach and Shavuos."

Based on this passage, *Maharsha*[13] notes that the deaths of Rabbi Akiva's 24,000 students were particularly shocking because they occurred between Pesach and Shavuos, which is naturally a time of health and healing.

Bnei Yissaschar[14] writes that Iyar is a month when the stomach can be healed from all sorts of ailments and weakness of the gall-bladder. Iyar is an auspicious time for healing digestive ailments because most such problems are caused when a person ingests food that does not agree with his system. The manna was a spiritual food in physical form, and therefore did not need to be processed by the body. It began to fall during Iyar, so that this month became, and remained, an auspicious time for the healing of digestive ailments.

Upon further consideration, we suggest that Iyar's healing quality also derives from its status as a "connecting" month, for a person who is healed from an illness "reconnects" to his earlier state of good health.

Iyar's power of healing is not limited to physical ailments; more than most other months, it is a time in which we can rectify our spiritual well-being through *teshuvah* (repentance), since it was the month of preparation for receiving the Torah. Therefore, in the prayer customarily recited after counting the *Omer*, we state that Hashem commanded us to count the *Omer* "so that the souls of Your people Israel shall be cleansed of their contamination." The idea of using *Sefiras Ha'Omer* to perfect our spiritual standing fits perfectly with our previous musings on the month of Iyar. Since *Sefiras Ha'Omer* is the time when we prepare to accept the Torah on *Shavuos*, it is indeed appropriate that we perfect ourselves spiritually during this period.

Since Sefiras Ha'Omer is the time when we prepare to accept the Torah on Shavuos, it is indeed appropriate that we perfect ourselves spiritually during this period.

---

12. *Shabbos* 147b.
13. *Yevamos* 62b s.v. *Mipnei.*
14. *Chodesh Iyar,* 1:3.

In addition, people are born in a state of spiritual purity, but sin corrupts it, as the verse states, "God has made man simple [i.e., naturally inclined to righteousness], but they sought many intrigues" (*Koheles* 7:29). Through the process of *teshuvah* we return to — and connect with — the spiritual purity with which we were born, in coherence with Iyar's status as a "month of connection."

THE ABOVE ALSO EXPLAINS WHY THE MANNA BEGAN TO FALL DURING Iyar. Ostensibly, eating is a purely physical pursuit, but it has a spiritual dimension, as well. In order for our *neshamah* to remain with the body, we must eat. Thus, if we eat in order to strengthen our bodies so that our souls can thrive inside them, eating actually becomes a spiritual activity.

The Manna: Connecting the Spiritual and the Physical

If we eat in order to strengthen our bodies so that our souls can thrive inside them, eating actually becomes a spiritual activity.

Chazal tell us that the Torah could be given only to those who ate manna. Why? Because the Jewish people in the Wilderness, where no normal means of sustenance was available, knew that they were being kept alive by means of a purely spiritual food. They ate with that knowledge and the manna made them aware that they should eat for the sake of Heaven. Such eating connects the body with the spirit and enables a person to engage in attaining spirituality.[15]

This concept is hinted to in the Ineffable Name, י-ה-ו-ה. The phrase אֲכִילָה וּשְׁתִיָה, *eating and drinking*, ends with the letters י-ה, and the word מִצְוָה, *commandment*, the basis of all spiritual pursuits, ends with ו-ה. If we use food and drink for the purpose of *mitzvos*, we complete the Name י-ה-ו-ה, because we take the physical aspect of food and turn it into the service of the spiritual aspect of the Torah. [This is also the concept of eating *shirayim* (food that a *tzaddik* recited a blessing over; typically food passed around at a *chassidic tish*). When a *tzaddik* eats food, he raises it to great realms of spirituality, and those who eat from that food can be similarly uplifted.]

When a tzaddik eats food, he raises it to great realms of spirituality, and those who eat from that food can be similarly uplifted.

Since the manna enabled those who ate it to connect the body to the spirit, it is appropriate that it began to fall in Iyar, the month of connection.

---

15. Perhaps this is alluded to in *Sefer Yetzirah's* statement that Iyar was created with a *vav* and Sivan with a *zayin*. It is known that the letter *zayin* "leans" on the letter *vav*, because the body of the *yayin* is a *vav*; only the top of the letter identifies it as a *zayin*. Perhaps the ability to receive the Torah in Sivan was contingent upon eating manna, which began to fall in Iyar. This may be why Iyar is called *Chodesh Ziv* [זִיו], a word that connects the letters *vav* and *zayin*.

FOLLOWING THE ORDER OF THE ENCAMPMENTS, IYAR CORRESPONDS to Yissachar. Now that we have ascertained that Iyar is the month of connection, we can understand this correlation with ease.

Yissachar Connects the Masses to the Torah

Yaakov Avinu blessed Yissachar as follows:

יִשָּׂשכָר חֲמֹר גָּרֶם רֹבֵץ בֵּין הַמִּשְׁפְּתָיִם. וַיַּרְא מְנֻחָה כִּי טוֹב וְאֶת הָאָרֶץ כִּי נָעֵמָה וַיֵּט שִׁכְמוֹ לִסְבֹּל וַיְהִי לְמַס עֹבֵד, *Yissachar is a strong-boned donkey crouching between the boundaries. He saw a resting place that it was good and the land that it was pleasant, and he bent his shoulder to bear and he became an indentured laborer* (Bereishis 49:14-15).

Rashi comments:

יִשָּׂשכָר חֲמֹר גָּרֶם, *Yissachar is a strong-boned donkey* — who bears the yoke of Torah, like a strong donkey that carries a heavy burden.

רֹבֵץ בֵּין הַמִּשְׁפְּתָיִם, *crouching between the boundaries* — like a donkey that walks by day and by night and has no lodging indoors. When it wants to rest it lies down on the outskirts of the city.

וַיֵּט שִׁכְמוֹ לִסְבֹּל, *and he bent his shoulder to bear* — the yoke of Torah.

וַיְהִי, *and he became* — to all of his brothers,

לְמַס עֹבֵד, *an indentured laborer* — to provide his brethren with practical decisions [on questions of] Torah law, and the arrangement of leap years.

On a very basic level, the very comparison of Yissachar to a donkey speaks of the connection associated with Iyar. The blessing likens Yissachar's mission to that of a donkey. Just as a donkey transports people and merchandise from place to place, thus serving as a "connection" of sorts between the places, so Yissachar brings the rulings of the Torah from one place to another, thus uniting the people in a common understanding of God's will. It is thus appropriate that Yissachar, the "connector," represents the month of connection, for by teaching Torah to all the other tribes and ruling on halachic issues, Yissachar connects all of *Klal Yisrael* to the Torah.

Amalek's attack during Iyar now fits into the entire equation perfectly. *Chazal* teach that Amalek was able to attack *Klal Yisrael* because they had weakened in their obligation to study Torah. This would have been considered a demerit no matter when it would have come, but since Iyar, Yissachar's month, is a time when Jews should naturally strengthen their connection to the Torah, this neglect was

Just as a donkey transports people and merchandise from place to place, so Yissachar brings the rulings of the Torah from one place to another, thus uniting the people in a common understanding of God's will.

considered a particularly serious shortcoming, and they were immediately punished by being forced to do battle with Amalek.

YISSACHAR'S STONE ON THE *CHOSHEN* (BREASTPLATE) WAS SAPIR.

Appropriately, the letters that form the word סַפִּיר come from the same

Sapir, Sefirah, and Yissachar

root as the word סְפִירָה, for *Sefiras Ha'Omer*. The sapphire stone reflects flashes of light, thus dispelling darkness, at least to a degree. This property of the stone negates the sharp division between night and day. When it is totally dark, there seems to be no connection between the period of light and the period of darkness, but when there is a sudden flash of light, one realizes that the darkness — which symbolizes despair — is not permanent, and that there will be a "connection" between the light that was and the light that will be again. This also ties in with our understanding of Iyar as a month of connection, because the light of a sparkling *sapir* casts away the darkness, connecting night and day.

As we observe the days of *Sefiras Ha'Omer* that connect Pesach to Shavuos throughout the month of Iyar, we should do our best to connect ourselves to the Torah, and reconnect ourselves with a state of both spiritual and physical health.

SIVAN

הנה תמצא בסידור השבטים לדגליהם,
יהודה יששכר זבולון, נגד ניסן אייר סיון.

(בני יששכר, מאמרי חדש תמוז אב מאמר א, אות ג).

You will find in the order of the tribes according to their encampments, Yehudah, Yissachar, and Zevulun correspond to Nissan, Iyar, and Sivan.

(*Bnei Yissaschar, Maamarei Chodesh Tammuz–Av 1:3*)

Climbing the Spiritual Ladder

Zevulun is associated with the aquatic creature chilazon, from which the bluish dye techeiles, used in tzitzis, was extracted.

BNEI YISSASCHAR TEACHES THAT THE TRIBE OF ZEVULUN corresponds to the month of Sivan. To understand this correlation, we must define the uniqueness of Zevulun. In the process, we will also gain clarity as why the festival of Shavuos is celebrated in Sivan and also why the precious stone *yahalom* was the one that represents Zevulun in the Kohen Gadol's *Choshen Mishpat*.

Zevulun is associated with the aquatic creature chilazon, from which the bluish dye *techeiles*, used in *tzitzis*, was extracted. As we will see below, Zevulun received the chilazon as a compensation when he complained about its portion of *Eretz Yisrael*. The Talmud[1] discusses the following verse in the Book of *Shoftim:* זְבֻלוּן עַם חֵרֵף נַפְשׁוֹ לָמוּת, *Zevulun is a tribe that risked its life to the death.* וְנַפְתָּלִי עַל מְרוֹמֵי שָׂדֶה, *and so did Naftali on the heights of the fields* (*Shoftim* 5:18). The plain meaning of the verse is that the prophetess Devorah was praising both of these tribes for their heroism in the battle against Sisera, the Canaanite general who conquered and oppressed much of *Eretz Yisrael*.

However, the Talmud adds a homiletical interpretation, according to which the tribe of Zevulun risked its life, as it were, by protesting that Hashem had treated it unfairly in dividing *Eretz Yisrael* among the tribes. Zevulun complained that it received mountainous regions, oceanfront, and rivers, the sort of territory that made prosperity impossible, because it was not suited for agriculture. By contrast, other tribes, such as Naftali, received fertile fields and lush vineyards. Hashem answered by quoting the blessing Zevulun received from Moses: כִּי שֶׁפַע יַמִּים יִינָקוּ וּשְׂפֻנֵי טְמוּנֵי חוֹל, *by the riches of the sea they will be nourished, and by the treasures concealed in the sand* (*Devarim* 33:19). The Sages interpret this to mean that all the other tribes will need Zevulun to provide the *techeiles* dye from the chilazon, an amphibious creature that lives in the sea.

The Sages interpret this to mean that all the other tribes will need Zevulun to provide the techeiles dye from the chilazon, an amphibious creature that lives in the sea.

Rashi[2] explains that since the chilazon ascends from the water only once every seventy years, the availability of the dye extracted from it was very rare, so it was expensive. Consequently, the members of Zevulun were able to demand a high price for it. The chilazon would be Zevulun's source of prosperity.

---

1. *Megillah* 6a.
2. *Bava Metzia* 61b.

True, the chilazon was a wonderful gift; however, it is hard to follow the rationale of the dialogue between Zevulun and Hashem. The people of Zevulun requested land and vineyards that they could use to plant and reap. If so, Hashem's promise of the chilazon emerging in their territory did not satisfy the request. Furthermore, if the chilazon and *techeiles* are indeed so wonderful, why was Zevulun singled out as the only tribe to be blessed with them? And why did Hashem word His promise to Zevulun, "all the others will need you"? Zevulun did not request honor; it wanted arable land. Furthermore, what did Zevulun do to merit this enigmatic blessing?

1. Techeiles Is Similar to …

LET US SEEK AN UNDERSTANDING OF THE DEEPER SIGNIFICANCE of *techeiles*. Why must one of the *tzitzis* threads be *techeiles*? The Talmud[3] teaches that *techeiles* was chosen over all other colors because it is similar to the color of the ocean, and the ocean is similar to the color of the sky, and the sky is similar to the Throne of Glory. Rashi adds that the sea is similar to sapphire, which is the color of the Throne of Glory. Consequently, *Rashi*[4] explains, the *techeiles* on our garments serves as a reminder of Hashem, Who sits on the Throne of Glory.

This passage begs an obvious question. If all four items listed in the Talmud (*techeiles*, the ocean, the sky, and the Throne of Glory) are similar to each other, why doesn't the Talmud say directly that *techeiles* is similar to the Throne of Glory? Why the need for three intermediate steps — the sea, the sky, and sapphire?

Why doesn't the Talmud say directly that techeiles is similar to the Throne of Glory? Why the need for three intermediate steps — the sea, the sky, and sapphire?

CHAZAL[5] NOTE THAT YISSACHAR WAS OLDER THAN ZEVULUN. ZOHAR[6] adds that Yissachar was characterized by his devotion to Torah study,

---
The Exalted Level of Zevulun's Charity

---

and the Torah always takes precedence over other qualities. If so, both *Chazal* and *Zohar* ask, why did both Yaakov Avinu and Moshe Rabbeinu bless Zevulun before Yissachar?

---

3. *Menachos* 43b; *Chullin* 89a.
4. To *Menachos.*
5. *Vayikrah Rabbah* 25:2.
6. *Parashas Vayechi* 242:1.

Chazal answer that since Zevulun traveled far from home to earn enough to provide support not only for his own families, but also for Yissachar's, Zevulun deserved to be blessed first. *Zohar* adds that Zevulun would even take his own food and give it to Yissachar. He was willing to go hungry in order to enable Yissachar to learn! [7]

Zevulun's exalted devotion to charity — his willingness to give his own food to Yissachar — was obviously not an easy trait to come by. How can we reach Zevulun's level? We cannot decide one morning that we are willing to give up everything we own for someone else's sake. In order to emulate Zevulun, we must go step by step. First we must learn to give a small amount of money to charity, then a little more, and a little more, until we are ready to move to the level at which we feel inclined to provide another individual with all his material needs, so that he can be free to study Torah. Finally, after conditioning ourselves to be more and more generous, we can reach a level at which we would be willing to take our own rations and give them to someone else. As *Rambam* writes, it is better to give many small contributions to charity than to give one large contribution, because by giving over and over, a person trains himself to be generous. In the oft-repeated maxin of *Sefer HaChinuch,* אָדָם נִפְעָל כְּפִי פְּעוּלוֹתָיו, *a person is fashioned by his deeds.*

> *Zevulun would even take his own food and give it to Yissachar. He was willing to go hungry in order to enable Yissachar to learn!*

> *it is better to give many small contributions to charity than to give one large contribution, because by giving over and over, a person trains himself to be generous.*

Slow — but Steady — Progress

WE SUGGEST THAT *CHAZAL* TOOK US THROUGH THE STEPS OF *techeiles* being similar to the water, the water to the sky, and the sky to the sapphire and the Throne of Glory to show us that spiritual progression cannot be made in giant steps. The road to the Throne of Glory cannot be traversed in one day. A person must take measured steps toward Hashem, climbing the spiritual ladder slowly and methodically.

Baal Ha'Akeidah [8] writes that *techeiles* represents the "middle path," because the bluish hue of *techeiles* is somewhere between white, which diffuses the vision, and black, which causes the vision to focus on a central point.

> *A person must take measured steps toward Hashem, climbing the spiritual ladder slowly and methodically.*

---

7. This idea is hinted to in the use of the singular form of the verb שְׂמַח, *rejoice,* in the verse שְׂמַח זְבוּלֻן בְּצֵאתֶךָ וְיִשָּׂשכָר בְּאֹהָלֶיךָ, *Rejoice, O Zevulun, in your excursions, and Yissachar in your tents* (*Devarim* 33:18). Although there were actually two partners in the Yissachar–Zevulun arrangement, and Yissachar should surely have rejoiced at the good fortune of his generous brother, the joy is ascribed to Zevulun. This is to Zevulun's credit, because it illustrates how happy he was to support Yissachar's Torah study.

8. *Parashas Shelach.*

The "*derech hamemutzah*," the "middle road," is the ideal path to take in our service of Hashem. Extremes are not good. As *Rambam* puts it, excessive generosity will lead to poverty, but too little will lead to parsimony. Appropriately, we find that Mordechai left King Achashveirosh wearing a garment of *techeiles*, symbolizing that a leader of *Klal Yisrael* should cloak himself in *techeiles* — i.e., he must train himself to navigate the nation along the middle road.

We can learn to travel the middle road symbolized by *techeiles* by having its lesson in mind: taking step after step, just as the ascent from *techeiles* to the Throne of Glory must done one step at a time.

II. Zevulun as a Teacher

WE CAN NOW EXPLAIN WHY HASHEM GAVE THE *TECHEILES* TO Zevulun. *Techeiles* represents the need for slow and steady progress. Zevulun mastered this art, as shown by his ascent in levels of charity until he was ready to deprive himself for Yissachar's benefit. It is only befitting that the tribe that represents slow progress in spiritual matters should be the guardian of the *techeiles,* and act as its source for the rest of the nation. Hashem presented the *techeiles* to Zevulun to teach him — and us — how important it is to adopt this method of serving Hashem.

This provides perspective on the dialogue between Hashem and the tribe of Zevulun. Zevulun asked for fields and vineyards — but no matter how much produce is reaped from a field, no matter how many tons of grapes are grown in a vineyard, the land and the vines remain exactly the same as they were before. The *chilazon*, on the other hand, "ascends" from the ocean. It represents the ability to be upwardly mobile in spiritual matters. When Hashem told Zevulun, "All the others will need you," He meant that the other tribes would need Zevulun to demonstrate the symbolic message of the *techeiles* — the need to progress in our service of Hashem, steadily, but slowly.

The chilazon, "ascends" from the ocean. It represents the ability to be upwardly mobile in spiritual matters.

WE CAN NOW UNDERSTAND THE CORRELATION BETWEEN ZEVULUN and Sivan, the month in which we received the Torah. The Torah cannot be acquired overnight. *Chazal*[9] list forty-eight steps necessary for acquiring the Torah. It took *Klal Yisrael* all forty-nine days of *Sefirah* to raise themselves

48 Steps Toward Acquiring the Torah

9. *Avos* 6.

Only those
who master
Zevulun's form
of serving
Hashem
will have
the patience
and fortitude
with which
to acquire the
Torah, step by
step, from level
to level.

to the level at which they could receive the Torah at Mount Sinai. Only those who master Zevulun's form of serving Hashem will have the patience and fortitude with which to acquire the Torah, step by step, from level to level.

Chazal[10] also tell us that Hashem "bent the lower skies and the upper skies and spread them on Mount Sinai during *Mattan Torah*." Perhaps this combination of the bluish lower skies with the upper skies that are closest to the Throne of Glory was meant to serve as yet another reminder of the slow and steady progress needed to traverse the road to greatness. This concept is illustrated by *techeiles*, which comes from the portion of Zevulun.

We might also add that this is the reason why we did not have *techeiles* for centuries and why modern attempts to identify the chilazon have not gained full acceptance. *Chazal* tell us that the final redemption will happen little by little. Only when we master the art of taking those small steps toward the level of spirituality that will bring the final redemption and the rebuilding of the *Beis HaMikdash*, will all Jews merit to have *techeiles*.

Zevulun —
the ultimate
exemplar of
the highest
level of service
of Hashem
— should be
represented by
yahalom, the
ultimate stone.

The uniqueness of Zevulun may also provide an understanding of why *yahalom* was its stone in the *Choshen Mishpat*. The *yahalom* is a diamond, the most precious and durable of all precious stones. It is known as the "rock of rocks." Only another diamond can cut a diamond; it is impervious to anything else. It is appropriate, therefore, that Zevulun — the ultimate exemplar of the highest level of service of Hashem — should be represented by *yahalom*, the ultimate stone.

---

10. *Mechilta Parashas Yisro.*

TAMMUZ

וְהִנֵּה תִּמְצָא בְּסִידוּר הַשְּׁבָטִים לְדִגְלֵיהֶם, רְאוּבֵן נֶגֶד תַּמּוּז.

(בני יששכר, מאמרי חדש תמוז אב מאמר א, אות ג)

*You will find in the order of the tribes
according to their encampments,
Reuven corresponds to Tammuz.*

(Bnei Yissaschar, Maamarei Chodesh Tammuz- Av 1:3)

The Power of Sight

LET US EXAMINE THE ASSOCIATION BETWEEN REUVEN AND Chodesh Tammuz.

Kabbalistic sources teach that Tammuz is a month characterized by strict judgment.

Kabbalistic sources teach that Tammuz is a month characterized by strict judgment. *Zohar*[1] states that the verse describing Yocheved's attempt to shield the newborn Moshe, "And she hid him for three months" (*Shemos* 2:2), refers to the three months of the year in which strict judgment reigns — Tammuz, Av, and Teves. The Talmud[2] states that demons named *Ketev Meriri* are most powerful during Tammuz.

Chazal spoke about the importance of the Minchah prayer and urged that we be especially zealous regarding that service; they use the prophet Eliyahu as an example. In the presence of hundreds of thousands of Jews, Eliyahu challenged hundreds of idolatrous prophets on Mount Carmel. He was confident that Hashem would perform a miracle to enable him to prove that the so-called prophets were false, and his prayer was answered at the time of Minchah.[3] Indeed, the Midrash[4] teaches that when we pray *Minchah*, it is as if we actually offer a *Minchah* (meal-offering) on the Altar.

This is commonly understood to mean that *Minchah* is a time of Divine mercy, but *Zohar*[5] has an entirely different perspective on the importance of the prayer:

One should take special care in regard to Minchah, for it is [recited at] a time when harsh judgment reigns in the world.

> One should take special care in regard to *Minchah*, for it is [recited at] a time when harsh judgment reigns in the world.

It would seem logical that if, as *Zohar* teaches, *Minchah* counteracts the harsh judgment that reigns each afternoon, then during Tammuz, which is also a time of such judgment, we should also exercise great care when praying *Minchah*. If so, we must try to understand the correlation between *Minchah* and this unique characteristic of Tammuz.

---

1. *Shemos* 12a.
2. *Pesachim* 111b.
3. *Berachos* 6a.
4. *Bamidbar Rabbah* 13:4.
5. *Bereishis* 132b; 230a; *Shemos* 36b.

1. Tammuz, Seeing, and Understanding

In ORDER TO REACH A SATISFACTORY UNDERSTANDING OF THESE topics, we must first examine another characteristic associated with the month of Tammuz.

Bnei Yissaschar cites from *Sefer Yetzirah*:

> [Hashem] coronated the letter ח through "sight" [in Tammuz], and then the letter ט through hearing; therefore, the letters ח and ט reign during the months of Tammuz and Av, as is hinted to in the verse חֵטְא חָטְאָה יְרוּשָׁלַם, *Jerusalem sinned greatly* (*Eichah* 1:8).[6]

Obviously, *Sefer Yetzirah* deals with profoundly esoteric Kabbalistic concepts that are beyond the scope of this essay, but it states that the concept of *sight* — or perhaps better said, *vision* — is especially associated with Tammuz. Later in the essay, *Bnei Yissaschar* adds:

> Let us delve into the words of the *Sefer Yetzirah*. The human sense of sight corresponds to the month of Tammuz, and the human sense of hearing to the month of Av. If we examine the tribes that correspond to the months of the year, we find that Yehudah, Yissachar, and Zevulun — the group of tribes that traveled first [in Israel's journeys in the Wilderness] — correspond to Nissan, Iyar, and Sivan. Moving on to the next group of tribes, we find Reuven corresponding to Tammuz, the month of *vision*. This is why Leah named Reuven to allude to sight: וַתַּהַר לֵאָה וַתֵּלֶד בֵּן וַתִּקְרָא שְׁמוֹ רְאוּבֵן כִּי אָמְרָה כִּי רָאָה ה' בְּעָנְיִי, *Leah conceived and bore a son, and she called his name Reuven, as she had declared, "Because Hashem has **seen** my humiliation"* (*Bereishis* 29:32). This explains why *Sefer Yetzirah* associates Reuven with Tammuz.

> The next month, Av, corresponds to hearing and to the tribe of Shimon. Indeed, Leah named Shimon to allude to hearing: וַתַּהַר עוֹד וַתֵּלֶד בֵּן וַתֹּאמֶר כִּי שָׁמַע ה' כִּי שְׂנוּאָה אָנֹכִי וַיִּתֶּן לִי גַּם אֶת זֶה וַתִּקְרָא שְׁמוֹ

---

6. To illustratrate the point that the letters *ches* and *tes* are "dominant" in the months of Tammuz and Av respectively, *Sefer Yetzirah* cites a verse from *Eichah* that gives the reason for the destruction of the Temple, a tragic process that began in Tammuz and culminated in Av. The verse begins with two words both of which have the letters ח and ט in succession.

שִׁמְעוֹן, *And [Leah] conceived again and bore a son and declared, "Because Hashem has **heard** that I am unloved, He has given me this one also," and she called his name Shimon* (ibid. 29:33). Appropriately, Reuven's name begins with the letter ר, as does the sense of sight, רְאִיָּה, and Shimon's name begins with a שׁ, as does the sense of hearing, שְׁמִיעָה.

We find that the princes of these two tribes were blemished early on in the travels through the Wilderness.

We find that the princes of these two tribes were blemished early on in the travels through the Wilderness. The prince of Reuven, Elitzur ben Shedeur, joined Korach in challenging Moshe, and Zimri ben Salu (whom Chazal tell us was actually Shlumiel ben Tzurishaddai, the prince of Shimon), sinned in Shittim. [The relationship between the senses of seeing and hearing and the leaders of Reuven and Shimon will be explained below.]

We find the correspondence between each of these two months and the senses of seeing and hearing in other instances. The *Meraglim* (Spies) first arrived in *Eretz Yisrael* during the month of Tammuz,[7] and spent the entire month engaged in their mission. While there, they sinned through their vision; everything they *saw,* they perceived negatively. When they came back to the Wilderness to report back to *Klal Yisrael* on the eighth of Av, the rest of the nation sinned through *hearing,* by listening and accepting the report of the Spies. *Ramban* (*Numbers* 13:4) comments that the Torah lists the spies in the order of their personal greatness. It is noteworthy, therefore, that the representative of Reuven is listed first and the representative of Shimon is second. Clearly, Reuven's representative was the most influential one in this historic perversion of the power of vision. An indication of his greatness is that Calev is third on the list and Yehoshua is fifth.

Everything they saw, they perceived negatively. When they came back to the Wilderness to report back to Klal Yisrael on the eighth of Av, the rest of the nation sinned through hearing, by listening and accepting the report of the Spies.

In addition, *Parashas Korach* is most commonly read during the month of Tammuz. As *Chazal*[8] explain, "Korach was a brilliant man; what did he *see* that influenced him to initiate his foolish rebellion against Moshe? His eyes led him astray, because he saw into the future that his descendant, the prophet Shmuel, would be equal to Moshe and Aharon put together." He reasoned that if his offspring was destined to be so great, then surely he could prevail against Moshe and Aharon.

---

7. Moshe sent the *meraglim* on their mission on the 29th of Sivan, and they reached *Eretz Yisrael* at the beginning of Tammuz.

8. *Bamidbar Rabbah* 18:8.

THE STEIPLER GAON *ZT"L* OFFERED A BRILLIANT INSIGHT INTO THE sense of sight. An object or occurrence is *seen* the same way by

Sight: In the Eye of the Beholder

everyone, but how it is understood varies widely from person to person; some may interpret it one way, while others will interpret it another way. Sight stimulates a process of identification and interpretation that plays itself out differently in the minds of the witnesses.

Another aspect of sight is that a person can see something or someone even if the person being seen prefers not to be noticed. On the other hand, no one can force us to see something that we do not wish to see — a witness always has the option of closing his eyes or turning away. Hearing is different. We cannot hear others against their will. If someone prefers not to be heard, he can simply stop talking.

II. Sight in the Tammuz Parashiyos

WHEN WE TAKE A CLOSE LOOK AT THE FOUR *PARASHIYOS* commonly read during Tammuz, we find that sight plays a major role in each of them. And in those *parashiyos* — *Shelach*, *Korach*, *Chukas*, and *Balak* — the interpretion of what is being seen depends on the witness.

PARASHAS SHELACH BEGINS WITH THE STORY OF THE *MERAGLIM*, whom Moshe sent to survey *Eretz Yisrael*. He charged them, "*See* the

The Spies

land — how is it? And the people that dwell in it — is it strong or weak? Is it few or numerous?" (*Bamidbar* 13:18).

The *Meraglim* returned from their journey, and "*showed* them [the Jewish people] the fruit of the land" (ibid. 13:26). They should have used the fruit to prove that Hashem was giving them a wondrously rich and fertile country. Instead they then gave their infamous interpretation: "They brought forth to the Children of Israel an evil report on the Land that they had spied out, saying, 'The Land through which we have passed, to spy it out, is a land that devours its inhabitants! All the people that we *saw* in it were huge! There we *saw* the

They should have used the fruit to prove that Hashem was giving them a wondrously rich and fertile country. Instead they then gave their infamous interpretation.

Nephilim … [i.e., giants] we were like grasshoppers *in our eyes*, and so we were *in their eyes*'" (ibid. 32-33).

Calev and Yehoshua went on the very same trip, saw the same things, but understood everything in a diametrically different way.

Calev and Yehoshua went on the very same trip, *saw* the same things, but understood everything in a diametrically different way: "The land that we passed through, to spy it out — the Land is very, very good!" (ibid. 14:7).

The *Meraglim* entered *Eretz Yisrael* and saw amazing wonders. They saw fruit that grew to unbelievable size. They saw people dying left and right. The issue was not what the *Meraglim* saw; the problem was their perception. Rather than being amazed by the fruit they would soon be able to enjoy, rather than realizing that Hashem orchestrated the mass deaths of inhabitants of *Eretz Yisrael* so that the population would be distracted and not notice the Jewish strangers among them, the *Meraglim* came back and claimed that the land devoured its inhabitants. Only Kalev and Yehoshua were untainted enough to properly interpret the sights they had seen.

A seer has great power over what he sees, for it is subject to his interpretation, which usually depends on his personal predelection.

As the Steipler said, a seer has great power over what he sees, for it is subject to his interpretation, which usually depends on his personal predelection.

At the very end of *Parashas Shelach* we read the *parashah* of *tzitzis*. We are commanded to wear *tzitzis* so that "You may *see* it and remember all the commandments of Hashem and perform them" (ibid. 15:39). We are also warned of the harmful effect sight can have on us: "and not explore after your heart and *after your eyes after which you stray*" (ibid.).

WE MOVE ON TO *PARASHAS KORACH*, WHOSE NAMESAKE *SAW* CORrectly, according to *Chazal*, but his misfortune was that he misinter-

Korach's Flawed Vision

"If all this greatness is to come from me," reasoned Korach, "is it possible for me to be destroyed?"

preted what he saw. The Midrash[9] tells us that Korach foresaw that his family would put forth a leader, the prophet Shmuel, who would be equal to both Moshe and Aharon combined.[10] He also saw that 24 groups of his descendants would prophesy through Divine Spirit. "If all this greatness is to come from me," reasoned Korach, "is it possible for me to be destroyed?"

He was sure that the glory of his posterity ensured that he would prevail over Moshe, but he failed to foresee that his children would

9. *Tanchumah*, cited in *Rashi, Bamidbar* 16:7.

10. Shmuel, who descended from Korach, is described as equal to Moshe and Aharon put together: *"Moshe and Aharon were among His priests, and Samuel among those who invoke His Name"* (*Tehillim* 99:6).

repent and be spared his fate. It seemed clear to him that only someone greater than Moshe and Aharon could have a descendant equal to them both. The Midrash concludes, וּמֹשֶׁה הָיָה רֹאֶה, *And Moshe did see.* He, too, foresaw the greatness of Korach's descendant, but he realized that the greatness was meant for Korach's descendant, not for Korach himself.

IN *PARASHAS CHUKAS*, HASHEM TEACHES THE IMPORTANCE OF SEEing and perceiving properly. The Jewish people began to complain
Raising Lights about Moshe, about the lack of water, and about the monotomy of the manna. Hashem punished them by dispatching snakes to bite them.

Moshe begged Hashem to end the plague, and Hashem commanded him, "Make for yourself a fiery [serpent] and place it on a pole, and it will be that anyone who was bitten *will look at it* and live" (ibid. 21:8).

The Mishnah (*Rosh Hashanah* 3:8) comments, "Could the serpent kill or give life? This [verse] teaches that when the Jewish people would gaze upward and subjugate their hearts to their Father in heaven, they would be healed; and if not, they would waste away." *Chazal* teach that it was not enough to simply *look* at Moshe's snake; seeing it had to trigger *a thought process* in the person gazing at it, which would eventually lead him to subjugate himself to Hashem.

PARASHAS BALAK BEGINS WITH SIGHT USED IN ITS WORST FORM. THE Torah states, "Balak the son of Tzippor *saw* all that Israel had done to
Seductive Sights the Amorite" (ibid. 22:2). *Chazal*[11] comment, "It would be better if the wicked would be blind, for their eyes bring evil into the world." The misuse of eyes continues throughout the *parashah*. *Chazal* teach that Bilaam contaminated his vision to such a degree that he could not prophesy. In order to enable him to receive prophetic visions for the benefit of Israel, Hashem blinded one of his eyes so that he would have one uncontaminated eye. Bilaam never quite understood what Hashem wanted of him, and tried time and again to harm *Klal Yisrael* by casting an evil eye upon them.[12]

Later in the *parashah* we find *Klal Yisrael* being provoked to sin through viewing the seductive Midianite women, but the plague that

Chazal comment, "It would be better if the wicked would be blind, for their eyes bring evil into the world."

11. *Bamidbar Rabbah* 20:2.
12. See *Bamidbar* 24:2.

ensued was brought to a halt through sight as well. The Torah tells us, "Pinchas the son of Elazar the son of Aharon the Kohen *saw*, and he stood up from amid the assembly and took a spear in his hand" (ibid. 25:7). Pinchas *saw* and acted — and by doing so shocked the Jewish people into withdrawing from their sinful conduct. By using his sense of vision properly, Pinchas atoned for the sin that had begun through improper use of sight, and he saved the Jewish nation from annihilation.

By using his sense of vision properly, Pinchas atoned for the sin that had begun through improper use of sight, and he saved the Jewish nation from annihilation.

To summarize, the lessons of these *parashiyos* point to the same concept. Sight can be used for good — great spiritual heights can be attained through it — but it can also be used for evil, leading a person to the depths of depravity. The Mishnah[13] sums it up by stating that those who have an *ayin tovah* (a good eye) are among the disciples of Avraham Avinu — i.e., their sight can lead them to greatness. Those who have an *ayin ra'ah* (an evil eye) are among the disciples of Bilaam — whose life as a prophet was wasted on evil and immorality.

III. Sight and Minchah

RE'IYAH (SIGHT) IS ALSO ONE OF THE FOUNDATIONS OF THE *Minchah* prayer. The Torah states, וַיֵּצֵא יִצְחָק לָשׂוּחַ בַּשָּׂדֶה לִפְנוֹת עָרֶב, *Yitzchak went out to supplicate in the field toward evening* (*Bereishis* 24:63). *Chazal* derive that the word *sichah* refers to prayer, and they deduce that Yitzchak established the *Minchah* prayer at that time, since he went to pray "toward evening."[14] The very same verse concludes, וַיִּשָּׂא עֵינָיו וַיַּרְא, *and he raised his eyes and he saw* (ibid.), which implies that the *Minchah* prayer is associated with raising one's eyes to see what is good and inspiring.

The Minchah prayer is associated with raising one's eyes to see what is good and inspiring.

Sight became a major issue later in Yitzchak Avinu's life. The Torah tells us, "When Yitzchak had become old, and his eyes dimmed from seeing …" (ibid. 27:1). Midrashim, cited by *Rashi*, differ as to the reason for Yitzchak's loss of vision.

---

13. *Avos* 5:22.

14. *Chazal* (*Berachos* 26b) derive this from the use of the word לָשׂוּחַ in this verse, which is used in the context of prayer in the verse תְּפִלָּה לְעָנִי כִי יַעֲטֹף וְלִפְנֵי ה׳ יִשְׁפֹּךְ שִׂיחוֹ, *A prayer of the afflicted man when he swoons, and pours forth his supplications before Hashem* (*Tehillim* 102:1).

ACCORDING TO *MIDRASH RABBAH*, YITZCHAK'S BLINDNESS WAS A result of a disturbing spiritual experience; according to *Midrash*

Both Extremes

Tanchuma, it was caused by the sinful conduct of Esav's wives. *Midrash Rabbah*[15] states that when Yitzchak was bound at the *Akeidah* and Avraham was on the verge of slaughtering him, the angels in heaven began to cry. Their tears entered Yitzchak's eyes and left an impression on them, until he eventually lost his sight. Another opinion there is that Yitzchak looked up during the *Akeidah* and saw the Divine Presence; that awesome sight affected his eyesight, eventually blinding him.

Midrash Tanchumah[16] takes an opposite approach, stating that Yitzchak was blinded by the incense that his daughters-in-law (Esav's wives) sacrificed to idols. In his exalted spiritual state, Yitzchok could not tolerate the sight of the idolatrous smoke, and it resulted in his blindness.

Thus, two extremes of vision existed in Yitzchak, one positive and one negative. On one hand his vision was characterized by striving to see the Divine Presence, but on the other hand, he restricted his vision to avoid seeing evil, and his vision was impaired by the incense of idol worship. According to our premise above, that Yitzchok inaugurated the *Minchah* service when he raised his eyes in the spiritual sense, it was surely with the sense of elevation — the positive aspect of sight — that he experienced at the *Akeidah*, as set forth by *Midrash Rabbah*. And that is why *Minchah* has remained a medium through which we can attain great spiritual levels.

On one hand his vision was characterized by striving to see the Divine Presence, but on the other hand, he restricted his vision to avoid seeing evil.

WE HAVE ALREADY NOTED THE IMPORTANCE THAT THE TALMUD ascribes to *Minchah*, based on the story of Eliyahu at Har HaCarmel.

Minchah: Neutralizing Harsh Judgment

Zohar[17] notes that the importance of *Minchah* is also expressed in a verse in *Tehillim*. David HaMelech beseeched Hashem, תִּכּוֹן תְּפִלָּתִי קְטֹרֶת לְפָנֶיךָ מַשְׂאַת כַּפַּי מִנְחַת עָרֶב, *Let my prayer stand as incense before You; the lifting of my hands as an afternoon offering* (*Tehillim* 141:2). David prayed that his prayer be comparable to two offerings in the *Beis HaMikdash*, the incense offering and the afternoon *Minchah* (meal-offering). *Zohar* explains that incense prevents disaster by curtailing

---

15. *Bereishis Rabbah* 65:9.
16. *Bamidbar* Ch. 8.
17. *Parashas Vayechi*, 229b.

Heavenly wrath before any damage is done.[18] And David teaches that *Minchah* — which is prayed in the afternoon, a time of harsh judgment — can accomplish the same; it can prevent death, prosecution, and wrath.

Zohar goes on to explain the reason to be zealous regarding *Minchah*:

Harsh judgment usually strikes in the afternoon. For instance, the Beis HaMikdash was destroyed and set ablaze at Minchah time.

Harsh judgment usually strikes in the afternoon. For instance, the *Beis HaMikdash* was destroyed and set ablaze at *Minchah* time. Regarding this, Yirmiyahu said, "Woe to us for the day draws to a close, for the shadows of late afternoon grow longer!" (*Yirmiyahu* 6:4). "Shadows of late afternoon" refers to the prosecutorial forces and the fury of Divine Judgment that reign in the world at that time. One must concentrate in every *Tefillah*, but it is especially important to do so at *Minchah*, because harsh judgment reigns in the world at that time of the day, and it was for that reason that Yitzchak Avinu inaugurated the afternoon *Minchah* prayer.

Appropriately, Yitzchak, whose unique character trait was דִּין, *judgment,* inaugurated the prayer that has the power to prevent harsh judgment.

PERHAPS WE CAN EXPLAIN THIS BASED ON OUR EARLIER FINDINGS that Yitzchak was able to establish *Minchah* because he had achieved heightened spiritual vision, and such vision has the

Pinchas and Eliyahu

power to nullify harsh judgments. As *Chazal* tell us, Pinchas and Eliyahu were one and the same; it is logical, therefore, that Scripture equates their achievements. Pinchas used his vision to atone for a sin that was stimulated by the sight of temptation. He was rewarded with the "*covenant*" of peace. Of Eliyahu, too, Hashem says, *My "covenant" was with him* (*Malachi* 2:5) — and Eliyahu's best-known miracle took place at the time of *Minchah*.

Pinchas and Eliyahu were one and the same; it is logical, therefore, that Scripture equates their achievements.

Now, we can better appreciate the need to pray *Minchah* with intense concentration during the month of Tammuz. *Minchah*, which

---

18. Following the death of Korach and his camp, the Jewish people pointed an accusing finger at Moshe Rabbeinu, claiming that he was responsible for the calamity. Hashem was enraged, and threatened to wipe out all of *Klal Yisrael* and rebuild it through Moshe Rabbeinu. Moshe immediately commanded Aharon, "Take the fire-pan and on it put fire from upon the Altar and place incense — and go quickly to the assembly and provide atonement for them, for the fury has gone out from the presence of Hashem; the plague has begun!" (*Bamidbar* 17:11). The incense halted the plague.

was established by a man of judgment and has the power to prevent judgment from causing destruction throughout the year, must be employed in order to prevent calamity from befalling us during *Tammuz*, a month that is most especially susceptible to harsh judgment.

Interestingly, the combined *gematria* (numerical value) of the names פינחס and אליהו (260) is twice that of the word עין, *eye,* for each of them is identified with vision. We suggest that this *gematria* alludes to the months of Tammuz and Av, which — according to *Arizal*[19] — correspond to the eyes; Tammuz to the right eye and Av to the left. *Bnei Yissaschar* adds that just as the Talmud (*Taanis* 24a) states that a bride who has beautiful eyes does not need to be examined further, by extension we may say that a person who guards his eyes from seeing inappropriate things during Tammuz and Av may be safeguarded from sin and need not be checked for the rest of the year.

Yirmiyahu Hanavi lamented, "עֵינִי עֵינִי יֹרְדָה מַּיִם כִּי רָחַק מִמֶּנִּי מְנַחֵם מֵשִׁיב נַפְשִׁי, *My eye, my eye* runs with water, because a comforter to restore my soul is far from me" (*Eichah* 1:16). Let us hope that Pinchas/Eliyahu — the names that carry the numerical value of the eyes shedding tears of sorrow — should come and bring this bitter exile to an end by announcing the arrival of *Mashiach,* speedily in our days.

A person who guards his eyes from seeing inappropriate things during Tammuz and Av may be safeguarded from sin.

---

19. Cited in *Bnei Yissaschar, Maamarei Chodesh Tammuz–Av,* 1:4.

AV

שׁמעון נגד חודש אב, הוא נגד חוש השמיעה,
על כן אמרה לאה בלידתו לשון שמיעה (בראשית כט:לג)
כי שמע ה'... וכן אות הראשון בשמעון ש',
כמו אות הראשון של שמיעה.

(בני יששכר, מאמרי חדשי תמוז אב, מאמר א, אות ג)

Shimon corresponds to the month of *Av*,
which corresponds to the sense of hearing.
Therefore, when Shimon was born, Leah mentioned
hearing: "For Hashem **heard** . . ."(*Bereishis* 29:33).
Also, the name Shimon starts with a שׁ,
like the word שמיעה, hearing.

(*Bnei Yissaschar, Ma'amarei Chodesh Tammuz - Av* 1:3)

Strength and Judgment, Positive and Negative

WE SHOULD SEEK TO UNDERSTAND HOW THE MONTH OF AV corresponds to the tribe of Shimon. We also find that this month is connected to חוּשׁ הַשְּׁמִיעָה, the *sense of hearing*, and the concept of *listening*. This seems to be self-contradictory, for the month of Av was a time when the Jews in the Wilderness chose *not* to heed the word of Hashem — for it was in the month of Av that the *Meraglim* brought back their negative report regarding *Eretz Yisrael*, causing the entire Jewish nation to lose confidence in Hashem and to weep unnecessarily. Accordingly, Hashem designated it as a national day of mourning for generations to come, not only for the sin of the spies but also for the sins that caused the destruction of both *Batei Mikdash* (Holy Temples) in the month of Av. It is therefore hard to understand how the month of Av corresponds to hearing; to the contrary, it was a month of refusal to hear.

Another interesting factor is the correlation between Pesach and Tishah b'Av. In our calendar system, Tishah b'Av always falls on the same day of the week as does the first day of Pesach. The *Shulchan Aruch*[1] states that the Torah alludes to this in the verse עַל מַצּוֹת וּמְרֹרִים יֹאכְלֻהוּ, *with matzos and bitter herbs shall they eat [the Pesach offering]* (*Bamidbar* 9:11).[2] The *Rema*[3] records a custom to eat hard-boiled eggs at the Seder as a reminder that we are in mourning for the *Beis HaMikdash*. He clarifies this custom by explaining that Tishah b'Av always falls on the same day of the week as the first day of Pesach. This is a puzzling connection. Pesach is the festival of freedom and redemption, and Tishah b'Av commemorates bondage and destruction.

Another point of interest is the name of the month, "Av," (literally, *a father*). A father is usually associated with mercy, as we see

---

It is therefore hard to understand how the month of Av corresponds to hearing; to the contrary, it was a month of refusal to hear.

Tishah b'Av always falls on the same day of the week as the first day of Pesach. This is a puzzling connection.

---

1. *Orach Chaim* 428:3.

2. I.e., the night that we eat the *matzos* and *Korban Pesach* is the same night of the week as a very bitter day.

3. Ibid. 476:2. It is customary for mourners to eat hard-boiled eggs when they return home from the burial.

in the verse כְּרַחֵם אָב עַל בָּנִים רִחַם ה' עַל יְרֵאָיו, *As a father is merciful toward his children, so has Hashem shown mercy to those who fear Him* (*Tehillim* 103:13). Why is a name symbolizing mercy given to a month of tragedy and destruction?

Furthermore, there is only one person of whom the Torah tells us the date of his death:[4] "Then Aharon the Kohen went up to Mount Hor at the word of Hashem and died there, in the fortieth year after the Children of Israel went forth from the land of Egypt, *in the fifth month on the first of the month*" (*Bamidbar* 33:38). Why was Aharon singled out in this way, and what should we learn from the fact that he died on Rosh Chodesh Av?

THERE IS A STRIKING CONTRADICTION BETWEEN THE TWO HALVES OF the month of Av. The first half of the month is enveloped in tragedy,

A Strange Juxtaposition

and the Mishnah[5] states, "When Av begins, we diminish our happiness." When we reach the fifteenth of Av, however, there is an explosion of joy. In the words of the Mishnah,[6] "There were no greater festivals for the Jewish nation than the fifteenth of Av and Yom Kippur." Why is there this juxtaposition of sadness and happiness in the month of Av?

The first half of the month is enveloped in tragedy. When we reach the fifteenth of Av, however, there is an explosion of joy.

Among the several reasons for great celebration on the fifteenth of Av, the Talmud[7] relates that the Jews in *Eretz Yisrael* received permission to intermarry with the other tribes for the first time on the fifteenth of Av. Until then, men and women were permitted to marry only within their tribe. Was this event significant enough to be commemorated as a festival for all eternity?

Inasmuch as the Talmud describes the fifteenth of Av as one of the most joyus occasions, it is surprising that it is not mentioned in *TaNaCh*. In the words of the Modzitzer Rebbe *zt"l*,[8] "It is astounding that two festivals, the fifteenth of Shevat and the fifteenth of Av, are completely omitted from Scripture, not meriting even the slightest mention. The importance of the fifteenth of Av was so hidden, in fact, that the Talmud wonders why it was celebrated as a festival." Why, indeed, isn't the fifteenth of Av mentioned in the Torah?

"It is astounding that two festivals, the fifteenth of Shevat and the fifteenth of Av, are completely omitted from Scripture.

4. We know the *yahrtzeits* of other leaders, such as the Patriarchs, the Matriarchs, Moshe, and Dovid only from Oral Tradition, not from written verses.

5. *Taanis* 4:6.

6. Ibid. 4:8.

7. Ibid. 30b-31a.

8. Heard at the Rebbe's *tisch* in the year 5764.

The Unblessed Tribe

*Only one
tribe was not
blessed at all,
neither by
Yaakov Avinu
nor by Moshe
Rabbeinu: the
tribe of Shimon.*

ONLY ONE TRIBE WAS NOT BLESSED AT ALL, NEITHER BY Yaakov Avinu nor by Moshe Rabbeinu: the tribe of Shimon. Yaakov harshly berated Shimon and Levi: *Shimon and Levi are comrades; their weaponry is a stolen craft. Into their conspiracy, may my soul not enter! With their congregation, do not join, O my honor! For in their rage they murdered people and at their whim they hamstrung an ox. Accursed is their rage for it is intense, and their wrath for it is harsh; I will separate them within Jacob, and I will disperse them in Israel"* (*Bereishis* 49:5-7). Yaakov then went on to bless Yehudah and the other tribes, leaving Shimon and Levi without a blessing.

Levi fared better when Moshe Rabbeinu blessed all the other tribes, but not Shimon. *Rashi* (*Bamidbar* 27:24) comments that Moshe had no intention of blessing Shimon. The reason the tribe of Shimon lost its entitlement to a blessing from Moshe was because of what it did at Shittim, when the people of the tribe, led by Zimri ben Salu, engaged in flagrantly immoral conduct with the young women of Midian (*Bamidbar* 25:1-6,14). *Midrash Shocher Tov*[9] adds that Zimri's behavior at Shittim also cost his tribe the privilege of having a *shofet* (judge) of *Klal Yisrael* come from his tribe. Of all the many judges, not a single one came from Shimon.

*Of all the many
judges, not
a single one
came from
Shimon.*

Shimon and Yehudah

ALTHOUGH SHIMON WAS NOT BLESSED DIRECTLY, NEVERTHELESS, AS *Chazal*[10] teach, "When Moshe blessed the tribes, he did not bless Shimon because of Zimri's sin,[11] but he alluded to them in Yehudah's blessing, "שְׁמַע ה׳ קוֹל יְהוּדָה *Hearken, O Hashem, to Yehudah's voice*" (*Devarim* 33:7); as the Midrash explains:

*"When Moshe
blessed the
tribes, he
did not bless
Shimon
because of
Zimri's sin,
but he alluded
to them in
Yehudah's
blessing.*

"וְזֹאת לִיהוּדָה וַיֹּאמַר, *And this to Yehudah, and he said*" (ibid.). This teaches that Yehudah would pray for the tribe of Shimon, for the verse continues, שְׁמַע ה׳ קוֹל יְהוּדָה, *Hearken, O Hashem …* The word שְׁמַע, *hearken,* alludes to Shimon, for when Shimon was born, Leah said, "כִּי שָׁמַע ה׳ כִּי שְׂנוּאָה אָנֹכִי, *Because Hashem heard that I am unloved*" (*Bereishis* 29:33). When Shimon will be in trouble [Moshe said to Hashem], Yehudah will pray before

---

9. *Tehillim* 90.
10. *Midrash Aggadah, Bamidbar* 1:2.
11. See *Bamidbar* 25.

You [on their behalf], and may You save them [Shimon] from their woes.

[The verse continues, Moshe said] "וְאֶל עַמּוֹ תְּבִיאֶנּוּ *and bring him to his people —*" Yehudah brought Shimon close to his [Yehudah's] inheritance [in *Eretz Yisrael*], as we see in the verse, וַיֹּאמֶר יְהוּדָה לְשִׁמְעוֹן אָחִיו עֲלֵה אִתִּי בְגוֹרָלִי, *Yehudah said to Shimon his brother, "Go up with me for my portion"* (*Shoftim* 1:3), i.e., unlike the other tribes, Shimon did not have a separate, contiguous portion in *Eretz Yisrael*. Instead, the people of Shimon had scattered towns and cities within the portion of Yehudah.

There was obviously a very unique bond between Yehudah and Shimon. We will try to explain this bond, and why Moshe indirectly included Shimon in his blessing of Yehudah.

ANOTHER ASPECT OF SHIMON THAT MUST BE UNDERSTOOD IS HIS role in the sale of Yosef. After Yosef repeatedly angered his brothers,

——————
Shimon and Yosef
——————

Yaakov sent him to check on them in Shechem, where they were tending the family's flocks. As Yosef approached his brothers, "They said to one another, 'Look! That dreamer is coming! So now, come and let us kill him, and throw him into one of the pits; and we will say, "A wild beast devoured him" ' " (*Bereishis* 37:19-20). *Rashi*[12] comments that Shimon and Levi were the brothers who conspired against Yosef. The *Midrash*[13] adds that when the tribes accepted Reuven's suggestion to throw Yosef into a pit rather than kill him, Shimon was the one who actually flung him into the pit. Shimon eventually paid for his sin by being the one whom Yosef — then viceroy of Egypt — kept as a hostage to ensure that his brothers would return with Binyamin.[14]

As an interesting addendum, *Rabbeinu Bachaye* notes that in the Torah's depiction of Moshe's census in the Wilderness when all the tribes were counted individually, the word פְּקֻדָיו, *its numbers,*[15] appears only regarding the population of the tribe of Shimon. *Rabbeinu Bachaye* suggests that פְּקֻדָיו refers not to numbers, but that it comes from the root פקד, *to remember.* He explains that Hashem always "remembers" Shimon's involvement in the sale of Yosef, and

There was obviously a very unique bond between Yehudah and Shimon. We will try to explain this bond, and why Moshe indirectly included Shimon in his blessing of Yehudah.

When the tribes accepted Reuven's suggestion to throw Yosef into a pit rather than kill him, Shimon was the one who actually flung him into the pit.

---

12. *Bereishis Rabbah* 49:5, s.v. *Shimon v'Levi Achim.*
13. Ibid. *Rabbah* 84:16.
14. See *Bereishis* 42; specifically, verse 24.
15. *Bamidbar* 1:22; the word פְּקֻדָיו appears in verse 22.

his descendants would be punished for that sin.[16] Shimon's apparent vindictiveness against Yosef, which exceeded that of his brothers, requires an explanation. What motivated him? How did he justify his actions? Why did he behave as he did?

What motivated Shimon? How did he justify his actions? Why did he behave as he did?

II. Shimon: Strength (Middas Hadin)

THE *ZOHAR* EXPLAINS WHY YOSEF CHOSE TO KEEP SHIMON AS A hostage, instead of anyone else:

Yosef knew that any situation in which Shimon would be involved will be initiated through strict *din* (justice). "When my father sent me to check on my brothers," Yosef reasoned, "Shimon was the one who began my judgment," as the verse states, "And they said to one another, 'Look! That dreamer is coming! So now, come and let us kill him'" (*Bereishis* 37:19-20).

In the incident of Shechem, too, the Torah tells us, "Two of Yaakov's sons, Shimon and Levi, Dinah's brothers, each took his sword and they came upon the city confidently, and killed every male" (*Bereishis* 34:25). … [Yosef decided] "All of Shimon's actions were governed by a strict sense of justice, so it is better to separate [Shimon], to ensure that he will not instigate strife among the brothers."

All of Shimon's actions were governed by a strict sense of justice.

The *Zohar* goes on to explain why Shimon chose Levi as his accomplice in the war against Shechem:

Shimon chose Levi because he knew that Levi had an inclination toward justice.

Why did Shimon choose Levi as his partner? Reuven was also his brother, close to him in age! Shimon chose Levi because he knew that Levi had an inclination toward justice, and that he [Shimon] had a tendency to even stricter justice. Shimon thought to himself, "Let us join one another and destroy the world!" What did Hashem do? He took Levi for himself [as the tribe of the Temple service] and said, "From now on let Shimon be bound in ropes, all alone."

---

16. *Degel Machaneh Ephraim* writes that the word שמעון can be split so that it reads שם עון *there* [in the tribe of Shimon] *is sin*. Perhaps this "sin" is the sale of Yosef, following *Rabbeinu Bechaye's* idea.

FROM THE PROFOUND WORDS OF THE *ZOHAR*, IT EMERGES THAT ALL of Shimon's deeds flowed from the attribute of strict justice. Having

Shimon's Standard

attained a lofty spiritual level, Shimon felt that people's actions and deeds should be scrutinized under a microscope of strict justice. He judged Yosef — as well as the people of Shechem — by his own standard of stern justice, and found them guilty.

In addition to the *Zohar*, there are other sources that depict Shimon as an individual governed by a strict sense of justice.

The first three *Sefiros,* i.e., the spiritual forces through which Hashem guides the world, are *Chessed, Gevurah,* and *Tiferes.*[17] *Gevurah* (lit., strength) is synonymous with *din,* justice. The *sefer Ma'or V'Shemesh*[18] writes that Reuven, Shimon, and Levi correspond to the three forefathers, Avraham, Yitzchok, and Yaakov, paralleling their paramount traits. Thus, just as Avrohom excelled in *Chessed,* Yitzchak in *Gevurah,* and Yaakov in *Tiferes,* the first three tribes — in order of their birth — were governed by those very same traits, and accordingly Shimon corresponds to Yitzchak, who was governed by *Gevurah,*[19] which is synonymous with judgment.

Shimon corresponds to Yitzchak, who was governed by Gevurah, which is synonymous with judgment.

WHEN UTILIZED PROPERLY, THE FIERY TRAIT OF *GEVURAH* CAN BE beneficial, but fiery temperament can cause people to act impul-

The Actions of Shimon and Levi Stem From Fire

sively, thereby making mistakes. In Yaakov's blessing of his sons, he said, "Shimon and Levi are comrades, their weaponry is a stolen craft" (*Genesis* 49:5). The *Ohr HaChaim* explains this as follows:

Fiery temperament can cause people to act impulsively, thereby making mistakes.

In seeking to understand the behavior of Shimon and Levi in the episodes of Shechem and Yosef, Yaakov saw that their nature

---

17. These three characteristics are very profound and far-reaching. The following is an explanation on an elementary level. *Chessed,* or kindness, is an outer-directed trait. Avraham, the epitome of *chessed,* acted out of a genuine desire to define the needs of others and to help them. *Gevurah,* epitomized by Yitzchok, is an inner-directed drive for self-perfection, and a zeal to avoid transgression in whatever form it may take. *Tiferes,* or splendor, is often called *emes,* or truth, and it is epitomized by Yaakov. *Tiferes* combines and balances *Chessed* and *Gevurah.* Pure *Chessed* can lead to undesirable excess and self-indulgence, while pure *Gevurah* can stifle achievement. The trait of Yaakov serves as a sort of checks and balances, expressing both kindness and judgment, with each channeling the other toward an ideal blend. [See ArtScroll Overview to *Lech Lecha,* ArtScroll *Genesis,* pp. 361-366.]

18. *Parashas Vayeitzei, Bereishis* 29:35.

19. *Avodas Yisrael* (*Parashas Vayishlach, Bereishis* 33:6-8), citing *Arizal,* states explicitly that Shimon corresponds to *Gevurah.*

was to be overpowered by the element of passion. Similarly, *Chazal* state that [King] Shaul sinned only once, but that sin cost him his kingdom, while [King] David sinned several times and did not lose the throne. This is because Shaul possessed a calm, serene nature, while David's nature was heated, as implied by his ruddy complexion.[20] Hashem judges a person according to his personal nature. A person with a fiery disposition will tend to err from time to time — even if he endeavors intensely to excel in the service of Hashem. But with minimal effort a person with a calm, serene makeup will be able to avoid making mistakes. Therefore, Saul's sin could not be excused.

Yaakov said, "שִׁמְעוֹן וְלֵוִי אַחִים," using the word אַחִים, literally *brothers,* but Yaakov alluded to חוּם, *heat,* because this was a description of their nature. Thus, Yaakov cursed their tempers — not them personally — for it is well-known that anger is magnified in people with fiery dispositions.

Yaakov went on to say, "כְּלֵי חָמָס מְכֵרֹתֵיהֶם, *their weaponry is a stolen craft.*" He described their tendency to become enraged as a "stolen craft," because they did not inherit that trait from him; it was מְכֵרֹתֵיהֶם, something *familiar*[21] only to them, and it was this trait that led them to act incorrectly in the case of Yosef.

> Thus *Ohr HaChaim* teaches that although their actions against Shechem were motivated by a commendable zeal to protect their sister, it was a product of their natural hotheadedness. So, too, in the case of Yosef, Shimon's zealotry got the better of him, as *Yalkut Shimoni*[22] states, when Yosef was lowered into the pit prior to his sale, Shimon commanded his brothers to hurl stones at him to kill him.

Rabbi Samson Raphael Hirsch explains Yaakov Avinu's words similarly:

"Accursed is their rage for it is intense, and their wrath for it is harsh" (*Bereishis* 49:6). [Yaakov Avinu] placed a curse on the thoughtless temper of Shimon and Levi, for it is impossible to deal with anger that so embroils a person that he loses control of himself so that he cannot be placated. Admonishing a person in such a state of anger will not help, nor can we convince him to display minimal consideration for others when he is overcome.

Sidenote: Hashem judges a person according to his personal nature. A person with a fiery disposition will tend to err from time to time, but with minimal effort a person with a calm, serene makeup will be able to avoid making mistakes.

Sidenote: [Yaakov Avinu] placed a curse on the thoughtless temper of Shimon and Levi, for it is impossible to deal with anger that so embroils a person that he loses control of himself

---

20. See *I Shmuel* 16:12.

21. *Ohr HaChaim* connects the word מְכֵרֹתֵיהֶם with the word הַכָּרָה, which means "to know" or be familiar with.

22. 128.

Noting the similarity between the words אָרוּר, *cursed,* and עָרִיר, *childless,* Yaakov placed a curse of עָרוּר[23] upon Shimon and Levi to make them עֲרִירִים, *childless,* in the sense that that their actions would not bear fruit, so that their fiery temperament would not bring destructive results.

Since Yaakov's blessings were the blueprints for the Jewish nation, his curse rendered Shimon and Levi incapable of becoming leaders of *Klal Yisrael,* for such leadership could have endangered the nation .... Their consciousness of their own power and strength was too hot, and in the service of the general welfare, it could be ruthless, knowing no bounds.

Since it was a time when the cornerstone of the Jewish nation was being laid, it was imperative that Yaakov should curse any transgression of morality and justice, even if it was done for the sake of the general good. Other nations could justify such conduct on the grounds that the interests of the state sanctify whatever is needed, but Yaakov curses trickery and violence whatever its justification. Thus the Torah sets forth a standard for all time: when the public interest is at stake, we must make sure that *not only* the end that we wish to reach is for the common good, but the means to that end must also be pure. All this being said, however, Yaakov placed a curse only on the *anger* of Shimon and Levi, not on them or on their goals.

Since it was a time when the cornerstone of the Jewish nation was being laid, it was imperative that Yaakov should curse any transgression of morality and justice.

III. Two Types of Fiery Passion

NETZIV EXPLAINS THAT THEIR ANGER WAS FUELED BY TWO different sets of ideals — one more commendable than the other — but even the purer of the two can be dangerous:

The motives that caused [Shimon and Levi] to become enraged [to the point that they killed all the males of Shechem]were not the same. One [Shimon] was fueled by a human need to defend the honor of his father's household. This is the sort of fire that leads to an "alien [i.e., impermissible] fire." The other [Levi] had no personal considerations; his actions were fueled

The motives that caused [Shimon and Levi] to become enraged [to the point that they killed all the males of Shechem]were not the same.

---

23. Rabbi Hirsch holds that words with similar sounds, even if they are not complete homonyms, are related to and shed light on each other. Thus, in this verse, R' Hirsch comments that the curse of Yaakov meant to say that their anger should have no consequences, just as a childless person has no offspring.

by a passion to take righteous vengeance for Hashem's honor. Although this sort of fire is called *Shalheves Kah* (the flame of God), it, too, must be employed with great caution. If one does not identify the correct time and place to use it, it can be extremely destructive. Yaakov Avinu sought to distance himself from *both* mindsets — he wasn't willing to take part even in the better sort of fire.

Although this sort of fire is called Shalheves Kah (the flame of God), it, too, must be employed with great caution.

SIMILARLY, WE FIND THAT *GEVURAH* AND *DIN*, WHICH ARE CONCEPTUally the same as *Yirah* (awe of Hashem), can cause a person to become angry and isolated from other people.

Awe Can Cause Anger and Isolation

Ma'or Va'Shemesh explains Yaakov's hesitance to bless Shimon and Levi as follows:

Shimon and Levi were on a lofty spiritual level, serving Hashem with awe. So much so that they were angered by sinners, as we see in the story of Shechem. Shimon and Levi found it hard to mingle with others, because they always seemed to be angry at people, but in reality, as the Talmud[24] puts it, "The Torah caused them to become heated," for those who serve Hashem with awe constantly find fault with their own service. People who interact with them think that they are angry at the world, but they are truly angry only at themselves for their own shortcomings. Yaakov Avinu knew that Shimon and Levi had this tendency and had angry looks on their faces. Such people tend to live in solitude.

For those who serve Hashem with awe constantly find fault with their own service. People who interact with them think that they are angry at the world, but they are truly angry only at themselves for their own shortcomings.

Shimon and Levi had an awe and sense of justice that brought them to such a lofty spiritual level that it prevented them from taking part in normal daily life. They preferred the seclusion emanating from pure awe of Hashem. Yaakov Avinu did not approve of this, as explained by the *Ma'or Va'Shemesh*:

Yaakov declared, "Into their private world, may my soul not enter!" *(Bereishis* 49:6), as if to say that he did not want to associate with their way of serving Hashem, because it originated from depression. Even when they acted together, they still could not rejoice as they should in the service of Hashem This is why Yaakov said, בְּקְהָלָם אַל תֵּחַד כְּבֹדִי, *With their congregation, do not join, O my honor* (ibid.). The word תֵּחַד

24. *Taanis* 4a.

can be related to the word חֶדְוָה, *joy, i.e.,* Yaakov was lamenting that even when Shimon and Levi would congregate instead of living in isolation, they would not rejoice, but would still be morose and depressed.

Although Yaakov knew that their anger was caused by their devotion to Hashem, he still condemned it, stating, אָרוּר אַפָּם כִּי עָז *Accursed is their rage for it is intense* (ibid. 49:7). Although their rage came from עָז, which alludes to the Torah,[25] and although עֶבְרָתָם, *their wrath,* was caused because they considered their own slightest misdeed — even if it was relatively trivial — as כִּי קָשָׁתָה, *extremely harsh,* because they held themselves to such high standards, Yaakov still deemed it inappropriate. Therefore, he concluded, אֲחַלְקֵם בְּיַעֲקֹב וַאֲפִיצֵם בְּיִשְׂרָאֵל, *I will separate them within Yaakov, and I will disperse them in Israel,* so that they will mingle with others and learn to appreciate other members of the nation — whether they are common people deserving of the name Yaakov, or great men worthy of the title Yisrael. They will learn to mingle with all and sundry, and rejoice among their people, and this is the perfect way to serve Hashem. The highest level of the awe of Hashem is when it stems from inner satisfaction and happiness. True fear of Hashem leads to hope and joy.

The highest level of the awe of Hashem is when it stems from inner satisfaction and happiness. True fear of Hashem leads to hope and joy.

Thus, even in the highest levels of fear of Hashem and punctilious observance of the commandments, one must be careful that it does not lead one into depression, anger, and a lack of lively joy in the service of Hashem. A Jew must maintain a pleasant, friendly appearance and associate with others.

WE MIGHT ADD A COMMENT FROM THE *ROSH* ON A TEACHING OF *Chazal:* The prophet said, אִמְרוּ צַדִּיק כִּי טוֹב כִּי פְרִי מַעַלְלֵיהֶם יֹאכֵלוּ, *Tell*

Consider Others

[each] righteous man that he is good; for they shall eat the fruit of their deeds (*Yeshayah* 3:10). The Talmud[26] wonders, "Is there a righteous man who is good, and a righteous man who is not good?" The Talmud answers, a righteous man who is good to Heaven (God) *and* to other creatures is "good," whereas a righteous person whose goodness extends only to Heaven, but not to other creatures is not good.

A righteous man who is good to Heaven (God) and to other creatures is "good."

---

25. As can be derived from the verse, ה' עֹז לְעַמּוֹ יִתֵּן *Hashem gives might to his people* (*Tehillim* 29:11).

26. *Kiddushin* 40a.

"For the Holy
One, Blessed
is He, prefers
mitzvos that
take other
people into
consideration
over those that
fulfill only His
own will."

Rosh[27] comments, "For the Holy One, Blessed is He, prefers mitzvos that take other people into consideration over those that fulfill only His own will."

Considering the above comments, it would seem that the "downside" of being governed by the traits of *Gevurah* and *Din/Yirah* is that such service of Hashem often comes at the expense of the respect that other people deserve. Those who excel in serving Hashem through harsh forms of service may consider the downside negligible in comparison to their spiritual gains, but Hashem does not. To Him, the feelings of fellow human beings must be part of a tzaddik's Divine service.

Good Gevurah and Bad Gevurah

THE MIDRASH[28] TEACHES THAT *PHYSICAL* STRENGTH (*GEVURAH*), CAN be used for good or for bad. David used his strength to vanquish *Klal Yisrael's* enemies — as described in the verse, "The rejoicing women called out, and said, 'Shaul has slain his thousands, and David his tens of thousands'" (*I Shmuel* 18:7) — and his strength earned him the love of his brethren: "All of Yisrael and Yehudah loved David, for he came and went before them" (ibid. 18:16).

Goliath, the Philistine giant, possessed phenomenal strength, continues the Midrash, strength that led him to taunt and deride the Jewish nation for forty days. What happened to him in the end? He was slain by David, and his carcass was abandoned like that of a dog, as the verse states, "The Philistines saw that their hero was dead, and they ran away" (ibid. 17:51). Thus, physical strength can be used beneficially, as we see from David, or it can be misused, as we see from Goliath.

*Physical
strength
can be used
beneficially,
as we see from
David, or it can
be misused, as
we see from
Goliath.*

Midrash Shocher Tov[29] expresses this thought tersely: "Some amass strength for their benefit, and some for their disadvantage. The strength of Yehudah and David was beneficial; that of Goliath and Shimshon was detrimental."

These Midrashim refer to physical strength, but there is also spiritual strength. "Who is strong?" asks the Mishnah. "He who conquers his evil inclination."[30]

Indeed, *Maharal*[31] teaches that *Gevurah* contains both physical *and* spiritual aspects. He writes:

---

27. *Peah* 1:1.
28. *Shemos Rabbah* 31:3.
29. *Shmuel* 7.
30. 4:1.
31. *Nesivos Olam, Nesiv HaOsher* 2.

There are three gifts in this world. There are things that are intellectual, such as wisdom. Wisdom is not physical at all. At the opposite extreme are things that are only physical, such as wealth, for wealth consists of material possessions. Between those two extremes is *Gevurah*, which combines the spiritual and the physical. *Gevurah* is a function of the spirit, but it is not completely disconnected from the physical as is the intellect; rather, it is ingrained in a person's body, a mixture of the physical and the spiritual.

Our analysis of *Gevurah* shows that it is an exalted trait, but because it combines the spiritual and the physical, it demands great vigilance. It can be dangerous. It can lead to serious mistakes, as *Ohr HaChaim* explained regarding Shimon and Levi, and it can also lead to isolation and depression, as *Ma'or Va'Shemesh* commented.

Michtav M'Eliyahu[32] points out that *Gevurah* has another potential pitfall. Just as there is an aspect of *Gevurah* that can be used for holy pursuits, there is also an aspect that can lead to impurity. If a person does not blend his *Gevurah* with *Chessed* and love for his fellows, it will lead him to think selfishly *only* about himself, and negate the feelings and needs of others. Such a person will develop a tendency to take and not to give. He can easily fall onto the slippery slope that leads to haughtiness, hatefulness, and — when someone becomes consumed with himself and indifferent to others — he may even sink into idolatry.

Gevurah is an exalted trait, but because it combines the spiritual and the physical, it demands great vigilance. It can lead to serious mistakes.

IV. Din and Gevurah Must Be Blended With Kindness

URING THE SIX DAYS OF CREATION, HASHEM DETERMINED that this world could not survive if He were to rule it exclusively through strict justice. *Chazal*[33] note that the first verse in the Torah mentions only the Name *Elokim*, which is associated with strict justice. But later in the narrative, the Torah includes the Name, יְ־ה־ו־ה, *Hashem* which is associated with Divine Mercy: בְּיוֹם עֲשׂוֹת יְ־ה־ו־ה אֱלֹקִים אֶרֶץ וְשָׁמַיִם, *on the day that Hashem/Elokim created earth and heaven* (*Bereishis* 2:4). *Chazal* explain that Hashem originally planned on

During the Six Days of Creation, Hashem determined that this world could not survive if He were to rule it exclusively through strict justice.

32. Vol. 2, p. 164.
33. *Bereishis Rabbah* 12:15.

guiding the world with strict justice, but since He knew that the world could not endure under such harsh scrutiny, He softened his treatment of the world by tempering strict justice with *rachamim* (mercy).

Through this Midrash, we can understand R' Tzaddok HaKohen's exposition[34] stating that "in this world" no king or judge could come from Shimon. Since this world can survive only if *din* is softened by *rachamim*, Shimon, who would govern through pure *din*, cannot be a ruler of *Klal Yisrael* in this world.

Since this world can survive only if din is softened by rachamim, Shimon, who would govern through pure din, cannot be a ruler of Klal Yisrael in this world.

Shimon and Rav Shimon

TO ILLUSTRATE THIS IDEA, R' TZADDOK ADDS AN AMAZING POINT. RAV Shimon bar Yochai, who, according to tradition, descended from Shimon, and whose soul emanated from Shimon, did not become as well-known as he could have been in the revealed Talmud. Most of his extraordinary wisdom is concealed in Kabbalah — the Holy *Zohar* — the hidden mystical part of the Torah.

Indeed, Rav Shimon bar Yochai was an extremely zealous person. The Talmud[35] relates that someone once praised the Romans for building markets, roads, and bathhouses. Rav Shimon protested, insisting that the Romans had only their own selfish interests in mind when doing so. His criticism was reported to the Romans, who sought to incarcerate and execute him. Rav Shimon fled and hid in a cave with his son Rav Elazar, where they studied Torah for twelve consecutive years.

When R' Shimon and R' Elazar left the cave, they could not fathom that people could neglect Torah study and work the fields to earn a living. "How could they place eternal life aside and toil in temporal living?" Rav Shimon wondered. The Talmud goes on to relate that as Rav Shimon and Rav Elazar walked around, anyone and everything they viewed with their zealous eyes was immediately consumed in fire.

It would seem that Rav Shimon bar Yochai possessed the very same sense of harsh justice as his ancestor Shimon: a vengefulness for Hashem's glory that was not tempered by mercy. Hashem did not approve of this sort of behavior. The Talmud relates that a Heavenly voice rang out, "Have you emerged [from your cave] to destroy My world? Return to your cave!"

Rav Shimon and R' Elazar emerged once again a year later and began to judge others favorably. Only then were they permitted rejoin

Rav Shimon bar Yochai possessed the very same sense of harsh justice as his ancestor Shimon: a vengefulness for Hashem's glory that was not tempered by mercy. Hashem did not approve of this sort of behavior.

34. *Takanos HaShavim* 28a.
35. *Shabbos* 33b.

the society of *Klal Yisrael*. We see clearly that this world cannot survive under the constant scrutiny of harsh, pure justice. The world can remain viable only if Mercy tempers the Attribute of Justice.

ZEALOTRY WAS A KEY COMPONENT OF ONE OF THE MOST INFAMOUS incidents involving the tribe of Shimon — albeit with the tide turned.

The Tides Are Turned

The Talmud[36] labels Pinchas, a descendant of Levi, a "zealot, son of a zealot" for avenging Hashem's honor by killing Zimri, a prince of Shimon, who engaged defiantly in a public display of immorality. *Rashi* explains that Pinchas was considered "son of a zealot" because his great-grandfather Levi avenged the abduction and violation of Dinah.

Maharsha notes that Pinchas followed in his ancestor's footsteps, by avenging an act of immorality, but Zimri, however, did not follow in his great-grandfather Shimon's footsteps. Like Levi, Shimon was revolted by the immorality of Shechem, but his descendant Zimri flagrantly committed an immoral act in full view of Moshe and the elders.

Like Levi, Shimon was revolted by the immorality of Shechem, but his descendant Zimri flagrantly committed an immoral act in full view of Moshe and the elders.

NOW THE BOND BETWEEN SHIMON AND YEHUDAH IS UNDERSTANDable. As we saw earlier, although the tribe of Shimon was not blessed

Shimon and Yehudah Complement One Another

directly by Moshe Rabbeinu, it was blessed indirectly through Yehudah. This relationship seems to have been a harbinger of a long-standing alliance between these two tribes. Shimon did not have a contiguous territory in *Eretz Yisrael*. Its towns and fields were scattered throughout Yehudah's portion: "Their [Shimon's] heritage was situated in the midst of the heritage of the children of Yehudah" (*Yehoshua* 19:1). And when the tribe of Yehudah went into battle to conquer its allotted portion of the Land, it invited Shimon to join in the fray (*Shoftim* 1:3).

Rav Tzaddok HaKohen[37] writes that the mission of Shimon is to uphold the separation between *Klal Yisrael* and the nations of the world. Shimon formed a bond with Yehudah, a tribe that also works to maintain that separation. The Talmud declares that any Jew who denies the validity of idols is called a Yehudi, and all Jews are called

Shimon did not have a contiguous territory in Eretz Yisrael. Its towns and fields were scattered throughout Yehudah's portion.

---

36. *Sanhedrin* 62b.
37. *Takanos HaShavin* 30a.

"Yehudim." In the case of Shimon, though, this separation is even more pronounced, as it will be in the future. At the end of his life, Moshe prophesied, "Hashem will guide them alone; no other power will be with them" (*Devarim* 32:12). This is also why Shimon took the lead in avenging Dinah's abduction. The absolute separation, however, will not be revealed in this world, until the coming of *Mashiach*.

It is clear from R' Tzaddok that Shimon could not have an independent identity because his ideal of total separation could not be attained in this world, and therefore the tribe of Shimon had to live among the people of Yehudah. This conforms to our earlier conclusion that Shimon's method of serving Hashem through *din* is too harsh for this world, and therefore must be tempered by mercy. Yehudah complemented Shimon, and Shimon was able to succeed only through this bond. In the words of *Bnei Yissaschar*, "Yehudah and Shimon — even during times of anger, they are connected and have mercy on each other."

V. Yehudah, Nissan, and Redemption; Shimon, Av, and Exile

Since Shimon's trait is strict, exacting justice, it is logical that his month should be Av, the month in which we were punished time and again.

SINCE SHIMON'S TRAIT IS STRICT, EXACTING JUSTICE, IT IS LOGICAL that his month should be Av, the month in which we were punished time and again because we were judged through Divine justice.

We can also gain a deeper appreciation of the relationships between Yehudah and Shimon, between Pesach and *Tishah b'Av*, and — on a broader level — between the months of Nissan and Av. *Bnei Yissaschar* writes:

> Based on the order of the tribal formations in the Wilderness, Yehudah corresponds to Nissan and Shimon to Av. Nissan was designated as a month of redemption and freedom; a month in which we can take hold of the Land that Hashem promised us. The month of Av, on the other hand, was designated for exile and servitude, [until Hashem takes mercy on His nation and the month of Av will become a month of joy and happiness].
>
> Hashem wanted us to find consolation even when He allowed the *Beis HaMikdash* to be destroyed, so when we first began to conquer *Eretz Yisrael*, He said, *Yehudah should go up; behold, I have delivered the land into his hand* (*Shoftim*

1:2). [Hashem said, "I *have delivered*" (in past tense), because when we left Egypt during Nissan, which is Yehudah's month, it became the month designated for *Klal Yisrael* to conquer *Eretz Yisrael*.] Yehudah immediately told Shimon, "Go up with me for my portion" (ibid. 1:3), For although Shimon's month, Av, would centuries later become the month of exile, Yehudah promised, "Then I, too, will go with you for your portion" (ibid.), promising Shimon through *Ruach Hakodesh* (Divine Spirit) that his month, like Yehudah's, would eventually become a month of glory and redemption.

Thus the bond between Yehudah and Shimon represents a broader link between redemption and exile, a bond that links Nissan, a month of Divine Mercy, to Av, which has always been a month of Divine justice.

Bnei Yissaschar continues:

> We can now understand why in our calendar system, the first night of Pesach always corresponds to the night of Tishah b'Av, and why there is a custom to eat an egg at the Seder, a food associated with mourners.

The fact that Tishah b'Av falls on the same day of the week as the first night of Pesach alludes to the ultimate redemption that will flow from the redemption from Egypt. That ultimate redemption alludes to the destruction of the *Beis HaMikdash* that occurred through *Din*, but will eventually be rectified through Divine Mercy.

Shimon and Hearing: The Hidden Pair

WE NOTED AT THE BEGINNING OF THIS ESSAY THAT SHIMON ALSO CORresponds to the sense of hearing, which is understandable considering that the trait of Shimon and the sense of hearing are hidden in this world. As Rav Tzaddok HaKohen writes:[38]

> The root of Shimon's holiness is completely hidden in this world, for it is rooted in the concealed world .... Shimon also corresponds to the trait of *Gevurah*, which limits and hides things, so it adds even more concealment to what is already concealed.

The sense of hearing cannot sense physical objects. Sight senses the physical, but hearing senses speech and sound, which

The fact that Tishah b'Av falls on the same day of the week as the first night of Pesach alludes to the ultimate redemption that will flow from the redemption from Egypt.

---

38. Ibid. 27b.

Hearing, therefore, is a "spiritual sense," for it senses only non-physical stimuli. By listening to others, we can perceive secrets concealed in their hearts, but which they express in speech.

are spiritual in nature in that they have no physical makeup. Hearing, therefore, is a "spiritual sense," for it senses only non-physical stimuli. By listening to others, we can perceive secrets concealed in their hearts, but which they express in speech. This cannot be achieved through sight, which can sense only physical objects, and not thoughts and feelings.

Now we can answer a question we asked at the very start of our perusal of Av. How can *Bnei Yissaschar* say that the month of Av symbolizes the sense of hearing? We found this difficult since Av was the month when Israel failed to listen to Hashem, and instead allowed itself to be misled by the spies. Nonetheless, ultimately Av does correspond to the sense of hearing, because when Hashem redeems us in the ultimate redemption, it will become clear that, though it was not previously apparent, He constantly listened to our cries, as Rav Tzaddok writes:

> The source of the holiness of Shimon's soul is at the root of the Heavenly sense of hearing. Although [Leah thought that she] was hated [and named Shimon for that reason], the truth was that Hashem did hear her. The hatred that she sensed was no more than the outward appearance, as it was perceived in This world. The truth is, however, as the prophet says, Hashem loves Israel: "I loved you, says Hashem" (*Malachi* 1:2). Indeed, the Midrash[39] tells us that the nations [not Hashem] came to hate Israel because Hashem gave us the Torah on Mount Sinai. [The word *Sinai* comes from the word *sinah* (hatred).] Hashem's hatred is never directed to Israel, it is directed at Esav, who symbolizes evil ....

> Just as Shimon's holy nature is hidden, his blessing is hidden; it is there in potential, but not revealed — it is concealed within Yehudah's blessing, [for Yehudah's power is revealed through the majesty of his kingship]. The hidden salvation will be revealed through the strength of Hashem's love for *Klal Yisrael* and will become apparent with the coming of *Mashiach*. Despite the times when appearances seem to indicate that Hashem hates us, the truth is that love of *Klal Yisrael* is hidden deep in His heart.

Just as Shimon's holy nature is hidden, his blessing is hidden; it is there in potential, but not revealed — it is concealed within Yehudah's blessing.

Shimon represents the roots of the ultimate redemption, which already exist even though we cannot discern them. Like Shimon's blessing, these roots are hidden for the time being.

---

39. *Shemos Rabbah* 2:4.

VI. Av — Month of Sadness and Happiness

NOW WE CAN UNDERSTAND THE OTHER ISSUES WE RAISED earlier. Perhaps the holiday of the fifteenth of Av — which *Chazal* considered one of the greatest festivals in the Jewish year — is celebrated during Av to allude to the great redemption that will take place during this month. The sad days of the first half of the month are no contradiction to the great joy of the second half — on the contrary, happiness will blossom from the sadness.

Considering the concealment of the tribe of Shimon, perhaps the reason the fifteenth of Av is not mentioned at all in Scripture is because its true glory is concealed, and will become fully apparent only when *Mashiach* redeems us, which will be the time when Shimon's greatness will be revealed.

We can also understand why the permission for tribes to intermarry was reason enough to create such a grand festival. Shimon represents harsh justice and vengefulness for Hashem's Glory. As important as those traits are, when used incorrectly, they can lead to divisiveness and fighting among Jews. The Second *Beis HaMikdash* was destroyed during Av because of baseless hatred among Jews. As the Gerrer Rebbe, the *Beis Yisrael* explains, actions that cause division among Jews are spiritually harmful, but the opposite is also true — we can neutralize the harsh justice of the month by showing unity and love for our fellow Jews. Such unity was achieved when the tribes set aside the differences between them and began to mingle with one another and marry one another. That display of unity was truly a cause for uninhibited joy.

We also noted that the only *yahrzeit* mentioned in the Torah is that of Aharon HaKohen, on the first of Av. Aharon was the symbol of unity among Jews; his efforts to create harmony between man and wife and between Jews who were at odds with each other was unparalleled. As we start Shimon's month, we are cautioned to follow his lead and bring unity to *Klal Yisrael*, not to engage in acts of vengefulness that cause discord.

Finally, we can appreciate why the month is called "Av." Despite all the pain that we have suffered during this month — pain that may not seem becoming for a merciful *Av* (father) — we are aware that even during the sad days of Av, our Merciful Father in Heaven — our *Av* — is paving the way to the ultimate redemption, waiting to lead us out of exile once and for all.

The sad days of the first half of the month are no contradiction to the great joy of the second half — on the contrary, happiness will blossom from the sadness.

We can neutralize the harsh justice of the month by showing unity and love for our fellow Jews.

Even during the sad days of Av, our Merciful Father in Heaven — our Av — is paving the way to the ultimate redemption.

eLuL

הנה, אלול יתייחס לשבט גד.

(בני יששכר, מאמרי חדש אלול מאמר א, אות ח)

Behold, Elul corresponds to the tribe of Gad.

(Bnei Yissaschar, Maamarei Chodesh Elul 1:8)

BNEI YISASSCHAR EXPLAINS AS FOLLOWS:

It is known that ג represents wealth, and ד represents poverty, as the Sages say: the letters ג ד stand for גְּמוֹל דַּלִים, *Bestow kindness upon the poor*; i.e., a wealthy person has an obligation to help a poor one. The letter י represents plenty [i.e., when added to a word as a prefix, the letter י changes the word into future tense, and the future hints to abundance and plenty, because one must always be optimistic that the future will be better than the past]. If we multiply the numerical values of ג and ד (3 and 4) by ten (the numerical value of י) we come to a total of 70 — or ע [which alludes to עולם, *the world*].

One must always be optimistic that the future will be better than the past.

Furthermore, these numerical values also allude to מזל, *good fortune*, because the numerical value of גד is seven, ז. The numerical value of ten times ג is ל; and ten times ד is מ. Those three letters combine to spell מזל.

Aside from the numerical allusions of the letters, the definition of the word גד is *good mazal* (good fortune), as we find when Leah named her son Gad. She declared, "בָּא גָד" (*Bereishis* 30:11). *Targum Yonasan* and *Rashi* both explain that she meant that good *mazal* had come.

Before we can understand the correspondence between the tribe of Gad and the month of Elul, we must explore the concept of mazal.

Before we can understand the correspondence between the tribe of Gad and the month of Elul, we must explore the concept of *mazal*.

1. Is Klal Yisrael Governed by (Dazal?

CHAZAL TEACH[1] אֵין מַזַּל לְיִשְׂרָאֵל, *KLAL YISRAEL IS NOT CONTROLLED by mazal*, i.e., although Hashem ordained that His control of events be channeled though heavenly forces, such as the constellations (*mazalos*), the Jewish people are not subject to this

---

1. *Shabbos* 156a.

control. (This will be explained below.) This teaching prompts several questions:

1) If the Jewish people are not controlled by a *mazal*, why would Leah give the name Gad, which is based on the idea of *mazal*?

2) The months of the Jewish calendar are associated with the constellations, which are called *mazalos* and which allude to the idea that God controls the word through the agency of heavenly beings. How do we reconcile this association with *Chazal's* teaching that Israel is not controlled by *mazal*?

3) The association between Elul and the tribe of Gad, whose name represents *mazal*, suggests that *mazal* is more significant during Elul than it is during the rest of the year. Why?

We will also attempt to understand the correlation between Elul and *shevo*, the stone in the *Choshen Mishpat* on which Gad's name was engraved. Since it is known that the colors of the *Choshen's* stones are related to the tribes they represent, we will examine how the color of Gad's stone — grayish, dark-blue — relates to other factors associated with Elul.

THE ISSUE OF WHETHER OR NOT *KLAL YISRAEL* IS GOVERNED BY *mazal* is the subject of dispute between Talmudic Sages. Rabbi

Conflicting Opinions

Chanina says, "*Mazal* makes a person wise; *mazal* makes person wealthy; and *Klal Yisrael* is governed by *mazal*." *Rashi* explains that a person's intellectual prowess is a function of *mazal*, as we see from the Talmudic teaching[2] that those who are born in the *mazal* of *Chamah* (Saturn) will be bright and wise. Moreover, since a person's life is controlled by *mazal*, he cannot change his lot in life through prayer and the performance of commandments.

Rabbi Yochanan and Rav[3] disagree. They maintain that *ein mazal*

"Mazal makes a person wise; mazal makes person wealthy; and Klal Yisrael is governed by mazal."

---

2. Ibid.

3. Rav Yochanan and Rav differ as to the source of *ein mazal l'Yisrael*, i.e., that Israel is not subject to *mazal*. Rav Yochanan derives this idea from a verse that states, "Thus said Hashem, *Do not learn from the way of the nations; do not be frightened by the signs of the heavens, though the nations are frightened by them*" (*Yirmiyahu* 10:2). Rav Yochanan deduces that the nations of the world have reason to be frightened by the signs of the heavens (because they are governed by the *mazalos*), but we do not. Rav derives this concept from a conversation recorded in the Talmud between Hashem and Avraham Avinu. Avraham questioned Hashem's promise that he would bear a child who would inherit him, because he had determined through his astrological sign that he was incapable of bearing children with Sarah. Hashem responded, "Leave your astrological calculations [aside]; *ein mazal l'Yisrael.*"

Mazal does not apply to the Jewish people. Rashi explains that Israel is not controlled by mazal, in the sense that Jews can change their lot through prayer or by accumulating merits.

l'Yisrael, mazal does not apply to the Jewish people. *Rashi* explains that Israel is not controlled by *mazal,* in the sense that Jews can change their lot through prayer or by accumulating merits.

In several places, the Talmud indicates that Jews are indeed subject to *mazal*:

> Rava[4] stated, "Fertility, longevity, and prosperity are not dependent on merit, but on *mazal,* as we find that Rabbah and Rav Chisdah were both very righteous, as evidenced by the fact that their prayers would cause rain to fall. Nevertheless, Rav Chisda lived 92 years, and Rabbah lived only 40 years. Rav Chisda made sixty wedding feasts [for children and grandchildren]; Rabbah mourned sixty times [for deaths in his family]. The dogs in Rav Chisdas house were fed food made with fine flour that was not needed [by members of the household, i.e., so prosperous was he that there was more good flour than his household could eat], but in Rabbah's house they could not find even enough barley flour to feed the people!"

Clearly, therefore, we must attempt to define the parameters of *mazal*. When is its power subject to change and when is it impervious to merit? We will seek to reconcile the seeming contradictions between the above and other passages in the Talmud.

How can Rava say that fertility, longevity, and prosperity depend not on personal merit, but on mazal?

Children, Life, and Sustenance Depend on Mazal, Not Merit

YALKUT REUVENI RAISES A MAJOR DIFFICULTY: HOW CAN *RAVA* SAY that fertility, longevity, and prosperity depend not on personal merit, but on *mazal?* The Torah promises specifically that those who observe His commandments will receive these rewards:

This shall be the reward when you hearken to these ordinances, and you observe and perform them; Hashem, your God, will safeguard for you the covenant and the kindness that He swore to your forefathers. He will love you, bless you and multiply you, and He will bless the fruit of your womb[5] and the fruit of your Land: your grain, your

---

4. *Moed Kattan* 28a. However, the *Vilna Gaon,* quoted by Ben Aryeh, has an entirely different interpretation of *mazal.* According to him, the Talmud uses that term to refer to one of God's Thirteen Attributes of Mercy, נוֹצֵר חֶסֶד, *Preserver of Mercy,* i.e., God's mercy extends for many generations, so that even if an individual does not merit His intervention, God may show him mercy because of the good deeds of his ancestors. Elsewhere, the Gaon explains that *mazal* can also refer to the merit of a person's prior good deeds.

5. I.e., you will bear offspring. This idea is further expressed in the following verse, "There will be no infertile male or infertile female among you."

wine, and your oil; the offspring of your cattle and the flocks of your sheep and goats;[6] on the Land that he swore to your forefathers to give you. You will be the most blessed of all the peoples; there will be no infertile male or infertile female among you or among your animals. Hashem will remove from you every illness[7] ... (*Devarim* 7:12-14).

Since this passage promises the blessings of fertility, prosperity, and longevity to those who deserve them, how can Rava suggest that those blessings are not merit-based?[8]

In another case, there is a mishnah that seems to say clearly that prosperity is a function of merit, not *mazal*, but *Tosafos* explains the mishnah differently:

> The mishnah[9] states, "One should pray to the One who controls wealth and possessions, because a person can become rich from any trade, and he can also become poor. Wealth and poverty do not come from a person's trade, but from his merits."
>
> *Tosafos* explain that when the mishnah uses the word *zechus* in this context, it actually means to say that a person's financial status is controlled by his *mazal*.

How can we reconcile the passages that state that Israel is not governed by *mazal* with those that suggest that it is? And how are we to understand *Tosafos*, which seem to interpret the mishnah by virtually contradicting it?

One of the first clues to resolving this problem appears in another *Tosafos*, which state, "Sometimes a person's lot in life will be changed by *mazal*, but sometimes it cannot be altered." Certain merits are considered *zechusim gedolim* (great merits), and they can change a person's *mazal*, but ordinary merits are not capable of altering it. However, *Tosafos* do not define what sort of merits are considered "great merits."

How can we reconcile the passages that state that Israel is not governed by mazal with those that suggest that it is?

---

6. Here we find a promise of prosperity.

7. This implies that those who guard the Torah will merit longevity.

8. See *Yalkut Reuveni*, who suggests possible solutions to this contradiction. Some say that an individual is subject to *mazal*, but not the nation. Others say that in *Eretz Yisrael* one is not subject to *mazal*.

9. *Kiddushin* 82a.

11. Torah and Tefillah Override Mazal

WHEN HASHEM GAVE AVRAHAM AVINU THE WONDERFUL news that after a lifetime of infertility together, he and Sarah would have a son. Avraham was surprised. How could they have a son when their *mazal* showed that this was impossible? Hashem told him to ignore the message of the stars, because Israel is not subservient to *mazal*. *Zohar* explains that until the Torah was given, the entire world, including Israel, was indeed governed by *mazal* — even in matters of fertility, longevity, and prosperity. Once the Torah was given, however, *Klal Yisrael* was removed from that rule.

When telling Avraham — whose name from birth was Avram — not to worry about his astrological sign, Hashem told him, "You are correct in your calculations; Avram [written without the Hebrew letter *hei*] cannot bear children, but *Avraham* can bear children." By adding the letter *hei* to Avram's name, Hashem changed his destiny. *Zohar* explains that the *hei* (with a numerical value of five) represents the Five Books of the Torah, meaning that one who toils in the study of Torah can remove the authority of *mazalos* from upon himself. *Maharsha*[10] adds that *Tefillah*, too, can override *mazal*.

As we have seen, the mishnah recommends that one should pray to the One who controls wealth and possessions, because wealth and poverty do not come from a person's trade, but from his merits. The Talmud[11] expands on this mishnah. One of twelve questions that the people of Alexandria asked R' Yehoshua ben Chaninah was how one can become wealthy. R' Yehoshua responded that he should accumulate much wisdom and be sure to deal honestly with others.

"But many tried this method and failed," objected the questioners.

R' Yehoshua responded, "Then let him ask for mercy from Him Who controls the wealth."

Maharsha comments, "Through exerting oneself and earning Divine assistance through *tefillah* and great merits, one can alter what has been decreed upon him. The same holds true for prosperity and fertility. One can change his lot through a combination of effort and Divine assistance."

Zohar explains that until the Torah was given, the entire world, including Israel, was indeed governed by mazal — even in matters of fertility, longevity, and prosperity. Once the Torah was given, however, Klal Yisrael was removed from that rule.

"Through exerting oneself and earning Divine assistance through tefillah and great merits, one can alter what has been decreed upon him."

---

10. *Niddah* 69b, s.v. *Shalosh Derech*.
11. Ibid. 70b.

The basis for the concept that a Jew can change his lot through *tefillah* can be found in the Talmud.[12] Rabbi Yitzchak says, "Four things can wipe out a [harsh] decree levied on a person: charity, crying out [to Hashem], change of name, and change of deeds. Some add change of location." Talmud Yerushalmi[13] relates that Rabbi Yochanan once told someone who was having difficulty in business to change his location, because "sometimes a change of name can cause [a change for the better]; other times a change of location can cause [a change]."

There are several other sources in the Talmud that show clearly that *tefillah* can change one's lot:

- *Shabbos* 151b: Rabbi Eliezer HaKappar says that a person should pray [that he not suffer poverty (*Rashi*)], for even if poverty does not befall *him,* it may befall his son or grandson [for poverty is a common phenomenon; it may skip generations, and therefore even prosperous people should pray for their future generations (*Rashi*)]. Clearly, therefore, Rabbi Eliezer considers it possible to change one's financial lot through prayer.

- *Eruvin* 41b: Three things can cause a person to violate his own will and the will of his Maker: idol worship, evil spirits, and extreme poverty. The reason we must know this, explains the Talmud, is so that we should beg for mercy that none of these three conditions should affect us. Clearly, then, *tefillah* can avert difficulties.

- Bava Kamma 80b: Rav Pappa says, "A closed door is not easily opened." *Rashi* explains that when the door to success is closed, it cannot be opened easily. What is the point of this passage? *Rashi* explains that it cautions us to pray intensely.

Ibn Ezra (*Shemos* 33:21) teaches the extent to which prayer and obedience to the Torah can override *mazal*:

> *Chazal's* statement that *Klal Yisrael* is not governed by *mazal* applies only when we observe the Torah. If we do not follow the Torah, however, *mazal* can bring evil upon us. According to the arrangement of the constellations, Israel should have remained in Egypt for many more years than it did, but when we cried out to Hashem and returned to Him, he redeemed us from exile. Just as the entire Jewish nation was saved from

Chazal's statement that Klal Yisrael is not governed by mazal applies only when we observe the Torah. If we do not follow the Torah, however, mazal can bring evil upon us.

---

12. *Rosh Hashanah* 16b.
13. *Shabbos* 6:9.

the difficulties dictated by *mazal*, an individual can also be saved from difficulties his personal *mazal* may pose. Therefore, praiseworthy is a person who follows the Torah.

Maharal adds that prayer certainly has the power to nullify any the troubles that mazal may have in store; however, even mitzvah observance alone — unaccompanied by prayer — can also change one's lot for the better.

Maharal adds that prayer certainly has the power to nullify any the troubles that *mazal* may have in store; however, even mitzvah observance alone —unaccompanied by prayer — can also change one's lot for the better. Thus, when *Chazal* said *ein mazal l'Yisrael*, they did not mean to suggest that *Klal Yisrael* is not under the influence of *mazal* altogether, continues *Maharal,* but that the dominance of their *mazal* is conditional on their merits. If their *mazal* dictates that they are in for difficult times, only a great *zechus* (merit) can save them from that fate. For instance, Pharaoh told Moshe that according to his astrological calculations the Jews would meet with calamity in the Wilderness. But the merit of the forefathers reversed our *mazal* and saved us from that fate. From *Maharal* it emerges that the uniqueness of Israel is the ability of its Torah study and mitzvah observance to override one of the basic laws of Creation — the normal dominance of *mazal*.

ALTHOUGH *KLAL YISRAEL* IS SUBJECT TO *MAZAL* IF THE NATION sins, there is a way to overcome its power. *Zohar Chadash*[14] teaches

Teshuvah Transcends Mazal

that even if a person's sins caused him to be placed under a harsh *mazal*, Hashem removes him from that *mazal* if he repents. There are many levels of *teshuvah*, how-

There are many levels of teshuvah. The more meaningful the repentance, the better the new mazal will be.

ever. The more meaningful the repentance, the better the new *mazal* will be.

We can understand this *Zohar* on a deeper level. The Talmud teaches that Hashem created *teshuvah* before He created the world, as we see from the verses, *Before the mountains were born, and You had not yet fashioned the earth and the inhabited land, and from the remotest past and to the most distant future, You are God. You reduce man to pulp and You say, "Repent, O sons of man"* (*Tehillim* 90:2-3).

Talmud Yerushalmi[15] expands on this teaching, stating that wisdom was asked what punishment should befall a person who sinned, and it answered, *Evil should pursue sinners* (*Mishlei* 13:21). The same question was asked of prophecy, and it answered, *The soul that sins — it shall die* (*Yechezkel* 18:4). When Hashem was asked

---

14. *Parashas Yisro*, 40b.
15. *Makkos* 2:6.

this question, He answered, "Let him repent, and he will be forgiven." *Yerushalmi* concludes that this is why the verse states that Hashem *guides sinners on the way* (*Tehillim* 25:8).

Thus, repentance is a supernatural phenomenon — one that wisdom and even prophecy could not fathom! Only Hashem Himself could provide this special dispensation. It had to precede Creation itself, because it transcends all natural and logical limitations. How else could an accumulation of sins simply disappear? Could one wish away a host of bad business decisions by declaring he is sorry he made them? Precisely because it is supernatural, repentance supersedes *mazal,* which functions on a natural pathway.

We can now understand why *Rashi* comments that according to Rabbi Chanina — who maintains that *Klal Yisrael* is governed by *mazal* — *tefillah* and *tzedakah* cannot change it. *Rashi* specifies *tefillah* and *tzedakah;* by mentioning only those two, *Rashi* means to imply that are other means that can enable a person to alter an unfavorable *mazal.* *Rashi* teaches that when *mazal* deals painful blows, it must be because sins have empowered it. In such situations, prayer and charity alone cannot avail; but *repentance* can nullify the power of *mazal.*

There is another reason why *teshuvah* should override *mazal.* We have seen that change of name or location can cause *mazal* to change for the better. *Teshuvah* affords a sinner the opportunity to change himself to the extent that he can be considered an entirely different person; he has discarded the label of "sinner" and become a righteous person. Furthermore, by placing the penitent on a different spiritual level, *teshuvah* can also be seen as a "change of location." As *Rambam* expresses it:

> How great is *teshuvah*! Yesterday this person was estranged from Hashem ... and today he can cling to the Divine Presence.

In a sense, however, *teshuvah's* power to change a sinner's *mazal* is not at all supernatural. Rather, the penitent is not the same person. He is in a different spiritual location, so it is natural that he now falls under a different, more favorable *mazal.*

Teshuvah affords a sinner the opportunity to change himself to the extent that he can be considered an entirely different person; he has discarded the label of "sinner" and become a righteous person.

OUR STUDY OF THE EFFECTS OF *MAZAL* AND THE MEANS TO CHANGE it leads us to a clear understanding of why Elul corresponds to Gad.

Elul and Gad, Teshuvah and Mazal

Gad means a good *mazal* — and since Elul is the month of repentance, it is the most appropriate time to eradicate the harmful influence of a negative *mazal* and replace it with a favorable *mazal.*

Elul corresponds to Gad. Gad means a good mazal.

With this insight into the correlation between Elul and Gad, we can better understand several other factors associated with Gad and/ or with Elul:

- When Moshe Rabbeinu blessed Gad saying, *Blessed is He who broadens Gad* (*Devarim* 33:20), perhaps he was referring to Gad's special association with *teshuvah,* which broadens a person's perception by making him aware that it is never too late; that one can always repent and improve one's lot in this world and the next.

- The *mazal* of Elul is *Besulah* (Virgin), a symbol of purity and newness. She symbolizes the stage in life when she is on the threshold of marriage and is about to produce new life and inspire hopes for the future. This signifies the state of purity that can be achieved through *teshuvah.*

- Gad's stone in the *Choshen* is *shevo,* whose color was a murky and indistinct grayish, dark blue. Perhaps this vague color alludes to our personal uncertainty during the month of Elul. Will we succeed in purifying ourselves so that we can enjoy a year of spirituality, or will the *yetzer hara* convince us to burrow more deeply into a morass of sin?

The very name of the stone, *shevo,* alludes to Gad's relationship with Elul. The word *shevo* comprises the three middle letters of the word *teshuvah.* Those three letters spell the word that means return, which is the definition of *teshuvah*/repentance. Elul begins with a question mark, with murkiness. Will we be the victims of our *mazal* or will we repent and overcome it? Will we go the way of life that thrusts us under a negative *mazal,* or will we fill our lives with the "great merit" of Torah, generosity, and obedience to the will of Hashem?

The name *shevo* reminds us that we can indeed repent and merit a year full of spirituality and good *mazal.* Indeed, Gad and its stone represent the eternal lesson that no *mazal* can withstand the force of sincere *teshuvah,* because Israel's spiritual elevation is the purpose of Creation.

The Months
and the
Name of Hashem

Cycle Two: Introduction

MANY CLASSIC WORKS OF KABBALAH, BEGINNING WITH THE *Holy Zohar*, expound on Hashem's method of controlling the functioning of the universe by means of the *Ten Sefiros,* which are emanations of His holiness.

Kabbalistic works concentrate on the power and influence of the Four-letter Name of Hashem, with which Hashem created the universe.

Later Kabbalistic works concentrate on the power and influence of the Four-letter Name of Hashem, the Tetragrammaton, with which Hashem created the universe. Foremost among them are *Mishnas Chassidim*, authored by Rabbi Emanuel Chai Rikki, a kabbalist born in Italy in 5448 (1688), and *Bnei Yissaschar*, written by Rabbi Tzvi Elimelech Shapiro of Dinev, a great chassidic leader who studied under the Chozeh of Lublin and R' Mendel of Rimonov. They teach that the four letters of the Name can be arranged twelve different ways, and these "Name Combinations" correspond to the twelve months of the year. Furthermore, the Name Combinations can be sourced to verses in the Torah, Prophets, and Writings.

The underlying principles of Name Combinations are too deep for us to understand, but we will try to explain the basic concepts involved.

Hashem continues to "manage" the universe through the Divine Name, with the exact form of control determined by the order in which the letters of the Divine Name appear.

Sacred works state that all of Creation is rooted in the Tetragrammaton, the holy Four-letter Name of Hashem. Hashem continues to "manage" the universe through the Divine Name, with the exact form of control — be it mercy, strict justice, kindness, etc. — determined by the order in which the letters of the Divine Name appear. For example, when the Name is spelled in the correct order, יה־ו־ה, it represents mercy, but if that order is reversed to ה־ו־ה־י, it represents strict justice. Each spelling represents a different form of control.

Bnei Yissaschar explains the change in the pattern of Divine control of the world on a deeper level: "There are twelve Name Combinations, each of which illuminates a different month of the year. The Four-letter Name has a numerical value of 26, so that the 12 combinations together equal 312, the same numerical value as the Hebrew word for month, חֹדֶשׁ. חֹדֶשׁ can also be translated as *new,* which suggests that the Name Combination associated with each month brings a new form of Divine Control with it."

It would seem that since these forms of Divine control are based on the specific Name Combination, we can do nothing to change the form of control. *Bnei Yissaschar* writes that the opposite is true. The Torah states, הַחֹדֶשׁ הַזֶּה לָכֶם רֹאשׁ חֳדָשִׁים, *This month is **for you** the beginning of the months* (*Shemos* 12:2). The term ***for you*** suggests that it is within our power to change negative influences that may reign in that particular month in the world. By studying Torah and serving Hashem in a manner that is most effective in each month, we can transform even the strictest justice into Divine Mercy. Thus, its Name Combination characterizes a particular month as a time of mercy or harshness or something in between. However, this is not so much a *fait accompli* as a challenge. The Jew can change it through his conduct — and Hashem wants us to.

By studying Torah and serving Hashem in a manner that is most effective in each month, we can transform even the strictest justice into Divine Mercy.

We might add that the Maggid of Kozhnitz considers this opportunity to be one of the most important aspects of our existence on earth. The Talmud (*Shabbos* 31b) teaches that one of the questions we will be asked on the Day of Judgment is, "Did you designate times for Torah?" Simply understood, we will be asked if we set aside times to study Torah. The Maggid of Kozhnitz explains this question homiletically: "Did you use Torah study to change the designated forms of Divine Control from negative to positive?"

"Did you use Torah study to change the designated forms of Divine Control from negative to positive?"

———•◦•———

As we have mentioned, *Mishnas Chassidim* and *Bnei Yissaschar* provided us with a list of how the Name Combinations correspond to the months, and found sources for them in Scripture.

In this series of essays, based on lectures that were delivered during 5763 (2002-3), we followed the path of the *Bnei Yissaschar*, expanding and explaining the correspondence between the month of the year and the verse from which its Name Combination is taken.

We are hopeful that the study of these ideas will add meaning and depth to our understanding of the months, and will help us serve Hashem properly during each of the respective months.

This concept will be explained at greater length in the Appendix to this work.

TISHREI

וַיִּרְאוּ אֹתָהּ שָׂרֵי פַרְעֹה (והי״ה).

The Name Combination for the month of Tishrei is derived from the verse that tells of the misfortune that befell the Matriarch Sarah when she and Avraham went to Egypt to escape a famine in Eretz Yisrael: וַיִּרְאוּ אֹתָהּ שָׂרֵי פַרְעֹה וַיְהַלְלוּ אֹתָהּ אֶל פַּרְעֹה וַתֻּקַּח הָאִשָּׁה בֵּית פַּרְעֹה, When the officials of Pharaoh saw her, they lauded her for Pharaoh, and the woman was taken to Pharaoh's house (Bereishis 12:15). The last letters of the first four words of the verse are the letters of Hashem's Name.

REVERSING SIN — PORTENTS FOR THE CHILDREN

תִּשְׁרֵי – וַיִּרְאוּ אֹתָהּ שָׂרֵי פַרְעֹה (והי״ה).

THERE IS A KABBALISTIC PRINCIPLE THAT EVERY MONTH IS related to the letters of the Holy Four-letter Name, and that the order of these letters as they relate the month is derived from the words of a Scriptural verse.[1] As shown above, the Name Combination for the month of Tishrei is derived from the verse that tells of the misfortune that befell the Matriarch Sarah when she and Avraham went to Egypt to escape a famine in *Eretz Yisrael*: וַיִּרְאוּ אֹתָהּ שָׂרֵי פַרְעֹה וַיְהַלְלוּ אֹתָהּ אֶל פַּרְעֹה וַתֻּקַּח הָאִשָּׁה בֵּית פַּרְעֹה, *When the officials of Pharaoh saw her, they lauded her for Pharaoh, and the woman was taken to Pharaoh's house* (*Bereishis* 12:15). The last letters of the first four words of the verse are the letters of Hashem's Name.

The correlation of this verse with Tishrei is perplexing:

1) What does the story of Avraham and Sarah in Egypt have to do with Tishrei, the month of repentance during the Days of Awe and Atonement?

Ramban criticizes the choices Avraham Avinu made in deciding to go to Egypt and saying that Sarah was his sister:

2) In his commentary on the Torah, *Ramban* criticizes the choices Avraham Avinu made in deciding to go to Egypt and saying that Sarah was his sister:

> Know that Avraham inadvertently committed a great sin, nearly causing his wife to sin [by living with Pharaoh] because of his fear of being killed. He should have had faith that Hashem would save him, his wife, and all his possessions, for Hashem has the power to provide salvation. For him to leave *Eretz Yisrael* when the hunger struck was also a sin, because Hashem would have saved him from dying of hunger. Because of this, Avraham was

---

1. This concept and its background are discussed in the Introduction to this section of the book and at greater length in the Appendix (p. 349).

punished by having his descendants exiled in Egypt; the place of the judgment was the place of the sin.

Ramban's exposition is surprising. The mishnah[2] declares that Hashem tested Avraham Avinu ten times, and he passed all the tests. One of those challenges was the hunger that struck *Eretz Yisrael* just as he settled there on Hashem's command. If so, how can *Ramban* describe Avraham's sojourn in Egypt as a sin if the mishnah lists it as a test that he passed?

HaK'sav VehaKabalah adds a more powerful question. At *Bris Bein HaBesarim* (the Covenant between the Parts [*Bereishis* 15:8-13]), Hashem informed Avraham that his descendants would be exiled in Egypt, but that event occurred five years before his trip to Egypt. How can *Ramban* consider the exile of Avraham's descendants to Egypt a punishment for going there if Hashem had foretold it to him five years earlier?

3) The Midrash[3] reveals the date when Sarah was taken to Pharaoh's palace:

> Rabbi Yehoshuah ben Karchah said, "The night Sarah was taken [to Pharaoh] was Pesach Eve. 'Hashem afflicted Pharaoh and his household with severe plagues' (*Bereishis* 13:17) to warn Pharaoh that He would eventually do the same years later, as the verse tells us [regarding the plague of the firstborn], 'One more plague shall I bring upon Pharaoh and upon Egypt'" (*Shemos* 11:1). [Since the word *plague* is used in both verses, the Midrash infers that the first event was an allusion to the second.]

Several questions come to mind. What is the significance of the fact that this occurred on Pesach Eve? Second, why did Hashem choose this test in particular to allude to the future enslavement of Avraham's descendants in Egypt?

This question increases tenfold when we realize the extent of the parallelism between the story of Sarah's abduction and that of our nation's stay in Egypt.

Ramban [4] points out the extent of the similarity between the two chains of events: Avraham descended to Egypt to escape a hunger in *Eretz Yisrael*, the Egyptians seized his wife, Hashem punished this crime by smiting Pharaoh and his people, He forced

We realize the extent of the parallelism between the story of Sarah's abduction and that of our nation's stay in Egypt.

---

2. *Avos* 5:3.
3. *Pirkei D'Rabbi Eliezer* 26.
4. *Bereishis* 12:10.

them to allow Avraham to leave with riches, and Pharaoh sent servants to escort Avraham from the country. What happened centuries later? Yaakov and his children traveled to Egypt to escape a hunger in *Eretz Yisrael*, the Egyptians tried to take possession of the Jewish women by killing all male children and leaving the females alive, Hashem avenged their deeds by smiting them with ten plagues, the Jews left Egypt with riches, and Pharaoh sent servants to usher them out of the land quickly.

The similarities between the stories are indeed remarkable. Why did Hashem orchestrate such a parallel series of events?

Why did Hashem orchestrate such a parallel series of events?

4) In listing the ten tests that Hashem posed to Avraham, *Rambam*[5] states that the fact that he faced a hunger soon after arriving in the very land where Hashem promised to make him into a great nation was "a great challenge." Why, of all the tests, does *Rambam* describe only this one as "great"?

l. Cɒaʹasei Avos Siɒan Lʹ'Ban 1ɒ — Tɦe Events of tɦe Foɾefatɦeɾs Aɾe Poɾtents foɾ tɦe Cɦildɾen

A WELL-KNOWN SEMINAL PRINCIPLE OF *RAMBAN* PROVIDES the foundation with which we can answer these questions.

Sefer Bereishis devotes much detail to describing events that occurred to our forefathers – and even to their servants. Why is this necessary? *Ramban* explains:

I will tell you a rule, so that you will understand all the coming *parashiyos* regarding Avraham, Yitzchak, and Yaakov — an important concept mentioned briefly by *Chazal* in a midrash:[6] מַעֲשֵׂי אָבוֹת סִימָן לְבָנִים, *All events that occurred to the forefathers are portents for their descendants.* This is why the Torah says so much about the travels of the forefathers, the digging of wells, and other events, which we may consider unnecessary information, with no apparent purpose. [In truth], these events

All events that occurred to the forefathers are portents for their descendants.

---

5. In his commentary to *Avos* 5:3.

6. *Tanchuma, Lech Lecha* 9.

foretold what was going to transpire, for when an event took place as a prophecy to our forefathers, from it could be derived an event decreed upon their descendants …. This is why Hashem preserved Avraham in the Land and had him experience situations similar to those that his descendants would undergo.

In his introduction to *Sefer Shemos*, *Ramban* adds:

> We have concluded *Sefer Bereishis*, which is *Sefer Hayetzirah* (the Book of Creation), a discussion of the creation of the universe and all other creations, and of the events that occurred in the lives of the forefathers, which serve as a "creation" of sorts for their descendants. All that happened to the Patriarchs served as portents of what would happen to their children. Thus, our forefathers "created" our future, in keeping with the general theme of *Bereishis*, the Book of Creation.

According to this principle, *Ramban* explains the parallelism we found between Avraham and Sarah's trip to Egypt and that of their descendants. To establish precedents for his descendants centuries later, Avraham had to travel to Egypt and have his wife abducted, which was followed by the Egyptians being punished, and culminating with him leaving with riches.

BUT BY JUXTAPOSING THIS *RAMBAN* WITH HIS CRITICISM OF AVRAHAM, we can learn an important lesson. How can his experience in Egypt

Learning From Mistakes

be a blueprint for our nation's stay there, if — as *Ramban* asserts — Avraham erred in his decision to make that journey? And, as we asked earlier, why does the mishnah state that Avraham passed the test of the hunger if, as *Ramban* contends, he sinned in leaving *Eretz Yisrael*?

Apparently, if a person errs in judgment he has not yet failed the test. If he repents and applies the lessons of his failure to similar situations in the future, he is considered to have passed the test. Why?

if a person repents and applies the lessons of his failure, he is considered to have passed the test.

Hashem knows that it is virtually impossible for a human being to lead a completely sin-free life. When someone is tested, Hashem wants to see not only if he can surmount the challenge, but also what he will do in the event he initially failed the test. Will he have the courage to admit failure and repent, or will he be reluctant to admit the mistake?

Ramban's criticism of Avraham does not contradict the mishnah's statement that Avraham passed this test. Avraham may not have passed the *initial* test when he left *Eretz Yisrael*, as *Ramban* maintains, but it is axiomatic that he repented and redeemed himself, thus reversing his mistake. This, too, was part of his test, and he surely passed it. As *Mesilas Yesharim* writes in his discussion of *teshuvah*, when a person sincerely uproots his desire to sin, he uproots the sinful deeds.

When a person sincerely uproots his desire to sin, he uproots the sinful deeds.

There is another valuable lesson to be extracted from this story. Why does *Ramban* find it necessary to expose Avraham's failure by stating openly that he erred? Would it not have been more respectful not to mention his misdeed?

IN THE COURSE OF EXPLAINING AVRAHAM'S ACTIONS, R' SAMSON Raphael Hirsch explains why *Ramban* commented on the mistake in such strong terms:

The Torah Does Not Sugarcoat

At first glance, this story is surprising. Avraham left the land that Hashem set aside for him; he did not have enough faith that Hashem would provide his sustenance in the barren land. Furthermore, it seems that he endangered his wife's moral wellbeing to save his own life.

Now, even if we cannot explain all of Avraham's actions, even if we follow *Ramban's* approach (that he sinned), we still should not be surprised by the Torah's mention of this story. The Torah does not try to present our leaders as being the epitome of perfection; it does not deify mere mortals and does not proclaim of any individual: "here lies perfection; here lies the human version of God."

The Torah does not try to present our leaders as being the epitome of perfection.

R' Hirsch adds:

The Torah does not conceal [our forefather's] mistakes, or the errors and weaknesses of our leaders. In exposing the less-flattering aspects of our leaders, the Torah stamps all of the stories that appear in it with the stamp of truth. Truthfully, however, our knowledge of the sins of our forefathers should not diminish their stature in our eyes; conversely, our impression of them should only grow when we realize that they sinned. If all of our forefathers "shone like the bright rays of the sun," without the slightest trace of failure, we might conclude that they were of a different makeup than normal human beings, and that their impressive achievements are beyond our capabilities. If we thought that their good character traits were a result of inborn perfection — not a result of determined inner battles to eradicate all their personal desires — then we would not accept our forefathers as role models for us ordinary mortals.

For instance, if we thought that Moshe Rabbeinu was unable to be angry, we might think that he was born with a propensity toward his famous trait of humility, and we would not try to emulate him. But when we read the verse in which Moshe angrily declares, "Listen now, O rebels" (*Bamidbar* 20:10), we begin to appreciate his true greatness. We see that he wasn't born perfect; his sterling character traits were earned through determined efforts to control himself and soften his disposition. We now consider Moshe Rabbeinu a role model whose character traits we can all hope to acquire, since we are all capable of reaching his level.

Let us learn from the greatest Torah scholars — and the *Ramban* is certainly among the greatest. We are not charged with the task of defending our leaders; they do not need our defense and they don't appreciate it. The Torah is inscribed with the stamp of truth, and [expressing the] truth is the basic foundation of the commentators on the Torah.

R' Hirsch teaches that knowing our forefathers' sins does not diminish them. On the contrary, when we realize that they repented — in keeping with King Shlomo's adage, "For though the righteous man may fall seven times, he arises" (*Mishlei* 24:16) — we are even more impressed with them than we were before.

True, Avraham erred when tested by the hunger, but he still passed the test by repenting, so he taught us a lesson that has become ingrained into our national spirit: the recognition that mistakes are not permanent — we can repent, pick up the pieces, and move on.

Mistakes are not permanent — we can repent, pick up the pieces, and move on.

The propensity to learn from mistakes is so compelling, in fact, that *Chazal*[7] state, "One cannot succeed in Torah matters until he errs in them."

II. STUMBLING BLOCKS OR STEPPING STONES?

NOT ONLY DID AVRAHAM MANAGE TO TURN THE TIDE AS FAR AS his personal success in passing the test of the hunger was concerned, but the commentators point out that his journey to

---

7. *Gittin* 43a.

Egypt prepared the way for the future success of his descendants, by showing that a Jew can withstand and overcome the impurity of Egypt's immorality and sorcery.

In his classic *Sefer Haparashiyos,*[8] Rabbi Eliyahu KiTov writes that Hashem caused Avraham and Sarah to travel to Egypt (by bringing a hunger to *Eretz Yisrael*) in order to spread word of their greatness throughout the world. Egyptians were known for their expertise in *kishuf,* a form of sorcery that harnesses the forces of evil and impurity in order to bring about supernatural events. It was common knowledge in those days that no one could save himself from Egyptian sorcery. But then — suddenly — word spread that not only had a couple managed to extricate itself from the clutches of the Egyptians, but they brought Pharaoh himself to his knees, forcing him to give them lavish gifts. Thus, Avraham and Sarah sanctified the Name of Hashem by proving that the forces of evil and impurity do not have the ultimate power in this world.

Avraham and Sarah sanctified the Name of Hashem by proving that the forces of evil and impurity do not have the ultimate power in this world.

Legacy of Survival

BUT RAV TZADDOK HAKOHEN OF LUBLIN[9] TEACHES THAT AVRAHAM'S trip had a much more important outcome. By managing to escape Egypt unsullied by the perverse atmosphere of that land, Avraham and Sarah instilled a new ability into *Klal Yisrael* — an ability that became imperative for their spiritual survival several generations later and throughout our history:

> When the hunger struck, Avraham traveled to Egypt because he realized that the entire purpose of the famine was for him to pave the way for *Klal Yisrael* to endure the rampant immorality of Egypt. The purpose of the Egyptian exile was to test us to see if we could withstand the depravity that pervaded Egyptian society. *Chazal*[10] tell us, in fact, that Israel was redeemed from Egypt in the merit of its steadfast refusal to descend to the immorality of its oppressors.
>
> That they were able to do so was because of the great holiness of Avraham, who embodied the attribute of *chessed,* kindness. Kindness can be channeled in two ways. It can be used for the cause of holiness and the Divine kindness, or it can be used for self-indulgence and immorality. Avraham's kindness was dedicated to the former. The underlying reason that the

Kindness can be channeled in two ways.

---

8. *Parashas Lech Lecha,* pg. 230.
9. *Machshevos Charutz,* p. 98b.
10. *Mechilta, Parashas Bo.*

force of impurity caused Sarah to be brought to Pharaoh was to defile her, and through her to defile Avraham. For husband and wife are one spiritual body; it is only in the material world that they are divided into two physical bodies. It is through lust that evil has entrée into holiness, as happened when the serpent was tempted by Chavah, and through her succeeded in toppling Adam from his spiritual pedestal. In the same way, the force of evil sought to defile Sarah and through her to contaminate Avraham. But it failed, because Sarah would not submit, and in her merit Jewish women through the ages were able to maintain their sanctity.

It is clear from R' Tzaddok's formulation that Pharaoh epitomized evil and Egypt epitomized impurity and physical lust. Avraham and Sarah, on the other hand, epitomized goodness, holiness, and purity. Avraham had to descend to Egypt to prepare the way for his descendants, so that they, too, would be strong enough to overcome impurity with holiness, and thereby merit redemption by insulating themselves against the immorality and temptation of Egypt.

Accordingly, Avraham's journey was a "portent" for his children, enabling them to remain pure throughout their enslavement. We may also add another insight to our earlier explanation of the *Ramban*. It may indeed be, as *Ramban* comments, that Avraham's trip to Egypt started as a sin, but as R' Tzaddok explains, it ultimately became clear that the trip was imperative for the spiritual survival of his descendants. He had the wherewithal to recognize his error when he arrived in Egypt, recover quickly, and turn the trip into a successful mission.

Avraham's journey was a "portent" for his children, enabling them to remain pure throughout their enslavement.

BY DOING SO, AVRAHAM AVINU TAUGHT ANOTHER INVALUABLE LESson. Not only can a failure be reversed so that it can become a suc-

Reversal of Failure

cess on a general level, but the *specific* issue or action in which one erred can not only be corrected, it can even be turned into something positive. What initially seemed like a stumbling block turned out to be a stepping stone toward perfection.

We can now answer two other questions we raised earlier.

Rambam describes the hunger as a "great test." Why? Perhaps because Avraham's decision to leave *Eretz Yisrael* was a sin, and it is common for one who sins to fall further, rationalizing that he has failed, to lose hope, and to sink further and further into sin. Or he may defend his action and thereby justify his sin, thus leading to more sins in the future. This was Avraham's "great test." Would he be able to recover and repent, and turn the situation into a positive one? Stopping in mid-stride and turning sinful circumstances around is truly a remarkable achievement.

We can also answer the *HaK'sav VehaKabbalah's* question of how the exile in Egypt could have been a punishment for Avraham's sin if it was already foretold five years earlier in the *Bris Bein HaBesarim*. Hashem knew before the test of the hunger that Avraham would err initially and travel to Egypt, but that he would then repent. These actions, the descent and the repentance, would serve as portents for his children years later. Thus, the Divine decree at the *Bris Bein HaBesarim* was a prophecy: Avraham would sin, and as a result, his offspring would be exiled. But he would repent and overcome the evil of Egypt, and as a result, his merit would enable his offspring to emerge from the contamination of Egypt. Thus, the descent to Egypt was not simply a punishment for Avraham's sin, but a process, a sequence of events that would eventually result in an enormous spiritual triumph.

The Divine decree at the Bris Bein HaBesarim was a prophecy.

III. The Golden Calf — Opening the Door of Penitence

CHAZAL (*AVODAH ZARAH* 4B) TELL US THAT THE JEWS IN THE Wilderness were tempted into serving the Golden Calf in order to pave the way for sinners who would want to repent, even after having sinned grievously. *Rashi* explains that the people of the time were really above the sin of idol worship, but Hashem let them be enticed to sin so that future transgressors would learn that it is possible to repent and achieve atonement.

Future transgressors would learn that it is possible to repent and achieve atonement.

Avraham Avinu's sin of traveling to Egypt teaches us not to become despondent when we make a mistake, but to turn that mistake into something positive. The story of the Golden Calf takes that lesson one step further, showing that even as reprehensible a sin as idolatry — a sin so devastating that *Chazal* tell us that all punishment meted out in this world contains some measure of reprisal for the sin of the Golden Calf — can also be reversed. We must repair the damage and move on.

In *Chedvas Yotzer*, my friend Rabbi Yitzchok Rosenzweig uses this idea to explain a series of teachings from *Chazal*. *Chazal*[11] tell us that the *Parah Adumah* (Red Calf) purifies the impure, but that it

11. *Yoma* 14a.

defies the pure.[12] *Rashi*[13] quotes *R' Moshe HaDarshan* that the *Parah Adumah* atones for the sin of the Golden Calf.

Rabbi Rosenzweig elucidates these three teachings of *Chazal* magnificently by connecting them to one another. Hashem's decree that the Jews in the Wilderness would sin in order to pave the way for future sinners to repent was a case of "defiling the pure" in order to enable impure people to purify themselves. The agency for this was the *Parah Adumah*.

It is appropriate that the atonement for the sin of the Golden Calf should be via the *Parah Adumah*, in which *Kohanim* who start off in a state of purity become impure as they prepare the water with which to purify people who have become impure.

Chazal give us one more example of this concept, stating that, "It was not fitting for King David to be involved in the episode [of Bas Sheva[14]]," but just as the Jews in the Wilderness worshiped the Golden Calf so they could serve as role models of repentance on a national level, King David sinned with Bas Sheva to serve as a role model for individual repentance.

The common theme that runs through these teachings provides us with the correct perspective on the sins of the greats. When people of the caliber of Avraham Avinu or King David sin, the misdeed is not an obstacle that prevents further growth; on the contrary, the sin spurs them to improve and perfect themselves — and it leads others to do the same. Righteous people's descent into sin leads them to ascend to a higher level than they had reached prior to the sin.

Righteous people's descent into sin leads them to ascend to a higher level than they had reached prior to the sin.

OUR STUDY OF AVRAHAM'S JOURNEY TO EGYPT PROVIDES US WITH the insight we need to understand the correlation between the phrase

Tishrei's Name Combination — A Call to Repent

וַיִּרְאוּ אֹתָהּ שָׂרֵי פַרְעֹה — which contains the month's Name Combination — and the month of Tishrei.

Tishrei is the month of *teshuvah*. The first ten days of Tishrei are the *Aseres Yemei Teshuvah* (Ten Days of Repentance), beginning with Rosh Hashanah, the Day of Judgment, and ending with Yom Kippur, the Day of Atonement.

As we have seen, a key lesson of Avraham's experience in Egypt is that it is never too late to repent. Not only can mistakes be

---

12. See *Bamidbar* 19.
13. Ibid. 19:22.
14. See *II Shmuel* 11.

reversed, they can also be turned into positive experiences — to the extent that we can be considered to have passed even "great tests," as did Avraham. It is fitting, therefore, that the Sages find the relationship between the Four-letter Name and the month of *teshuvah* in the phrase that tells of Sarah's abduction in Egypt. The episode began as a result of Avraham's mistake, and ended in triumph — a portent of the Jewish people's ability to surmount unspeakable tragedy.

WE CAN ALSO APPRECIATE ON SEVERAL LEVELS THE SIGNIFICANCE of Sarah being taken to Pharaoh on Pesach Eve. R' Tzaddok taught

Method to the Miracles

that Sarah's strength in remaining pure in Pharaoh's house paved the way for her descendants to do the same generations later, enabling them to overpower the impurity of Egypt and be redeemed from its clutches on that very same night.

Sarah's strength in remaining pure in Pharaoh's house paved the way for her descendants to do the same generations later.

On a deeper level, we celebrate the miracles that occurred during the Exodus by conducting the Seder on Pesach Eve. *Maharal* teaches that the name "Seder," literally "order," teaches that while miracles may seem to be spontaneous reactions to urgent needs, Hashem does not perform them haphazardly without any semblance of order. He performs miracles in very specific instances and at specific times, and that order reveals that His hand is heavily involved in *all* the events that occur in Jewish history — even those that seem natural.

This concept is expanded upon in a *piyyut* recited toward the end of the Seder, *Vayehi Bachatzi Haleiylah*, (It Happened at Midnight), which records many miracles that occurred in our history throughout the ages, all of them on the night of Pesach. The message of this *piyyut* is that miracles are no mere coincidence — Hashem brings them about with a *seder*, a specific order, so that we, His People, will appreciate His ever-constant guidance and His concern for our well-being — no matter when, and no matter where.

Miracles are no mere coincidence — Hashem brings them about with a seder, a specific order, so that we, His People, will appreciate His ever-constant guidance.

The merit of that first Pesach Eve miracle, when Sarah proved her greatness in Pharaoh's palace, earned Israel a great miracle in a generation when the people had fallen to such a low spiritual level that they had no merit of their own. In the time of Gideon, the Midianites conquered the Land and Israel was helpless to defend itself. The invaders looted the land and subjugated the people.[15] Gideon was a young man, threshing wheat, when an angel appeared to him on Pesach Eve and said, "Hashem is with you, O mighty hero."

_____
15. See *Shoftim* Ch.13

Gideon protested, "If Hashem is with us, why has all this happened to us? And where are all His wonders of which our forefathers told us, saying, 'Behold, Hashem brought us up from Egypt'? For now, Hashem has deserted us, and He has delivered us into the grip of Midian."

Then, because the young Gideon had protested in defense of Israel, God appointed him to be the leader who would miraculously defeat the powerful oppressor. Gideon's miracle demonstrated anew that even in its lowliest state, the miracles of Pesach Eve remain eternal and make it possible for Israel to repent and return to its natural state of spiritual greatness — and thereby overcome its enemies, as Avraham and Sarah did in ancient Egypt.

The experience of Gideon, even more than that of Avraham and Sarah, gives us hope that even in the throes of exile and spiritual poverty, Israel can rise again and earn its place at the pinnacle of Creation.

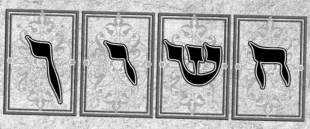

cheshvan

וּדְבָשׁ. הַיּוֹם הַזֶּה יְהוָֹ"ה (וֹהה"י).

The Name Combination for the month of Cheshvan comes from the verses הַשְׁקִיפָה מִמְּעוֹן קָדְשְׁךָ מִן הַשָּׁמַיִם וּבָרֵךְ אֶת עַמְּךָ אֶת יִשְׂרָאֵל וְאֵת הָאֲדָמָה אֲשֶׁר נָתַתָּה לָנוּ כַּאֲשֶׁר נִשְׁבַּעְתָּ לַאֲבֹתֵינוּ אֶרֶץ זָבַת חָלָב וּדְבָשׁ. הַיּוֹם הַזֶּה יְהוָֹ"ה אֱלֹקֶיךָ מְצַוְּךָ לַעֲשׂוֹת אֶת הַחֻקִּים הָאֵלֶּה וְאֶת הַמִּשְׁפָּטִים וְשָׁמַרְתָּ וְעָשִׂיתָ אוֹתָם בְּכָל לְבָבְךָ וּבְכָל נַפְשֶׁךָ, *Gaze down from Your holy abode, from the heavens, and bless Your people Israel, and the ground that You have given us, as You swore to our forefathers, a land flowing with milk and honey. This day, Hashem, your God, commands you to perform these decrees and statutes, and you shall observe and perform them with all your heart and with all your soul (Devarim 26:16-17).*

BEIN ADAM L'CHAVEIRO —
BETWEEN MAN AND HIS FELLOW

חֶשְׁוָן – וּדְבָשׁ. הַיּוֹם הַזֶּה יהו"ה (והה"י).

THE NAME COMBINATION FOR THE MONTH OF CHESHVAN COMES from the verses אֶת הַשְׁקִיפָה מִמְּעוֹן קָדְשְׁךָ מִן הַשָּׁמַיִם וּבָרֵךְ אֶת עַמְּךָ יִשְׂרָאֵל וְאֵת הָאֲדָמָה אֲשֶׁר נָתַתָּה לָנוּ כַּאֲשֶׁר נִשְׁבַּעְתָּ לַאֲבֹתֵינוּ אֶרֶץ זָבַת חָלָב וּדְבָשׁ. הַיּוֹם הַזֶּה יהו"ה אֱלֹקֶיךָ מְצַוְּךָ לַעֲשׂוֹת אֶת הַחֻקִּים הָאֵלֶּה וְאֶת הַמִּשְׁפָּטִים וְשָׁמַרְתָּ וְעָשִׂיתָ אוֹתָם בְּכָל לְבָבְךָ וּבְכָל נַפְשֶׁךָ, *Gaze down from Your holy abode, from the heavens, and bless Your people Israel, and the ground that You have given us, as You swore to our forefathers, a land flowing with milk and honey. This day, Hashem, your God, commands you to perform these decrees and statutes, and you shall observe and perform them with all your heart and with all your soul (Devarim 26:16-17).*

Let us analyze the connection between these verses and the month of Cheshvan.

It is somewhat surprising that Cheshvan should be symbolized by honey, the symbol of sweetness and pleasantness.

It is somewhat surprising that Cheshvan should be symbolized by honey, the symbol of sweetness and pleasantness. Cheshvan is commonly referred to as מַר חֶשְׁוָן, *the bitter month of* Cheshvan, while sweet, pleasant honey represents the opposite of bitterness. *Sefer HaToda'ah* cites two explanations for the prefix *Mar* (Bitterness), which is appended to the name of Cheshvan:

1) There are no festivals in the month of Cheshvan and no reasons to rejoice.

2) Historically, Cheshvan has been a month of hardship — in world history in general, and to *Klal Yisrael* in particular. On a general level, the *Mabul* (Flood) in Noach's time began on the seventeenth of Cheshvan. In Jewish history, Yeravam ben Nevat — the first king of the Ten Tribes, who seceded from David Hamelech's dynasty — created a new festival on the fifteenth of Cheshvan to replace the holiday of *Succos*. This act of open defiance against the Torah caused great anger in heaven toward *Klal Yisrael*.[1]

---

1. Toward the end of King Shlomo's reign, Hashem allowed the ten northern tribes to

Bnei Yissaschar [2] adds that because Yeravam's rebellion against the Davidic kingdom took place in Cheshvan, it became the month when decrees and special taxes targeting the Jews were imposed throughout Jewish history. Because Israel rebelled in Cheshvan against its legitimate government in the time of Yeravam, the nation was punished measure-for-measure by hostile governments during this month.

How can we resolve the apparent contradiction between the historical events that led to Cheshvan being entitled the "bitter" month — *Mar* Cheshvan — and the seemingly anomalous fact that the Name Combination for this month speaks of honey?

IN JEWISH HISTORY, SEVEN IMPORTANT EVENTS OCCURRED OR WILL occur during Cheshvan:

Events Associated with Cheshvan

1) Mesushelach, the only righteous person alive at the time of the *Mabul* (other than Noach and his family), died on the eleventh of Cheshvan. The *Mabul* was delayed, so as not to intrude on seven days of mourning for him.[3]

2-3) Our matriarch Rachel died in childbirth when her son Binyamin was born, on the eleventh of Cheshvan.[4]

4) The construction of the first *Beis HaMikdash* was concluded.[5]

5) *Bnei Yissaschar*[6] teaches that in order to rectify the sin of rebellion against the Davidic dynasty during Cheshvan, all the tribes of Israel will unite under the reign of *Mashiach* ben David during the month of Cheshvan. This reunification will occur simultaneously with the construction and dedication of the Third *Beis HaMikdash*.

All the tribes of Israel will unite under the reign of Mashiach ben David during the month of Cheshvan.

---

rebel against the House of David and set up their own kingdom, with Yeravam ben Nevat serving as their first king. Yeravam felt that he would not be able to fully establish his kingdom as long as the Jews under his new regime would travel to the *Beis HaMikdash*, which remained in the hands of the House of David. He set up two idols, one in the north and one in the south of his kingdom, and created a festival to replace the national pilgrimage of Succos, which begins on the fifteenth of Tishrei. He successfully induced the people to worship his idols and, in case there were loyal Jews who wanted to go to the *Beis HaMikdash*, Yeravam stationed military men to seal the border!

2. 1:2.

3. *Sanhedrin* 108b.

4. *Yalkut Shimoni* 162.

5. *Melachim* I, 6:38.

6. *Chodesh MarCheshvan*, 1:2.

Add to this list the two events we have already mentioned:

6) The *Mabul* began on the seventeenth of Cheshvan.[7]

7) Yeravam ben Nevat fabricated a festival on the fifteenth of Cheshvan.[8]

We are left with a diverse array of events, some positive and some negative, that have occurred or will occur during Cheshvan. Can we find a common thread connecting them all, so that we can understand why the קֹרֵא הַדֹּרוֹת מֵרֹאשׁ, *He Who proclaimed the generations from the beginning* (*Yeshayah* 41:4) arranged for all these events to occur during Cheshvan?

1. Tishrei and Cheshvan: Two Aspects of Avodah

W E WILL NOT SUCCEED IN OUR SERVICE OF HASHEM IF WE try to perfect ourselves in all areas at once. Any attempt to reach all the ultimate pinnacles of success at the same time will fail. This concept is expressed in the respective goals of Tishrei and Cheshvan. Each month directs our focus to a specific form of service, uniquely suited to that month. During the first two months of the Jewish calendar year,[9] Tishrei and Cheshvan, we are called upon to concentrate on different — albeit complementary — forms of service.

Each month directs our focus to a specific form of service, uniquely suited to that month.

THE MONTH OF TISHREI COMPRISES MANY FESTIVALS, ALL OF WHICH focus on perfecting our standing in *Bein Adam l'Makom* — matters pertaining to our relationship with Hashem:

Tishrei: Bein Adam L'Makom

• Rosh Hashanah — Our service of Hashem in the new calendar year begins with our acceptance of His Kingship over the world in general, and over ourselves as individuals, as we pray in each *tefillah,* מְלוֹךְ עַל כָּל הָעוֹלָם כֻּלּוֹ בִּכְבוֹדֶךָ, *reign over the entire universe in Your Glory.*

---

7. *Bereishis* 7:11.

8. *Melachim* I, 12:36.

9. The month of Nissan is actually considered the first of all Jewish months, to which the months of the year and the festivals are counted (See *Shemos* 12:2). The calendar year, however, begins in Tishrei.

- Yom Kippur — We atone for the sins committed against Hashem. In fact, the Mishnah[10] teaches that repentance can atone *only* for sins committed against Him; sins that affect other humans can be rectified only by seeking their forgiveness and by paying for any monetary damages. Only then can repentance avail.

- Succos — Called זְמַן שִׂמְחָתֵנוּ, it is *the Time of our Gladness.* We rejoice in commemoration of the Clouds of Glory[11] and other miracles Hashem performed for Israel after the Exodus from Egypt. *Mishnah Berurah* writes that in order to fulfill the mitzvah of *succah* properly, one should reflect on the miracles Hashem performed for us in the process of removing Israel from Egypt, and especially on the miracle of the Clouds of Glory that the *succah* symbolizes.

- Shemini Atzeres — As *Klal Yisrael's* opportunity to enjoy our nation's personal relationship with Hashem in solitude, this festival is described in Torah as עֲצֶרֶת הִוא, *it is an assembly* (*Vayikra* 23:36). *Rashi* cites *Chazal's* explanation, "[Hashem says,] I am 'detaining' you for an additional day [after the seven days of Succos]. This is akin to a king who invites his children to join him for a celebration for a certain number of days. As that period comes to an end, the king tells his children, 'Please stay with me one more day; it is difficult for me to part from you.'"

- Simchas Torah — The final festival in Tishrei (which, in *Eretz Yisrael*, is celebrated in conjunction with Shemini Atzeres), Simchas Torah was established by the *Geonim*. It allows us to express our joy for having received the Torah. By celebrating the Creator's choice of Israel to receive His ultimate gift, we express our gratitude for having this unique and personal relationship with Hashem.

Clearly, the emphasis of Tishrei is on perfecting our relationship with Hashem.

Clearly, the emphasis of Tishrei is on perfecting our relationship with Hashem.

Cheshvan: Bein Adam L'chaveiro

DURING THE MONTH OF CHESHVAN, ON THE OTHER HAND, THE emphasis of Israel's *avodah* shifts to *bein adam l'chaveiro* — the mitzvos of interacting with other human beings. This is highlighted by the fact that Cheshvan is the first month of the calendar year in which we celebrate Rosh Chodesh.

---

10. *Yoma* 88b; see also *Rambam's Hilchos Teshuvah*, 2:11.
11. Hashem sent pillars of clouds to protect Israel from the elements of the inhospitable Wilderness.

Although the first day of Tishrei is a Rosh Chodesh, it is not identified as a "Rosh Chodesh." We do not announce the arrival of the first of Tishrei on the Shabbos preceding it, as we do on the Shabbos before every other Rosh Chodesh. Nor do we recite *Hallel* or mention Rosh Chodesh in *Ya'aleh Veyavo*, and although we mention the Rosh Chodesh offering in the *Mussaf* of Rosh Hashanah, we do not include the Torah's verses regarding the offering, as we do in the monthly Rosh Chodesh *Mussaf*.

What preeminence can be learned from Rosh Chodesh and applied to Cheshvan?

What preeminence can be learned from Rosh Chodesh and applied to Cheshvan as the first month of each calendar year[12] in which we specifically celebrate Rosh Chodesh?

II. Sun and Moon

THE TALMUD[13] NOTES AN APPARENT CONTRADICTION IN THE Torah's description of the sun and moon. First the Torah refers to them as שְׁנֵי הַמְּאֹרֹת הַגְּדֹלִים, *the two large luminaries,*[14] but then, in the same verse, the Torah refers to the sun as הַמָּאוֹר הַגָּדֹל, *the large luminary,* and to the moon as הַמָּאוֹר הַקָּטֹן, *the small luminary.*

The Talmud explains that both are true. The sun and the moon were originally the same size, but the moon came before Hashem and asked, "Can two kings share the same crown?" Hashem responded, "Go and make yourself smaller." "Because I raised a valid point," countered the moon, "must I shrink myself?"

The he-goat offered on Rosh Chodesh "atones" for Hashem's command that the moon should shrink itself.

The Talmud goes into great detail in describing Hashem's efforts to compensate the moon for its loss in stature, and the moon's refusal to be consoled, until Hashem finally said, "Please bring an atonement offering for me, for shrinking the moon." This is why the Torah describes the atonement sacrifice of Rosh Chodesh as a חַטָּאת לַה', *an atonement for Hashem* (*Bamidbar* 28:15). The Talmud concludes that in the *Beis HaMikdash*, the he-goat offered on Rosh Chodesh "atones" for Hashem's command that the moon should shrink itself.

---

12. See note 9.
13. *Chullin* 9b.
14. *Bereishis* 1:16.

RIF[15] EXPLAINS THAT WHEN WE FOLLOW THE MONTHLY CYCLE OF THE moon and bring an atonement offering on Rosh Chodesh, we return

Consoling the Moon

some of the glory to the shrunken moon. Thus, a key function of the monthly Rosh Chodesh offering was to honor, respect, and pacify the moon that had once been diminished.

Toldos Yaakov Yosef [16] explains this concept further. When the moon complained to Hashem, it thought that it, like the sun, was an independent source of light that could illuminate the world on its own; it was therefore competing with the sun. When Hashem told the moon, "Go shrink yourself," He was saying that if the moon would view itself with humility, it would realize that it is not at all equivalent to the sun; it merely reflects light that emanates from the far-superior sun. When the moon realized that it had overestimated its stature, and that in reality it was inferior to the sun, it felt humiliated. Hashem consoled the moon by commanding Israel to bring the atonement offering on Rosh Chodesh.

Rosh Chodesh is a monthly opportunity for us to reflect on the lessons of this passage from the Talmud. If Hashem was so careful to assuage the feelings of the inanimate moon, how much more should we be careful to treat other human beings with respect and honor? And if the moon was punished so drastically for its haughtiness, Rosh Chodesh should serve as a reminder to be humble.

Another connection between Rosh Chodesh and the need to be considerate of others can be derived from the *Chazal's* reasoning in establishing the number of people who are called to the Torah on Rosh Chodesh. On festivals five people are called to the Torah, but on Rosh Chodesh only four people are honored with *aliyos*. The Talmud[17] explains that *Chazal* did not want to burden working people by adding more time to the prayers on Rosh Chodesh. The consideration *Chazal* had for the needs of those working for a livelihood falls in line with the general theme that Rosh Chodesh is a time to consider our relationships with other people.

Rosh Chodesh is a time to consider our relationships with other people.

We can now understand why we do not celebrate Rosh Chodesh Tishrei in the same manner as we celebrate Rosh Chodesh the rest of the year. On Rosh Hashanah, we focus our efforts toward our relationship with Hashem, and not on our relationships with others. Rosh Chodesh Cheshvan is our first opportunity to focus on those relationships and employ the lessons of Rosh Chodesh in our daily interactions with others.

---

15. *Shevuos* 1b of *Rif* folios.
16. *Parashas Bereishis*.
17. *Megillah* 21a-22b.

III. Bein Adam L'chaveiro and Cheshvan in History

LET US REEXAMINE THE HISTORIC EVENTS THAT OCCURRED IN Cheshvan and see how they all fit the theme of *bein adam l'chaveiro*.

WHY DID NOACH'S GENERATION DESERVE TO BE WIPED OUT? HASHEM told Noach כִּי מָלְאָה הָאָרֶץ חָמָס מִפְּנֵיהֶם, *the earth is filled with robbery from them* (*Bereishis* 6:11). The Talmud[18] notes that

The Mabul

Thievery is punished so severely because theft signifies not only defiance against Hashem, but evil against other humans as well.

Noach's generation had sinned in many ways aside from robbery, but this verse shows that the sin that sealed their fate was robbery. *Ramban* explains that thievery is punished so severely because a person should understand on his own that he should not take what belongs to others — this concept is often called the "Social Contract" — and because theft signifies not only defiance against Hashem, but evil against other humans as well. Only a sin that represented wickedness toward other humans could cause such anger that the entire world had to be wiped out.

Three people are associated with Cheshvan: Mesushelach, Rachel, and Binyamin. All three excelled in their care and concern for others.

Mesushelach is counted as one of the seven "shepherds" of world history.

MESUSHELACH DIED ON 11 CHESHVAN, A WEEK BEFORE THE FLOOD. "He was a complete tzaddik whose every word was in praise of the

Mesushelach

Creator and who reviewed nine hundred orders of the Mishnah."[19] He is counted as one of the seven "shepherds" of world history. David was in the middle, flanked by Adam, Shes, and Mesushelach on his right, and Avraham, Yaakov, and Moshe on his left.[20] Why are these seven people known as shepherds? Because they excelled in their care for others, like a shepherd caring for his flock.

The Midrash describes Mesushelach's concern for the fate of his wicked generation. "The righteous Mesushelach would warn them each day, 'Repent, for if you do not, Hashem will flood the world; your corpses will float in the water like flasks.'" Clearly, he

---

18. *Sanhedrin* 108a.
19. *Yalkut Shimoni, Bereishis* 202.
20. *Succah* 52b.

cared deeply for his fellow humans, and warned them repeatedly not to sin. For what sin was he rebuking them? The sin that precipitated the Flood: that of mistreating other people by stealing their property

OUR MATRIARCH RACHEL IS BEST KNOWN FOR HER SELFLESS ACTION

Rachel
to save her sister from disgrace. As the Midrash[21] relates, when Hashem wanted to destroy the *Beis HaMikdash* because of Israel's sins, Rachel jumped to *Klal Yisrael's* defense, telling Hashem:

> Master of the Universe, You know that your servant Yaakov loved me so deeply that he was willing to tend to my father's flock for seven years in order to marry me. When those seven years were up, the time came for me to marry my husband, but my father decided to switch me with my sister and have my husband marry her. I found out about this plot, and I was very hurt by it. I told my intended husband, and I gave him a set of codes that would allow him to differentiate between my sister and me, so my father could not succeed in switching us. Later, I regretted that decision, swallowed my desire to be married to Yaakov, and had mercy on my sister lest she be turned away in disgrace. That night, when my father switched me for my sister, I gave her all the codes that I had given to my husband, so he should think that she was Rachel. I even crept under their marital bed, and when Yaakov addressed Leah, she remained silent and I spoke from under the bed so he would not recognize her voice. I treated her with kindness; I did not allow jealousy to get the better of me and allow her to be turned away in shame.

There can be no greater perfection in the area of *bein adam l'chaveiro* than that displayed by Rachel.

Binyamin inherited his mother Rachel's outstanding character trait of caring for others.

BINYAMIN INHERITED HIS MOTHER RACHEL'S OUTSTANDING CHARACter trait of caring for others.[22] He had ten children while his brother

Binyamin
Yosef was in Egypt, and he named all of them with words that expressed the pain his brother was experiencing.[23] *Bela*, which means to swallow, was named

21. *Midrash Eichah, Pesichta* 24; see also *Bava Basra* 123a and *Megillah* 13b.
22. *Zohar,* Vol. I, 202b.
23. *Sotah* 36b.

for the fact that Yosef was "swallowed" among the nations of the world. *Becher* — related to the word *bechor,* firstborn — was named for the loss of Rachel's firstborn, and so on.

Futhermore, *Yalkut Shimoni* [24] quotes Binyamin as saying, "From the day my brother Yosef went into exile, I did not wash or comb my hair, and I behaved like a mourner.[25] *Zohar* [26] notes that Binyamin "resembled" his mother, a term that means he shared her primary character traits. She was the exemplar of sensitivity to others; and that trait was found in Binyamin, as well.

The three people associated with Cheshvan excelled in their interactions with others.

Appropriately, therefore, the three people associated with Cheshvan excelled in their interactions with others.

Sharing the Burden

IF WE EXAMINE THESE MIDRASHIM WE FIND THAT THE SPECIFIC AREA of *bein adam l'chaveiro* in which Mesushelach, Rachel, and Binyamin excelled was their ability to share the burden of others (*nosei ba'ol im chaveiro*).

Chochmah Umussar [27] writes that the trait of *nosei be'ol im chaveiro* requires one to go above and beyond the mitzvah of וְאָהַבְתָּ לְרֵעֲךָ כָּמוֹךָ, *Love your fellow as you love yourself,* which requires us only to love our friends in thought and in our hearts. Sharing another person's burden, however, requires us to put ourselves into the shoes of a friend in need, and imagine that we are experiencing all his pain and suffering. We should then think about what we would expect or want our friends to do for us if we were to fall into such a situation, and do it for the friend in need. This character trait applies not only to physical matters; one must tend to his fellow's spiritual well-being as well.

True leaders accept the mantle of leadership out of concern for the welfare of their fellow Jews.

We may assume, continues *Chochmah Umussar,* that this is why the leaders of Israel accepted the burden of leadership. True leaders, such as King David, are not fueled by the desire for the honor that comes with being king. They accept the mantle of leadership out of concern for the welfare of their fellow Jews. Being a leader allows a person to follow in Hashem's ways by helping and perfecting others. In fact, many of our leaders were shepherds, because this trained them to care for others — even if those others were livestock, not human beings — so they could then excel in caring for humans as well.

24. 150.

25. *Zohar,* (Vol. I, 123b) explains that he did not derive pleasure from his marital duties.

26. 202b.

27. Vol. 1, p. 1.

IV. The Beis HaMikdash

THREE EVENTS ASSOCIATED WITH THE *BEIS HAMIKDASH* happened or will happen in Cheshvan: The completion of the construction of the First *Beis HaMikdash*, the rebellion against the House of David, and, according *Bnei Yissaschar*, the Third *Beis HaMikdash* will be built in Cheshvan.

True to the theme of the month, the Mishnah teaches that the *Beis HaMikdash* was the site of unparalleled Jewish unity. Three times a year, millions of Jews converged on Yerushalayim for the festivals, yet, "No one ever said to his friend, 'There is insufficient space for me to stay overnight in Yerushalayim.'"[28] When there is mutual love and dedication to a common ideal, no one resents or complains that others are intruding on his space, just as, in an earlier generation, when the tribes of Israel came together with a sense of mission, to right a grievous wrong, they were united as one — וַיֵּאָסֵף כָּל אִישׁ יִשְׂרָאֵל אֶל הָעִיר כְּאִישׁ אֶחָד חֲבֵרִים, *Then all the men of Israel gathered together at the city, as one man, as comrades (Shoftim* 20:10).

But when the unity among *Klal Yisrael* dissipated because of baseless hatred, the Second *Beis HaMikdash* was destroyed. The Third *Beis HaMikdash* will be built only when we eradicate that hatred and learn to love one another. Since Cheshvan is the month most identified with *bein adam l'chaveiro*, it stands to reason that, as noted above, the Third *Beis HaMikdash* will be built in Cheshvan.

The Third Beis HaMikdash will be built only when we eradicate hatred and learn to love one another.

This would also explain why Yeravam chose Cheshvan as the most suitable month for his fabricated festival. He knew that his regime would survive only if he could unite the tribes under his reign, to replace the unity they felt when traveling to the *Beis HaMikdash*. What better time to try to bring his subjects together than Cheshvan, the month of *bein adam l'chaveiro*?

RETURNING TO OUR FIRST QUESTION: WHY IS THE LETTER COMBINA-tion of *Mar* Cheshvan — a month known for its bitter past — formed from verses mentioning honey, the symbol of sweetness?

The Cedar Tzaddik vs. the Date Tzaddik

In the Scriptural verse alluding to Cheshvan (cited above), *Rashi* comments that the word *d'vash*, honey, refers to honey produced from dates *(temarim)*. *Baal Shem Tov* teaches that there are two types of

---

28. *Avos* 5:7.

tzaddikim, both of whom are alluded to in the verse צַדִּיק כַּתָּמָר יִפְרָח כְּאֶרֶז בַּלְּבָנוֹן יִשְׂגֶּה, *A righteous man will flourish like a date palm; like a cedar in Lebanon he will grow tall (Tehillim 92:13)*. Some tzaddikim are like cedar trees, he explains. They grow tall and strong, perfecting their own spiritual standing. But like cedar trees that do not provide fruit for others to enjoy, such tzaddikim are unwilling to give of their time and energy to help others improve.

Tzaddikim are willing to give of themselves to help others perfect themselves spiritually.

A higher level of righteousness is displayed by tzaddikim who are likened to date palms. Just as a date palm gives off fruit that others can enjoy, these tzaddikim are willing to give of themselves to help others perfect themselves spiritually.[29]

A tzaddik who excels in tending to the needs of others sweetens the world in a spiritual sense.

TAKING THIS ANALOGY ONE STEP FURTHER, THE HONEY EXTRACTED from dates may supply sweetness in a physical sense, but a tzaddik who excels in the *avodah* of Chodesh Cheshvan — tending to the needs of others, and helping them perfect themselves — sweetens the world in a spiritual sense.[30]

Injecting Sweetness Into Cheshvan

Everything in this world has the potential to be used for good or for bad. Historically speaking, Cheshvan has certainly been a difficult and bitter month. It is from that very bitterness, however, that we know that Cheshvan must have the same potential to be the sweetest month of the year. If we learn from the letter combination of Cheshvan — וּדְבַשׁ הַיּוֹם הַזֶּה יהו״ה — to inject the sweetness symbolized by honey into the world, by respecting and caring for others, and helping them improve both physically and spiritually, we can fill the month of *Mar* Cheshvan with everlasting sweetness.

29. *Chazal* teach, "In the place that a *baal teshuvah* [lit. master of repentance] stands, even a perfectly righteous person cannot stand" (*Berachos* 34b). Simply understood, this means that a person who sins and repents can attain spiritual levels unavailable to those who have never sinned. Based on his differentiation between the two types of tzaddikim, *Baal Shem Tov* offers an alternative explanation: A *baal teshuvah* is a tzaddik who gives of himself to help others repent. He is a master of repentance because he influences others to repent and serve Hashem properly. Such a tzaddik can attain levels that tzaddikim consumed with their own growth — even if they become perfect — cannot attain.

30. Interestingly, bee honey, too, is created by a display of unity among hundreds of bees, who selflessly gather pollen from a multitude of flowers and bring it to the hive to be turned into honey.

kislev

וַיַּרְא יוֹשֵׁב הָאָרֶץ הַכְּנַעֲנִי (ויה"ה).

The Name Combination for the month of *Kislev* comes from the verse describing the mourning period for *Yaakov Avinu*: וַיַּרְא יוֹשֵׁב הָאָרֶץ הַכְּנַעֲנִי אֶת הָאֵבֶל בְּגֹרֶן הָאָטָד וַיֹּאמְרוּ אֵבֶל כָּבֵד זֶה לְמִצְרָיִם עַל כֵּן קָרָא שְׁמָהּ אָבֵל מִצְרַיִם אֲשֶׁר בְּעֵבֶר הַיַּרְדֵּן, *When the Canaanite inhabitants of the land saw the mourning in Goren HaAtad, they said, "This is a grievous mourning for Egypt." Therefore, it was named Avel Mitzrayim, which is across the Jordan (Bereishis 50:11).*

Children: The Key to Our Future

כִּסְלֵו – וַיַּרְא יוֹשֵׁב הָאָרֶץ הַכְּנַעֲנִי (ויה"ה).

THE NAME COMBINATION FOR THE MONTH OF KISLEV COMES from the verse describing the mourning period for Yaakov Avinu: וַיַּרְא יוֹשֵׁב הָאָרֶץ הַכְּנַעֲנִי אֶת הָאֵבֶל בְּגֹרֶן הָאָטָד וַיֹּאמְרוּ אֵבֶל כָּבֵד זֶה לְמִצְרָיִם עַל כֵּן קָרָא שְׁמָהּ אָבֵל מִצְרַיִם אֲשֶׁר בְּעֵבֶר הַיַּרְדֵּן, *When the Canaanite inhabitants of the land saw the mourning in Goren HaAtad, they said, "This is a grievous mourning for Egypt." Therefore, it was named Avel Mitzrayim, which is across the Jordan* (Bereishis 50:11).

The connection between the month of Kislev and the Canaanite inhabitants of Eretz Yisrael is strange.

On the surface, the connection between the month of Kislev and the Canaanite inhabitants of *Eretz Yisrael* is strange. In our study of Kislev, we will find a general theme that will explain this cryptic correlation, along with several other factors associated with this month:

- As we have seen in the first half of this volume, *Tur*[1] states that the twelve months of the year correspond, respectively, to the twelve tribes, and, according to *Arizal's* system of identifying the correspondence, Kislev is the month of Binyamin. We shall show the relationship between the tribe and the month.

- One of the vestments of the Kohen Gadol was the *Choshen Mishpat*, which he wore on his chest. In it were set twelve precious stones, each one inscribed with the name of a tribe. The stone of Binyamin was *yashfeh*.[2] We will show its relationship with both Binyamin and the month of Kislev. We will also find how the festival of Chanukah, which begins in Kislev, is related to the month.

Chanukah and Purim are emanations of the festivals.

- *Sfas Emes*[3] writes:

   Chanukah and Purim are emanations of the festivals. Three pilgrimage festivals are mentioned in the Written

---

1. *Orach Chaim* 417.
2. *Bereishis Rabbah* 71:5.
3. *Chanukah* 5641.

Torah, but two additional festivals were instituted later, Purim by prophets and Chanukah by *Chazal*. Chanukah is an emanation of Succos, and Purim is an emanation of Shavuos.

We must understand the relationship between Chanukah and Succos. In the chapter for the month of Teves, we will discuss what Chanukah and Purim have in common.

I. Chanukah:
Educating the Next Generation

LET US BEGIN WITH AN INTERESTING POINT MY FATHER *Z"TL* [the *Avnei Nezer*] mentions frequently.[4] In the *Al Hanissim* of Chanukah — "In the days of Mattisyahu, *son* of Yochanan, and *his children*" — *Chazal* emphasize the concept of parents and children. Why? My father writes as follows:

> "Chanukah" comes from the same root as *chinuch* (education). *Chazal* emphasize that three generations — Yochanan, Mattisyahu, and his children — all followed Hashem. The Chashmonaim's victory was in merit of the continuous righteousness of their family. This continuity guaranteed both physical and spiritual success. The mitzvah of lighting the Chanukah menorah is described by *Chazal* as *"ner ish ubeiso,"* a flame for each man and his household, to teach the centrality of family within the home, and to publicly proclaim the miracle.

The Chashmonaim's victory was in merit of the continuous righteousness of their family.

The Syrian-Greek occupiers in the days of the Chashmonaim understood that Jewish eternity was based on the strength of the chain binding generation to generation. The enemy was determined to break the bond that carries our nation's ideals from father to son — and on a larger scale, from one generation to the next. To do so, they outlawed three key links in that chain: Rosh Chodesh, Shabbos, and Bris Milah.

---

4. This question appears in his work, *Iyunim B'Parashah*, on *Parashas Vayeishev* (pg. 42).

CHAZAL[5] TEACH THAT *KLAL YISRAEL* IS COMPARED TO THE MOON. The specific attribute of the moon that corresponds to us is

Rosh Chodesh

expressed clearly in the text of *Kiddush Levanah*: "To the moon [Hashem] said that it should renew itself as a crown of splendor for those borne [by Him] from the womb, those who are destined to renew themselves like it [the moon] and to glorify their Maker for the sake of His glorious kingdom." *Rashi* explains that the moon serves as a symbol of Israel's power of renewal, and foretells a period in which *Klal Yisrael,* like the moon, will renew itself and glorify its Maker.

The moon has a quality that the sun does not: it grows. The moon is barely visible at the beginning of the month, but it grows and grows, and even though it slowly grows smaller after mid-month until it disappears, it will renew itself again next month. The sun is infinitely bigger and more powerful than the moon, but it is stagnant. it does not grow, it does not develop, and it does not renew itself. In a word, the sun represents the present, and the moon — always changing in one way or another — represents the future.

Like the moon, the Jewish People focuses constantly on the future, when they are "destined to renew themselves and to glorify their Maker for the sake of His glorious kingdom."

SHABBOS, TOO, REPRESENTS THE FUTURE, AS WE SAY AT THE end the Shabbos *Mussaf,* "On Shabbos [the Levites] would say

Shabbos

[in the *Beis HaMikdash*], 'A Psalm, a song for the Sabbath day. A psalm, a song *for the time to come,* for the day that will be entirely Shabbos and contentment for the eternal life." Furthermore, in the Shabbos *Zemiros,* we describe the day as *Me'ein Olam Haba,* "a semblance of the World to Come is the Sabbath day of contentment," for the holiness of Shabbos is a reflection and a taste of the World to Come.

Shabbos also symbolizes the next generation, as the Talmud[6] states, "One who is scrupulous with candle-lighting will have children who are *talmidei chachamim.*" *Rashi* explains, כִּי נֵר מִצְוָה וְתוֹרה אוֹר, *For a commandment is a lamp and the Torah is a light* (Mishlei 6:23), i.e., one who is scrupulous about the

5. *Sanhedrin* 42a.
6. *Shabbos* 23b.

commandment to light Shabbos and Chanukah lamps will merit to see the light of the Torah.

We find further mention of the connection between Shabbos and children in the *Zemiros*: where men and women are referred to with the metaphor of children: הַשּׁוֹמֵר שַׁבָּת הַבֵּן עִם הַבַּת, *Whoever keeps Shabbos*, **the son and the daughter**, and דְּרוֹר יִקְרָא לְבֵן עִם בַּת, *Freedom shall He proclaim for the* **son and the daughter**.

THE THIRD COMMANDMENT OUTLAWED BY THE SYRIAN-GREEKS was the covenant Hashem established with Avraham *and his*

Bris Milah

offspring, as the Torah emphasizes: "God said to Avraham, 'And as for you, you shall keep My covenant — *you and your offspring after you throughout their generations*. This is My covenant which you shall keep between Me and you *and your offspring after you*: every male among you shall be circumcised' " (*Bereishis* 17:9-10).

To sever the connection between generations, the Syrian-Greeks tried to prevent the Jews from performing the three mitzvos that are crucial links in the chain that connects one generation to the next. Chanukah, therefore, is a celebration dedicated to inculcating our children with faith in Hashem's salvation, strengthening the chain that the Syrian-Greeks tried to break.

Chanukah is a celebration dedicated to inculcating our children with faith in Hashem's salvation.

LIKE THE MONTH OF KISLEV, BINYAMIN IS THE TRIBE MOST ASSOCIated with children and the future. Perhaps the clearest indication of

Binyamin Represents the Future

this is the fact that Binyamin had ten children, several more than any of his siblings. We also find that Binyamin himself represents the concept of being a child more than any other tribe does.

As his mother Rachel was dying in childbirth, she named her newborn son *Ben Oni* (Son of My Pain). That name, *Ben Oni*, conveyed her pain at the realization that she would not live to raise and educate him. Yaakov chose to rename him with a more positive name, *Binyamin*, which conveyed that although Binyamin would not have a mother, he would merit special Divine Assistance and would turn out to be a *Ben Yamin, the son* [of Yaakov's] *right hand,* a term of respect and endearment.

Yalkut Shimoni[7] states, "Why did Binyamin merit having the

---

7. *Parashas Vezos HaBerachah,* 957.

Divine Presence rest in his portion [i.e., having the *Beis HaMikdash* built on his land]? This is like a king who had many children, each of whom grew up and settled in a different place. The youngest son was most beloved to his father; he would eat and drink with him, he would lean on him as he came and as he went. The righteous Binyamin, too, was the youngest of the tribes, and Yaakov Avinu would eat and drink with him and lean on him as he came and went. Hashem declared, "I want to rest My Presence in the same place that this righteous man leaned his hands." Thus the verse states (regarding Binyamin), " ... and [Hashem] rests between his shoulders [i.e., the *Beis HaMikdash* will be built among the mountains — the "shoulders" — of Binyamin]" (*Devarim* 33:12).

Hashem declared, "I want to rest My Presence in the same place that this righteous man leaned his hands."

Yaakov's special affinity for his youngest son is also expressed clearly in the Torah, which quotes the tribes telling Yosef — then acting the part of a callous viceroy of Egypt — that Yaakov could not survive the loss of Binyamin because "his soul is so bound up in his soul" (*Bereishis* 44:30).

Binyamin exemplifies the concept of carrying the Jewish heritage on to the next generation.

Binyamin himself exemplifies the concept of carrying the Jewish heritage on to the next generation. Yaakov never stopped grieving over the loss of Yosef, his most beloved son, and Binyamin named all of his ten children in memory of Yosef. The Talmud[8] teaches that the names of Binyamin's children expresses the loss that was felt in the household when Yaakov thought that Yosef had been killed.[9]

Thus, of all the tribes, Binyamin was the most suited to be associated with Kislev and to represent the concept of children and the future of *Klal Yisrael*. This idea also manifests itself in Binyamin's stone in the *Choshen*. *Yashfeh* was a multi-colored stone, which symbolizes that the Jewish people, too, is comprised of many tribes and people of many characteristics. King Shlomo, the wisest of all men, counseled: *"Train the youth according to his way"* (*Mishei* 22:6), because each child is unique and must receive an education that is best for him. *Yashfeh's* numerous colors are thus an accurate repre-

---

8. *Sotah* 36b.

9. Their names were:
Bela — for [Yosef] was swallowed between the nations. (*Nivla ben ha'umos.*)
Becher — [Yosef] was the eldest child of my mother. (*Bechor l'imi.*)
Ashbel — For God made him a captive (*Sheshvao E-l*)
Gera — [Yosef] resided in inns. (*Shegar b'achsanya*)
Naaman — for he was extremely sweet (*Na'im beyoser.*)
Echi — he was my brother, and,
Rosh — was a leader.
Muppim — he learnt from my father's mouth (*mipeh*, from the mouth).
Chuppim — He did not see my *chuppah*, and I did not see his.
Ard — he descended among the nations. (*Sheyarad l'vein ha'umos.*)

sentation of the children of *Klal Yisrael*, and perhaps this is why it was chosen as Binyamin's stone in the *Choshen*.

II. Succos and Chanukah

SFAS EMES TEACHES THAT CHANUKAH EMANATES FROM Succos. We suggest the reason for this relationship is that Succos, like Chanukah, represents the future of Israel through the education and nurture of its children. The commandment of *Succah* emphasizes, "So that *your generations* will know that I caused the Child of Israel to dwell in booths when I took them from the land of Egypt" (*Vayikra* 23:43). Thus, when we sit in a *succah* we must inform our children why we are doing so. An allusion to this is the fact that the initials of the first three words of this verse, לְמַעַן יֵדְעוּ דֹרֹתֵיכֶם, can be rearranged to form the word יֶלֶד, *a child*.[10] Clearly, therefore, Succos is associated with Chanukah, for both emphasize the critical bond of the generations and the need to convey the ideals and obligations of the Torah to our children.

Succos and Chanukah both emphasize the critical bond of the generations and the need to convey the ideals and obligations of the Torah to our children.

Kislev, the Rainbow, and the Letter ס

SEFER YETZIRAH[11] ASSOCIATES TWO MORE CONCEPTS WITH THE month of Kislev: a *keshes* (rainbow), and the letter ס. Both of these concepts fit perfectly with our understanding of Kislev. Just as the emphasis on education during the month of Kislev guarantees the continued spiritual existence of our nation, a rainbow guarantees the physical existence of the world. After the Flood in Noach's time was over, Hashem assured him that never again would He bring such a catastrophe upon the entire world. The sign of that covenant between Hashem and man was the rainbow, as the Torah states:

> And God said, "This is the sign of the covenant that I give between Me and you, and every living being that is with you, *to generations forever.* I have set My rainbow in the cloud, and it shall be a sign of the covenant between Me and the earth. And it shall happen when I place a cloud over the earth and the bow will be seen in the cloud, I will remember My covenant

---

10. *Lev Simchah, Succos* 5743, s.v *L'maan.*
11. 5:9.

between Me and you and every living being among all flesh, and the water shall never again become a flood to destroy all flesh (*Bereishis* 9:12-15).

The letter ס, too, symbolizes the continuing chain of generations, and therefore is associated with Kislev and the rainbow. The first appearance of the letter ס in the context of living creatures is in the word וַיִּסְגֹּר, which appears in the Torah's description of the creation of Chavah (Eve). The letter *samech* is enclosed from all sides, symbolizing the unity that existed between Adam and Chavah when she was created. This unity of man and wife exists in order to make possible the continuation of human life through producing future generations.[12]

All factors associated with Kislev focus on the issue of bearing and raising children, to guarantee the continuity of the world.

We see that all factors associated with Kislev focus on the issue of bearing and raising children, to guarantee the continuity of the world.

CHAZAL TEACH THAT THE POWER OF A CHILD MAY BE GREATER THAN that of his father. The Mishnah[13] lists three kings who will not merit a portion in the World to Come: Yeravam, Achav, and Menasheh. The Talmud[14] asks why Amon (Menasheh's son, who carried on his father's wicked legacy) is not included with those kings. The Talmud answers that Amon was excluded in honor of his son, the righteous Yoshiyahu.

The Power of Children Is Greater Than That of Their Fathers

If so, wonders the Talmud, why wasn't the honor of Chizkiyahu, one of the most righteous of all the kings, sufficient to exclude his son Menasheh from the list?

A son can provide merit for his father, but a father cannot provide merit for his son.

The Talmud answers that a son can provide merit for his father, but a father cannot provide merit for his son. Therefore, Yoshiyahu's merit could rescue his father Amon, but Chizkiyahu's merit could not rescue his son Menashe. Hashem declared, "There is no rescuer from My hand" (*Devarim* 32:39); Avraham could not save Yishmael, and Yitzchok could not save Eisav.

Similarly, a midrash[15] teaches that Avraham Avinu was saved from Nimrod's fiery furnace not in his own merit, but in the merit of his future grandson Yaakov. The midrash illustrates this point with a parable. A governor once sentenced a person to be burnt at the stake. Before the person was put to death, however, the governor decided

---

12. *Olam Ha'osiyos/ Wisdom in the Hebrew Alphabet*, pg. 145.

13. *Sanhedrin* 90a.

14. Ibid. 104a.

15. *Bereishis Rabbah* 63:2.

to calculate his astrological sign, and to his surprise, the condemned prisoner was destined to have a daughter who would marry the king. Said the governor, "It is worthwhile to leave this man alive in honor of his daughter who will marry the king."

So too, continues the midrash, Avraham had been sentenced to die in Nimrod's furnace, but Hashem saw that Yaakov was destined to descend from him, and He said, "It is worthwhile to save Avraham in the merit of Yaakov."[16] This why the verse states, "Therefore, thus said Hashem to the house of Yaakov, who redeemed Avraham" (*Yeshayah* 29:22).

We see clearly that children can provide merit for their fathers. It is true, as we have established above, that the Jewish people and the world at large depend on the transmission from generation to generation, but we dare not lose sight of another aspect of the relationship between parents and children. The growth and good deeds of children are an enormous source of merit for their parents. Can there be a greater incentive to invest in the training, education, and growth of the next generation?

The growth and good deeds of children are an enormous source of merit for their parents.

WE HAVE SEEN THAT MANY FACTORS ASSOCIATED WITH KISLEV FOCUS on the issues of education and child-rearing. Let us now return to the Name Combination of Kislev, which associates the month with the

Canaan: Epitomizing Educational Failure

Canaanites, who were then living in *Eretz Yisrael*. The Canaanites are the polar opposites of *Klal Yisrael* when it comes to education, as we can deduce from an incident that occurred shortly after the *Mabul*:

> Cham, the father of Canaan, saw his father's nakedness and told his two brothers outside …. Noach awoke from his wine and realized what his small son had done to him, and he said, "Cursed is Canaan; a slave of slaves shall he be to his brothers." (*Bereishis* 9:22, 24-25.)

---

16. *Sfas Emes* (*Toldos* 5640) writes that this obviously cannot be taken literally; Avraham Avinu "the greatest of the giants" was certainly worthy of being saved without Yaakov's merit. He explains that Avraham's outstanding character trait was *chessed*, and had he been saved on his own merit it would have been due to Hashem's kindness, which would imply that he was spared even though he was undeserving. Yaakov, however, who epitomizes Torah, represents God's Attribute of *Din*. In saying that Avraham was saved in the merit of Yaakov, the midrash means to say that justice, not only mercy, decreed that he be spared. Thus the midrashic parable refers to a person who was legally guilty of a capital offense, but was saved nonetheless, not because of the ruler's mercy, but because calculated justice required that he remain alive.

Chazal[17] note the seemingly unfair punishment. "Cham sinned, and Canaan is cursed?" they wonder.

Rashi (ibid.) cites one of the midrashic answers: Canaan saw his grandfather's humiliation and told his father and uncles about it.

But the question still remains: if Canaan did not actually commit a sin, but merely related what he saw, why was he cursed?

Perhaps *Chazal* are teaching that Noach understood the underlying reason for Canaan's base behavior. It stemmed from an extreme spiritual malady, and Noach realized that Canaan's underlying character faults would be passed on to his descendants, who would follow his path of immorality and perversity. Therefore, he delivered his curse to Canaan.

History proves that Noach's assessment of Canaan was correct. The Talmud[18] records the five clauses that comprised Canaan's last will and testament to his children: "Love each other, love robbery, love immorality, hate your masters, and don't speak the truth." Just as Noach foresaw, Canaan commanded his children to develop the worst character traits possible! This is diametrically opposed to the values that Judaism inculcates in its young.

Where did Canaan learn to enjoy and propagate wickedness? *Ibn Ezra* writes that by restating the obvious, that Cham was the father of Canaan, the Torah means to teach that both of them were wicked, and "the sons follow the ways of their fathers." *Sforno* echoes this thought, writing that "Cham was similar to Canaan, who was known for his wickedness — Cham 'fathered' Canaan's wickedness." It is true that all Canaan did was laugh at Noach's shame and tell others about it, but that in itself was a mirror of his character. It was a dangerous, accursed character, one that Noach rightfully condemned.

WE CAN NOW UNDERSTAND WHY THE VERSE REGARDING CANAAN was chosen as the source for the Name Combination of Kislev. As we

Kislev's Name Combination: A Study in Opposites

have seen, the positive symbols of Kislev highlight the Jewish attitude toward education and childrearing — the rainbow that represents the continuous chain of generations, the letter *samach* that highlights the unity of husband and wife and their preparation for the future, and above all the educational theme of Chanukah. This

The positive symbols of Kislev highlight the Jewish attitude toward education and childrearing.

---

17. *Bereishis Rabbah* 36:7.
18. *Pesachim* 113b.

concern for our children's future and their spiritual growth, and the intense efforts we are willing to invest into them are primary themes of Kislev.

By placing Canaan — the embodiment of corrosive education — in the forefront of our consciousness as we enter this month, we become more motivated to invest exhaustive efforts to ensure that our children choose the path of the Torah, and not, *chas v'Shalom*, the path of Canaan.

TEVES

לַה' אִתִּי וּנְרוֹמְמָה שְׁמוֹ (היה"ו).

The Name Combination for the month of Teves comes from the final letters of a phrase in the verse גַּדְּלוּ לַה' אִתִּי וּנְרוֹמְמָה שְׁמוֹ יַחְדָּו, Declare the greatness of Hashem with me, and let us exalt his Name together (Tehillim 34:4).

A Good Eye vs. an Evil Eye

טֵבֵת – לַה׳ אִתִּי וּנְרוֹמְמָה שְׁמוֹ (היה"ו).

T HE NAME COMBINATION FOR THE MONTH OF TEVES COMES from the final letters of a phrase in the verse גַּדְּלוּ לַה׳ אִתִּי וּנְרוֹמְמָה שְׁמוֹ יַחְדָּו, *Declare the greatness of Hashem with me, and let us exalt his Name together* (*Tehillim* 34:4).

In order to understand how this verse corresponds to Teves, we must first examine several other factors associated with this month and with Chanukah, which begins in Kislev and ends in Teves.

- Rosh Chodesh Teves is celebrated during Chanukah, making it the only Rosh Chodesh that coincides with a Yom Tov. [As we have noted in our discussion of Tishrei, the Rosh Chodesh aspect of that month is subsumed in Rosh Hashanah.] However, on the surface, at least, the fundamental principals of Rosh Chodesh Teves and Chanukah are diametrically opposed. Teves is considered a difficult month — for *Klal Yisrael* in particular, and for the world as a whole. Rav Tzaddok HaKohen of Lublin[1] considers Teves "the lowliest of the months," and *Zohar*[2] writes that Teves is one of three months[3] in which strict and dangerous justice reigns in the world.

Based on *Ravad* (to *Yeshayah* 13:21), Rav Tzaddok writes further that the *mazal* of Teves is *Gedi*, a young goat, which alludes to Eisav's portion in this world, since Eisav is called *Sa'ir*, a mature he-goat.

Zohar refers to Teves as the "*yemei hara'ah*, the bad days." Elaborating on this melancholy aspect of Teves, *Sfas Emes* notes that Teves is a month in which the Divine Presence is hidden from us, and therefore Hashem compensated for it by having Chanukah precede and include Rosh Chodesh Teves. In

Teves is a month in which the Divine Presence is hidden from us, and therefore Hashem compensated for it by having Chanukah precede and include Rosh Chodesh Teves.

---

1. *Tzvi LaTzaddik,* 7th day of *Chanukah,* 17.
2. *Shemos* 12a.
3. Tammuz and Av are the others.

a sense, He prepared the antidote of Chanukah before the malady of Teves. Chanukah is a joyous occasion when we praise and thank Hashem in order to publicize the miracles that occurred in the days of the Chashmonaim.

GIVEN THE ABOVE, WHY, OF ALL THE MONTHS, WAS THE LOWLY, JUDG-mental month of Teves designated to coincide with the festivity of Chanukah?

Teves and Chanukah

- There are two versions of *Sefer Yetzirah's* description of the creation of Teves. *Arizal's* version states that Hashem crowned רוגז, *anger* with the letter *ayin,* combining them and using them to create the *gedi* in the world and Teves in the yearly calendar. The text of the *Geonim,* however, is much different. According to them, *Sefer Yetzirah* states that Hashem presented Teves with a combination of the letter *ayin* and שְׂחוֹק, *laughter.* Although the two versions seem to contradict one another, R' Tzaddok writes that both versions are correct: "These and those are the words of the Living God." How can these opposites — anger and laughter — reside together in the same month?

- Chanukah is called a Yom Tov, as the Talmud[4] states, "[*Chazal*] established the days of Chanukah as *Yamim Tovim* [on which] to praise and thank Hashem." *Shem MiShmuel* notes that the term Yom Tov implies that it is forbidden to perform *melachah* (forms of labor prohibited on Shabbos and/or festivals).[5] If so, why is labor permitted on the "yom tov" of Chanukah?

- The Talmud[6] rules that a person who *sees* Chanukah flames should recite the blessing of שֶׁעָשָׂה נִסִּים, *Who performed miracles.*[7]

How can these opposites — anger and laughter — reside together in the same month?

---

4. *Shabbos* 21b.

5. The Talmud notes that *Megillas Esther* refers to Purim as a Yom Tov in one place, but later refers to it only as a day of feasting and happiness, with no mention of Yom Tov. The Talmud explains that the leaders of the time wanted to make into a full Yom Tov, including a moratorium on *melachah,* but the people accepted only the feasting and joy upon themselves, not the prohibition of *melachah.* Thus, the appearance of the term Yom Tov in the *Megillah* refers to the original proposal of the leaders of the time; the omission later on conveys the actual *halachah.* Hence, the term Yom Tov is considered synonymous with a moratorium on *melachah.*

6. *Shabbos* 23a.

7. This refers only to a person who has not lit Chanukah candles himself and is not going to light at any point later that evening.

Tosafos[8] notes that this is the only instance in which we recite a blessing upon merely seeing a mitzvah that was performed by someone else. We do not recite a blessing if we see a *succah*, *lulav*, or matzah. Why were Chanukah flames singled out for this distinction? *Tosafos* explains that there is a special love for the miracles of Chanukah, but does not explain *why* these miracles are more beloved than the miracles that we celebrate on Purim, Pesach, or any other festival.

Since a portion of Chanukah is celebrated in the month of Teves, we will also explore the relationship between Teves and the question of why Chanukah is the only Yom Tov in which we are permitted to perform *melachah* and on which we make a *berachah* for merely seeing the mitzvah of the day.

I. Rosh Chodesh vs. Chanukah — Natural vs. Supernatural

OUR FIRST STEP TOWARD ANSWERING THESE QUESTIONS IS TO examine the underlying concepts of Rosh Chodesh and Chanukah. As an introduction, however, we will first examine the difference between Chanukah and Rosh Hashanah.

NESIVOS SHALOM[9] WRITES THAT THERE ARE TWO KINDS OF DIVINE Jurisdiction with which Hashem controls the world. The standard

Two Kinds of Conduct

form of Divine Jurisdiction functions on the principles of "time and order," meaning that God's blessings will flow according to the laws of nature, without any apparent supernatural occurrences. Rain will fall and crops will grow in season, and business dealings will be successful, but not in a manner that suggests Divine intervention. Of course, a person's degree of success or failure, of good health or illness, and so on will be based on his individual level of merit, as determined by the Divine judgment on Rosh Hashanah.

But there is also a second, higher form of Divine Jurisdiction that is beyond the principles of time and order. This form is controlled directly by Hashem, Who — in His infinite mercy — can provide a steady flow of abundant blessings. Each member of *Klal Yisrael* can

---

8. *Succah* 46a s.v. *Haroeh*.
9. *Chanukah*, p. 9.

receive this abundance at any point during the year by strengthening his or her faith in Hashem. To make this possible, Hashem invests people not only with natural spiritual potential, but also the potential for extraordinary accomplishment.

A person can serve Hashem on two levels. If a person is satisfied with the level of service that comes naturally to him, without attempting to go beyond his natural abilities and elevating his nature, then Hashem does not change nature for him, either. Such a person's world will follow the standard principles of time and order. But if someone throws all his strength into the service of Hashem, going above and beyond his natural abilities, Hashem responds in kind. If such a person is in situation that endangers his survival, Hashem will perform a miracle and save him.

The festivals of Chanukah and Purim signify the supernatural form of Divine Jurisdiction, concludes *Nesivos Shalom*. They light up the darkness of the long exile. If Israel were to rely on its natural strength, we would not have been able to survive the difficult exile. We can hope to survive only if we draw the supernatural form of Divine Jurisdiction upon ourselves, just as the Chasmonaim did on Chanukah and Mordechai and Esther did on Purim.

THE SACRED LITERATURE STATES THAT THE FINAL SEAL ON A PERSON's judgment for the year comes on Chanukah. *Nesivos Shalom*

Chanukah — The Final Seal

notes that this idea fits perfectly with his explanation of the uniqueness of Chanukah and Purim. On Rosh Hashanah we are judged through the "regular" form of Divine Jurisdiction, and we are evaluated based on how much reward or punishment we deserve, but Chanukah and Purim offer an opportunity for people to receive *more* than their deeds entitle them to. The extraordinary dedication of the Chasmonaim and Mordechai and Esther paved the way for us, making these times of the year particularly propitious for those who want to merit special Divine Jurisdiction. Chanukah and Purim provide us with yearly opportunities, to show Hashem that we are ready to invest supernatural energy into serving Him. If we capitalize on these opportunities, then Hashem — in His infinite mercy — will follow suit and provide us with more than we naturally deserve to have.

This follows the rule of צִלְּךָ 'ה, *Hashem is your protective Shade* (*Tehillim* 121:5), which the *Baal Shem Tov* and others render homiletically as "Hashem is your Shadow." Just as a shadow corresponds completely to the movement of the person, so, too, God's conduct with us reflects our own behavior. If we are kind to others, He is kind

Chanukah and Purim provide us with yearly opportunities to show Hashem that we are ready to invest supernatural energy into serving Him.

to us. If we make the effort to extend ourselves to serve Him without reservation, He will set aside the natural laws and deal with us in a supernatural manner — in the manner symbolized by Chanukah and Purim.

Rosh Hashanah represents the natural, and Chanukah represents the supernatural.

In summation, Rosh Hashanah represents the natural, and Chanukah represents the supernatural. Quite appropriately, Chanukah is celebrated for eight nights, and it is well known in Rabbinic literature that seven represents nature and eight represents the supernatural.

Rosh Chodesh is associated with the natural order of the world — not only because its date is determined by the natural cycle of the moon, but also because Rosh Chodesh is an occasion for atonement, similar to the Days of Awe. There is a long-standing custom to observe the day before Rosh Chodesh as *Yom Kippur Kattan* (a "Miniature" Day of Atonement). Special supplications are recited at *Minchah*, in which we beg for atonement for the sins we committed in the previous month.[10]

Rosh Chodesh Teves contains both forms of Divine Jurisdiction. It follows the natural form associated with Rosh Chodesh; it is also associated with the supernatural form of Divine Jurisdiction.

We can assume, then, that Rosh Chodesh works on the same pathway as Rosh Hashanah, with the "natural" form of Divine Jurisdiction. If so, Rosh Chodesh Teves contains *both* forms of Divine Jurisdiction. On one hand, it follows the natural form associated with Rosh Chodesh; on the other hand, since it is celebrated during Chanukah, it is also associated with the supernatural form of Divine Jurisdiction.

II. The Natural and Supernatural Complement Each Other

ALTHOUGH THE NATURAL AND SUPERNATURAL MODES SEEM TO be contradictory, the truth is that these two forms of Divine Jurisdiction do not contradict each other at all — they parallel and complement one another. In the familiar dictum of the Sages: "The One who commanded oil to burn, commanded vinegar to burn."

Chazal teach that there is no real difference between "nature" and

---

10. *Mishnah Berurah* (417:4) cites *Ramak* as the source for this custom and explains that this *tefillah* is in place of the he-goat that would be slaughtered in the *Beis HaMikdash* as a *mussaf*-offering on Rosh Chodesh. Additional proof comes from the *Mussaf* prayer on Rosh Chodesh, in which we refer to Rosh Chodesh as זְמַן כַּפָּרָה לְכָל תּוֹלְדוֹתָם, *a time for atonement for all their actions*. (*Beis Yosef* explains that while the word תּוֹלְדוֹתָם usually means "offspring," it occasionally refers to one's actions. Its appearance in this passage follows that usage.)

miracles — Hashem controls both equally, as expressed eloquently in the book entitled *Eileh Heim Moadoi*:[11]

Nature is no more logical than miracles. "Natural" events are miracles that occur frequently, while "miracles" are unusual events that occur once, for a limited period of time. The briefer the phenomenon, the more miraculous it seems; if it happens over and over again, the novelty fades until we barely notice it. What we refer to as "miracles" actually prove that "nature" is supernatural. Conversely, nature highlights the miracles. We can appreciate miracles only when they are painted on a backdrop of the laws of the familiar laws of nature. The break from everyday routine allows us to appreciate the sudden departure from the normal order.

Truthfully, then, there is no difference between the week of Creation and the week of Chanukah, except that the phenomena of Creation repeat themselves continuously. Had we been alive at the time of Creation, we would have perceived the first week as a series of supernatural, miraculous events. It was only after the same phenomena repeated themselves week after week that humankind began to view them as routine. Had the Chanukah oil kept burning continuously, it would no longer be considered a miracle, and we would no longer understand the need to recite a blessing over it.

Chazal[12] rule that a person who has enough money for only one candle for Shabbos Chanukah should use it as a Shabbos candle, and not for the Chanukah flame. The reason may be because the miracle of Creation that we celebrate through Shabbos observance is no less phenomenal than the miracle of Chanukah. The light of the seven days of Creation transcends all other forms of light. The superficial observer sees nothing unusual about the original light, because it is veiled by the constant repetition of nature, but its bright rays are not missed by a perceptive person who pierces the shell of nature and reaches the inner depth of Creation.

The miracle of Creation that we celebrate through Shabbos observance is no less phenomenal than the miracle of Chanukah.

Thus there is no real difference between nature and miracles — they are two sides of the same coin. Hashem's control of the universe, which usually hides under the mantle of nature, occasionally breaks through nature and becomes evident in the miracles He performs.

---

11. *Chanukah*, p. 11.
12. *Shabbos* 23b; *Orach Chaim* 678:1.

WE CITED TWO SEEMINGLY CONTRADICTORY VERSIONS OF *SEFER Yetzirah*. One version stated that Hashem crowned the month of

Two Ayins — Ayin Tovah and Ayin Ra'ah

Teves with the letter ע and with anger; the other stated that He crowned it with the letter ע and with laughter. We also cited R' Tzaddok's teaching that both are true, and wondered how this could be. We can resolve this contradiction through a proper understanding of the letter ע.

The letters of the Hebrew alphabet can be written out to follow their pronunciation. The letter ע is thus spelled out as עַיִן, which is also the Hebrew word for an *eye*.

Perceptive vision permits us to interpret and appreciate the depth of the object we are viewing.

We can assume that the letter ע represents the perceptive vision that permits us to interpret and appreciate the depth of the object or subject we are viewing. When using this sort of vision, different people "see" the same thing differently, depending on their levels of intelligence and depth. One person will interpret a stimulus one way, and another person might interpret it in exactly the opposite way.

To take this concept one step further, not only can two people see things differently, but a person may have "split vision." With one eye — his *ayin tovah* — he will interpret all events positively, while with the other eye — his *ayin ra'ah* — he will interpret them negatively. As the Kotzker Rebbe remarked, a person was given two eyes so that he could "see" the world with two viewpoints: with one eye he can focus on the greatness of Hashem, and with the other eye, he can focus on his own insignificance.[13]

With one eye he can focus on the greatness of Hashem, and with the other eye, he can focus on his own insignificance.

Since the letter ע represents the ability to see things from different perspectives, the two versions of *Sefer Yetzirah* do not contradict each other at all. A person can choose to use his eyes to see either anger or laughter; if he uses his "good eye" to view an event, he will see laughter, and if he uses his "evil eye" to view those very same events he will see anger.

Moreover, it is possible to transform anger into laughter, as *Shem MiShmuel* writes:

> Hashem crowned the letter ע upon anger — that is to say that when we use our "good eye" we can change bad into good. This is

─────────────

13. The *Midrash* (*Tanchuma Parashas Korach*) states that Korach began his rebellion against Moshe Rabbeinu because, "*eino hita'aso* — his eye made him err." Why his *eye*, in singular, and not his *eyes*?

According to the Kotzker, we can suggest that Korach's mistake was to use one eye to focus only on the greatness of Hashem. His fault was that he did not use his other eye to focus on his own lowliness.

the principle of Teves, which, according to *Arizal*, corresponds to the right eye, which is the "good eye" that can change anger into laughter. Similarly, even a wicked person still has hope, because he can become a good person — and Teves is a particularly auspicious time for such a transformation to take place.

BASED ON THESE INSIGHTS, WE CAN UNDERSTAND WHY TEVES — a "lowly month," a month when strict justice reigns in the world — enjoys the great illumination of the Chanukah lights.

Transforming Anger Into Laughter and Bad Into Good

By the virtue of its association with the letter ע, Teves provides us with an opportunity to transform events or concepts from one extreme to the other by using our *ayin tovah* to view them positively. This principle is discussed by *Shem MiShmuel*, who notes that according to *Arizal*, who specifies the organ of the body that corresponds to each month, Teves corresponds to the right eye, which is the *ayin tovah*, the good eye.

An *ayin tovah*, continues *Shem MiShmuel*, is the diametric opposite of jealousy. When the Chashmonaim defeated the Greeks — who were jealous of the Jews — and established the holiday of Chanukah that we celebrate (partially) during Teves, we received an *ayin tovah*, the opposite of jealousy. Anger is rooted in jealousy; and, indeed, the first angry person in the Torah is Kayin, who was so jealous of his brother Hevel that he killed him. When *Sefer Yetzirah* states that Hashem crowned Teves with the letter ע, it means that the *ayin tovah* of *Klal Yisrael* defeated the anger of the Syrian-Greeks, and that is the fundamental concept of the month of Teves.

Thus the correlation between Chanukah and Teves represents our ability to use an *ayin tovah* to transform anger into laughter and bad into good. It stands to reason, therefore, that this time of the year becomes a test for everyone. Therefore, *Shem MiShmuel* writes, a person must be extremely careful not to become angry during Teves, since it is a month when anything can be transformed and we must be very careful not to let things turn for the worse. We should attempt to make positive changes in our character and behavior during Teves, for even a person who normally does not act properly can transform himself into a good person during this month.

The correlation between Chanukah and Teves represents our ability to use an ayin tovah to transform anger into laughter and bad into good.

We can further expand this concept with an amazing insight quoted by Rabbi Avrohom Schorr *shlit"a*.[14] The Torah quotes Yehu-

---

14. In his discourse on *Parashas Vayeishev* 5762.

dah's[15] friend as saying, אַיֵּה הַקְּדֵשָׁה הִוא בָעֵינַיִם עַל הַדָּרֶךְ, *Where is the prostitute, the one at the crossroads by the road? Tiferes Shlomo* elucidates this verse homiletically: אַיֵּה הַקְּדֵשָׁה, *where is holiness?*[16] הִוא בָעֵינַיִם, *it is in the eyes.* The more a person guards his eyes from seeing improper sights, the more holiness can take hold in his body.

Ohr Yitzchak writes that the only body parts that can be affected by the tiniest speck of sand are the eyes, because the eyes are so spiritual that they cannot bear even the smallest interference from the material world. The dwelling place of the soul is in the eyes; and the reason we are careful to close a person's eyes as soon as he dies is because the forces of impurity will enter the lifeless body through the organ where the spirit resided.

The eyes have such great power that they can enable a person to leap to the summit of holiness.

The eyes have such great power that, used optimally, they can enable a person to leap to the summit of holiness. Because of their ability to change bad into good, and because they are the resting place of the spirit, one must guard them very carefully.

III. Blessing on Seeing Chanukah Lights — Controlling One's Sight

Chanukah lights can "repair" a person's spiritual vision, which is why we recite a blessing upon seeing them.

W E CAN NOW APPRECIATE ON A DEEPER LEVEL THE connection between Chanukah and Teves. Rabbi Schorr writes that the Chanukah lights can "repair" a person's spiritual vision, which is why we recite a blessing upon *seeing* them. We may also suggest that the power of the Chanukah lights comes from their association with the month of Teves, which Hashem crowned with *ayin*, the eye.

To take this one step further, perhaps the reason Chanukah is deemed a Yom Tov — even though labor is permitted — is because its capacity to perfect and repair the spirituality of our eyes is so extraordinary that it can truly be on par spiritually with a Yom Tov.

---

15. *Bereishis* 38:21.

16. *Tiferes Shlomo* interprets the word *kedeishah* in this verse to refer to *kedushah* (holiness).

IN CONCLUSION, WE FIND THAT THE IDEAS WE DEVELOPED FIT together like pieces of a puzzle.

The Eyes Connect Natures and Miracles

We started with the idea that Rosh Chodesh Teves and Chanukah seem to represent opposites — Rosh Chodesh represents nature and Chanukah represents miracles. We found, however, that nature and miracles are not contradictory at all; on the contrary — they complement one another. We label something as a miracle only because it is outside of our normal experience while "nature" is normal because we are accustomed to it. The truth is, however, that both are manifestations of God's will; what we consider nature is actually a series of miracles that occur with reliable frequency.

This idea fits nicely with the correlation between *ayin* and Chodesh Teves. Just as an *ayin tovah* can change bad into good, so too, all events that occur in this world can be seen as miracles or as nature, depending on the way we *see* (or interpret) them.

FINALLY, WE GO BACK TO THE NAME ASSOCIATION FOR THE MONTH of Teves, which comes from the verse גַּדְּלוּ לַה׳ אִתִּי וּנְרוֹמְמָה שְׁמוֹ יַחְדָּו

Exalting Hashem in Unity

Declare the greatness of Hashem with me, and let us exalt his Name together (*Tehillim* 34:4). This verse expresses the idea that all the myriad, disparate parts of the universe can come together to declare and exalt Hashem's greatness. Man's challenge is to turn chaos into harmony, disunity into unity.

Man's challenge is to turn chaos into harmony, disunity into unity.

By separating the upper waters from the lower waters on the second day of Creation, God set in motion the conflicting drives and desires that cause rifts and conflict. However, this should not be the permanent condition of the world. Through the verse associated with Teves, David HaMelech calls all parts of Creation to join together to exalt His Name in unison.

The splitting of the waters introduced a competitive spirit into the world, but the destructiveness of that spirit can be reduced and removed by using our *ayin tovah* — especially during the month of Teves — to discover the ultimate purpose of all components of the spiritual world. Good and bad, laughter and anger, nature and miracles will come together to *declare the greatness of Hashem ... exalt His Name together.*

shevat

הָמֵר יְמִירֶנּוּ וְהָיָה הוּא (היו"ה).

*T*he Name Combination for the month of *Shevat* comes from the penultimate verse of *Sefer Vayikra:* לֹא יְבַקֵּר בֵּין טוֹב לָרַע וְלֹא יְמִירֶנּוּ וְאִם הָמֵר יְמִירֶנּוּ וְהָיָה הוּא וּתְמוּרָתוֹ יְהְיֶה קֹדֶשׁ לֹא יִגָּאֵל, *He shall not distinguish between good and bad and he should not substitute for it; and if he does substitute for it, then it and its substitute shall be holy, it may not be redeemed (Vayikra 27:33).*

Decrees and Statutes

שְׁבַט – הָמֵר יְמִירֶנּוּ וְהָיָה הוּא (הי״ה).

THE NAME COMBINATION FOR THE MONTH OF SHEVAT COMES from the penultimate verse of *Sefer Vayikra*: לֹא יְבַקֵּר בֵּין טוֹב לָרַע וְלֹא יְמִירֶנּוּ וְאִם הָמֵר יְמִירֶנּוּ וְהָיָה הוּא וּתְמוּרָתוֹ יִהְיֶה קֹדֶשׁ לֹא יִגָּאֵל, *He shall not distinguish between good and bad and he should not substitute for it; and if he does substitute for it, then it and its substitute shall be holy, it may not be redeemed* (27:33). This teaches that once an animal has been designated as an offering, it is forbidden to substitute a different animal for it — whether the substitute is better or worse than the original offering. If one attempts to do so, both animals are holy.

Once an animal has been designated as an offering, it is forbidden to substitute a different animal for it.

In order to understand the enigmatic correlation between the laws of *temurah* (substitution for an offering) and the month of Shevat, we will analyze the laws of *temurah*, but first, we must note several factors regarding Shevat; specifically, Rosh Chodesh Shevat:

- Moshe began to explain the Torah on the first day of the eleventh month. On that day —Rosh Chodesh Shevat — Moshe began to teach *Sefer Devarim*, which is also called *Mishneh Torah*, literally, a repetition of the Torah. *Tosafos*[1] state that *Mishneh Torah* is a review of what has already been taught in the first four books of the Chumash. *Ramban*[2] writes that Moshe repeated the commandments of the earlier books of the Torah to caution Israel to fulfill them. He also explained them, and added some commandments that were not mentioned in the other books.

Netziv[3] offers a different perspective on *Mishneh Torah*:

Devarim requires the nation to toil in Torah study in order to understand the nuances of the Written Torah and to elucidate its implicit lessons.

Much of *Sefer Devarim* is devoted to elaboration and explanation of commandments that were given previously. Thus, *Devarim* requires the nation to toil in Torah study in order to understand the nuances of the Written Torah and to elucidate its implicit lessons. This level of analysis and understanding is called Talmud [just as the Talmud analyzes and elaborates upon the

---

1. *Gittin* 2a, s.v. *Hameivi Get*.
2. Introduction to *Sefer Devarim*.
3. Ibid.

Mishnah]. Moshe Rabbeinu's many lengthy admonitions were focused on persuading Israel to devote itself to this task. *Devarim* is therefore known as *Mishneh Torah*, from the word *shinun*, which means deep, clear analysis.

According to all explanations of the name *Mishneh Torah*, we must understand why it was necessary for Moshe to repeat the commandments that he had taught and reviewed for forty years.

- In a significant sense, the first of Shevat is considered the "*Mattan Torah*" for the generation that had not been at Sinai. *Ibn Ezra* writes:

> Moshe began to teach the children born in the Wilderness what had happened to their parents. He taught them all of the *mitzvos* — including the Ten Commandments that their parents heard from Hashem — so that they [their offspring] would hear them now from His trusted representative.

Moshe chose Rosh Chodesh Shevat as the day to review the Torah, and to analyze and explain it to the Jews born in the Wilderness. *Likkutei Yehudah* quotes *Chiddushei HaRim* that a date specified in the Torah is an "important matter"; therefore we will examine what is so significant about the day when Moshe Rabbeinu began to review the Torah.

Moshe chose Rosh Chodesh Shevat to review the Torah and to analyze and explain it to the Jews born in the Wilderness.

- We find that the Moshe repeated the Torah in more depth than before: הוֹאִיל מֹשֶׁה **בֵּאֵר** אֶת הַתּוֹרָה הַזֹּאת *Moshe began **explaining** the Torah* (*Devarim* 1:5). What was it about this day that made it necessary to explain the Torah in greater depth?

I. Devarim, Chukim, and Mishpatim — Three Aspects of the Torah's Teachings

WE FIND INSTANCES IN WHICH THE COMMANDMENTS ARE divided into the categories of דְּבָרִים, *statements*; חוּקִים, *decrees*; and מִשְׁפָּטִים, *laws* or *ordinances*. For instance:

- שָׁם שָׂם לוֹ חֹק וּמִשְׁפָּט וְשָׁם נִסָּהוּ, *There He established for [the nation] a decree and a law, and there he tested it* (*Shemos* 15:25).

- מַגִּיד דְּבָרָיו לְיַעֲקֹב חֻקָּיו וּמִשְׁפָּטָיו לְיִשְׂרָאֵל, *He related His Word to Jacob, His decrees and laws to Yisrael* (*Tehillim* 147:19).

What is the difference between words, decrees, and laws, and why is the term "words" applied to Yaakov and the terms "decrees and laws" applied to Yisrael?

The commentators throughout the ages have dealt with the division of the mitzvos, and have given us many possible explanations of the categories:

1) A midrash[4] states that *devarim*, words, refers to the teachings that are explicit in the Torah; *chukim*, decrees, are the Midrashic teachings derived from the Torah; and *mishpatim*, laws, are the halachic portions of the Torah.

Devarim refers to the Written Torah, chukim are expositions based on the use of traditionally ordained methods of derivation, and mishpatim are the laws.

According to *Netziv*,[5] *devarim* refers to the Written Torah, *chukim* are expositions based on the use of traditionally ordained methods of derivation, and *mishpatim* are the laws.

2) *Mikdash Me'at* on *Tehillim* cites another explanation from *Mahari ibn Yachiye*: Three terms are listed (in *Tehillim* 147:19), *davar*, *chok*, and *mishpat*, for the *mitzvos* of the Torah are split into three groups:

Eidos — sometimes referred to as *devarim* — refer to mitzvos that commemorate a specific happening or concept, such as fulfilling the Pesach mitzvos to commemorate the Exodus from Egypt.

Chukim are mitzvos for which no reason is given.

Mishpatim are mitzvos that are self-understood and need no explanation.

Mishpatim seem so logical that all the nations of the world would adopt them, but the Psalmist declares, לֹא עָשָׂה כֵן לְכָל גּוֹי וּמִשְׁפָּטִים בַּל יְדָעוּם, *He did not do so for any other nation; such judgments — they know them not* (ibid. 147:20). Inasmuch as all nations have man-made laws formulated according to their level of wisdom, their laws often do not produce the desired results, and in that sense they are not correct. The laws of the Torah, however, are righteous, as the Torah states, "And which is a great nation that has righteous decrees and ordinances" (*Devarim* 4:8). When the Psalmist wrote that "they know them not," he meant that their laws are not correct.

The laws of the Torah are righteous.

---

4. *Tanchumah Shoftim* 1.
5. *Herchav Davar, Vayikra* 18:1.

These explanations define the respective terms, but they do not explain why *devarim* are associated with Yaakov and *chukim* and *mishpatim* with Yisrael

AS WE SAW, THE NAME COMBINATION FOR SHEVAT COMES FROM A verse that prohibits the substitution of an animal for a designated offering.

Temurah: An Enigmatic Decree

There are actually three parts to this mitzvah: two prohibitions — not to distinguish between bad and good animals, and not to substitute — and also a positive commandment that if one transgressed and impermissibly declared an animal to be a substitute, both animals remain consecrated.

Many of the laws of *temurah* seem to be inexplicable. For instance, the Mishnah teaches that only if an *individual* substitutes an animal are both animals consecrated. But if the community or even two partners attempt to make a substitution, the second animal does not become holy. Nevertheless, those who attempted to make such a substitution are punished with lashes for transgressing a Torah prohibition — even though their intention did not take effect.

INDEED, THE PROHIBITION AGAINST SUBSTITUTION OF AN OFFERING is somewhat surprising, because the very concept of using an animal

Korban — Atonement Through Substitution

as an offering is based on the idea of substitution — that a person who is guilty of a sin escapes punishment by offering an animal in his place. As Ramban explains in discussing the *olah*-offering, which is completely burned on the Altar:

The very concept of using an animal as an offering is based on the idea of substitution.

Our deeds are comprised of thought, speech, and deed. Therefore, when we bring an offering to atone for a sin, we must lean on the animal with our hands to atone for the physical action; we must confess verbally to atone for the speech; and we must burn the innards and kidneys on the altar, because those organs inspire the thoughts and desires that bring us to sin; the forelegs and hind legs that are burnt atone for our hands and feet that sinned; the blood that is sprayed on the walls of the altar correspond to our blood, and reminds us that our own blood should have been spilled for having disobeyed Hashem — if not for Hashem's kindness in accepting *a substitute* as an atonement.

Nowadays, in the absence of the *Beis HaMikdash*, we cannot bring offerings, but in the custom of *kapparos* before Yom Kippur, we swing a chicken around our heads and declare, "This is instead of me, this is *my substitute (zeh temurasi)*, this is my atonement. This rooster shall go to its death, and I will go to a good life and to peace."

If the very concept of offerings is based on substitution, as Ramban explains, why can't we substitute one animal for another?

If the very concept of offerings is based on substitution, why can't we substitute one animal for another?

II. A Continuous Circle

THERE IS A CUSTOM TO TRY AND CONNECT THE END OF A BOOK of the Torah with its beginning. *Pardes Yosef HaChadash* explains this custom:

> "Hashem looked into the Torah and created the world"[6] [i.e., the Torah is the blueprint of the world]. Since the world is round, with no beginning or end, the Torah must also be "round," in the sense that its end and beginning are fused with one another. The Torah is therefore an endless cycle. As soon as we finish the Torah we start over again, and this is the source of the custom to connect the end [of a portion of Torah or a tractate] with the beginning.

We will try to explain, therefore, how the end of the *Sefer Vayikra* — which deals with *temurah* — connects to the beginning of the Sefer, which deals with the laws of *korbanos* (offerings).

To observe Hashem's decrees means that we should fulfill them; to safeguard them means that we should be vigilant with them and not imagine that they less important than the mishpatim (laws).

THE KEY TO ANSWERING THESE QUESTIONS IS IN *RAMBAM'S*[7] EXPLAnation of the difference between *chukim* and *mishpatim*:

The Need to Understand

[Hashem commands us:] "You shall observe all My decrees (*chukim*) and all My ordinances (*mishpatim*), and you shall safeguard them" (*Vayikra* 19:37). The Sages explain that we have to *observe* and *safeguard* both the decrees and the laws. To *observe* Hashem's decrees means that we should fulfill them; to *safeguard* them means that we should be vigilant with them and not imagine that they less important than the *mishpatim* (laws). *Mishpatim* are *mitzvos* for which we understand the reasoning

---

6. *Zohar* Vol. II, *Parashas Terumah* 161b.
7. *Hilchos Me'ilah* (8:8).

and from which we can benefit in this world — such as the prohibitions against stealing and murder, and the commandment to honor our parents. *Chukim* are the mitzvos that we do not understand, but, as the Sages state,[8] "I [Hashem says] decreed decrees, and you have no right to cast doubt on them."

AT THE END OF *HILCHOS TEMURAH* (4:13), *RAMBAM* WRITES:

Trying to Understand

Although the *chukim* of the Torah are decrees, as we explained at the end of *Hilchos Me'ilah*, it is worthwhile to think about them and try to develop logical reasons for them whenever you can. As the Sages tell us, King Shlomo understood most of the reasons for all the decrees in the Torah.

Rambam goes on to offer the lesson that derives from the prohibition of *Temurah*:

It seems to me that the Torah commands, "Then it and its substitute shall be holy, it may not be redeemed" (*Vayikra* 27:33) for the very same reason that it requires a person who consecrated his own house to add a fifth onto its value when redeeming it.[9] The Torah takes a person's psyche and evil inclination into account, and works with the understanding that a person is naturally inclined to acquire possessions and take pity on his property. Therefore, although he has already vowed to consecrate [something he owns], he might change his mind and want to redeem it for less than its actual value. The Torah prevents him from doing so by requiring a person who redeems it for himself to add a fifth onto its value.

The Torah works with the understanding that a person is naturally inclined to acquire possessions and take pity on his property.

Similarly, when a person consecrates an animal, he might change his mind. Since he knows that he cannot redeem it, he may try to exchange it for a less valuable animal. If the Torah were to allow a person to exchange an animal for one of greater value, he might exchange it for one of lesser value and say that the substitute is worth more. Therefore, the Torah prohibits us from substituting animals, and penalizes a person who does so by decreeing that both animals are consecrated.

All these measures were necessary in order to suppress a person's evil inclination and perfect his character traits. Most of the laws in the Torah are pieces of advice sent from afar

---

8. *Yoma* 67b.
9. *Vayikra* 27:15.

by the Greatest of Advisors, to teach us how to perfect our traits and deeds, as Scripture states, "Surely, I have written for you [in the Torah] extremely noble things, with counsel and knowledge, to teach you the veracity of true words, so that you may answer words of truth to those who send word to you" (*Mishlei* 22:20-21).

Mishpatim are mitzvos that are readily understood, whereas chukim cannot be understood by everyone, but can be understood by those who make a concerted effort to do so.

To summarize, *Rambam* suggests that *mishpatim* are mitzvos that are readily understood, whereas *chukim* cannot be understood by *everyone,* but can be understood by those who make a concerted effort to do so, just as he does with the laws of *temurah.* [*Chinuch* and some of the commentators on the Torah offer reasons for various other *chukim.*]

Dealing With Chukim

RAMBAN AGREES WITH *RAMBAM.* ON THE VERSE "YOU SHALL OBSERVE my decrees; you shall not mate your animal into another species" (*Vayikra* 19:19), *Ramban* quotes *Rashi's* comment that *chukim* are decrees from the King for which there are no reasons, but he comments:

[*Rashi*] does not mean that the decrees of the King of kings are for no reason, for "Every word of God is refined" (*Mishlei* 30:5). Rather, *chukim* are decrees that a king promulgates without revealing the reasons to the citizenry. The nation does not appreciate those decrees and doubts them in their hearts, but they fulfill them out of fear of the king. Similarly, Hashem's decrees are the secrets He hid in the Torah. The nation does not appreciate them rationally as it does the *mishpatim*, but there is a valid reason and much to gain from them.[10]

In regard to the list of relatives with whom we may not cohabit, *Ramban* writes:

The King knows the reason for his decrees and the benefit of what he commands, but he does not divulge that reason to the nation, only to his wisest advisors.

Arayos [illicit relationships] are *chukim*, decrees from the King. Decrees are laws that a king passes based on his wisdom and understanding of how to administer his kingdom. He knows the reason for his decrees and the benefit of what he commands, but he does not divulge that reason to the nation, only to his wisest advisors.

---

10. It appears that *Rashi* (*Bereishis* 26:5) disagrees with *Ramban* and maintains that human intelligence cannot understand the reasons for *chukim. Ramchal* (*Adir Bamarom,* p. 23) writes that Hashem concealed the reasons for the *chukim* to prevent the forces of impurity from clinging to them.

Ramban clarifies his idea further in his comment on the verse, "If you consider my decrees loathsome, and if your being rejects My ordinances, so as not to perform all My commandments, so that you annul My covenant" (*Vayikra* 26:15):

> Since the *chukim* are *mitzvos* for which the reasons have not been divulged to the general population, fools tend to find them repugnant. They say, "What difference does it make to Hashem if I wear a garment of linen and wool interwoven, and what use is there in burning a red cow and sprinkling its ashes upon ourselves?" *Mishpatim*, on the other hand, are accepted by all, and everyone understands the need for them; no nation or country can survive without laws.

Finding Reasons — Our Mission

WE SEE FROM BOTH *RAMBAM* AND *RAMBAN* THAT THERE CERTAINLY are logical reasons for every portion of the Torah — both the *chukim* and the *mishpatim* — but we are unaware of the reasons for the mitzvos that fall into the category of *chukim*. *Ramban* supports this contention through a midrash that states, "Hashem said to Moshe, 'I am revealing the reason for *Parah Adumah* to you, but it will be concealed from all others. Things that are concealed in this world will be revealed in the World to Come'" Clearly, writes *Ramban*, our inability to understand the *chukim* does not stem from a lack of logic in them, but to our own lack of intelligence. However, the reason for even the most enigmatic *chok* was revealed to the wise men of *Klal Yisrael*.

As Rav Dessler elaborates,[11] only Moshe Rabbeinu, with his superior level of understanding, was able to fathom the inner content of *all* the mitzvos, even of *Parah Adumah*, which was revealed only to him. All others — even giants of Rabbi Akiva's stature — had to accept some of the laws simply because they were transmitted to Moshe at Sinai, i.e., to accept the commandment without knowing the reason.

Sfas Emes[12] offers guidance on how one can merit to understand *chukim*: There is certainly a reason for every *chok*, but we cannot understand the reasons until we accept upon ourselves to fulfill the commandments without knowing those reasons. We can then merit to understand them in proportion to the level of faith and willingness we displayed to keep the mitzvos without knowing the reasons for them. As we find in the Midrash, children who had never sinned were

We merit to understand them in proportion to the level of faith and willingness we displayed to keep the mitzvos without knowing the reasons for them.

11. *Michtav Me'Eliyahu*, Vol. V, pg. 315.
12. *Chukas* 632.

able to expound upon the Torah. Our task [in this world] is to reveal the hidden reasons for the mitzvos.

III. Ḥilchos Temurah — Understanding Chukim

W E HAVE SEEN THAT ALTHOUGH *CHUKIM* ARE BEYOND normal human comprehension, many were understood by the wisest men of *Klal Yisrael* over the ages. Moshe, the father of all prophets, was privileged to understand the reasons for all the *chukim*, even that of the Red Cow. Ordinary people cannot understand such decrees, but the wise men of the Torah, who explain the reasoning of the Torah and its decrees, can understand some of them to some degree and explain them to others.

Moshe, the father of all prophets, was privileged to understand the reasons for all the chukim.

This principle is at the root of the laws of *Temurah*. As we noted above, Rambam writes at the end of *Hilchos Temurah* that at first glance human intelligence cannot comprehend the reason for this law. We noted that the very institution of offerings is a "substitution," because the sinner is substituting the offering for himself. Furthermore, only an individual's attempt to make a *temurah* sanctifies the substitute, but if partners or the community make a *temurah* the substitute does not become holy.

Rambam comments that this *chok* teaches that every *mitzvah* was established for a reason, and we should make concerted efforts to understand the reason, as best we can, even though portions of the *chukim* will remain a mystery. For example, as noted above, we still do not understand why only the *temurah* of an individual becomes consecrated, but not the *temurah* of partners or the general public.

THIS HELPS UNDERSTAND HOW THE END OF *SEFER VAYIKRA* IS CONnected to the beginning. In truth, the entire concept of *Korbanos* is enigmatic. Does Hashem need our offerings? Certainly not! Furthermore, the concept that an offering can atone for its owner's sins is even harder to understand.

Closing the Circle

Hashem — in His infinite Kindness — enables us to substitute the animal's life for our own.

How can an animal burnt on the altar atone for the sin of a human being? Difficult though it may be to fathom, however, the Sages explained that Hashem — in His infinite Kindness — enables us to substitute the animal's blood for our own, and its life for ours, as we cited above from *Ramban*.

In this sense, the end of *Vayikra* corresponds to its beginning. By explaining the concept of the offerings, with which *Vayikra* begins, our Sages showed that even *chukim* can be understood, at least to a degree. As the Book draws to a close, therefore, we must accept the principle that the laws of *temurah,* as well, although seemingly incomprehensible, have a reason, and that the greatest Torah scholars can understand them.

LET US NOW GO BACK TO OUR QUESTIONS REGARDING *MISHNEH Torah.*

Mishneh Torah: Finding Reasons

The first four books of the Torah contain the mitzvos — *chukim* and *mishpatim* — often without elaboration or reasons. On Rosh Chodesh Shevat, Moshe Rabbeinu "began explaining this Torah" (*Devarim* 1:5), teaching the depths of the Torah and the reasons for the mitzvos, as we saw from *Tosafos* and *Ramban* cited at the beginning of the essay.[13]

This explains why *Chiddushei HaRim* considers the first of Shevat such a momentous occasion. Indeed, the day that we began to learn reasons for the mitzvos is worthy of his proclamation that it was a "great thing," and we can understand why *Ibn Ezra* considers it akin to the the Giving of the Torah at Sinai.

WE WONDERED WHY KING DAVID CHOSE THE TERM *"DEVARIM"* IN RELAtion to Yaakov and *chukim* and *mishpatim* to Yisrael. As the classic commentators have taught, the term *Yaakov* refers to ordinary people and the term *Yisrael* refers to those on a more exalted spiritual level. Based on this, *Ohr HaChaim* explains the difference between Yaakov and Yisrael in his commentary on the verse, "So shall you say to the House of *Yaakov,* and relate to the Children of *Yisrael*" (*Shemos* 19:3):

Words to the Masses; Reasons to the Wise

The term Yaakov refers to ordinary people and the term Yisrael refers to those on a more exalted spiritual level.

> The House of Yaakov represents the lower levels of our holy nation, people who — if left to their own devices — would serve Hashem only out of awe, not out of love. Therefore, Hashem commanded Moshe to convey the mitzvos of the Torah to such

---

13. The word בָּאֵר, *explain,* used in this verse can also be read בְּאֵר, *well* (of water). This is appropriate, because if a person wants to find water he must dig deep into the ground, and a person who wants to understand the Torah properly must plumb the depths of the wellspring of Torah.

people softly, so they would understand that they can serve Hashem out of love, as well.

Bnei Yisrael refers to people who would naturally be inclined to serve Hashem out of love. Such people had to be taught in a manner that would remind them to infuse their service of Hashem with awe, and not to suffice with serving Him out of love alone.

Based on this delineation, it is appropriate that the mitzvos referred to as *devarim* — simple words, with no explanations — should correspond to Yaakov, the relatively simple members of *Klal Yisrael*. The *chukim* and *mishpatim,* however, should correspond to Yisrael, the people who are wise enough to examine and develop them until they understand them fully. Now, on Rosh Chodesh Shevat, as the nation stood on the threshold of *Eretz Yisrael,* Moshe again conveyed the mitzvos to the Jewish people, but this time he did so to all layers of the nation, with full clarification and explanations and reasons.

We can now understand the correspondence between the month of Shevat and the Name Combination that is derived from a verse discussing the laws of *temurah.* As we have seen, *temurah* is a portion of the Torah that appears to be incomprehensible at first, but the *Rambam* was able to understand it properly. Since the ability to reach such a level of understanding of the enigmatic portions of the Torah became possible on Rosh Chodesh Shevat, when Moshe began to explain the Torah, it is only appropriate that Shevat and *temurah* should correspond to each other.

The power of Torah is so great that those who devote themselves to it with total application and sincerity can rise to amazing heights — even to understand matters beyond ordinary human capacity.

Bnei Yisrael refers to people who would naturally be inclined to serve Hashem out of love.

The power of Torah is so great that those who devote themselves to it with total application and sincerity can rise to amazing heights.

ADAR

עִירֹה וְלַשְׂרֵקָה בְּנִי אֲתֹנוֹ (ההי"ו).

*T*he Name Combination for the month of *Adar* comes from the last letters of four words in *Yaakov's* blessing to *Yehudah:* אֹסְרִי לַגֶּפֶן עִירֹה וְלַשְׂרֵקָה בְּנִי אֲתֹנוֹ כִּבֵּס בַּיַּיִן לְבֻשׁוֹ וּבְדַם עֲנָבִים סוּתֹה *He will tie his donkey to the vine; to the vine branch his donkey's foal; he will launder his garments in wine and his robe in the blood of grapes (Bereishis 49:11).*

Reversals and Opposites

אָדָר – עִירֹה וְלַשְׂרֵקָה בְּנִי אֲתֹנוֹ (ההי״ו).

THE NAME COMBINATION FOR THE MONTH OF ADAR COMES FROM the last letters of four words in Yaakov's blessing to Yehudah: אֹסְרִי לַגֶּפֶן עִירֹה וְלַשְׂרֵקָה בְּנִי אֲתֹנוֹ כִּבֵּס בַּיַּיִן לְבֻשׁוֹ וּבְדַם עֲנָבִים סוּתֹה, *He will tie his donkey to the vine; to the vine branch his donkey's foal; he will launder his garments in wine and his robe in the blood of grapes* (*Bereishis* 49:11).

Rashi explains the verse as follows:

> [Yaakov] prophesied that the land of [the tribe of Yehudah] would draw forth wine as if from a spring. A man of Yehudah will tie one he-donkey to a vine and load it up from a single vine; from a single vine branch he will load up a foal of a she-donkey.

[Yaakov] prophesied that the land of [the tribe of Yehudah] would draw forth wine as if from a spring.

Thus, donkeys and copious quantities of wine in Yehudah's territory are key subjects in this verse. *Rashi* also cites *Onkelos'*[1] interpretation of this verse:

> *Onkelos* interprets that this verse speaks allegorically about the King *Mashiach*. גֶּפֶן, vine, refers to *Eretz Yisrael*; עִירֹה, his city,[2] to Jerusalem; שׂרֵקָה, vine branch, refers to *Klal Yisrael*[3]; and בְּנִי אֲתֹנוֹ refers to the *Beis HaMikdash*,[4] which *Mashiach* will rebuild.

We will examine how this verse correlates to the month of Adar according to the renderings of both *Rashi* and *Onkelos*. We will also try to find a connection between those explanations and some other factors associated with Adar:

- *Shem MiShmuel*[5] cites *Arizal's* teaching that Adar's symbolism of the Four-letter Name should have reversed the order

---

1. The same approach is taken by *Targum Yonasan ben Uziel*.

2. *Rashi* associates the word עִירֹה with the root word עַיִר, which means a donkey. *Onkelos* associates it with the pronunciation עִיר, *a city*.

3. Upon whom Hashem said, "וְאָנֹכִי נְטַעְתִּיךְ שֹׂרֵק, *And I planted you as a vine branch*" (*Yirmiyahu* 2:21).

4. According to *Onkelos*, אֲתֹנוֹ is related to the שַׁעַר הָאִיתוֹן *Gate of Entry*, one of the gates to the *Beis HaMikdash* (See *Yechezkel* 40:15).

5. *Rosh Chodesh Adar* 5672.

of the letters completely to read ה‑ז‑ה‑י, but through their prayers, Mordechai and Esther were able to change the letter-combination to ה‑ה‑י‑ו. We will seek to understand what *Arizal* means by saying that the Name's letters should have been completely reversed. Furthermore, *Shem MiShmuel* wonders why Mordechai and Esther prayed that the order of letters be changed to this particular order.

- The *mazal* of Adar is דָּגִים, *fish*.[6] How are fish related to Adar?

- As we have often noted, each month corresponds to a tribe. According to *Arizal's* system, Adar corresponds to the tribe of Naftali. How so?

- There is a relationship between Purim — which we celebrate during the month of Adar — and Yom Kippurim, our yearly Day of Atonement, as is apparent in the name, Yom Kippurim, which can be rendered, [יוֹם כְּפוּרִים], "A day *like* Purim." *Zohar*[7] explains that we will eventually celebrate Yom Kippur by indulging in all the forms of pleasure that are now forbidden on that day.

  These two days are also related by the virtue of the fact that they are the only two festivals that will still be observed after the final redemption.[8]

  At first glance, Purim and Yom Kippur seem to be diametric opposites of each other. Purim is a day of feasting and merrymaking, and Yom Kippur is a day of fasting and solemnity. What can two such dissimilar days have in common?

Purim and Yom Kippur seem to be diametric opposites of each other. What can two such dissimilar days have in common?

l. Chamra: Donkeys and Wine

IN THE VERSE FROM WHICH THE NAME COMBINATION OF ADAR IS derived, two subjects are mentioned twice: wine and donkeys. *Gefen* and *soreika* are types of vines upon which grapes grow — thus, they are an indirect reference to wine, and *iro* and *asono* are types of donkeys. Interestingly, both wine and donkeys have the potential to propel people to great heights, each in its own way, but they can also be abused and cause terrible harm. Let us examine one at a time:

---

6. The source for this is *Sefer Yetzirah* 5.

7. *Tikkun* 21.

8. See *Yerushalmi Taanis* 2:1, and *Midrash Mishlei* 9:2.

THERE ARE *MITZVOS* CAN BE FULFILLED *ONLY* WITH WINE, SUCH AS the wine libations poured onto the Altar with each offering in the *Beis HaMikdash. Kiddush* and *Bircas HaMazon* should preferably be recited on a cup of wine.[9]

Wine — A Blessing and a Curse

Wine "gladdens God and men" (*Shoftim* 9:13). In fact, *Chazal* teach that, ideally, happiness can best be achieved through the consumption of wine.[10] Indeed, the daily songs of the Levites in the *Beis HaMikdash* were chanted when the wine libations were poured on the Altar.[11]

The daily songs of the Levites in the Beis HaMikdash were chanted when the wine libations were poured on the Altar.

The Talmud[12] records an instance in which wine was served to reluctant young sages to make them reveal the Torah that they knew. The Talmud[13] also states that wine helps makes a person wise.

On the other hand, wine also "brings curses to the earth."[14] According to one view, the Tree of Knowledge was a grapevine, so wine was responsible for Adam's sin, which, as we know, brought multiple curses upon the world. Ten generations later, Noach drank wine when he emerged from the Ark and became drunk, which led to his curse against his grandson, Canaan. Also, a *ben sorer u'moreh* (wayward and rebellious son)[15] is guilty of a capital sin only if he eats meat and *drinks wine.*[16]

A Kohen who drinks wine may not serve in the *Beis HaMikdash,*[17] or even bless the congregation[18] until the effect of the wine wears off. A rav who is even slightly inebriated may not render halachic decisions;[19] nor is one allowed to pray while intoxicated.[20]

This dual nature of wine is illustrated by the statement of Chazal.

This dual nature of wine is illustrated by the statement of *Chazal*[21] that the vision of wine in a dream can be either a good or a bad omen, but it is not clear which. Rabbi Yochanan says that such a vision is always good for *talmidei chachamim* (Torah scholars).

---

9. *Pesachim* 107a.
10. Ibid. 109a.
11. *Berachos* 35a.
12. *Sanhedrin* 38a.
13. *Yoma* 76b.
14. *Berachos* 40a.
15. See *Devarim* 21:18-21.
16. *Sanhedrin* 70a.
17. *Vayikra* 10:8-9.
18. *Taanis* 26b; *Orach Chaim* 128:38.
19. *Kereisos* 13b; *Rema, Yorah Deah* 242:13.
20. *Eruvin* 64a; *Orach Chaim* 99:1.
21. *Berachos* 57a.

There is a duality in the physical manifestation of wine as well. Drinking a little wine will cause a feeling of satiation, but drinking much wine will leave the drinker hungry.[22]

ALTHOUGH THE REFERENCES TO DONKEYS IN THIS VERSE COME IN the forms of *ason* and *ayir*, the word commonly used for a donkey is

Donkeys

chamor, a word that is related to the word *chomer*, which means *earthiness* and *physicality*. The Talmud[23] notes that the Torah compares people who are devoid of spirituality to donkeys, based on a verse in the narrative of Avraham taking his son Yitzchak to the *Akeidah*. They were accompanied by two attendants, and when they reached their destination, Avraham addressed the attendants: וַיֹּאמֶר אַבְרָהָם אֶל נְעָרָיו שְׁבוּ לָכֶם פֹּה עִם הַחֲמוֹר, *And Avraham said to his young men, "Stay here by yourselves with the donkey"* (*Bereishis* 22:5). Chazal comment that he likened them to the donkey, in their insufficient level of spirituality.

On the other hand, a midrash[24] teaches that a donkey is associated with *Mashiach*, who will bring the world to a state of spiritual perfection, for *Mashiach* will ride the very same donkey that Avraham rode to *Akeidas Yitzchak*, as the prophet foretold, *"Behold, your king [i.e., Mashiach] will come to you, righteous and victorious is he, a humble man riding upon a donkey"* (*Zechariah* 9:9).

Appropriately, stubbornness — a trait that characterizes donkeys — is also associated with extremes. On the one hand, a person's stubbornness can be used to attain perfection, as we see from Yaakov Avinu's blessing to Yissachar: יִשָּׂשכָר חֲמֹר גָּרֶם ... וַיֵּט שִׁכְמוֹ לִסְבֹּל, *Yissaschar is a strong-boned donkey ... he bent his shoulder to bear* (*Bereishis* 49:14-15). As *Rashi* explains, this means that Yissaschar is like a strong-boned donkey who bends his shoulders to accept the burden of Torah study.

Stubbornness is also a character trait of the Jewish people — as Moshe Rabbeinu said, "They are a stiff-necked people"[25] — and stubbornness has enabled us to remain faithful to Hashem despite enduring the travails of exile for nearly two thousand years. Positive though

Stubbornness has enabled us to remain faithful to Hashem despite enduring the travails of exile for nearly two thousand years.

---

22. Ibid. 35b. There is a halachic manifestation of this fact. On Erev Pesach, one is allowed to drink much wine, because it will leave him hungry enough to eat the matzah heartily, but one is not allowed to drink a small amount of wine, lest one feel satiated and unable to eat matzah with a proper appetite.
23. *Kesubos* 112a.
24. *Pirkei D'Rabbi Eliezer* 31.
25. *Shemos* 34:9.

it can be, however, Israel's stubbornness caused much agony in the Wilderness when the people rebelled against Hashem and Moshe. And everyone knows from personal experience how harmful stubbornness can be.

Thus, wine and donkeys have something in common, in that they both have dual characteristics. It is fascinating to note that in Aramaic, the language of the Talmud and Midrash, both wine and donkeys are referred to as *chamra*.

11. וְנַהֲפוֹךְ הוּא, Turned About

ADAR, TOO, IS A MONTH WITH A DUAL CHARACTER, AS WE SEE in the story of Purim. It was the month when it was decreed that the Jewish people would be wiped out, but then, as *Megillas Esther* declares: וְנַהֲפוֹךְ הוּא אֲשֶׁר יִשְׁלְטוּ הַיְּהוּדִים הֵמָּה בְּשׂנְאֵיהֶם, *and it was turned about: The Jews prevailed over their adversaries* (9:2). This duality of Adar is expressed in Chazal's teaching,[26] "When the lots [that Haman drew to set a date to annihilate the Jews] fell during the month of Adar, [Haman] was extremely happy. He said, 'My lot fell on the month in which Moshe died.' He did not know that although Moshe died on the seventh of Adar, he was also born on the seventh of Adar."

Nesivos Shalom explains:

> Purim is named for the *pur* [lot] [that Haman drew]. *Irin Kadishin* [by the *Ruzhiner Rebbe*] explains that Haman chose Adar because each month corresponds to one of the combinations of Hashem's Names; in Nissan the Name appears in the proper order (יהד-ה), which corresponds to the Attribute of Kindness (*chessed*). Each month thereafter, the combination moves further and further from that order. Since no letters of the Name Combination of Adar are in their proper order, it should have been a month in which strict, exacting justice would reign in the world.

> That is why Haman was so sure he would be able to capitalize on that and wipe out the Jews. However, it was exactly at the point of utter darkness, when there was not even a hint of light, that Hashem chose to demonstrate that even when there seems to be no hope for *Klal Yisrael*, He is with His people in times of distress.[27] In the words of the Talmud,[28] "A cloudy day

26. *Megillah* 13b.
27. See *Tehillim* 91:15.
28. *Yoma* 28b.

is infused with sunlight," i.e., the sun is there even though it is obscured by clouds. So it was that hopeless Adar became a month of scintillating joy, as Hashem caused Adar to "turn about." Instead of being a month plagued by tragedy, it was the time when Hashem showered us with an amazing show of love, and Adar was transformed into the month when *Klal Yisrael's mazal* thrives more than any other month.

A similar idea appears in *Ohr Gedalyahu:*

WHEN WE CONTEMPLATE THE STORY OF THE MEGILLAH, WE FIND that each event that contributed to the eventual plan to annihilate the Jewish people was reversed when they repented, and actually contributed to their redemption. The trouble began when the Jews ignored Mordechai's ruling and

Planned "Coincidences"

partook in Achashveirosh's party. At that party, Vashti sinned, and Haman's role in advising Achashveirosh catapulted him to greatness. But then *Klal Yisrael* repented and began to obey Mordechai, and Vashti's death — which initially seemed to produce terrible results for the Jews — actually resulted in Esther's rise to power, thus enabling her to save them from Haman's plot.

Klal Yisrael's realization that their own sins brought on the threat of annihilation led to a turnabout. All the factors that led to their threatened obliteration contributed to their redemption, in keeping with the concept expressed by the verse עֵת צָרָה הִיא לְיַעֲקֹב, *It is a time of trouble for Yaakov,* וּמִמֶּנָּה יִוָּשֵׁעַ *from it* he shall be saved (*Yirmiyahu* 30:7) i.e., the trouble itself will bring about the salvation. As *Sfas Emes* points out, the letters מִמֶּנָּה can be rearranged to read מֵהָמָן *from Haman;* Haman himself brought about the salvation by recommending that Vashti be put to death and a new queen be chosen in her place, thus putting Esther in a position to save the Jews.[29]

The same will occur in the Final Redemption. All the prophecies regarding the Final Redemption begin with the word וְהָיָה, [a word that, the Sages teach, implies a happy event] because when we are finally redeemed we will realize that everything we endured during the exile was actually for the best, and that the exile was all in preparation for — and therefore a portion of — the redemption. The word וְהָיָה connotes that the

Klal Yisrael's realization that their own sins brought on the threat of annihilation led to a turnabout.

---

29. *Ohr Gedalyahu* adds that the same idea can be derived through a homiletical reading of a verse in *Tehillim:* עֶזְרָה בְצָרוֹת נִמְצָא, *Salvation is found in the troubles* (46:2).

past will turn into the future.[30] We will eventually see that all that we endured in the past will have brought about the redemption.

The Month of Reversals

HAVING ASCERTAINED THAT ADAR IS A MONTH OF TURNABOUT, WE can see how the questions we raised at the beginning of the essay find expression in many factors associated with Adar.

The Name Combination for Adar is derived from the phrase עִירֹה וְלַשֹּׂרֵקָה בְּנִי אֲתֹנוֹ, which, according to *Rashi,* refers to donkeys and wine, both of which are means that can achieve diametrically opposed ends. This verse, therefore, is an apt description of the month of Adar, which demonstrates the potential to reverse events entirely and turn an event that seems to spell doom into one that will be celebrated with feasting and merrymaking forevermore.

Shem MiShmuel's quotation from *Arizal* — that the ineffable Name associated with this month would have been exactly the opposite, had Mordechai and Esther not reversed it — also becomes clear. In the normal course of events, Adar would have been a month of such strict judgment that the Four-letter Name would have been completely reversed, totally obscuring its message of mercy and changing it to strict judgment. The spectacular reversal of the events in the Purim story was so far-reaching that it even changed the Holy Name of Hashem associated with the month.

The new Name Combination ה-ה-י-ו places the letter *hei* twice at the beginning of the Name. The letter *hei* in Hebrew is the feminine gender, which symbolizes mercy. That was the result of the prayers of Mordechai and Esther. A further symbolism of the *hei* is found in the Scriptural word from which the second *hei* is taken: עִירֹה, which can be translated *his city,* an allusion to Jerusalem, the city where Hashem rests His Presence, and which is therefore the repository of His Attribute of Mercy.

Onkelos interpreted this verse as a reference to *Mashiach.* According to *Ohr Gedalyahu,* the connection between this verse and the month of Adar is readily apparent, since the Purim story foreshadows the events that will occur when *Mashiach* will redeem us.

This idea blends in perfectly with an insight Rabbi Avigdor Nebenzahl writes in the name of Rabbi Shlomo Zalman Auerbach *zt"l:*[31]

The month of Adar demonstrates the potential to reverse events entirely and turn an event that seems to spell doom into one that will be celebrated with feasting and merrymaking forevermore.

The Purim story foreshadows the events that will occur when Mashiach will redeem us.

---

30. The word הָיָה means *was,* so anything following would be describing an event that had already occurred. The addition of the letter ו at the beginning of the word reverses the tense of the word, however, so that וְהָיָה with the prefix means "and it shall be."

31. From an essay on *Parashas Shemini* 5763.

Although Purim will never be abolished,[32] the obligation to reach the level of *ad d'lo yada,*[33] will no longer apply in *Mashiach's* times. With the terrible suffering we endure nowadays, it is difficult to reach the required level of joy on Purim without reaching the level of *ad d'lo yada,* which, in a sense, removes us from reality. When *Mashiach* comes, however, there will be no more travail, and we will no longer need to detach ourselves from the realities of the world in order to rejoice; reality itself will be reason enough for celebration.

In times of suffering we must drink wine — with its innate ability to reverse things from one extreme to another — to *symbolize* the Time to Come, when our suffering will be turned into joy and happiness. In the time of the ultimate redemption it will no longer be necessary.

That Fish is the constellation of Adar can also be explained through our understanding of Adar as a month of reversals. *Shem MiShmuel*[34] observes that fish are cold beings without natural warmth, as opposed to animals that have some level of warmth. In spiritual terms, therefore, Adar would seem to be a month in which we feel a "chill" in our attitude toward serving Hashem, and the quality of our service should decline. This led Haman to believe that he could capitalize on Israel's lackadaisical approach to the service of Hashem, but he did not realize that *Klal Yisrael* is not subject to the control of *mazal*, and we can *reverse* our *mazal* for the better.

In times of suffering we must drink wine to symbolize the Time to Come, when our suffering will be turned into joy and happiness.

III. Naftali: Gold, Honey, and Duality

ADAR'S STATUS AS A MONTH OF DUALITIES ALSO EXPLAINS ITS correspondence to the tribe of Naftali. A midrash[35] states, "The name Naftali alludes to the Torah, for נַפְתָּלִי can be split into the words נֹפֶת לִי, *the honey is mine.* The word נֹפֶת, *honey,* refers to the Torah, as we see from the verse הַנֶּחֱמָדִים מִזָּהָב וּמִפַּז רָב וּמְתוּקִים מִדְּבַשׁ וְנֹפֶת צוּפִים, *They [the words of Torah] are more desirable than gold, than*

The name Naftali alludes to the Torah.

---

32. *Yalkut Shimoni* 944; *Taanis* 2:1; *Midrash Mishlei* 9:2.

33. We are obligated to imbibe on Purim until we cannot differentiate between *Baruch Mordechai* (blessed is Mordechai) and *arur Haman* (accursed is Haman) (*Shulchan Aruch, Orach Chaim* 695:2).

34. *Rosh Chodesh* 5672.

35. *Bamidbar Rabbah* 14:11.

even much fine gold; and sweeter than honey and drippings from combs (*Tehillim* 19:11). The word לי has the numerical value of 40, alluding to the Torah, which was given to Moshe during his forty days in heaven. *Shem MiShmuel* wonders why Naftali is associated with the Torah more than any other tribe.

Naftali's character traits are symbolized by a verse referring to gold and honey because all three are known for duality.

Perhaps we can explain that the midrash is teaching that Naftali's character traits are symbolized by a verse referring to gold and honey because all three are known for duality.

Gold

PURE GOLD IS EXTREMELY MALLEABLE, TO THE EXTENT THAT IT CANnot be formed into a useful permanent shape unless it is mixed with another metal that will help it maintain its shape. Thus, it has an unusual duality in that it lacks practical utility in its purest form; it reaches its maximum value only when mixed with another metal.

Honey

HONEY IS A SATIATING AND NUTRITIOUS TREAT; IT CAN "LIGHT UP THE eyes" of someone on the verge of collapse.[36] Nevertheless, it would be wise to eat only a little bit of honey at a time, for, in the words of the wisest of men, "When you find honey, eat what is sufficient for you, lest you be satiated and vomit it up" (*Mishlei* 25:16); and, "Eating too much honey is not good" (ibid. verse 27). Thus honey, too, has dual characteristics, because, more than other foods, it is beneficial only if eaten in small quantities, but harmful if eaten in quantities that are normal for other foods.

A duality existed in the tribe of Naftali, although not in Naftali himself.

Naftali

CHAZAL TEACH THAT A DUALITY EXISTED IN THE TRIBE OF NAFTALI as well, although not in Naftali himself. This can be derived from two midrashic interpretations of the names of his sons: According to one version of the midrashic text, the children of Naftali combated and derided idolatry, but according to a second version, they fell prey to idol worship. We may assume that both tendencies existed among elements of the tribe; thus, the tribe of Naftali exhibited duality.[37]

---

36. See *I Shmuel* 14:29.

37. *Bereishis Rabbah* (94:8). According to the Midrashic text of *Matanos Kehunah* and *Rashash*, the names of the sons have a negative connotation but according to the reading of *Yefeh Toar* and *Radal*, the names have a positive connotation.

THE COMPARISON BETWEEN PURIM AND YOM KIPPURIM CAN ALSO BE understood in the context of reversals and turnabouts.

Purim and Yom Kippurim

Purim celebrates a reversal of our national lot from imminent annihilation to a miraculous salvation. The essence of Yom Kippur is transformation: the transformation of the Divine Attribute of Justice into the Attribute of Mercy and the reversal of our personal lots for the year through repenting and begging Hashem to wipe away our sins and make us worthy of His Mercy.

We can add that Purim complements Yom Kippur in another way. It is said that the first two letters of the Ineffable Name of Hashem, י and ה, allude to physical pursuits, as evidenced by their appearance in the words אכילה, *eating*; שתיה, *drinking*; and לינה, *sleeping*. The last two letters, ו and ה, represent spiritual pursuits, which is why they appear in the words תורה and מצוה. It follows, then, that the complete Name of Hashem symbolizes the perfection of the world, in which both spiritual and physical — ostensible opposites — come together in the service of Hashem.

Similarly, Purim represents the physical, and Yom Kippur — when we refrain from all physical pleasure — represents the spiritual. The two complement each other when people use their entire capacity to devote all their actions in this world to Hashem.

This explains why Adar is uniquely suited to be the month when the commandment to wipe out Amalek is read, in conjunction with Purim. As long as Amalek exists, Hashem's Name remains incomplete, and the spiritual perfection of the world can be realized only once they are wiped out.[38]

In order to wipe out Amalek's influence in this world, we must transform the materialism of this world into spirituality — and Adar is an ideal time for such a reversal.

Purim represents the physical, and Yom Kippur represents the spiritual. The two complement each other.

---

38. See *Rashi* to *Shemos* 17:16, where the Four-letter Name of Hashem is reduced to two letters. Rashi explains that as long as Amalek exists, Hashem's Name is not complete.

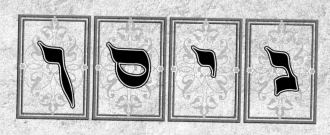

NISSAN

יִשְׂמְחוּ הַשָּׁמַיִם וְתָגֵל הָאָרֶץ (יהו"ה).

The Name Combination for the month of Nissan comes from the verse יִשְׂמְחוּ הַשָּׁמַיִם וְתָגֵל הָאָרֶץ, *The heavens will be glad and the earth will rejoice (Tehillim 96:11).*

Nature and Divine Supervision

נִיסָן – יִשְׂמְחוּ הַשָּׁמַיִם וְתָגֵל הָאָרֶץ (יהו"ה).

THE NAME COMBINATION FOR THE MONTH OF NISSAN COMES from the verse יִשְׂמְחוּ הַשָּׁמַיִם וְתָגֵל הָאָרֶץ, *The heavens will be glad and the earth will rejoice* (*Tehillim* 96:11).

What is the relationship of Nissan to a joy so overwhelming that it encompasses heaven and earth? Ostensibly it would seem more logical to associate joy with the month of Adar, about which *Chazal* teach,[1] מִשֶּׁנִּכְנַס אֲדָר מַרְבִּים בְּשִׂמְחָה, *When Adar begins, we increase our joy.* However, *Rashi* comments that the period that begins with Adar "are days of miracles for *Klal Yisrael*, [because we celebrate] Purim and Pesach." Clearly, then, the increased joy should not end when Adar is over, but should extend to the month of Nissan as well, in celebration of the great miracles of the Exodus.

Increased joy should not end when Adar is over, but should extend to the month of Nissan as well, in celebration of the great miracles of the Exodus.

Nevertheless, we must still delve into the association between joy and the month of Nissan, because, although the Torah contains four mentions of the obligation to rejoice on festivals, *not one* appears in the Torah's discussion of Pesach. Three out of four mentions are in the verses regarding Succos;[2] the other is in a verse regarding Shavuos.[3] Furthermore, we do not recite the full *Hallel* on Pesach, except for the first day(s), which indicates that the joy of the festival is less than complete.

Considering the fact that the Torah makes no mention of a mitzvah to be joyous on Pesach, there must be some deeper reason why the Name Combination of Nissan is derived from a verse that speaks of the joy of Creation.

---

1. *Taanis* 29a.
2. See *Vayikra* 23:40; *Devarim* 16:14; Ibid. verse 15.
3. *Devarim* 16:11.

1. Simchah vs. Gilah

THE TWO VERBS FOR JOY MENTIONED IN THE VERSE OF THIS Name Combination — יִשְׂמְחוּ, *let them be glad,* and תָגֵל, *let them rejoice,* are more familiar in their noun forms, שִׂמְחָה and גִּילָה. *Malbim* and the *Vilna Gaon,* offer opposing definitions of these two near-synonyms

Malbim[4] writes that *simchah* refers to a lasting, consistent happiness, and *gilah* refers to a joy that comes as a result of some new event or occurrence. When a person enjoys the world in its normal, predictable state, we would describe his happiness as *simchah.* If he receives an unexpected favor as a reward for his good deeds, the proper term to describe the resulting joy would be *gilah.*

Since the heavens are controlled by Hashem in a predictable, orderly fashion, they are in a constant state of joy, so the appropriate term is *simchah.* On earth, however, Hashem, regulates life according to the deeds of people and what they deserve, for the good or not. Therefore, the verse associates the term *gilah* with the earth. *Malbim* follows the same approach in explaining several other instances where both of these terms appear.[5]

The *Vilna Gaon* seems to say exactly the opposite. Commenting on the verse גִּיל יָגִיל אֲבִי צַדִּיק וְיוֹלֵד חָכָם יִשְׂמַח בּוֹ, *The father of a righteous person will be mirthful; one who begets a wise child will be glad with him* (*Mishlei* 23:24), *Vilna Gaon* writes, "The difference between *gilah* and *simchah* is that *gilah* applies to something that is constant, and *simchah* applies to something new. When a child is born, the father's initial reaction is an ecstatic *simchah*; the rest of the child's life and gradual development bring *gilah* to him." The *Gaon* continues, "The verse applies *simchah* to the heavens and *gilah* to the earth because nothing new has been added to the earth since its creation, as King Shlomo says, *There is nothing new beneath the sun* (*Koheles* 1:9). The heavens, on the other hand, constantly innovate in declaring the infinite greatness of God, as the verse states, "The heavens declare the glory of God, and the firmament tells of his handiwork. Day following day utters speech" (*Tehillim* 19:2-3).

While there seems to be an irreconcilable disagreement between *Vilna Gaon* and *Malbim,* perhaps we can show that there is a degree of agreement.

Simchah refers to a lasting, consistent happiness, and gilah refers to a joy that comes as a result of some new event or occurrence.

---

4. *Tehillim* 96:11.

5. See *Mishlei* 23:24-25; *Iyov* 3:22; *Tehillim* 16:9; *Yeshayah* 16:10.

A MIDRASH[6] TEACHES THAT MOSHE RABBEINU DID NOT KNOW HOW much of the moon must be visible in order for the court to declare the

Moshe Rabbeinu's Difficulty

day as Rosh Chodesh, until Hashem showed him the moon and said, "When you see this, you should sanctify [the month]." This midrash is difficult. Moshe was certainly familiar with the phenomenon of the monthly renewal of the moon. What was it that he did not understand?

Another famous teaching related to the month of Nissan is *Rashi's* first statement in his commentary on the Torah:

> Rabbi Yitzchak said, "[God] should have begun the Torah with the verse, 'This month shall be for you [the beginning of the months],' because it is the first mitzvah to *Klal Yisrael*." [Although the commandment of circumcision was given to Avraham, Rosh Chodesh is the first mitzvah given to the nation as a whole.]

Rosh Chodesh is the first mitzvah given to the nation as a whole.

Many early commentators wondered how R' Yitzchak could suggest that the Torah should omit the story of Creation, upon which our faith in Hashem is founded, and omit the lives of our forefathers, which forged the heritage of all Jews throughout the generations.

WE WILL BEGIN OUR EXPLANATION OF NISSAN WITH A CONCEPT FROM *Maharam Schick*.[7] Two *tannaim* disagree over the month of Cre-

Tishrei and Nature; Nissan and Miracles

ation.[8] Rabbi Yehoshua says that it was Nissan, and Rabbi Eliezer maintains that it was Tishrei. The Sages ruled that Rabbi Yehoshua is correct, and we assume that the world was actually created in Nissan. Why, then, wonders *Maharam Schick*, do we observe Rosh Hashanah on the first of Tishrei?

The soul involves the use of thought and intelligence, for, indeed, there are mitzvos that are fulfilled not through physical acts, but through intelligent faith and intent.

He answers that there are two ways that Hashem regulates the world — טֶבַע, the Law of Nature and הַשְׁגָּחָה פְּרָטִית, Divine Providence. The natural system operates according to the rules of the physical Creation, while Providence operates according to the Torah and the Jewish people's fulfillment of its commandments. We fulfill the Torah through body and soul. The soul involves the use of thought and intelligence, for, indeed, there are mitzvos that are fulfilled not through physical acts, but through intelligent faith and intent. The Jewish people mark the new year not in Nissan, when the physical

---

6. *Mechilta, Bo* 1, cited in *Rashi* to *Shemos* 12:2.
7. *Responsa Orach Chaim* 184.
8. *Rosh Hashanah* 10b.

act of creation took place, but in Tishrei, to make it clear that the key to existence is God's Providence. And that is why Hashem established Rosh Hashanah, the Day of Judgment, in Tishrei, for it is the day when Jews harness their minds and hearts to repent and earn forgiveness. By working to elevate our mind and heart over the body, and thereby making the body a servant of the Torah, we unite the physical nature of Nissan — the month of physical creation — with Tishrei, the month that represents spirituality and Divine Providence.

The underlying concept expressed by *Maharam Schick* appears elsewhere as well. Noting that the ה of יוֹם הַשִּׁשִּׁי, *the* sixth day seems to be superfluous,[9] the Talmud explains that Hashem conditioned the existence of the world on *Klal Yisrael's* future willingness to accept the Torah on *the* sixth day of Sivan, the date the Ten Commandments were to be given at Sinai. Had *Klal Yisrael* refused to accept the Torah, Hashem would have returned the world to the emptiness that existed prior to Creation. *Maharal*[10] explains:

> This condition was necessary because the Torah is the completion of Creation. The Torah provides the primary perfection of the world. Had *Klal Yisrael* not accepted the Torah, the world would have returned to nothingness, for if it could not attain perfection, there would be no reason for it to exist.

Maharal makes a similar point in *Tiferes Yisrael.*[11]

The Torah that Hashem gave us is the perfection of this world. Hashem gave the Torah to direct people toward the path of righteousness, so that they should be good in this world and so that the world should fulfill the purpose of its existence. For this reason, he gave us the Torah, because the world is deficient .... Obviously, because Creation is deficient, the only way it can be brought to completion is through the Torah.

Maharal's concept of perfection is implicit in *Maharam Schick's* words. In addition to the course defined by the Laws of Nature, which began with the physical Creation, the course of spiritual completion of Creation began when the bond between Hashem and the Jewish people began to form. That occurred when He gave us the mitzvah to start counting the months from the month of Nissan, for this

Hashem gave the Torah to direct people toward the path of righteousness, so that they should be good in this world and so that the world should fulfill the purpose of its existence.

---

9. At the conclusion of each day of Creation, the Torah states, "And there was evening, and there was morning, a first [second, third, etc.] day." The day of the Creation usually appears without a ה: יוֹם שְׁלִישִׁי, יוֹם שֵׁנִי, יוֹם אֶחָד, etc. The appearance of the definite article "ה" at the conclusion of the sixth day — יוֹם הַשִּׁשִּׁי, *the* sixth day — indicates that it refers to a specific sixth day.

10. *Gur Aryeh Vayikra* 12:2.

11. Chapter 58.

The Book of
Shemos is a
continuation —
a "sequel" to
Bereishis,

commandment introduced the concept of Divine Providential form of regulating the world, which is done through the Torah.

Indeed, *Netziv*[12] cites *BaHaG's* teaching that the Book of *Shemos* is called "The Second Book" because it is a continuation — or a "sequel" — to *Bereishis*, since the story of the Exodus and the giving of the Torah continue and complement the book of Creation.

11. Starting From the Purpose

WE WONDERED HOW R' YITZCHAK COULD SUGGEST THAT THE Torah should have started from the mitzvah of the New Moon. How can we omit Creation, which is the basis of Jewish faith, and the equally important lessons we learn from the lives of our forefathers?

According to the above understanding of the importance of Rosh Chodesh, we can understand R' Yitzchak's question. He did not mean that the *accounts* of Creation and the development of the Jewish people should be omitted. Rather he suggested that the *order* of the Torah should be reversed: since the world was created for the sake of the Torah and the fulfillment of its commandments, it should have begun with the first mitzvah, and then reverted to the history of Creation and the story of the Patriarchs.

It is clear from Scripture that Hashem created the world for His Glory. The prophet Yeshayah delivered a message from Hashem: "Everyone who is called by My Name and whom I have created for My glory" (*Yeshayah* 43:6); King Shlomo wrote, "Everything Hashem made [He made] for His sake" (*Mishlei* 16:4).

Maharal[13] notes that Hashem derives glory from the world only when humans fulfill His commandments and serve Him, and Israel is the nation that accepted the yoke of doing so, which is why Hashem says, "This people which I fashioned for Myself that they might declare My praise" (*Yeshayah* 43:21).

Hashem derives
glory from the
world only
when humans
fulfill His
command-
ments and
serve Him,
and Israel is
the nation that
accepted the
yoke of doing
so.

Since the world was created to serve Hashem through the Torah, and the Jewish people are the ones who do so, logic dictates that the entire purpose of Creation was for the Torah and for *Klal Yisrael's* observance of the mitzvos. It stands to reason, therefore, contended R' Yitzchok, that the opening words of the Torah should be the first

12. *Ha'Amek Davar*, introduction to *Shemos*.
13. *Gur Aryeh*, *Bereishis* 1:1; *Netzach Yisrael* 10.

mitzvah given to Hashem's people. Furthermore, as *Maharam Schick* explained, since the spiritual primacy of Creation — the message of Tishrei — gives the ultimate meaning to the physical creation of Nissan, it would seem that the Torah should begin with that mitzvah, and then go back to discussing Creation and the lives of forefathers.

To this, R' Yitzchak responds that it was even more essential to begin with Creation and the story of the Jewish people to establish that Hashem created the world and it is His to present to whichever nation He finds deserving — and therefore no nation can contest His decision to designate *Eretz Yisrael* as the heritage of *Klal Yisrael*.

The Torah Completes Creation — and Changes Halachah

IT IS INTERESTING TO NOTE THAT, SINCE THE GIVING OF THE TORAH TO Israel was the fulfillment and completion of Creation, the world achieved a higher status with *Mattan Torah*. This new status played itself out in the realm of Halachah, since we find that certain laws changed after Sinai.

The early commentators wonder how Yaakov could have purchased the rights to the *bechorah* (right of the firstborn) from Eisav, since there is a halachic principle that one cannot transfer possession of something that has not yet come into existence (*davar shelo ba le'olam*). The status of the firstborn involved the privilege of being the nation that would receive the Torah and perform the sacrificial service in the *Mishkan* and *Beis HaMikdash*, a privilege that did not yet exist at the time when Yaakov bought the *bechorah*. How, therefore, could Yaakov's purchase be valid?

Ohr HaChaim answers that since the sale of the *bechorah* occurred before *Mattan Torah*, it is possible that one could transfer possession of a *davar shelo ba le'olam* prior to *Mattan Torah*.

Rabbi Yehoshua of Kutno[14] explains why the law should have been different before *Mattan Torah*. As mentioned above, the Talmud[15] relates that Hashem had stipulated that the world would continue to exist only if *Klal Yisrael* would accept the Torah. In a sense, therefore, prior to *Mattan Torah*, all of Creation was like a *davar shelo ba le'olam*, since its very existence was dependent on *Klal Yisrael's* acceptance of the Torah. It would stand to reason, then, that one could also transfer possession of a *davar shelo ba le'olam* at that point.

> The Talmud relates that Hashem had stipulated that the world would continue to exist only if Klal Yisrael would accept the Torah.

---

14. *Yeshuos Malko*, Toldos s.v. Ha'acharonim.
15. *Shabbos* 88a.

Not only was the nature of the world different prior to *Mattan Torah*, but even the observance of Torah and mitzvos was different. *Rambam*[16] writes:

When we distance ourselves [from sin] or perform [mitzvos] nowadays, we do so because Hashem commanded us to do so through Moshe Rabbeinu, not because He commanded them to the prophets that preceded him. When we refrain from eating the limbs of a live animal, we do not do so because Hashem commanded Noach to refrain from eating them, but because Moshe forbade us from eating them, when he told us at Sinai that the prohibition remained in effect. Similarly, we do not circumcise ourselves because Avraham Avinu circumcised himself and his household, but because Hashem told Moshe at Sinai that we should continue to circumcise ourselves, just as Avraham did. The same applies to *gid hanasheh* [sinew of the hip socket]. By not eating it, we are not following a prohibition set in place by Yaakov Avinu, but the commandment we heard from Moshe Rabbeinu. We see that this is so, because *Chazal* tell us[17] that we received 613 commandments at Sinai, and these are among them.

Clearly, not only was the nature of the world different prior to *Mattan Torah*, but even the nature of Torah and mitzvos changed when we received the Torah.

Only Torah Brings Simchah

CHAZAL TEACH US THE TRUE DEFINITION OF *SIMCHAH*, JOY. THE TALmud[18] relates that the Sages once wanted to conceal King Shlomo's book of *Koheles* because there were apparent contradictions within it. For example, in one verse he praises *simchah* (8:15), yet he also disparages it, saying, "*simchah*, what does it accomplish!" (2:2).

In the end, however, the Sages resolved the contradictions. Shlomo praised *simchah* that resulted from observing mitzvos, and he disparaged joy that is not associated with mitzvah observance. This teaches, continues the Talmud, that the Divine Presence does not rest where there is depression, laziness, laughter, lightheadedness, or idle chatter — only where there is *simchah* that derives from a mitzvah.

16. *Chullin* 7:6.
17. *Midrash Tanchuma, Shoftim* 10.
18. *Shabbos* 30b.

The same principle applies to Torah study, concludes the Talmud. Rabbah would begin his Torah lectures with a humorous remark, in order to introduce a feeling of joy into the day's Torah study. Clearly, positive and true *simchah* emanates only from mitzvah observance.

Furthermore, *Tanna D'vei Eliyahu* states that when the Jewish people study Torah and engage in charity and justice, Hashem — so to speak — rejoices over them, and tells them that their own *simchah* will last forever. Hashem says, "My children, what sort of joy is there in this world — only Torah! If a person derives joy from silver, gold, or precious gems and diamonds, what joy does he derive from them after he dies? His *simchah* will end when he dies, so what has he gained from his joy? But you, My children, come and rejoice with the Torah — a complete *simchah!* — just as I rejoice in you forever and ever."

Similarly, *Sefer Ha'Akeidah*[19] explains that true *simchah* can be attained only if three conditions are met, and those conditions can be met only through observance of Torah and mitzvos:

1) The action must be perfect.

2) The person performing the action must have perfect intentions. Harmful motives sadden the soul, which comes from an elevated source.

3) Joy results from achieving the purpose of the deed.

Therefore, concludes *Sefer Ha'Akeidah*, true *simchah* cannot emanate from temporal pursuits, for they do not provide complete benefit. True joy emanates only from Godly pursuits, in which the action and the purpose are achieved simultaneously.

Based on all we have seen, we can understand why *simchah* plays such an important role in our service of Hashem, as elucidated by *Ramchal*:[20]

True simchah cannot emanate from temporal pursuits, for they do not provide complete benefit.

> *Simchah* is an important principle in serving Hashem, as King David cautions, "Serve Hashem with gladness, come before him with joyous song" (*Tehillim* 100:2). *Chazal* teach that the Divine Presence rests only out of joy associated with a mitzvah. The Midrash comments on the verse, "Serve Hashem with gladness," that when we rise to pray, we should feel joy in our hearts that we have the ability to pray to God Who has no equal. True *simchah* is when a person feels glad that he merits to serve Hashem, to study His Torah, and observe His mitzvos, for they lead to true perfection and eternal value.

---

19. 16.
20. *Mesilas Yesharim* 19.

III. Nissan —
Creation Becomes Complete

WE CAN NOW UNDERSTAND WHY WE REACH THE HIGHEST level of *simchah* during the month of Nissan. As we saw, the world was created for two purposes: for the Torah and for *Klal Yisrael*. Both of these purposes reached perfection during Nissan:

The Torah

KLAL YISRAEL'S FIRST COMMANDMENT AS A NATION WAS THE MITZVAH of Rosh Chodesh. Since the world was created for the Torah and the commandments, it follows that true *simchah* would begin to be achieved when the first commandment was given.

The Torah tells us that the Jewish people left Egypt with "their leftovers bound up in their garments upon their shoulders" (*Shemos* 12:34). *Chazal* comment,[21] "They made the mitzvos beloved upon themselves," i.e., the matzos of the first Pesach were so precious to them that they did not pack the leftovers with their belongings, but wrapped them up and carried them on their shoulders.

Since Klal Yisrael accepted their first mitzvah — Rosh Chodesh — with joy, they set a precedent for all future generations to feel joy when they perform mitzvos.

Sfas Emes explains that since *Klal Yisrael* accepted their first mitzvah — Rosh Chodesh — with joy, they set a precedent for all future generations to feel joy when they perform mitzvos. Joy associated with a mitzvah is very great; a person can perfect his entire being through this joy. *Klal Yisrael* knew full well that the purpose of the Exodus was to enable them to become Hashem's servants, and their joy at being redeemed was because they had become privileged to be His servants. That they carried the matzos on their shoulders symbolized their exultation at assuming the yoke of God's service. Since then, *Klal Yisrael* — throughout the generations — has continued to fulfill the mitzvah of matzah on Pesach night with joy; as *Chazal* tell us,[22] "Mitzvos that were accepted with joy are still performed with joy."

Thus it is clear that the ultimate joy was experienced when the Jewish people received the first mitzvah in Egypt, and as we suggested earlier, this was also the most joyous moment of Creation, for Hashem's plan can be completed only through Torah and mitzvos.

---

21. *Midrash Tanchuma, Bo* 8.
22. *Shabbos* 130a.

MAHARAL[23] WRITES THAT WE DID NOT BECOME A NATION PRIOR TO
the Exodus. Since the world was created for *Klal*

Klal Yisrael

Yisrael, it follows that its inauguration as a nation would be a cause for great joy, for it allowed all of Creation to actualize its potential.

IV. NISSAN —
JOY THROUGH TORAH AND MITZVOS

W E CAN NOW EXPLAIN WHY THE NAME ASSOCIATION OF
Nissan comes from the verse יִשְׂמְחוּ הַשָּׁמַיִם וְתָגֵל הָאָרֶץ, *The heavens will be glad and the earth will rejoice* (*Tehillim* 96:11). The heavens certainly rejoiced on the day that they were created, but that joy was only temporary, because the world was still without Torah and mitzvos. When we received the mitzvah of Rosh Chodesh, the joy was finally complete, for the nation had received the first mitzvah of the Torah. Nissan is therefore the month in which the joy of Creation reaches its greatest height.

We wondered why Moshe found the renewal of the moon so difficult to understand. We suggest that it was not the astronomical reappearance that puzzled him, for he was no stranger to the heavenly bodies. Rather, he did not understand why the renewal of the moon at the beginning of Nissan would bring joy to all of Creation. Thus, he questioned not the physical reappearance of the moon, but its spiritual significance, and why, of all the commandments, that of Rosh Chodesh should be the very first one.

The answer, as we have seen, is that the Torah and mitzvos elevated all of Creation — the *physical* creation that began in Nissan. Thus, it was not merely the importance of Rosh Chodesh as the first mitzvah that was of great significance. It was that Rosh Chodesh Nissan was the beginning of Creation, a phenomenon that could find fulfillment only with the giving of the Torah.

The Torah and mitzvos elevated all of Creation that began in Nissan.

In light of the above, perhaps we may suggest that there is an area of commonality in the conflicting definitions of the *Vilna Gaon* and *Malbim*. As we noted, *Malbim* writes that *simchah* refers to constant happiness, and *gilah* refers to the outburst of joy that one experiences upon the occasion of a new event. The *Vilna Gaon* writes exactly the opposite. Can we reconcile these two opinions?

---

23. *Netzach Yisrael* 10.

Malbim refers to the simchah associated with Torah and mitzvos, which is the only true and lasting simchah.

We suggest that *Malbim* refers to the *simchah* associated with Torah and mitzvos, which, as we saw, is the only true and lasting *simchah*, whereas the *Vilna Gaon* refers to *simchah* that emanates from some other, temporal source. Such *simchah* is not complete, and therefore it does not endure once the stimulus is gone.

IYAR

יִתְהַלֵּל הַמִּתְהַלֵּל הַשְׂכֵּל וְיָדֹעַ   (יהה"ו).

The Name Combination for the month of Iyar comes from the verse כִּי אִם בְּזֹאת יִתְהַלֵּל הַמִּתְהַלֵּל הַשְׂכֵּל וְיָדֹעַ אוֹתִי כִּי אֲנִי ה' עֹשֶׂה חֶסֶד מִשְׁפָּט וּצְדָקָה בָּאָרֶץ, *For only with this may one glorify himself — contemplating and knowing Me — for I am Hashem Who does kindness, justice, and righteousness in the land (Yeremiah 9:23).*

STRENGTHENING OUR FAITH

אִיָּיר – יִתְהַלֵּל הַמִּתְהַלֵּל הַשְׂכֵּל וְיָדֹעַ (יהה"ו).

THE NAME COMBINATION FOR THE MONTH OF IYAR COMES FROM the verse כִּי אִם בְּזֹאת יִתְהַלֵּל הַמִּתְהַלֵּל הַשְׂכֵּל וְיָדֹעַ אוֹתִי כִּי אֲנִי ה' עֹשֶׂה חֶסֶד מִשְׁפָּט וּצְדָקָה בָּאָרֶץ, *For only with this may one glorify himself — contemplating and knowing Me — for I am Hashem Who does kindness, justice, and righteousness in the land* (*Yeremiah* 9:23).

In order to understand how this verse correlates to the month of Iyar, we must first examine several factors associated with this month.

- *Bnei Yissaschar* [1] cites *Arizal's* analysis of the spiritual aspects of tefillin. He writes that the tefillin known as "*Rashi* tefillin" correspond to the simple reading of Hashem's Name — יה־ו־ה — which, as we have seen above, is the order of the Name Combination for the month of Nissan. The tefillin known as "*Rabbeinu Tam* tefillin" correspond to the Name Combination יה־ה־ו, the Name Combination for Iyar. [2]

  Arizal adds that *Rabbeinu Tam* tefillin are on a higher spiritual level. They are particularly propitious for attaining wisdom, perhaps because they correspond to the Name Combination of Iyar, which includes the phrase "contemplating and knowing me." From this *Bnei Yissaschar* deduces that Iyar must be a month in which we can attain wisdom more easily than in other months.

Iyar must be a month in which we can attain wisdom more easily than in other months.

The correspondence between tefillin and the month of Nissan is easily understood. One of the verses in which we are commanded to wear tefillin states, "And it shall be a sign upon your arm and an ornament between your eyes, for with a strong hand Hashem removed us from Egypt" (*Shemos* 13:16). In his well-known essay on the purpose of the mitzvos, *Ramban*

---

1. *Maamarei Chodesh Iyar*, 1.

2. There is a dispute between *Rashi* and his grandson *Rabbeinu Tam* regarding the order in which the *parashiyos* of tefillin are to be written. We will explain this dispute at length below.

explains that tefillin are a daily reminder of the Exodus, which took place in Nissan.

We do not understand, however, the correlation between tefillin and Iyar, and specifically how the tefillin of *Rabbeinu Tam* correspond to this month. Why only *Rabbeinu Tam's* tefillin and not *Rashi's?*

We will examine the basic differences between *Rashi* and *Rabbeinu Tam* tefillin, in order to understand how they correspond to the months of Nissan and Iyar, respectively.

- We will also try to explain why Iyar was the most appropriate month for the following two historic events:
    1) Amalek attacked *Klal Yisrael* as they traveled toward Mount Sinai.[3]
    2) The construction of the First *Beis HaMikdash* began during Iyar.[4]

- *Sefer Yetzirah*[5] associates the letter ו with the month of Iyar. The letter ו generally serves as a conjunction, which implies that Iyar is connected to Nissan. We will try to explain the connection between the two months.

1. The Dry Bones: Giving Hope

THE *HAFTARAH* OF SHABBOS CHOL HAMOED PESACH IS THE story of dead, dried bones that Hashem instructed the prophet Yechezkel to bring back to life (*Yechezkel* 37:1-14).

Sifsei Tzaddik[6] explains why this episode was chosen for that day's *haftarah*. His explanation will provide a basis to understand the various factors associated with the month of Iyar. He writes:

> *Chazal* (*Megillah* 31a) chose Yechezkel's description of the dry bones coming to life as the *haftarah* for Shabbos Chol Hamoed Pesach because they foresaw that during the long and bitter exile, we would anxiously await the month of Nissan, and the Seder night, a time when the Sages tell us that it is propitious for

During the long and bitter exile, we anxiously await the Seder night, a time that it is propitious for Mashiach to come.

---

3. *Shemos* 17:8, 19:2.
4. See *I Melachim* 6:1.
5. Chapter 5.
6. *Pesach* #23.

Mashiach to come. When the Seder night comes and goes and we are still in exile, we will shudder as we wonder, "How long must we suffer such degradation?"

We will shudder as we wonder, "How long must we suffer such degradation?"

Chazal chose this *haftarah* to strengthen our *emunah* [faith] in Hashem, so that we would not lose hope. This *haftarah* reminds us that everything Hashem pledged through the prophets will come true — even something as wondrous as the revivification of a heap of dry bones. No one would have thought that they could live again, but when their remembrance came before Hashem He brought a great multitude back to life. It is clear that this narrative was no mere allegory, since the Talmud states that the Mishnaic sage Rabbi Yehudah ben Bava was one of their descendants. So, too, we can be sure that we will eventually be able to rise from the depths to which we have sunk.

HASHEM TOLD YECHEZKEL, "THESE BONES — THEY ARE THE whole House of Israel" (ibid. 37:12). At first glance, this seems

Dry Bones and Vibrant Nation

peculiar, because the dry bones were but a small segment of *Klal Yisrael*. In the context of the chapter, however, we can understand the application of this verse to all of *Klal Yisrael*. The verse tells us that in its despair, the nation cries, "Our bones are dried out and our hope is lost; we are doomed!" (ibid.). This cry of desperation was emitted not only once in our history. It is a cry that each of us emits from time to time during periods of travail. Occasionally we feel that we have descended into spiritual darkness, and we feel that we are doomed to enter Gehinnom. One Talmudic sage states that the "dry bones" described in this verse were the corpses of people who had not the slightest hint of "moisture" of mitzvos. Their lives were spiritually arid. Nevertheless, Hashem revivified them in His great kindness.

This cry of desperation is a cry that each of us emits from time to time during periods of travail.

We know that each organ and sinew in the human body corresponds to a specific mitzvah, and through performing the respective mitzvos we give spiritual life to those organs. An organ or limb that does not perform mitzvos will wither and be useless in the spiritual life of the Days to Come, and this will surely be so if a person sinned many times, or refrained from performing many mitzvos. This is the meaning of Israel's cry, "We are doomed!"

From the revivification of these bones, we learn that we should hope that Hashem will have mercy on us and endow us with eternal life, for the Torah states, "I shall show favor to whom I choose to show favor," (*Shemos* 33:19), and *Chazal* explain,[7] "Even to a person who is not worthy."

Sifsei Tzaddik teaches that *Chazal* chose this *haftarah* to encourage us at a time when we would naturally feel dejected, when the first days of Pesach have passed and we are still in exile. Hashem commanded Yechezkel to revivify those bones in the period after the destruction of the First Temple, when many doubted the future of the Jewish People: "Our hope is lost; we are doomed!" they said. If we strengthen our faith in Hashem by internalizing the message of the dry bones, we can survive even in the most trying times.

It stands to reason that the doubt that enters our minds after the Seder night might remain with us as we return to our daily routines during Iyar, struggling for spiritual growth and scratching out a livelihood. In anticipation of this disappointment, *Chazal* reminded us of the episode of new life being granted to dry bones. This fans the flame of faith that burns in the heart of every Jew who fervently awaits the redemption.

The flame of faith burns in the heart of every Jew who fervently awaits the redemption.

II. The Number Two —
Separation, Division, and Conflict

AN EXTRA MEASURE OF FAITH IS NECESSARY DURING IYAR FOR another reason. Iyar is the second month of the year. The number two represents separation and division. When there is only one person, there is only one opinion; two people means two opinions, which all too often leads to divisiveness and conflict. The more people, the more conflict.

Rabbeinu Bachya[8] points out that the first conflict in history began on the second day of Creation, when the upper waters were split from the lower waters. From that time on, he adds, there was conflict and division in the world.

Ohr Gedalyahu broadens this concept. He notes that the first day is described in the Torah as *yom echad* (lit., *one* day), rather than *yom rishon* (the *first* day), even though the rest of the days are listed

---

7. *Berachos* 7a.
8. *Kad HeKemach*, entry for *Sinas Chinam*.

as *yom sheini, yom sh'lishi* (the second day, the third day), and so on. Had the Torah written *Yom Rishon*, it would imply that a second already existed, which is not the case, since something cannot be called a "first" if there is as yet no "second." On the first day of Creation, unity reigned; there was no multiplicity and no possibility of conflict, for all of Creation flowed from the Oneness of Hashem. Even the angels had not yet been created. *Chazal* express this concept homiletically by interpreting *yom echad* as "the day of the One and Only" i.e., Hashem was alone in His world.

On the first day of Creation, unity reigned, for all of Creation flowed from the Oneness of Hashem.

MULTIPLICITY BEGAN ON THE SECOND DAY THROUGH THE SEPARATION of the upper waters from the lower waters. It was then that the possibility of multiple entities came into existence.

Day Two Brings Conflict

As the daily offerings were sacrificed in the *Beis HaMikdash*, the Levites would sing a psalm that corresponded to what Hashem created on that day. [9] On the second day of the week, they would sing Psalm 48, which begins, "A song, a psalm, by the sons of Korach. Great is Hashem and much praised." As *Chazal* explain, the word *great* implies expansion and growth, and is therefore appropriate for the second day of Creation, when, as the Sages expressed it, חִילֵק מַעֲשָׂיו וּמָלַךְ עֲלֵיהֶם, Hashem "split His creations and reigned over them." On that day, Creation was expanded and that made Hashem's greatness apparent.

With the creation of multiple entities came a multiplicity of interests, desires, and opinions, which inevitably leads to conflict.

With the creation of multiple entities came a multiplicity of interests, desires, and opinions, which inevitably leads to conflict. Not all conflict is bad, however. The mishnah (*Avos* 5:17) tells us that the disputes between the Academies of Shammai and Hillel were undertaken for the sake of Heaven, and were therefore meritorious. In contrast, the conflict that Korach and his camp initiated against Moshe was not for the sake of Heaven. Therefore, it is appropriate that the psalm chosen for the second day of the week was composed by Korach's children, who were originally involved in that conflict but repented and withdrew.

Maharal[10] notes that the Torah does not state, "*Ki tov* (for it is good)" regarding the second day of Creation because there is no blessing in divisiveness. *Chazal*[11] teach that Gehinnom was created on the second day, and since Gehinnom is not perfect, it is the appro-

9. *Rosh Hashanah* 31a.
10. *Tiferes Yisrael* 18.
11. *Bereishis Rabbah* 4:6.

priate environment for the wicked who have not perfected themselves.

"THE HARVEST HAS PASSED, THE SUMMER HAS COME, BUT WE HAVE not been saved" (*Yirmiyah* 8:20). So, too, with the passing of Nissan, we enter Iyar. We are still in exile and doubt creeps into our hearts. During Nissan, month number one, the month of redemption, we feel complete, but with the advent of Iyar our minds begin to "split" and generate multiple opinions. Multiplicity engenders doubt. We begin to see more than one side to an issue, and we wonder which is true. During Nissan our faith might be strong, but as Iyar approaches we might find ourselves turning away from our faith in Hashem — Heaven forbid — and beginning to trust in our own abilities: in our wisdom, our strength, our wealth.

From Nissan to Iyar, Faith and Trust

The Name Combination of Iyar reminds us that we must rely only on Hashem, and strengthen our faith in Him, as the complete verses state, "Let not the wise man glorify himself with his wisdom, and let not the strong man glorify himself with his strength, let not the rich man glorify himself with his wealth. *For only with this may one glorify himself — contemplating and knowing Me*, for I am Hashem Who does kindness, justice, and righteousness in the land, for in these is My desire — the word of Hashem."

In commenting on these verses, *Chazal* explain why it is so important to turn our trust toward Hashem and away from our own abilities. *Midrash Tanchuma*[12] states that Hashem endows the world with three gifts: wisdom, strength, and wealth. If a person has any of them — wisdom, strength, or wealth — he can acquire everything that is desirable. But this is true, notes the midrash, only if those gifts come from Hashem. Wisdom, strength, or wealth gained through human effort are worthless, as King Shlomo wrote, "Once more I saw under the sun that the race is not won by the swift, *nor the battle by the strong, nor does bread come to the wise, riches to the intelligent*" (*Koheles* 9:11), and as Yirmiyah said, "Let not the wise man glorify himself with his wisdom ...."

Hashem endows the world with three gifts: wisdom, strength, and wealth.

---

12. *Mattos* 5.

IF THESE THREE GIFTS DO NOT COME FROM HASHEM, THEIR HOLDER will surely end up losing them, concludes the Midrash, for faith in Hashem is the key to keeping all of our blessings.

Moshe, Shimshon, Achav

Only one who has absolute faith that wisdom, power, and wealth are Divine gifts can be assured of retaining them.

These are piercing words. Only one who has absolute faith that wisdom, power, and wealth are Divine gifts can be assured of retaining them; they are not intrinsic parts of their possessor and can easily be lost.

Chazal[13] illustrate this point by dissecting Yirmiyah's prophecy phrase by phrase and offering examples of people who had these gifts and lost them:

Only Hashem may glorify Himself, for all wisdom is His.

- "Let not the wise man glorify himself with his wisdom" refers to Moshe Rabbeinu. When the time came for him to die, he pleaded, "Master of the Universe, Your Torah requires that a worker must be paid in time. I served You loyally for forty years. Give me my reward." Hashem answered that Avraham, Yitzchak, and Yaakov were just as loyal, and they received their reward in the World to Come. When it came time for Moshe to pass away, his wisdom did not help him. Thus, only Hashem may glorify Himself, for all wisdom is His, as described by the verse: "There is no calculating His understanding" (*Yeshayah* 40:28).

- "Let not the strong man glorify himself with his strength" refers to Shimshon. Though his physical strength was unprecedented and unparalleled, when he died, all his strength disappeared. Rather, a person should glorify only Hashem for His strength, as the verse states, "Yours, Hashem, is the greatness and the strength" (*I Divrei Hayamim* 29:11).

- "Let not the rich man glorify himself with his wealth" refers to King Achav, who had seventy sons and built an ivory palace for each one. Nevertheless, when he died, his dynasty and wealth were gone. Rather, a person should glorify Hashem, to Whom all the wealth belongs, as we see from the verse, "Mine is the silver and Mine is the Gold — the word of Hashem, Master of the Legions" (*Chaggai* 2:8).

If the people listed in this midrash — each of whom epitomized the gift associated with him — lost those gifts when Hashem decided it was time for them to depart from this world, can we rely on our own wisdom, strength, or wealth, which pales in comparison to theirs?

13. *Yalkut Shimoni, Yirmiyah* 284.

Certainly, we can place our faith only in Hashem, Whose Glory will last forever and whatever we have is His gift.

III. Rashi Tefillin — Pure Faith Rabbeinu Tam Tefillin — Faith Through Contemplation

THE COMMANDMENT TO DON TEFILLIN IS A DAILY REMINDER TO strengthen our faith in Hashem. *Shulchan Aruch*[14] rules that while donning tefillin, we must have in mind that Hashem commanded us to bind these four passages of the Torah on our arms and on our heads to remind us of the miracles and wonders He performed when He took us out of Egypt. They demonstrate His Unity and Omnipotence in the upper and lower worlds. We don tefillin on our heads to subjugate our souls — which dwell in our minds — and on our arms adjacent to our hearts, the seat of desire and emotion, to keep the remembrance of Hashem in our hearts constantly, and thereby to control our thoughts and desire for [earthly] pleasure.

Rashi and *Rabbeinu Tam* disagree about the order in which the paragraphs are placed into the tefillin. All agree that *Kadesh* and *Vehayah ki yeviacha*[15] are the first two of the four passages. *Rashi* holds that those two are followed by *Shema,* and then *Vehayah im shamoa. Rabbeinu Tam* maintains that *Vehayah im shamoa* is placed before *Shema.*[16]

We suggest that their disagreement is based on their respective opinions as to how we should go about attaining faith in Hashem.

The paragraph of *Shema* calls for wholehearted acceptance of Hashem's Unity and Sovereignty out of blind faith, without attempting to understand it logically. The next paragraph, *Vehayah im shamoa,* requires us to accept the yoke of mitzvah observance upon ourselves. Preferably this acceptance should come with logical understanding, as we see from the comments of *Ibn Ezra* and *Ramban* on *Shemos* 15:26: אִם שָׁמוֹעַ תִּשְׁמַע לְקוֹל ה׳ אֱלֹקֶיךָ, *If you hearken diligently to the voice of Hashem, your God … and observe His decrees. Ibn Ezra* and

We don tefillin on our heads to subjugate our souls and on our arms to keep the remembrance of Hashem in our hearts constantly.

---

14. *Orach Chaim* 25:5.
15. *Shemos* 13:1-10, 11-16.
16. *Orach Chaim* 34:1.

Ramban explain that, grammatically, when the verb שָׁמוֹעַ, *hearken* or *hear* is followed by a *lamed,* meaning *to,* the verb indicates not merely that one should listen, but that one should attempt to *understand* the commandments. The same applies to the second paragraph of the *Shema,* which commands the Jewish people to *hearken **to*** the commandments. We are commanded not only to observe the commandments, but also to understand them, to the best of our ability.

Apparently, then, *Rashi,* whose order of the tefillin paragraphs gives priority to *Shema,* holds that we should begin our service of Hashem by accepting His sovereignty with total, unquestioning faith. Only then should we attempt to understand the commandments. *Rabbeinu Tam,* on the other hand, holds that it is preferable to begin with understanding, if possible, and proceed from there to acquire faith.

Interestingly, *Rabbbeinu Tam* agrees that when *writing* the paragraphs, the scribe should write them in the order in which they appear in the Torah, with *Shema* preceeding *Vehaya im shamoa.* Only when placing them into the tefillin should he reverse the order and place *Vehaya im shamoa* before *Shema.*[17] Apparently *Rabbeinu Tam* holds that there are two approaches to acquiring proper faith. The first is *Rashi's* approach, which *Rabbeinu Tam* advocates in his ruling that *Shema* should be *written* first. But the second and higher approach is symbolized by giving preference to *Vehaya* in the placement. Giving priority to that paragraph symbolizes the attempt to rise to a greater level of faith — a faith that comes from logical reasoning.

This explains why *Arizal,* quoted above, writes that *Rabbeinu Tam* tefillin are considered greater than *Rashi* tefillin, and why *Arizal* writes that one can attain wisdom through them. This also explains why *Shulchan Aruch* writes that only people who are known for their piety should wear *Rabbeinu Tam* tefillin. The essence of these tefillin represents the higher level of faith that comes through logic and reasoning.

We are commanded not only to observe the command- ments, but also to understand them, to the best of our ability.

Only people who are known for their piety should wear Rabbeinu Tam tefillin. The essence of these tefillin represents the higher level of faith that comes through logic and reasoning.

Nissan vs. Iyar: Heavenly Inspiration vs. Self-inspiration

THE ABOVE UNDERSTANDING OF THE TWO TYPES OF TEFILLIN WILL explain why Nissan corresponds to *Rashi* tefillin, and Iyar to *Rabbeinu Tam* tefillin. Nissan is a month when we rely on Heavenly inspiration, just as the Exodus occurred through Hashem's mighty hand, without human intervention, אִתְעַרוּתָא דִלְעֵילָא. Pure and simple faith — the faith represented by *Rashi* tefillin — was the key

---

17. See *Mishnah Berurah, Orach Chaim* 34:3.

merit through which Israel was redeemed from Egypt. The spiritual level of the nation had become so degraded by exile and slavery that the people lacked sufficient merit of their own to be redeemed.

Iyar, on the other hand, is a month in which we must gain Hashem's help by inspiring ourselves, אִתְעֲרוּתָא דִלְתַתָּא, to deserve it. We must begin to work on understanding Hashem's Unity and attaining faith through logic, as we see from the Name Combination of Iyar: "For only with this may one glorify himself — *contemplating and knowing Me*." Iyar, therefore, corresponds to *Rabbeinu Tam* tefillin, which represent a faith that results from the effort to reason and understand.

ARUCH HASHULCHAN[18] EXPLAINS THE DISAGREEMENT BETWEEN *Rashi* and *Rabbeinu Tam* according to *Zohar's* teaching that the order

Olam Hazeh and Olam Haba

of the *parashiyos* in *Rashi* tefillin corresponds to *Olam Hazeh* (this world), and the order of *Rabbeinu Tam* tefillin corresponds to *Olam Haba* (the World to Come). He explains that this world is governed by *Din*, Divine Justice, the system of reward and punishment, under which Hashem treats people according to what they deserve. This system is the basis of the form of service described in *Vehaya im shamoa*, which therefore appears last in *Rashi* tefillin. The World to Come, on the other hand, will be governed by Divine Mercy, and we will serve Hashem out of love. This form of service is the subject of the *parashah* of *Shema*, which is therefore placed last in *Rabbeinu Tam* tefillin.

The World to Come will be governed by Divine Mercy, and we will serve Hashem out of love.

According to our earlier thesis, we can add another explanation of the *Zohar*. In this world, we are unable to attain the highest levels of faith in Hashem. After the Final Redemption, however Hashem will be One and His Name One,[19] meaning that everyone will understand that everything Hashem does is for the good. Only then will we be fully able to reach the level of faith that *Rabbeinu Tam* tefillin represent.

SEFER YETZIRAH TEACHES THAT IYAR IS CROWNED BY THE CONJUNCtive letter ו, which means that Nissan and Iyar are connected, and

The Continuum from Nissan to Iyar

that the spiritual accomplishment of Iyar flows from that of Nissan. In Nissan we learn to accept Hashem's Unity and Sovereignty through pure and simple faith. We

18. *Orach Chaim* 34:6-9.
19. *Zechariah* 14:9.

should not be satisfied with that level, however. In Iyar we use that faith as a springboard to attain the deeper levels of faith, which can come only through contemplation.

It is appropriate, therefore, that King Shlomo chose to begin building the *Beis HaMikdash* during the month in which faith in Hashem reaches its peak through reasoning and understanding. Nothing on earth represents faith in Hashem's Sovereignty as much as the *Beis HaMikdash*, as King David implied, "Hashem, our God, all this vast amount that we have prepared to build You a Temple for Your holy Name is for Your own hand, *for everything is Yours*" (*I Divrei Hayamim* 29:16).

Although we can attain great levels in our faith in Hashem during Iyar, we must remember that Iyar is also the second month of the year, and the concept of "second" brought division and separation into the world. Iyar presents us with an opportunity to draw close to Hashem, but if we do not capitalize on that opportunity, we are open to attack from Amalek, whose goal it is to fight Hashem's Presence in the world, and to replace certainty with doubt, by fostering conflict and lack of faith.[20] Indeed, when *Klal Yisrael* treated their responsibility toward Torah study lackadaisically during the month of Iyar, they were attacked by Amalek, and were able to defeat them only by strengthening their faith in Hashem.[21]

After succeeding in doing so, the Jewish people went on to Sinai as a nation unified in its resolve to accept the Torah. This remains our incentive to strengthen our faith through Torah study and הַשְׂכֵּל וְיָדֹעַ אוֹתִי, *contemplation and knowing Me.*

---

20. Many commentators note that the numerical value of עמלק equals that of ספק, *doubt.*

21. See *Rosh Hashanah* 29a.

SIVAN

יְדֹתָיו וּלְצֶלַע הַמִּשְׁכָּן הַשֵּׁנִית (יוה״ה).

The Name Combination for the month of Sivan comes from verses in the Torah describing the construction of the kerashim, the planks of gilded wood that served as the walls of the Mishkan (Tabernacle): וְאַרְבָּעִים אַדְנֵי כֶסֶף תַּעֲשֶׂה תַּחַת עֶשְׂרִים הַקָּרֶשׁ שְׁנֵי אֲדָנִים תַּחַת הַקֶּרֶשׁ הָאֶחָד לִשְׁתֵּי יְדֹתָיו וּשְׁנֵי אֲדָנִים תַּחַת הַקֶּרֶשׁ הָאֶחָד לִשְׁתֵּי יְדֹתָיו. וּלְצֶלַע הַמִּשְׁכָּן הַשֵּׁנִית לִפְאַת צָפוֹן עֶשְׂרִים קָרֶשׁ *You shall make forty silver sockets under the twenty planks; two sockets under one plank for its two tenons, and two sockets under the next plank for its two tenons. For the second wall of the Tabernacle on the north side — twenty planks (Shemos 26:19-20).*

Keresh and Kesher

ילְצֶלַע הַמִּשְׁכָּן הַשֵּׁנִית (יוה"ה).

סִיוָן – יְדֹתָיו וּלְצֶלַע הַמִּשְׁכָּן הַשֵּׁנִית (יוה"ה).

THE NAME COMBINATION FOR THE MONTH OF SIVAN COMES from verses in the Torah describing the construction of the *kerashim*, the planks of gilded wood that served as the walls of the Mishkan (Tabernacle): וְאַרְבָּעִים אַדְנֵי כֶסֶף תַּעֲשֶׂה תַּחַת עֶשְׂרִים הַקָּרֶשׁ שְׁנֵי אֲדָנִים תַּחַת הַקֶּרֶשׁ הָאֶחָד לִשְׁתֵּי יְדֹתָיו וּשְׁנֵי אֲדָנִים תַּחַת הַקֶּרֶשׁ הָאֶחָד לִשְׁתֵּי יְדֹתָיו. וּלְצֶלַע הַמִּשְׁכָּן הַשֵּׁנִית לִפְאַת צָפוֹן עֶשְׂרִים קָרֶשׁ, *You shall make forty silver sockets under the twenty planks; two sockets under one plank for its two tenons, and two sockets under the next plank for its two tenons. For the second wall of the Tabernacle on the north side — twenty planks* (*Shemos* 26:19-20).

How do the *kerashim*/planks correspond to the month of Sivan?

Bnei Yissaschar implies that *Klal Yisrael* was able to reach the Sinai Desert and begin preparing to receive the Torah on Rosh Chodesh Sivan because the Name Combination for Sivan prepared them for it. Why does this Name Combination make Sivan the most auspicious time for receiving the Torah?

Klal Yisrael was able to reach the Sinai Desert and begin preparing to receive the Torah on Rosh Chodesh Sivan because the Name Combination for Sivan prepared them for it.

SINCE THE NAME COMBINATION FOR SIVAN COMES FROM THE VERSES in the Torah describing the construction of the Tabernacle, it behooves us to gain a deeper understanding of that description before we move on to explain the Name Combination.

A Detailed Description

Rav Avigdor Nevenzahl of Jerusalem[1] raises a question that should occur to everyone who studies the *parashiyos* discussing the construction of the Tabernacle. In *Terumah* and *Tetzaveh,* the Torah goes into great detail describing the exact dimensions of the *kerashim,* the number of *kerashim,* their type of wood, and more. The same holds true for the coverings of the Mishkan and many other minutiae associated with it. And the Torah repeats the entire description, with the same detail, in *Vayakhel* and *Pekudei,*

---

1. In a lecture delivered in Adar II of 5763 (2003).

where it describes the how the Mishkan's components were assembled to construct the building.

Granted, the commandment to build the Mishkan — "They shall make a sanctuary for Me" (*Shemos* 25:6) — is listed by *Rambam*[2] as a commandment that applies to all generations, meaning that it applies to the construction of the *Beis HaMikdash*, which happened 480 years later. However, only in the Mishkan were there *kerashim* and coverings. The *Beis HaMikdash* was built of stone. Rav Nebenzahl wonders, therefore, why does the Torah provide so many details — not only once, but twice — about an edifice that would be only temporary?

Furthermore, after telling how each of the many parts of the Mishkan was made, the Torah states that it was done "as Hashem had commanded Moshe." Why was it necessary to repeat this phrase over and over again? Why didn't the Torah suffice with the verse that appears at the end of the entire narrative: "The Children of Israel had done everything that Hashem commanded Moshe, so did they do" (ibid. 39:32)?

We will attempt to answer these questions in our discussion of the month of Sivan.

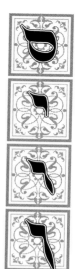

I. Qualities of the Kerashim

CHAZAL CONSIDERED THE *KERASHIM* TO BE OF UTMOST importance, and mention their unique qualities in many places:

- The very first time the *kerashim* are mentioned in the Torah, they are referred to as **ha**kerashim, with the definite article ה, *the,* at the beginning of the word. Rashi notes this and comments:

> It should have said *kerashim* [without the definite article at the beginning], as it says regarding all the other items that were constructed for the Mishkan. What is meant by "the" *kerashim*? [The verse refers to] planks that were originally designated for this purpose. Yaakov Avinu planted *shittim* [acacia] trees in Egypt, and on his deathbed, he commanded his sons to bring them up with them when they would depart from Egypt. He told them that Hashem would command them to make a Mishkan of *shittim* wood in the wilderness, and that they should be sure to have the wood at hand.

Yaakov Avinu planted shittim trees in Egypt, and he commanded his sons to bring them up with them when they would depart from Egypt.

---

2. *Sefer HaMitzvos*, Positive Commandment 20.

[The Torah states,] "So Yisrael set out with all he had and he came to Be'er Sheva where he slaughtered sacrifices to the God of his father Yitzchak" (*Bereishis* 46:1). Why did he go [to Be'er Sheva]? R' Nachman says that he went to cut down the cedar trees that his grandfather Avraham had planted in Be'er Sheva, as the verse states, "He [Avraham] planted an *'eishel'* in Be'er Sheva." [Yaakov cut those trees and replanted them in Egypt.]

Prepared by the Patriarchs

He went to cut down the cedar trees that his grandfather Avraham had planted in Be'er Sheva.

The midrash continues, "[The Torah states,] The middle bar inside the planks should extend from end to end" (*Shemos* 26:28). R' Levi notes that the middle bar measured 32 cubits. Where did they find such a long bar [in the Wilderness] on short notice? This teaches that they stored the wood with them from the days of Yaakov Avinu. Thus the Torah states, "And everyone with whom **there was** *shittim* wood" (ibid. 35:24), not "Everyone who **had** *shittim* wood" [to indicate that the Torah is referring to people who had wood with them from the time that they left Egypt].

- Another midrash[4] tells us that the planks were taken from trees that did not have knots or cracks, which is further proof that the wood used for the Mishkan was prepared beforehand.

- The Talmud[5] comments on the verse that refers to the *kerashim* as being made from עֲצֵי שִׁטִּים עֹמְדִים, *acacia wood, standing erect*" (*Shemos* 26:15). What is the meaning of the term "standing erect"? The Talmud offers three explanations: (1) the *kerashim* were erected in the direction in which they grew[6]; (2) they provided the support so that their [gold] plating would "stand" in place; (3) the *kerashim* will stand [i.e., last] forever and to all eternity.

The kerashim are referred to as "standing" because they stood straight and did not bend. In this way, the kerashim were like the Heavenly Seraphim, who cannot bend.

- *Zohar*[7] adds that the *kerashim* are referred to as "standing" because they stood straight and did not bend. In this way, the *kerashim* were like the Heavenly *Seraphim*, who cannot bend, because they do not have knees.

---

3. *Parashas Vayigash*, 94:4.

4. Ibid.

5. *Yoma* 72a.

6. I.e., the planks stood in the same direction as they appeared when they grew — the bases of the trees were on the ground, and the tops of the trees were the upper ends of the *kerashim*.

7. *Parashas Terumah* 171a.

To summarize, the *kerashim* contained the following characteristics: They were planted by Avraham Avinu, transplanted by Yaakov Avinu, contained no imperfections, did not bend, and will stand for all eternity. Why did the *kerashim* need to possess such rare qualities?

ANOTHER AMAZING FACT IS MENTIONED IN A MIDRASH[8] COMMENTING on the verse in which we were commanded to make the *kerashim*.

Too Precious To Be Hidden

Several items that Hashem created were hidden away for use in Days to Come, because He deemed them too special to be used in this world. An example is the light that Hashem created on the first day of Creation. Knowing that people were not worthy of enjoying this especially holy light, Hashem hid it for use by the righteous in Time to Come. There were other items that Hashem *wanted* to hide for the same reason, but he left them in the world to be used for the sake of His glory. For instance, gold should have been hidden away for the righteous, but Hashem left it in the world to be used for the construction of the Mishkan and the *Beis HaMikdash*.

The midrash adds that cedar trees should also have been hidden, but Hashem left them in the world to be used in the construction of the Mishkan and *Beis HaMikdash*. Obviously, the *kerashim* were so important that they prevented the *shittim* from being hidden! Clearly, the *kerashim* represent profound concepts. Let us try to understand them.

II. Keresh and Kesher

WE SUGGEST THAT THE *KERASHIM* SYMBOLIZE THE *KESHARIM*, the "ties," that bind one generation of Jews to the next. The idea that the *kerashim* represent connection is first mentioned by *Ohr HaChaim*, who writes[9] that the *kerashim* are *kesharim*, because the Mishkan was the medium that united and bound together all the holy elements of the upper and lower worlds. *Shem MiShmuel*[10] elaborates on this idea, writing that the *kerashim* were *kesharim* that tied Israel to the Creator:

Kerashim symbolize the kesharim, the "ties," that bind one generation of Jews to the next.

---

8. *Shemos Rabbah* 35:1.
9. *Shemos* 25:15.
10. *Parashas Terumah* 5674.

The name *adanim* (sockets upon which the *kerashim* rested) comes from the root *adnus*, which alludes to Hashem's *Lordship*. My father declared, "The *adanim* represent our acceptance of the yoke of our Master in Heaven." When we refer to "the yoke of Heaven" we refer only to the *physical* performance of the mitzvos, because attaining spiritual levels through contemplation is not a "yoke," it is sweeter than the sweetest honey. Physical performance of mitzvos is the foundation of everything; just as a building cannot be constructed without a foundation, so is it impossible to attain spiritual greatness without the physical performance of mitzvos. Even if a person were to contemplate the deep secrets contained in the mitzvah of tefillin all day long, and even if he cleaves to Hashem through that contemplation, if he does not actually perform the physical act of wrapping himself in tefillin, he has nothing to show for his efforts.

Attaining spiritual levels through contemplation is sweeter than the sweetest honey.

IT SEEMS, THEN, THAT THE *KERASHIM* SERVED AS *KESHARIM* TO connect the *adanim*, which represent the physical performance

Uniting the Upper and Lower Worlds

of mitzvos, to the *yerios* (coverings of the Mishkan), which represent the light of the Torah. Appropriately, *keresh* and *kesher* are made up of the very same letters.

It is clear, therefore, that the *kerashim* allude to the connection of the spiritual to the physical, and of the upper worlds to the lower worlds.

The kerashim allude to the connection of the spiritual to the physical, and of the upper worlds to the lower worlds.

Shem MiShmuel adds that the above explains why the *kerashim* are ascribed to Yaakov, for he, too, united the upper world with the lower world. As the *Zohar* comments, Leah symbolized a higher world of holiness, and Rachel represented service of Hashem in this world. Yaakov's mission was to unite both worlds, which he did by marrying them both.[11] Thus, Yaakov did in his life what the *kerashim* did in the Mishkan. Avraham Avinu, on the other hand, is characterized by the בְּרִיחַ הַתִּיכֹן, *the middle bar*, which went through all the planks of the Mishkan on all three of its walls (*Shemos* 26:28), binding them together. *Targum Yonasan* (ibid.) states that the middle bar was fashioned from a tree that Abraham planted in Be'er Sheva. The middle bar, which originated with Avraham, symbolizes the unification of all people on earth in the service of Hashem, which was his mission.

---

11. See Overview to *Vayeitzei*, pp. 1190-1204, ArtScroll *Bereishis*.

As *Chazal* teach, Avraham, the symbol of kindness, sought to unite everyone in such service by providing them with food, drink, and lodging, and then encouraging them to thank and bless Hashem Who made this all possible. Thus, in its totality, the structure of the Mishkan is associated with both Avraham and Yaakov.

PERHAPS WE CAN EXPAND ON THIS IDEA AND SUGGEST THAT *KERashim* also symbolize the connection between one generation and the next.

Kerashim — The Continuity of Klal Yisrael

Before Yaakov Avinu descended into the Egyptian exile, he wanted to ensure the continuity of the Jewish people. He felt it was vital to make a detour to Be'er Sheva to collect wood that Avraham Avinu had planted. Hashem had said of Avraham, "For I love him because he will instruct his children and his household after him ..." (*Bereishis* 18:19). Because Avraham had earned Hashem's love by his committment to transmit to future generations his own total dedication to Hashem and His commandments, and because Avraham was determined that all generations of Jews be involved in the effort to provide a resting place for the Divine Presence in this world, Yaakov made sure that the *kerashim* and the bars that held the Mishkan together would be fashioned from wood planted by Avraham. The *kerashim,* therefore, were a symbol of the eternal bond — the *kesher* — between generations of Jews, all of them committed to be a resting place for the *Shechinah.* Thus each *keresh* represents a link in the golden chain of Jewish generations.

This heavenly aspect was symbolized by the covering of the Mishkan. It consisted of ten curtains, each of which was 28 by 4 *amos.* The ten curtains were attached and placed above the Mishkan and draped over the *kerashim.* The Sages and commentators find many spiritual allusions in the number and dimensions of the coverings: They allude to King Shlomo's twenty-eight "seasons and times for everything under the heavens,"[12] so that they represent some of the most important aspects of the world in general, and Judaism in particular. The ten curtains represent the ten firmaments in the heavens,[13] the Ten Commandments,[14] and the Ten Utterances with which the world was created.[15] This latter allusion

The kerashim, were a symbol of the eternal bond between generations of Jews, all of them committed to be a resting place for the Shechinah.

---

12. *Koheles* 3:1-8.
13. *Zohar, Parashas Terumah* 706.
14. *Midrash HaGadol, Parashas Terumah.*
15. *Ohr HaChaim, ibid.* 26:1.

teaches that the Mishkan was equivalent to all of Creation and that Israel, which built it, has the merit of fulfilling the purpose of the Ten Utterances.

Knowing what the Mishkan would represent, Yaakov Avinu considered it vital that all Jewish generations should have a *kesher* to the Mishkan via the *kerashim*.

Support Beams and Sockets: Of Trials and Tribulations

THE GOLD-PLATED WOODEN SUPPORT BARS THAT WERE PLACED along the outside length of the Mishkan walls to hold the *kerashim* together were also deeply significant. They represent the different eras that we have traversed over the course of our history, each marked by its unique trials, difficulties, and tests. There was also a symbolism in the two *adonim*/sockets that supported each individual *keresh*. Just as each *keresh* needs its own *adanim*, so, too, each generation needs its own approach to deal with its trials and tests. Just as each *keresh* needed its own sockets, each exile had to chart its own course. The path that took Israel through the exile in Spain was not appropriate for Germany, and the stance that fit the European exile would not succeed in America. The solutions to problems we faced in Spain might have caused us to stumble in Germany. The solutions to the problems of the Sephardic world would not fit the Ashkenazic world, and approach needed in *Eretz Yisrael* might harm those living in other parts of the world.

The thing that united all the *kerashim* was the *b'riach hatichon*, the central bar that went through the *kerashim* and miraculously curved at the corners of the building to encompass all three walls. Different though conditions might be in all the countries and all the generations of Jewish history, the *b'riach hatichon* symbolizes the connection of all Jewish generations, from Avraham until today, united by a common faith and dedication to Hashem that infuses the nation and inspires it throughout history.

Just as a *keresh* serves as a *kesher* to hold together generations of Jews, there is another word formed from the same letters: *sheker* (falsehood). Falsehood — misrepresentation of Jewish authenticity — can sever that historic bond. In recent generations, we have unfortunately witnessed the assimilation and abandonment of faith caused by various segments of society that decided to cut the *kesher* that united all generations of Jews. Only if we are careful to keep the connection between our generation and those before us can we fortify and protect ourselves from such falsehood.

RABBI SAMSON RAPHAEL HIRSCH EXPLAINS THE SYMBOLISM OF TREES in general, and cedar trees in particular:

Standing Kerashim — Fortifying the Bond

The tree generally symbolizes steady, progressive growth and development. The cedar, of which *shittah* is one of ten varieties, represents, in addition, the characteristics of greatness and strength. Thus, the *shittim* wood in the Mishkan and its furnishings generally symbolize vigorous, enduring, ever-renewed, and continuous development.

We cited *Chazal's* teaching that the *kerashim* would last forever and for all eternity. Can that really be true? We do not have *kerashim* today! However, if we add the idea expressed by Rav Hirsch to the factors we raised earlier regarding the *kerashim*, we can learn vital lessons necessary for the survival of our nation.

Chazal teach that even after the tree was fashioned into a plank, it must retain the original integrity of the tree. The *kerashim* must be erected in the same direction in which they grew, they must be rigid and unbendable, and they support their gold plating — i.e., the essence of the *kerashim* is not the gold but the wood; the external gold covering is secondary to the essence of the wood.

Our lives must mirror these qualities. We must be like trees, with "our roots" — the earlier generations — placed firmly on the ground as a foundation, and, like trees that grow upward and reach for the heights, our forefathers' constant striving for spiritual growth should be our model. Thus, we must be planted firmly on earth, knowing the needs and desires of those around us, while at the same time aspiring toward the heavens, striving for ever-higher spiritual levels.

And, like the *kerashim* that did not bend, we must also stand strong against all negative and harmful influences that might seek to destroy our nation.

Finally, just as the external coverings of the *kerashim* were secondary to their wooden base, throughout the exile, our external coverings — our clothing, our language, our symbols of prosperity — may have changed to match those of our host country, but they remain secondary to our base, the firm, unbending Jew who remains faithful to Hashem. Though the *kerashim* were covered with gold, the Torah still speaks of them as wood, because their essence did not change, despite their external grandeur. And just as the wood used for the *kerashim* had to be free from imperfections, so, too, the planks of the Mishkan demand that we strive unceasingly toward perfection.

We can now understand why, at the beginning of Creation, Hashem considered hiding away cedar trees. The objectives that they sym-

We must be planted firmly on earth, knowing the needs and desires of those around us, while at the same time aspiring toward the heavens, striving for ever-higher spiritual levels.

bolize — remaining firmly rooted on earth, being involved in everyday activities of the world around us while simultaneously striving to attain spiritual greatness — are extremely difficult to achieve. To blend earthly pursuits with lofty ones, to lead others toward heightened spiritual levels while tending to their earthly desires and needs, is beyond the capacity of people unless they are dedicated to it totally. Since this goal is so difficult to achieve, Hashem considered concealing the cedar trees. In the end, however, He left them on earth so that they could be used to build the Mishkan and thereby be an inspiration to people, showing them how high they can rise if they follow the example of the great generations of old. The goal *can* be attained, and therefore we must make the attempt.

The goal can be attained, and therefore we must make the attempt.

Considering all the lessons of the *kerashim*, we might add that Hashem did not hide them so that we would be able to endure all the trials of exile and remain faithful to Him, no matter what hurdles we face.

III. Sivan: The Three-Ply Cord

NOW THAT WE HAVE SHOWN THAT THE *KERASHIM* REPRESENT the continuity of *Klal Yisrael*, we can understand why the Name Combination for Sivan comes from a verse regarding the *kerashim*. They symbolize the eternal bond between the generations of the Jewish people through allegiance to the Torah, so it is appropriate that the verse of Sivan, the month when Hashem gave the Torah to Israel, should be about the *kerashim*. As we saw from *Bnei Yissaschar*, the reverse is also true: the fact that the Name Combination for this month comes from a verse that represents our bond to our forefathers makes it the most appropriate month for receiving the Torah.

The fact that the Name Combination for this month comes from a verse that represents our bond to our forefathers makes it the most appropriate month for receiving the Torah.

The Talmud states,[16] "Blessed is the Merciful One, who gave a three-part Torah, to a three-part nation, through a third, in the third month." *Rashi* explains that the Torah has three parts: Chumash, *Nevi'im* (Prophets), and *Kesuvim* (Writings); we are a nation of three groups: Kohanim, Levites, and Israelites; we received the Torah through Moshe Rabbeinu, the third-born child of Amram andYocheved; and we received it in Sivan, the third month of the year, counting from Nissan.

Maharal notes that three is a number that represents wholeness, in the sense that when there are three sides, they can be joined in a

---

16. *Shabbos* 88a.

triangle, so that the previously existing two sides, which may be diametrically opposed to one another, can be conncected by the third side, thus bringing the opposites together to form a unit. White and black, for instance, are diametric opposites of each other, and cannot be unified. Three, however, cannot represent opposites, for, by definition, three things cannot be opposites of each other — one of the three will always fall between the other two. But if one takes two opposites — such as black and white — and adds a third color, such as red, the third color will fall somewhere between the two opposites and connect them. Thus the number three represents connection and therefore unity.

In the light of our explanation of the need to use Torah to seek spiritual advancement while remaining firmly rooted on earth, we can understand why it was vital that the Torah be given in the third month. The number three, with its ability to connect opposites that would otherwise be in conflict with each other, represents the possibility to take such diametric opposites as spirituality and materialism and combine them into one complete and perfect unit. In the simile of King Shlomo, "The three-ply cord will not quickly be severed" (Koheles 4:12). Here, too, the third side of the triangle, as it were, brings all three elements into one unified whole.

Since it is so important that the ties that bind one generation to another be perfect, the most appropriate time for receiving the Torah, which ties us to our ancestors, was Sivan, the third month, with its special potential for connection.

The number three represents the possibility to take such diametric opposites as spirituality and materialism and combine them into one complete and perfect unit.

MAHARAL[17] SETS FORTH ANOTHER PROPOSITION: THAT THREE REPREsents spirituality, and therefore the number three is uniquely associated with Israel. This is in addition to the prin-

Three — Bridging the Gap

ciple mentioned above, that the number three symbolizes Israel's responsibility to resolve the conflict between the spiritual and the material, like the *kerashim* that stand on earth and reach toward heaven. It is understandable, therefore, that we find the number three associated with our nation in many ways:

There are three partners in man: *Hashem*, a father, and a mother.[18] Our spiritual composition, too, is based on three parts: *nefesh*

---

17. In a lengthy and complex exposition (*Gur Aryeh, Bamidbar* 21:35), *Maharal* shows that there are three steps to a level of spirituality that elevates man above mundane, material existence.

18. *Kiddushin* 30b.

— the life-giving force that we share with animals; *ruach* — the spirit that raises us to a higher level than animals; and *neshamah* — the soul, a portion of Hashem, as it were, which makes the Jewish nation holy. The Jewish nation also is endowed with three qualities: we are merciful, bashful, and kind.[19]

Furthermore, the Torah clearly revolves around the number three, as we have seen from the passage from the Talmud we cited earlier. *Midrash Tanchuma*[20] cites several of the factors found in the Talmud, and adds several more:

- The Torah is comprised of three parts — Chumash, *Nevi'im*, and *Kesuvim*.
- [The study of] Mishnah can be divided into three categories — Talmud, Halachah, and Aggadah.
- The agent [who brought us the Torah] was the third-born in his family — Miriam, Aharon, and then Moshe.
- We pray three times daily.
- We declare Hashem's Holiness in *Kedushah* three times: *Kadosh, Kadosh, Kadosh.*
- Our nation is split into three groups — Kohanim, Levites, and Israelites.
- Moshe's name is spelled with three letters: מֹשֶׁה.
- Moshe is from the tribe of Levi, spelled with three letters: לֵוִי.
- We descend from three forefathers — Avraham, Yitzchok, and Yaakov.
- We received the Torah in the third month — Nissan, Iyar, Sivan.
- We received the Torah in a desert that has a three-letter name: סִין.
- We sanctified ourselves for three days before receiving the Torah, as the verse states, "Let them be prepared for the third day" (*Shemos* 19:11).

We might add that our relationship with Hashem was displayed through our pilgrimage to the *Beis HaMikdash* for the three annual festivals.

All these factors bear witness to the wonderful quality of the third month, in which three factors came together to form an indivisible whole — as *Zohar* states, "HaKadosh Baruch Hu, the Torah, and *Klal Yisrael* are one."

Now we can return to Rav Nevenzhal's question regarding the unusual detail and repetition in the Torah's discussion of the *kerashim*

---

19. *Yevamos* 79a.
20. *Yisro* 10.

and the other portions of the Mishkan. We were commanded to build the Mishkan to allow the Divine Presence to rest among us, so that we could have a close relationship with our Father in Heaven. The *kerashim,* as we have seen, binds us all with one another and with all the generations since Avraham. They also bind us to Hashem, for Hashem, the Torah, and Israel are one unit. Since *kerashim* represent the Jewish continuity that is critical if we wish to maintain that relationship, their construction is described at length. So important are they that the Torah repeats them.

The same is true of the Mishkan as a whole. The *Shechinah* rested upon it, just as it rests on the Jewish people as a whole. As *Ramban* and others note, the Mishkan and its parts symbolized the giving of the Torah at Mount Sinai. Sinai and Torah. Torah and Israel. They are inseparable. This is why every part of the Mishkan and all its vessels were important and precious to Israel. This explains the alacrity with which the Jews contributed for the Mishkan and built it. And the Torah emphasizes this by saying over and over that the people fashioned every part of the Mishkan complex "as Hashem commanded Moshe."

Just as the Mishkan became the resting place for the *Shechinah* in the Wilderness, so, too, the Jewish people, bound to its origins and Creator by the *kerashim,* continue to be the host of Hashem's Presence. We are a living Mishkan.

The Mishkan and its parts symbolized the giving of the Torah at Mount Sinai.

TAMMUZ

זֶה אֵינֶנּוּ שׁוֶה לִי (הוה"י).

The Name Combination for the month of Tammuz comes from a verse in Megillas Esther (5:13), "וְכָל זֶה אֵינֶנּוּ שׁוֶה לִי בְּכָל־עֵת אֲשֶׁר אֲנִי רֹאֶה אֶת מָרְדְּכַי הַיְּהוּדִי יוֹשֵׁב בְּשַׁעַר הַמֶּלֶךְ, Yet all this is worth nothing to me so long as I see Mordechai the Jew sitting at the king's gate," in which the wicked Haman bemoans the blow to his bloated pride every time Mordechai refuses to bow to him.

The Two Faces of Honor

תַּמוּז – זֶה אֵינֶנּוּ שׁוֶֹה לִי (הוה"י).

THE NAME COMBINATION FOR THE MONTH OF TAMMUZ COMES from a verse in *Megillas Esther* (5:13), וְכָל זֶה אֵינֶנּוּ שׁוֶֹה לִי בְּכָל עֵת אֲשֶׁר אֲנִי רֹאֶה אֶת מָרְדְּכַי הַיְּהוּדִי יוֹשֵׁב בְּשַׁעַר הַמֶּלֶךְ, *Yet all this is worth nothing to me so long as I see Mordechai the Jew sitting at the king's gate,* in which the wicked Haman bemoans the blow to his bloated pride every time Mordechai refuses to bow to him.

Rashi explains that all the obeisance Haman received when everyone in Achashveirosh's court bowed to him was meaningless, as long as Mordechai ignored him — so obsessed was he with his honor. It bothered him so much (*Lekach Yosef*) that he became severely depressed. We must understand how this verse and the subject of honor relate to the month of Tammuz.

Some other points to consider regarding Tammuz:

- *Bnei Yissaschar*[1] points out that the Name Combination for Tammuz, הוה"י, is the exact reverse of the Tetragrammaton, י-ה-ו-ה. When written in the correct order, the Name יהו־ה represents Heavenly Mercy (*rachamim*); if the order is completely reversed, it represents a shift toward Strict Justice (*Din*). In fact, this Name Combination was the catalyst for the strict justice that brought about Haman's downfall. The month of Tammuz, therefore, is a month in which strict justice reigns, continues *Bnei Yissaschar*. This applies even to the part of the month that precedes the Seventeenth of Tammuz,[2] for the *meraglim* (spies) were on their mission during the entire month. Heavenly Mercy is relatively limited during the month of Tammuz.

  Why did the spies' sin develop specifically during Tammuz, and how is that historic event related to the concept of honor that is the subject of the Name Combination of this month?

- *Bnei Yissaschar* also states that according to the order of the encampment in the Wilderness, Tammuz correlates to the tribe

All the obeisance Haman received when everyone in Achashveirosh's court bowed to him was meaningless, as long as Mordechai ignored him — so obsessed was he with his honor.

---

1. *Maamarei Chodesh Tammuz–Av* 1:1.

2. The Seventeenth of Tammuz was a particularly tragic day in Jewish history, second only to the Ninth of Av. See Mishnah, *Taanis* 26a, and the accompanying Talmudic analysis (beginning on 28b) for a list of tragedies that occurred on this day.

of Reuven. He writes, "Reuven correlates to Tammuz, which represents the sense of sight, and therefore, when Reuven was born, Leah said 'Hashem has *seen* my suffering' (*Bereishis* 29:32) which is why Leah chose the name Reuven, which means 'see, a son.'" We will explain this correlation as well.

1. Good Honor; Bad Honor

CHAZAL SEE HONOR BOTH POSITIVELY AND NEGATIVELY. ON THE one hand they taught,[3] "Jealousy, desire, and honor remove a person from the world." Also the Talmud states that the haughtiness of Yeravam ben Nevat, the first king of the Ten Tribes, drove him from the world.[4] The Talmud illustrates Yeravam's lust for honor by relating that Hashem grabbed him by his garment and said, "Repent, and I will walk with you and the son of Yishai [King David] in *Gan Eden.*" "Who will be first?" Yeravam asked. "The son of Yishai will be first," Hashem responded. "If so," declared Yeravam, "I do not want to repent." Clearly, lust for glory and honor can lead a person to make terrible mistakes.

On the other hand, *Chazal* spoke highly of the ideal of honoring our fellows, which implies that honor is a positive thing. One mishnah states,[5] "R' Eliezer says, 'Let your fellow's honor be as dear to you as your own.'" Another states,[6] "Who is honored? He who honors others, as it is said, 'Those who honor Me I will honor, and those who scorn Me shall be scorned.'"[7] *Chazal* also taught us that if a person runs away from glory, glory will pursue him.[8]

The answer to this apparent contradiction is obvious. A person should avoid honor for *himself,* but he should be zealous in honoring *others.*

A classic story illustrates what a person's attitude toward glory should be. It is told that when R' Shmelka, the brother of the *Hafla'ah,* arrived in Nikolsburg to become its rav, the city's Jews filled the streets to welcome him. When he saw the glory that was being bestowed

A person should avoid honor for himself, but he should be zealous in honoring others.

---

3. *Avos* 4:28.
4. *Sanhedrin* 101b.
5. Ibid. 2:15.
6. Ibid. 4:1.
7. *I Shmuel* 2:30.
8. *Eruvin* 13b.

upon him, he began to cry, and said, "I am unworthy of this honor."

When he arrived at the house that had been prepared for him, he asked for a few minutes to spend in solitude. The inhabitants granted his request, but one curious member of the community hid to see what the new rabbi would do. When R' Shmelka thought he was alone, he began to speak to himself: "Shalom Aleichem, Reb Shmelka"; "Welcome to our city, Rebbe"; "Come in peace, Rav of Nikolsburg."

The eavesdropper was puzzled by this and told the townspeople what he had overheard. Some of them asked R' Shmelka to explain his peculiar behavior. He answered, "The Mishnah teaches us that a person should value his fellow's honor as much as he values his own. But a person has the right to forgo his own honor. Does this give him the right to take liberties with his fellow's honor, as well? Certainly not!

"The Mishnah is teaching us that when other people praise us, we should take it no more seriously than if we were loudly proclaiming our own praises. Just as it is absurd for a person to display honor toward himself, it should be equally absurd to take it seriously when others glorify him.

"When I saw all the honor and glory that was being showered upon me by the people of Nikolsburg, I began to fear that I might become haughty. I decided to praise myself with the same words that I was hearing from the townspeople. When I heard those very same words coming out of my own mouth, I realized the absurdity of honor."

Interestingly, the Mishnah quoted above (*Avos* 4:28) mentions jealousy and desire as two more things that, like honor, remove a person from the world. We find the very same dichotomy in *Chazal's* statements regarding those two dangerous traits.

Jealousy

KING SHLOMO WROTE, "JEALOUSY IS HARSH AS THE GRAVE" (*SHIR HaShirim* 8:6), and, "Envy brings rotting of the bones" (*Mishlei* 14:30). We also saw the Mishnah's teaching that jealousy removes a person from the world.

On the other hand, *Chazal* taught,[9] "Envy between scholars increases wisdom." In a similar vein, *Sefer Chassidim*[10] writes, "Envy of mitzvos will increase [performance of] mitzvos." Furthermore, envy is listed as one of Hashem's character traits: "For Hashem, your God — He is a consuming

---

9. *Bava Basra* 21a.
10. 1189.

fire, a jealous God" (*Devarim* 4:24), and the liturgy of the High Holidays says, "His garment is Jealousy."

THE MISHNAH'S STATEMENT THAT DESIRE REMOVES A PERSON from the world can be sourced to the verse, "The desire of the

——————
Desire
——————

sluggard will kill him" (*Mishlei* 21:25). But desire for the right things is good. King Shlomo also wrote, "The desire of the righteous is only for good" (ibid. 21:25). Other verses praise desire as well: "Your Name and Your mention are the desire of our soul" (*Yeshayah* 26:8); "O Lord, before You is all my desire" (*Tehillim* 38:10).

Chazal[11] also found proper uses for desire, stating that a person who loves Torah will not become satisfied with the amount of Torah that he knows, and a person who loves mitzvos does not become satiated with the mitzvos that he has performed.

Thus, the three character traits that can remove people from the world when used improperly can also be used in a positive way.

II. Jealousy, Honor, and Desire Correspond to the Brain, the Heart, and the Liver

IN *DERECH CHAIM* (TO *AVOS* 4:22), *MAHARAL* COMMENTS THAT jealousy, lust, and honor correspond to three essential human functions, which are embodied in the mind, heart, and liver.

Know that a human being has a life-giving spirit, which has various forces that govern its actions. The three primary forces are:

Know that a human being has a life-giving spirit, which has various forces that govern its actions.

1) Nature. This force takes the nourishment that a person receives from the food he eats, removes what is indigestible, and enables the body to grow in height and girth. Lust for carnal pleasure comes from the extraneous natural force that encourages this drive. All desire, in fact, comes from this natural force, which is housed in the liver.

2) The life-giving force. This force enables us to move from place to place, and it also provides us with the desire for

---

11. *Devarim Rabbah* 2:26.

revenge, the tendency to bear a grudge, be jealous, and hate. The heart is home to this force.

3) The spiritual force. This power provides us with many important faculties, such as the five senses, the ability to think, to imagine, to remember, and to contemplate. This power is housed in the mind.

MAHARAL CONCLUDES THAT JEALOUSY IS UNDESIRABLE — WHY should a person envy what is not his? Jealousy drives a person from

Entitlement?

the world, because it diminishes his spirit. The same applies to lust, which also emanates from the life-giving force and leads a person to lust after something that is not his. The desire for honor emanates from a person's intelligence [a part of his spiritual force], which also leads him to feel that he is entitled to honor. Honor is a spiritual, not a physical, thing, which is why the desire for honor relates to the mind. And that is why lust for honor is harmful to the mind.

Nesivos Shalom expands on this point, explaining that a person's control over himself is defined by how well he controls these three basic traits. If his control in these areas is faulty, the *yetzer hara* takes control of the three main strongholds of his body, and therefore these sins remove him from the world. Torah observance is dependent on [the proper use of] these three central parts of the person, and all bad things come from losing control of one or more of the three.

But *Nesivos Shalom* concludes with comforting words. He writes that Hashem gave us three pillars upon which the world stands — Torah, *Avodah* (service), and *Gemilus Chassadim* (acts of loving-kindness) — which correspond to the same three primary organs that can cause a person's downfall. Torah is acquired primarily through the use of the mind, service is performed by the heart,[12] and kindness through the organs of the body that perform physical acts.

It seems from *Nesivos Shalom* that we can repair damage caused by jealousy, desire, and honor, measure for measure, by putting each damaged organ to a corresponding positive use: Torah atoning for the sin of honor; service of the heart atoning for human lust; and kindness atoning for jealousy.

Jealousy drives a person from the world, because it diminishes his spirit.

Hashem gave us three pillars upon which the world stands — Torah, Avodah, and Gemilus Chassadim — which correspond to the same three primary organs that can cause a person's downfall.

---

12. As the Torah commands us, "And to serve Him [Hashem] with all your heart" (*Devarim* 11:13).

PIRKEI D'RABBI ELIEZER[13] STATES THAT (ANGELS AND) SATAN SAW THE *honor* Adam HaRishon was being accorded, with angels roasting

Early Manifestations of Jealousy, Lust, and Honor

meat and filtering wine for him,[14] and they were consumed with *jealousy*. They therefore caused him to *desire* the fruit of the Tree of Knowledge, which was "desirous to the eyes" (*Bereishis* 6:3).

Sfas Emes[15] quotes the Kozhnitzer Maggid, stating that the Torah recorded the stories of Kayin killing Hevel, the generation of the *Mabul*, and the *Dor Haflagah* (Generation of the Dispersion), because each of us has some measure of the traits that caused those people to sin. Kayin killed Hevel because he was jealous of him, the people who perished in the *Mabul* sinned through desire, and those who built the Tower of Bavel, and were consequentially dispersed, sinned because they sought honor. Everyone has some measure of jealousy, desire, and craving for honor, and these portions in the Torah remind us to perfect ourselves and repair these negative traits.

In *Iyunim B'Pirkei Avos*, my father *zt"l* expands on this idea:

> These three traits (jealousy, desire, and honor) damage a person's character and cause him to degenerate and be removed from the world.
>
> Kayin and Hevel were two brothers, each of whom would eventually be able to lay claim to half the world. Nevertheless, the slightest hint of perceived favoritism caused Kayin to become jealous. The jealousy consumed him until he lost control of himself and murdered Hevel.
>
> The serpent also lost all that he had because of jealousy. As the Midrash[16] states, the serpent coveted Adam's wife and plotted to entice Adam to sin so that it, the serpent, could take Chavah as a mate.
>
> The corruption in Noach's time began with lust, as the Torah states, "Now the earth had become corrupt before God, and the earth had become filled with robbery. And God saw the earth and behold it was corrupted, for all flesh had corrupted its way upon the earth" (*Bereishis* 6:11-12). The people had become very corrupt, both in their desire for carnal pleasure[17] and for

Jealousy, desire, and honor damage a person's character and cause him to degenerate and be removed from the world.

---

13. Ch. 13.

14. *Sanhedrin* 59b.

15. *Parashas Noach,* 5654.

16. *Bereishis Rabbah* 18:6.

17. As *Beis Genazei* infers from the verse, "They took themselves wives from whomever they chose" (*Bereishis* 6:2).

wealth, but, as the verse indicates, the source of their downfall was lust for pleasures of the flesh.

The people who built the Tower of Bavel had but one thing in mind: honor. They expressed their interest clearly in outlining their plans for the Tower. "Let us build us a city," they said, "and a tower with its top in the heavens, *and let us make a name for ourselves*" (*Bereishis* 11:4).

The sin of idol worship that began during the generation of Enosh was also rooted in jealousy.

Beis Genazei adds that the sin of idol worship that began during the generation of Enosh was also rooted in jealousy. The most popular idols of that era were the heavenly bodies, which people thought controlled the world. They thought that paying them homage would bring greater levels of abundance to the earth, and each worshiper thought that his "god" would make him more prosperous than the others.

Seeking Honor: The Worst Trait

ACCORDING TO R' CHAIM SHMULEVITZ,[18] THE VERSE ABOUT HAMAN from which the Name Combination of Tammuz is derived proves that, in a way, seeking honor is the worst character trait:

Achashveirosh had elevated Haman to a higher position than all the other ministers of his kingdom, and all the king's subjects had to bow and prostrate themselves to him. He was second only to the king, and had great honor and power. His desire for honor was so great, however, that he demanded the last bit of honor that he was missing — he insisted that Mordechai also had to bow and prostrate himself. It is truly astounding that a man who receives so much obeisance could even notice — much less insist on — the tiny bit of honor that Mordechai withheld from him. Haman should have been so satiated with honor that he should not have noticed Mordechai.

Honor is nothing more than an illusion of greatness. Since it is an illusion, it cannot satisfy a person.

We see, however, that the desire for honor is unique. People usually desire something that will bring them pleasure. Once they obtain it they feel satisfied. Honor, however, is not a tangible pleasure; it is nothing more than an illusion of greatness. In and of itself, honor does not provide pleasure. Since it is an illusion, it cannot satisfy a person. Not only did Haman feel that he was missing the slight honor that Mordechai's bow would provide, but he decided that all the honor he received from everyone else was worthless, as long as Mordechai refused to acknowledge

---

18. *Sichos Mussar*, 5733, No.17.

him. Imagine a person who attends a lavish banquet, at which he is served every delicacy he could possible want, except for one. Would he say, "It is worth nothing to me"?

How different is the desire for honor from all other desires!

Honor is not tangible. It is a desire for something that a person has concocted from his own imagination, his personal fantasy. If that is what he wants, he enjoys it when it comes, but if even a small part of the fantasy is lacking, he will feel frustrated and unfulfilled. That is why Haman could say that all the prostrations in the king's court meant nothing to him as long as Mordechai stood erect. Had he wanted only physical pleasure and could obtain only part of it, he could have enjoyed at least that much, but Haman wanted a fantasy, and he had not achieved it.

R' Chaim concludes:

There is no limit to the desire for honor, because the desire is for falseness, and it can blind a person until he shamelessly demands it, even though he realizes it is false. A person who is controlled by his desire for honor has willingly sold himself into his slavery to it, for only his own wishes lit the flame that caused him to desire honor. He dug himself a pit that can give him no satisfaction.

Similarly, R' Chaim of Volozhin writes that of the three character traits listed in the mishnah, the trait of seeking honor is the worst, because jealousy is a sin of *bein adam l'chaveiro* (between man and his fellow human); desire is a sin of *bein adam l'Makom* (between man and God); but seeking honor is a sin that affects both our fellow man and God [because in the process of seeking it, one denigrates others and tries to seize the honor that is due to God].

Seeking honor is a sin that affects both our fellow man and God [because in the process of seeking it, one denigrates others and tries to seize the honor that is due to God].

III. Positive Uses of the Three Traits

ALTHOUGH JEALOUSY, DESIRE, AND HONOR REMOVE A PERSON from the world, there are times and places when they can serve holy causes.

Chasam Sofer teaches that jealousy, which is rooted in anger and cruelty, should be used against wanton sinners. We should not be accepting of those who sin; we should pursue them until we wipe them out, in keeping with the Torah's commandments, "You shall destroy the evil from your midst" (*Devarim* 13:6); "You shall not accede to him" (ibid. 13:9); and "You shall not be compassionate or conceal him" (ibid.). King Shaul was punished for showing undeserved mercy to Agag, King of Amalek,[19] disregarding the commandment "You shall not allow any person to live" (*Devarim* 20:16). Desire should be used when necessary, to maintain the body and provide it with its needs. Honor can be used by a *talmid chacham*, who should have an eighth of an eighth of pride when teaching his students, as the Talmud states,[20] "Conduct your role of leadership among exalted people, and cast awe on your students."

Honor can be used by a talmid chacham when teaching his students, as the Talmud states, "Conduct your role of leadership among exalted people, and cast awe on your students."

Chasam Sofer finds an allusion to the proper uses of these traits in the verse אֶרְחַץ בְּנִקָּיוֹן כַּפָּי וַאֲסֹבְבָה אֶת מִזְבַּחֲךָ ה', *I wash my hands in purity and circle around Your Altar, O Hashem* (*Tehillim* 26:6). The letters ר, ח, ץ in the word אֶרְחַץ are an acronym. The ר stands for רשע, *a wicked person*, against whom we may use jealousy; ח, the numerical value of which is 8, corresponds to the eighth of an eighth of pride a *talmid chacham* should display; and the ץ stands for צורך, *need*, which alludes to the use of desire in order to provide the body with its needs. The proper use of the words alluded to by this acronym, as implied by the verse, are means by which one can gain purity and be worthy of circling Hashem's Altar.

Similarly, *Likkutei Torah* (by the *Baal HaTanya*) writes that jealousy, desire, and honor will not harm a person who uses them for holiness — on the contrary, they can make one grow even more. *Chazal* teach that jealousy among scholars increases wisdom. A person dedicated to the attainment of Torah wisdom can be the subject of other people's admiration and not become haughty.[21] Thus the Torah commanded Moshe, "You shall make vestments of sanctity for Aharon your brother, for **glory** and splendor" (*Shemos* 28:2). And the Torah commands, "In the presence of an old person, you shall rise" (*Vayikra* 19:32), and so on.

Any use of jealousy, desire, and honor for non-spiritual purposes is a product of self-importance.

In contrast, increased honor for earthly accomplishments, however, feeds a person's ego and makes him haughty. Any use of jealousy, desire, and honor for non-spiritual purposes is a product of self-importance and may well remove a person from the world.

---

19. See *I Shmuel,* Ch. 15.

20. *Kesubos* 103b.

21. The letters of the Hebrew word חכמה spell the words כח מה, the power of considering oneself to be insignificant.

AS WE HAVE SEEN, HAMAN COULD NOT ENJOY THE HONOR HE received — he needed *a full measure* of honor. The Talmud asks,[22]

A Scriptural Allusion to Haman

"Where do we find an allusion to Haman in the Torah? From the phrase, 'הֲמִן הָעֵץ' (*Bereishis* 3:12), where Hashem asked Adam if he had eaten from the Tree of Knowledge, which had been forbidden to him. Granted, the name הָמָן is comprised of the same letters — and even in the same order — as the word הֲמִן, but is that enough of an allusion to be considered a source for Haman in the Torah?

Itturei Torah quotes one of the mussar greats, who states that Haman's behavior demonstrates one of the strange traits of human nature. He could not find satisfaction with what he *had*. His main objective in life was to acquire the only thing he did *not* have. Haman was well aware of this peculiar trait, as the Megillah relates: "Haman recounted to them the glory of his wealth and of his many sons, and all [the ways] in which the king had promoted him and elevated him above the officials and royal servants. Haman said, 'Moreover, Queen Esther brought no one but myself to accompany the king to the banquet that she had prepared, and tomorrow, too, I am invited by her along with the king' " (*Esther* 5:11-12)

What more could a person want? Haman goes on: "Yet all this *is worth nothing to me* as long as I see Mordechai the Jew sitting at the king's gate" (ibid. 5:13). One Jew refuses to bow, and Haman cannot find satisfaction!

One Jew refuses to bow, and Haman cannot find satisfaction!

The Talmud was not looking for a word that sounded similar to Haman's name. Rather it sought a Scriptural source for Haman's character trait. The Talmud answers that the same trait was the root cause of Adam's sin, regarding which we find the phrase הֲמִן הָעֵץ. Adam was supposed to live forever in Gan Eden, surrounded by everything he could possibly want. Hashem told him, "Of every tree of the garden you may freely eat" (*Bereishis* 2:16). Only one tree was off limits — "But of the Tree of Knowledge of Good and Bad, you must not eat thereof; for on the day you eat of it, you shall surely die" (ibid. 2:17).

Adam had everything except one tree, but he could not resist partaking from the only tree that was forbidden to him, and he thereby brought death upon all humankind.

There is a vital lesson to be learned from these stories. Not always must a person have everything he desires. We must learn to be satisfied with the bountiful blessings that Hashem grants us. If

We must learn to be satisfied with the bountiful blessings that Hashem grants us.

---

22. *Chullin* 139b.

we constantly seek to acquire the few things that we are missing in life, we may bring death and destruction upon ourselves and those around us, as was the fate of Adam. The same trait was at the root of Haman's downfall. He had the subservience of everyone but one man. And that was not enough.

WE WONDERED HOW THE MONTH OF TAMMUZ CORRELATES TO ITS Name Combination, which comes from the verse regarding Haman.

The Spies: Wanting Everything — A Dangerous Perspective

As noted, the spies were touring *Eretz Yisrael* during the entire month of Tammuz. What were they seeking to accomplish with their negative report about *Eretz Yisrael*?

Shem MiShmuel[23] writes that everyone realized that life would change in *Eretz Yisrael*. While traveling the Wilderness, the Jews ate manna, a spiritual food, and drank water from the Well of Miriam, whose waters enabled a person to attain great spiritual levels. (It is known that the *Arizal* gave R' Chaim Vital a cup of water from the Well of Miriam in order to open his mind to the secrets of Torah.) When the Jews would enter *Eretz Yisrael*, they would engage in physical labor, in plowing and planting the land, by which they would be able to perform the mitzvos that apply to the land. The spies, however, were afraid that they might become mired in the mundane realities of the world. They wanted to stay in the Wilderness to maintain the spiritual level that they had attained by living in constant proximity to miracles.

In other words, the spies wanted everything. They wanted to retain the high level of spiritual greatness that they were experiencing in the Wilderness, where their physical needs were supplied for them without having to invest any effort, lest they lose some of the spirituality in the process. They wanted to continue to live via miracles, as they did during the forty years in the Wilderness. They wanted to have food delivered to them ready to eat, to have their clothing washed and ironed by the clouds, to be able to study Torah uninterrupted, and therefore they preferred to remain in the Wilderness, rather than enter the Promised Land.

This is what the spies had in common with Haman. He could not do with the honor that he had; he wanted everything. And while the interests of the spies were incomparably loftier than Haman's, they, too, refused to be satisfied with the manner of life that was destined

The spies wanted to stay in the Wilderness to maintain the spiritual level that they had attained by living in constant proximity to miracles.

---

23. *Beha'aloscha* 5664.

for them in *Eretz Yisrael*. They would not be content with the ordinary form of living. They wanted to live through miracles.

The spies' outlook on life, their feeling that everything was owed to them, is very dangerous. People who are so self-centered that they think that they are owed everything find it hard to accept other people's opinions and feelings, and will usually treat others harshly.

Tammuz is associated with such behavior. The wall surrounding Jerusalem in the era of the Second *Beis HaMikdash* was breached during Tammuz, and that set off a process of destruction that culminated in the burning of the *Beis HaMikdash* on Tishah b'Av. Why was the Second *Beis HaMikdash* destroyed? Because people displayed baseless hatred and disrespect for one another.

AS MENTIONED, *BNEI YISSASCHAR* TEACHES THAT ACCORDING TO the order of the encampments in the Wilderness, Tammuz corresponds to the tribe of Reuven, whose name

Tammuz: Impaired Spiritual Sight

is based on the sense of sight: "Leah conceived and she bore a son, and she called his name Reuven, as she had declared, 'Because Hashem has *seen* my humiliation'" (*Bereishis* 29:32). It appears that Tammuz is related to the sense of sight. Why?

R' Meir Yechiel of Ostrovtza wonders why the Torah states, "You shall not explore after your heart and after your eyes, after which you stray" (*Bamidbar* 15:39). It would seem that the eyes should be mentioned before the heart, since, in *Rashi's* words, "The eyes see, and the heart desires." Why, therefore, is the heart mentioned before the eyes?

The truth is that the heart also "sees," says the Ostrovtza Rebbi. The intellectual vision of the heart is what we refer to as the "mind's eye," and it is far more acute and deep than the sense of vision of the eyes. Therefore, the Torah places the vision of the mind before the vision of the eyes. Certainly it is true that the eye is the "agent of sin," but in terms of vision that of the heart is potentially more dangerous.

The intellectual vision of the heart is what we refer to as the "mind's eye," and it is far more acute and deep than the sense of vision of the eyes.

This idea provides us with a basis for understanding the connection between Tammuz and vision. We have seen *Maharal's* teaching that honor, which is associated with Tammuz, is pleasure that the mind desires. The only way to combat a desire that begins in the mind and avoid chasing honor is by using our mind's eye properly, by perfecting the intellectual and emotional "vision" that, if left unbridled, can inspire a perverted desire for honor.

Especially in the light of *Likkutei Torah's* teaching that when jealousy, desire, and honor are used for sacred, spiritual purposes, not only do they not remove a person from the world, they elevate and enhance his stature. Surely it is the mind's eye, more than anything else, that can channel a person to direct his faculties toward the pursuit of holiness.

This takes us back to *Bnei Yissaschar's* teaching that the Name Combination for Tammuz represents strict justice, because it reverses the spelling of Hashem's Name that stands for His Attribute of Mercy. It is true that strict justice is dominant in this month, but we can overcome it. Although jealousy, desire, and honor are usually extremely harmful traits, the power of intellectual vision — which is closely related to Tammuz — can turn them around and make them instruments of spirituality. Seeking honor is destructive; rendering honor is positive. Even the character traits that remove a man from the world can be used constructively. The "negative" Name Combination of Tammuz need not be absolute; it is meant to spur people to change themselves and thereby change strict justice into pure mercy.

Although jealousy, desire, and honor are usually extremely harmful traits, the power of intellectual vision can turn them around and make them instruments of spirituality.

Nesivos Shalom, cited above, taught that the damage caused by jealousy, desire, and honor can be repaired by using the offending organ properly: Torah study repairs damage done through honor, service of Hashem cures the ills of desire, and kindness is an antidote to jealousy. Accordingly, we may suggest that an additional way to cure the damage wrought by these traits is to use these very same traits in a spiritual manner. Then we can hope to turn the strict justice associated with Tammuz into Heavenly Mercy.

AV

הִנֵּה יַד ה' הוֹיָה בְּמִקְנְךָ; הַסְכֵּת וּשְׁמַע יִשְׂרָאֵל הַיּוֹם (הוי"ה).

Unlike all other months, there are two versions of the Name Combination for the month of Av, although both agree that the order of the letters is הוי"ה. According to Bnei Yissaschar, it comes from a single word in a verse in which Moshe Rabbeinu warns Pharaoh about the impending plague of dever (epidemic that caused the sudden death of animals): הִנֵּה יַד ה' הוֹיָה בְּמִקְנְךָ, Behold, the hand of Hashem is on your livestock (Shemos 9:3). Incidentally, he notes that this is the only Name Combination that consists of a single word; those of the other months are formed from letters of four consecutive words.

Destruction and Consolation

אָב – הִנֵּה יַד ה' הוֹיָה בְּמִקְנְךָ;
הַסְכֵּת וּשְׁמַע יִשְׂרָאֵל הַיּוֹם (הוי״ה).

UNLIKE ALL OTHER MONTHS, THERE ARE TWO VERSIONS OF the Name Combination for the month of Av, although both agree that the order of the letters is הוי״ה. According to *Bnei Yissaschar*, it comes from a single word in a verse in which Moshe Rabbeinu warns Pharaoh about the impending plague of *dever* (epidemic that caused the sudden death of animals): הִנֵּה יַד ה' **הוֹיָה** בְּמִקְנְךָ, *Behold, the hand of Hashem is on your livestock* (*Shemos* 9:3). Incidentally, he notes that this is the only Name Combination that consists of a single word; those of the other months are formed from letters of four consecutive words.

Siddurim quote *Mishnas Chassidim* as sourcing this Name Combination to the verse הַסְכֵּת וּשְׁמַע יִשְׂרָאֵל הַיּוֹם, *Be attentive and hear, O Israel: This day …* (*Devarim* 27:9), which is part of the covenant *Klal Yisrael* forged with Hashem when they were on the verge of entering *Eretz Yisrael*.

We must wonder how these subjects — the epidemic in Egypt and the covenant forged in the Plains of Moav — are related to the month of Av, and whether any connection can be found between the two subjects.

Why is Av the only month that does not have a universally accepted Name Combination?

Furthermore, why is Av the only month that does not have a universally accepted Name Combination?

Bnei Yissaschar points out that while the Name Combination of Tammuz is written in the reverse order of the Tetragrammaton — an indication of a strong presence of strict justice in the world — the Name Combination for Av is split in two: the first half has the last two letters of the Name (ו and ה), but they are written in reverse order — first ה, then ו — while the second half of the Name Combination contains the first two letters of the Name in their proper order — י followed by ה. As explained in our essay on Tammuz, the proper order of the Name's letters alludes to Divine mercy, while the reversed order indicates strict justice. Thus, the Name Combination of Av implies that the first half of Av is a time of strict justice, while the second half of the month — starting with the fifteenth — is a time of mercy. Appropriately, *Chazal* teach that the fifteenth of Av, which begins the second half of the month, was celebrated with unparalleled joy. We will try to explain why a single month is a mixture of justice and mercy, and what we can learn from the dual nature of Av.

Bnei Yissaschar notes that we always read the *parashiyos* of *Pinchas, Mattos, Masei,* and *Devarim* during *Bein HaMetzarim*[1] (the Three Weeks). In order to insure that *Pinchas* is read during the Three Weeks, *Chukas* and *Balak* are sometimes separated and *Mattos* and *Massei* are read together. Apparently these *parashiyos* contain an important message for the *Bein HaMetzarim*. We will try to bring that message to light.

I. Dever — Heavenly Justice

CHAZAL[2] STATE THAT THE TERM יַד ה׳, *THE HAND OF HASHEM,* always refers to *dever*. They derive this through a בְּנְיַן אָב, a *general principle*, drawn from the verse הִנֵּה יַד ה׳ הוֹיָה בְּמִקְנְךָ, *Behold the hand of Hashem is on your livestock,* which appears in Moshe Rabbeinu's warning regarding *dever*. Since the term *hand of Hashem* in that verse refers to an epidemic that causes sudden death, we may assume that whenever it appears in Scripture, that is its meaning. This concept is also found in the Haggadah, which states that the term יָד חֲזָקָה, *strong hand,* refers to *dever,* as is derived from the above verse.

Ramban[3] comments that the term יַד ה׳, *the hand of Hashem,* also alludes to the Attribute of Justice, and cites several Scriptural sources to prove his point.

It is interesting to note that *dever* was the fifth plague, and *Maharal*[4] points out that the number five represents *din*. For instance, the Mishnah lists five bitter herbs that can be used to fulfill the mitzvah

Ramban comments that the term "the hand of Hashem" also alludes to the Attribute of Justice, and cites several Scriptural sources to prove his point.

---

1. *Bein HaMetzarim* is the three-week period of mourning that begins on the Seventeenth of Tammuz and ends on Tishah b'Av. In the times of both *Batei Mikdash* the walls of Jerusalem were breached on the Seventeenth of Tammuz and the *Beis HaMikdash* was destroyed on the Ninth of Av.
2. *Rus Rabbah* 2:20.
3. *Shemos* 14:31.
4. *Tiferes Yisrael* 26.

of eating *maror* at the Seder. Similarly, Midbar Sinai had five names (*Shabbos* 89a), some of which allude to the harsh judgment that the nations earned because they spurned the Torah. *Maharal* explains that a desert symbolizes judgment because it lacks the elementary conditions needed for human life. He explains further that since the number five represents judgment, the plague of *dever*, the embodiment of God's strong hand, was the fifth plague.

We will explain the correlation between the month of Av and *dever*, the time and the plague that symbolize judgment.

A desert symbolizes judgment because it lacks the elementary conditions needed for human life.

Retribution Measure for Measure

SOURCES IN THE MISHNAH INDICATE THAT *DEVER* IS A PUNISHMENT that comes to atone in specific, proportionate measure. The mishnah states[5] that *dever* comes to the world for the [illegal use] of fruits of the Sabbatical Year, meaning that they were not made available to everyone, including the poor. The next mishnah states that *dever* comes "at four periods [of the seven-year Sabbatical cycle]. *Dever* increases in the fourth year, in the seventh year, in the year following the Sabbatical year, and annually following the Succos festival. In the fourth year, for [having neglected to give] the tithe of the poor in the third year; in the seventh year, for [having neglected to give] the tithe of the poor in the sixth year; in the year following the Sabbatical year for [having violated the laws of] the Sabbatical produce; and annually, at the conclusion of the festival of Succos, for having robbed the poor of the gifts they were entitled to."

Tosafos Yom Tov explains that when *dever* strikes during one of these periods, it is measure for measure for a corresponding transgression. There are always some people who withhold food that should go to the poor, especially at the times mentioned in the mishnah. The sinners shortened the lives of the needy by not giving them food. Some of the sinners thought that if they gave away these portions of their produce to the poor instead of selling it, when they would grow older they would lack funds to purchase food. Their punishment fits the sin. By denying food to the needy, they affected their health and even caused starvation; therefore Hashem shortens their lives.

When dever strikes it is measure for measure for a corresponding transgression.

Meiri,[6] too, comments that *dever* is the fitting punishment for those who withhold gifts that should go to the poor, thereby causing them to die of hunger. He adds that by mentioning the long list of

---

5. *Avos* 5:8,9.

6. In his commentary to this mishnah.

specific sins and the retribution that they bring, the Mishnah means to encourage people who suffer misfortune to analyze their deeds in order to discover what sins may have caused the suffering. Doing so will influence serious people to repent.

Midrash Shmuel provides an additional perspective with which to view the proportionality of *dever* as a punishment for selfish use of Sabbatical Year produce. By maintaining ownership of their fields and produce as if they, not Hashem, are the proprietors of the world, they deny Divine Providence. They act as if the world functions according to the law of nature, independent of His will. Hashem punishes them by sending a very unnatural death to the world — a plague that cannot be explained rationally and can come only from Hashem — as Scripture states, "I will send *dever* among you" *Vayikra* 26:25), and "Hashem will attach the plague to you" (*Devarim* 28:21). Thus those who deny Divine Providence are punished with a form of death that proves its presence in our lives.

Maharam Shick sums up, stating that these two mishnayos highlight Hashem's infinite Mercy. Since we see that Hashem punishes only measure for measure, people can learn to identify their sins based on the punishment they receive, thus making it easier for them to repent and receive Hashem's forgiveness.

Since Hashem punishes only measure for measure, people can learn to identify their sins based on the punishment they receive, thus making it easier for them to repent and receive Hashem's forgiveness.

Destruction and Consolation — Measure for Measure

NOW THAT WE HAVE SEEN THAT THE PLAGUE OF *DEVER* SYMBOLIZES of the proportionality of Heavenly justice, its association with the month of Av is readily understood. The *haftarah* of the Shabbos after Tishah b'Av begins with the repetitive נַחֲמוּ עַמִּי יֹאמַר אֱלֹקֵיכֶם, *Comfort, comfort My people, says your God* (*Yeshayah* 40:1).

Rabbeinu Bachaye[7] explains that Hashem rules this world *midah k'neged midah*, measure for measure. Since *Klal Yisrael* had sinned repeatedly, as the verse states, חֵטְא חָטְאָה יְרוּשָׁלַם, *Jerusalem has sinned by committing a sin* (*Eichah* 1:8), [i.e. the repetitive use of the word *sin* implies that their sins were repetitive] and their punishment was doubled, as we see in the verse, כִּי לָקְחָה מִיַּד ה' כִּפְלַיִם בְּכָל חַטֹּאתֶיהָ, *For she has received double for all her sins from the hand of Hashem* (*Yeshayah* 40:2), it is only appropriate that they should be comforted twice. In other words, the relationship of destruction and comfort must be in exact proportion to each other, measure for

---

7. In the entry for *Nachamu*.

measure. Just as a double sin brought a double punishment, so, too, Hashem will provide a double measure of consolation.

The Name Combination for Av comes from a verse regarding *dever*, because the proportionality with which Hashem rules this world — which *dever* symbolizes — is present in Av. During the first, difficult part of the month, which is represented by the reversed ה and ו in the Name Combination, we mourn for the double punishment that we received in proportion to our repeated sins. In the second, comforting half of the month, represented by the י and ה in the correct order, we are comforted repeatedly, in equal measure to the punishment we received.

God's "strong hand" alludes to punishment that parallels the sin, measure for measure.

That *dever* is a paradigm for the concept of measure for measure explains why *Chazal* chose to use it as the *binyan av,* the "general principle" that sheds light on every Scriptural reference to Hashem's strong hand. As in the case of *dever,* God's "strong hand" alludes to punishment that parallels the sin, measure for measure.

II. Dual Purposes of Dever and Av

PERHAPS WE CAN EXPLAIN THE CONNECTION BETWEEN AV AND *dever* in another light, based on *Meshech Chochmah's*[8] formulation regarding *dever.* He points out that the plague of *dever* did not begin as soon as Moshe announced it. Instead, as he told Pharaoh, Hashem set an appointed time, saying, "Tomorrow Hashem shall carry out this word in the land" (*Shemos* 9:5). *Meshech Chochmah* explains that Hashem wanted to give the Egyptians time to sell their livestock to the Jews so that the animals would not die. Indeed, many Egyptians did so, and the Jews then returned the animals after the plague, as a favor to the Egyptians. As a result, the Egyptians were embarrassed to refuse the Jews' requests to borrow their clothing, gold, and silver when the time came for them to leave Egypt.

According to Meshech Chochmah, therefore, dever had two purposes.

According to *Meshech Chochmah,* therefore, *dever* had two purposes. On a simple level, it punished the Egyptians, but on a deeper, concealed level, it allowed the Jews to curry favor in the eyes of the Egyptians so they would later feel obligated to lend their possessions to the Jews.

---

8. *Shemos* 9:5.

The month of Av, as well, has two purposes: destruction and comfort. At first glance, Av is characterized by the destruction and mourning over the loss of both *Batei Mikdash*, and the first portion of the month is devoted to bemoaning that loss. But the second half of the month serves a second purpose; it is a time of consolation and joy.

The resemblance between *dever* and Av runs even deeper, however. The good that we experienced when we left Egypt, in the sense that the Egyptians gave the Jews much wealth, came *as a result* of the difficulty that the Egyptians were dealt during *dever*. It may even be that the threat to the Egyptian livestock was not the main objective of *dever*. Its primary purpose may have been to bring goodwill to the Jews who would return livestock to the Egyptians, so they could later request the Egyptian's possessions.

Similarly, the destruction of the *Batei Mikdash* was not the primary purpose of Av. The primary purpose will be experienced only with the coming of *Mashiach*, when, in the words of the prophet, "The fast of the fourth [month],[9] the fast of the fifth, the fast of the seventh and the fast of the tenth will be to the House of Judah for joy and gladness and for happy festivals" (*Zechariah* 8:19).

Because of Zechariah's reassuring prophecy, *Chazal* taught, "When Av begins we *diminish* our joy" — we do not eliminate it — we diminish our joy temporarily at the beginning of the month, in mourning over the loss of the *Batei Mikdash*. We know, however, that all the fast days, including Tishah b'Av, will eventually be celebrated as festivals.

All the fast days, including Tishah b'Av, will eventually be celebrated as festivals.

It is told that R' Avraham Kammai, the son of R' Eliyahu Boruch Kammai, the Rav and Rosh Yeshivah of Mir, once went to a bookstore on Erev Tishah b'Av to purchase a *Kinnos*. Uncharacteristically, he hesitated over the purchase. Surprised, the storekeeper asked him why he was suddenly being so frugal.

"When I come into your store to buy a *sefer*, I expect to use it for many years, including in the days of *Mashiach*. A *Kinnos*, however, is a book that I need only temporarily, for certainly by next year *Mashiach* will have redeemed us, and we will no longer recite *Kinnos*."

---

9. The fast of the fourth month is the Seventeenth of Tammuz, the fast of the fifth is Tishah b'Av, the seventh is Tzom Gedaliah, and the tenth is the fast of the tenth of Teves.

WE CAN NOW MOVE ON TO EXPLAIN THE SECOND NAME COMBINATION for Av. The verse הַסְכֵּת וּשְׁמַע יִשְׂרָאֵל הַיּוֹם appears in the Torah's descrip-tion of the covenant forged between Hashem and the Jewish people when they were about to enter Eretz Yisrael. As part of that covenant, Hashem commanded Moshe to take huge stones and write the Torah on them.[10]

אֶבֶן:
An Acronym

Hashem commanded Moshe to take huge stones and write the Torah on them.

There are certainly deep concepts hidden in the commandment to write the Torah on stones. We can suggest that one of those ideas is that the word אֶבֶן, *stone*, is an acronym for אַב, בֵּן, and נֶכֶד, *father, son,* and *grandson.* These stones served as a means to pass the Torah from one generation to the next; to provide a continuum between Jewish generations.

The stones therefore served a double purpose. On one hand they enabled the Jews of that generation to study the Torah and observe its commandments. On another level, they remained an everlasting sign of the bond forged with Hashem — a bond that we pass from one generation to the next, from father to son to grandson.

The writing of the Torah on the stones is therefore associated with Av because they both serve two purposes, uniting the past with the future. Indeed, the very month of mourning over the loss of the Tem-ples was a month of rejoicing over a tangible foundation of the future, because the fifteenth of Av was a day that the Sages instituted to be a day when young men and women would find their mates. It was also a time when the deadly schism between the tribe of Binyamin and the rest of the nation was healed,[11] thus ensuring the continuity of the Jewish people in a physical sense, much as the stones of the Torah did in a spiritual sense.

The very month of mourning over the loss of the Temples was a month of rejoicing over a tangible foundation of the future.

Even the name of the month, Av, which means "father," connotes the continuity of the Jewish generations, from father to son, to grand-son, generation after generation to this day — and tomorrow.

---

10. The *Rishonim* disagree whether the entire Torah was written on the stones (*Ramban*) or only some of the *mitzvos* (*Ibn Ezra*)

11. *Taanis* 30b-31a. During the era of the *Shoftim* (Judges), there was a civil war that pitted the tribe of Binyamin against all the other tribes. After the defeat of Binyamin, the victorious tribes adopted a prohibition against permitting their daughters to marry men from Binyamin. The prohibition was rescinded on the fifteenth of Av. (See *Shoftim* Ch. 19-21.)

WE CAN TAKE THIS IDEA ONE STEP FURTHER. ASIDE FROM THE FACT that our mourning over the destruction will eventually turn into

Light in the Face of Darkness

celebration, *Chazal* teach that the destruction of the *Beis HaMikdash* itself also contained a certain measure of comfort and consolation.

One of the Psalms that speaks of the destruction of the *Beis HaMikdash* begins with the words, *"A song of Asaf: O God! the nations have entered into Your heritage, they have defiled the Sanctuary of Your holiness, they have turned Jerusalem into a heap of rubble"* (79:1). The midrash[12] wonders how Asaf could compose a "song" about the destruction. This psalm should have begun with the words, "A *cry* of Asaf," "A *lament* of Asaf," or "A *dirge* of Asaf." Why was Asaf singing about the destruction?

The Midrash answers that Asaf sang because Hashem poured out his wrath on the wood and stones of the *Beis HaMikdash*, and spared *Klal Yisrael* from being wiped out; in the words of the verse in *Eichah*, "Hashem vented his fury, He poured out His burning anger; He kindled a fire in Zion which consumed its foundations" (4:11).

Anaf Yosef notes that not only did Hashem spare *Klal Yisrael*, but even the holiness of the *Beis HaMikdash* was not nullified. In the *Tochachah* (Admonishment), Hashem admonishes *Klal Yisrael* to heed the Torah, or He will "Make your sanctuaries desolate" (*Vayikra* 26:31). The Talmud[13] deduces that since the area is still described as a sanctuary even after it is made desolate, it remains holy, for the Divine Presence never left the site of the *Beis HaMikdash*. The midrash[14] states that the verse, "Behold! He [Hashem] was standing behind our wall" (*Shir HaShirim* 2:9) refers to the Western Wall, from which the Divine Presence has never departed.

The Divine Presence never left the site of the Beis HaMikdash.

Thus, even the destruction of the *Beis HaMikdash* contains a measure of consolation in that Hashem destroyed only the physical structure, but did not withdraw His Presence from the Jewish people and allow the nation to be destroyed.

---

12. *Eichah Rabbah* 4:15.
13. *Megillah* 28a.
14. *Shir HaShirim Rabbah* 2:10.

III. Tishah b'Av — a Mo'ed?

NESIVOS SHALOM[15] NOTES THAT AT FIRST GLANCE, THE association between Av and the verse, הַסְכֵּת וּשְׁמַע יִשְׂרָאֵל הַיּוֹם הַזֶּה נִהְיֵיתָ לְעָם לַה' אֱלֹקֶיךָ, *Be attentive and hear, O Israel: This day you have become a people to Hashem, your God* seems extremely incongruous. The verse implies a lasting closeness between God and Israel — but of all the months, Av would seem to be the month in which our relationship with God is least apparent, if not severed. We lost both of our *Batei Mikdash*, and we were sent into exile, far from our holy land. Why would we use a Name Combination for this month that highlights our status as God's People?

Furthermore, *Chazal* derive from a verse in *Eichah* that Tishah b'Av is considered a *mo'ed* (festival). In addition, the first day of Pesach always corresponds to the day of Tishah b'Av, which is another indicator that Tishah b'Av has some sort of exalted status.

Nesivos Shalom uses the above-cited Midrashim to explain these perplexing associations. He explains that our existence as a nation is contingent upon maintaining our relationship with Hashem. Although it appeared that our relationship with Him was severed when gentiles defiled and destroyed the *Beis HaMikdash*, Hashem showed us that His love is eternal and undying by having the Cherubs on the *Aron* hug each other at the time of the *Churban*[16] — a clear sign of His love for us.[17]

The Name Combination for Av comes from a verse highlighting our closeness to Hashem, because in this month, more than any other time, we can discern that no matter how low we sink as a nation, Hashem will always love us. Even when He must punish us and banish us from His Presence, He still loves us, and that love sustains our nation.

Tishah b'Av is called a *mo'ed* — a festival, a time when God and Israel "rendezvous" with one another — because just as our closeness to Hashem was displayed during the three annual pilgrimages to the *Beis HaMikdash*, that closeness was equally apparent during the destruction of the *Beis HaMikdash*, when it became clear that our bond with Hashem will never be severed, no matter how severe our lapses.

The name of this month, אב, *father*, also alludes to this idea. A father usually treats his son with mercy and love, but he must sometimes

> *Our existence as a nation is contingent upon maintaining our relationship with Hashem.*

> *Just as our closeness to Hashem was displayed during the three annual pilgrimages to the Beis HaMikdash, that closeness was equally apparent during the destruction of the Beis HaMikdash.*

---

15. *Bein HaMetzarim*, pg. 208.
16. *Yoma* 54b.
17. *Bava Basra* 99a.

display anger toward him — as King Shlomo wrote, "One who spares his rod hates his child" (*Mishlei* 13:24). So, too, our Father in Heaven displayed His Fatherliness toward us, chastising us at the beginning of Av through the destruction of the *Beis HaMikdash*, but then, from the fifteenth of the month on, showing us His love and mercy.

NOW ALL THE IDEAS EXPRESSED UNTIL NOW CAN BE UNDERSTOOD AS one unit.

Av: Exile and Redemption

We have seen that Av is a month comprised of two parts: the days of mourning in its first half, and the days of joyous celebration beginning with the fifteenth. This month symbolizes the everlasting bond between Hashem and the Jewish people. Even though we mourn intensely on Tishah b'Av, we do not recite *Tachanun* on this *mo'ed*, an implicit reminder that with all the pain and suffering that the day represents, it also ensures the continuity of our nation. As we have seen, the fifteenth of Av celebrates the very same concept, as young men and women would find their mates, adding another link to the great chain of Jewish generations.

An allusion to this idea is apparent in the name of this month. We refer it as מנחם אב *The comforting month of Av*. As we have seen, אבן is an acronym for three generations: אב, בן, and נכד, *father, son,* and *grandson*. The word אב represents only two generations: אב and בן, *father* and *son*, because until the middle of the month there is no guarantee of a third generation. On the fifteenth of Av, when the son finds his mate, the father can be comforted, assured that his lineage will be carried on.

We wondered why this month lends itself to two Name Combinations, whereas all other months have only one. We have seen that Av comprises two unlike parts, as if it were two separate months, because it contains destruction and comfort, exile and redemption. Thus we can understand that its two Name Combinations represent this duality: the plague of destruction and the covenant of survival.

Av comprises two unlike parts, because it contains destruction and comfort, exile and redemption.

BNEI YISSASCHAR NOTED THAT THE *PARASHIYOS* OF *PINCHAS, MATOS, Masei,* and *Devarim* are always read during *Bein HaMetzarim*. He

Torah Reading During Bein HaMetzarim

finds a common denominator between these *parashiyos*: they all mention the division of *Eretz Yisrael* between the tribes. During our period of mourning, we must remember that the current state of the nation — bereft of the *Beis HaMikdash,* exiled from our land, far from our Father in

Heaven — will not last forever. We will eventually return to our Land, and each of us will inherit our rightful portion there.

Another reason *Pinchas* must be read during the Three Weeks is because it includes the Temple offerings of all the festivals, a reminder that although we currently fast in mourning for the *Beis HaMikdash*, those fast days will eventually be celebrated as festivals, along with all the others mentioned in *Parashas Pinchas*.

———◆———

ON A FINAL NOTE, ASIDE FROM ALL THE IMPLICIT SIGNS OF THE CONTInuity of *Klal Yisrael* that Tishah b'Av presents, the fact that we still mourn for the loss of the *Batei Mikdash* is itself a sign of our eternity.

Joy in Mourning

It is told that Napoleon once passed a shul on Tishah b'Av and saw Jews sitting on the floor, crying and reciting *Kinnos*. He asked why they were mourning. They explained that they were bemoaning the loss of the *Batei Mikdash*. He was deeply moved by the reply.

"A nation that can mourn and cry over the loss of their land for thousands of years without forgetting will never be destroyed," said Napoleon. "Such a nation can be confident that its land will be returned to it."

Binah L'ittim concludes, "A nation that constantly remembers its land, and does not stop shedding tears over its destruction — such a nation has the right to hope, and be sure that its hope will not be for naught."

The uniqueness of the Jewish nation is that even the essence of its mourning is a source of joy and hope for the future.

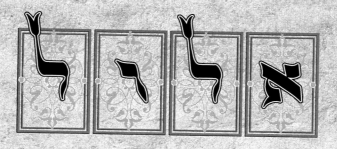

eLuL

וּצְדָקָה תִּהְיֶה לָּנוּ כִּי (ההו"י).

*T*he Name Combination for *E*lul comes from the verse וּצְדָקָה תִּהְיֶה לָּנוּ כִּי נִשְׁמֹר לַעֲשׂוֹת אֶת כָּל הַמִּצְוָה הַזֹּאת לִפְנֵי ה' אֱלֹקֵינוּ כַּאֲשֶׁר צִוָּנוּ, *And it will be a merit for us if we are careful to perform this entire commandment before Hashem, our God, as He commanded us* (Devarim 6:25).

Tzedakah and Teshuvah

אֱלוּל – וּצְדָקָה תִּהְיֶה לָּנוּ כִּי (ההו״י).

THE NAME COMBINATION FOR ELUL COMES FROM THE VERSE וּצְדָקָה תִּהְיֶה לָּנוּ כִּי נִשְׁמֹר לַעֲשׂוֹת אֶת כָּל הַמִּצְוָה הַזֹּאת לִפְנֵי ה' אֱלֹקֵינוּ כַּאֲשֶׁר צִוָּנוּ, *And it will be a merit for us if we are careful to perform this entire commandment before Hashem, our God, as He commanded us* (*Devarim* 6:25).

The word tzedakah, from the root tzedek, justice, can be rendered as justice or as charity.

The word *tzedakah*, from the root *tzedek*, justice, can be rendered as *justice* or as *charity*. What is its definition in this context, and how does this verse relate to the month of Elul and to repentance and supplication, which are the essence of Elul ?

Bnei Yissaschar[1] notes that the numerical value of the letters that make up the four words of the Name Combination — after deducting the letters of the Name itself — (i.e., the letters וצד״ק תה״י ל״נ כ) totals 715, the numerical value of the word בִּתְשׁוּבָה, *with repentance*. The association between Elul and *teshuvah* is obvious, but how does the verse of this Name Combination relate to *teshuvah*?

I. The Wise Son's Question

IN ORDER TO GAIN A DEEPER UNDERSTANDING OF THIS NAME Combination, we will examine the context in which this verse appears in the Torah. It comes in answer to a question: "If your child asks you tomorrow, saying, 'What are the testimonies and the decrees and the ordinances that Hashem, our God, commanded you?'" (*Devarim* 6:20). This familiar verse appears in the Haggadah as the question of the wise son. The answer found in the Torah is a brief summary of the Egyptian exile and the Divine redemption:

The answer is a brief summary of the Egyptian exile and the Divine redemption.

> You shall say to your son, "We were slaves to Pharaoh in Egypt, and Hashem took us out of Egypt with a strong hand. Hashem placed signs and wonders, great and harmful, against Egypt, against Pharaoh, and against his entire household, before our eyes. And he took us out of there in order to bring us, to give us

---

1. *Maamar Chodesh Elul* 1:1.

the Land that He swore to our forefathers. Hashem commanded us to perform all these decrees, to fear Hashem, our God, for our good, all the days, to give us life, as this very day. *And it will be a merit for us* if we are careful to perform this entire commandment before Hashem our God, as He commanded us." (ibid., 6:21-25)

Surprisingly, however, the Haggadah does not give the Torah's answer. Instead, the Haggadah's response is very concise — and does not seem to answer his question: אֵין מַפְטִירִין אַחַר הַפֶּסַח אֲפִיקוֹמָן, *One may not eat dessert after the [final taste] of the Pesach offering.* In our explanation of these verses, we will explain this perplexing answer.

THE PROPHET TELLS US, "SEEK HASHEM WHEN HE CAN BE FOUND; call upon Him when He is near" (*Yeshayah* 55:6). When is Hashem

Elul — The Month of Teshuvah

"near"? The Talmud[2] explains that this refers to the Ten Days of Repentance, beginning with Rosh Hashanah and ending with Yom Kippur. The days of Elul, which lead up to the Ten Days of Repentance, are also an auspicious time to repent. As *Chayei Adam*[3] writes, although *teshuvah* is accepted at any time, the month of Elul is a time when *teshuvah* is more readily accepted, because it has been designated as days of favor ever since we were chosen to be His nation.

In a similar vein, *Kitzur Shulchan Aruch*[4] writes that the period from Rosh Chodesh Elul through Yom Kippur is one of favor, and although Hashem will always accept the repentance of those who return to Him wholeheartedly, these days have been set aside for this purpose, as they are days of Divine mercy and favor.

It is somewhat difficult to understand this concept. *Teshuvah* is a commandment that is constant. If a person repents sincerely, it is accepted at any time of the year, and if the repentance is not sincere it is not acceptable during Elul either. What, then, is the uniqueness of Elul?

We must also try to understand *Rambam's* teaching[5] that a person who repents should cry out constantly before Hashem, *[give] tzedakah to the best of his ability*, and distance himself as much as possible from the matter in which he transgressed — indeed, he

Although teshuvah is accepted at any time, the month of Elul is a time when teshuvah is more readily accepted, because it has been designated as days of favor ever since we were chosen to be His nation.

---

2. *Rosh Hashanah* 18a.
3. 238:1.
4. 128:1.
5. *Hilchos Teshuvah* 2:4.

should change, as if to say, I am a different person, not the one who sinned. Why did *Rambam* single out *tzedakah* as the primary mitzvah for a repentant person?

II. What Is Tzedakah?

BEFORE WE CAN GO ON TO EXPLAIN THE IDEA OF *TZEDAKAH* IN the context of the Name Combination of Elul and its association with *teshuvah*, we must define its appearance in the Name verse וּצְדָקָה תִּהְיֶה לָּנוּ. The commentators on the Torah offer several possible definitions:

Tzedakah means to do what is correct, to perform Hashem's commandments, for He is our Master.

1) IBN EZRA STATES THAT *TZEDAKAH* HERE MEANS TO DO WHAT IS correct, i.e., it is proper for us to perform Hashem's commandments, for He is our Master.

The Proper Thing

The same definition seems to emerge from Rashi's commentary on the Talmudic statement,[6] "*Tzedakah* is rewarded based on the level of *chessed* contained therein, as the verse states, 'Sow for yourselves righteousness and you will reap according to kindness'" (*Hoshea* 10:12). *Rashi* comments: "Giving is *tzedakah*, and the effort expended [in order to provide benefit to the recipient] is *chessed*, kindness. For instance, if the person giving the *tzedakah* brings his donation to the recipient's house, or if he invests effort into giving him something that is ready for use, such as baked bread, or ready-to-wear clothing, or if he gives money at a time that wheat is priced reasonably so that the recipient does not waste money when it is more expensive. [In short,] *chessed* is when the giver places thought and heart into what is best for the poor person."

Chessed is when the giver places thought and heart into what is best for the poor person.

It appears from *Rashi* that *tzedakah* refers to the commandment to give charity — which is "just" — whereas acts that go beyond that basic standard are in the category of *chessed*.

2) *RAMBAN* WRITES THAT *TZEDAKAH* IN THIS VERSE DOES NOT refer to charity that people give. Rather, the charity of this verse refers to God; His reward to us for our good deeds is charity. We are Hashem's servants. We owe Him everything; He owes us nothing in return. Therefore, any reward He grants us for

A Higher Degree

6. *Succah* 49a.

heeding His commandments is considered charity.

Ramban seems to understand that *tzedakah* is something that is לִפְנִים מִשּׁוּרַת הַדִּין, something that goes beyond what the law requires. *HaKsav VehaKabbalah* (*Bereishis* 15:6) takes the same approach, writing:

> The difference between *tzedek* and *tzedakah* is well-known. *Tzedek* is something that should rightfully belong to the recipient based on standard rules of justice and fairness, whereas *tzedakah* refers to something that goes beyond justice. A letter *hei* added to a word takes it to a higher level, so the extra *hei* in *tzedakah* means that we are dealing with something greater than *tzedek*.

3) *Ohr HaChaim* also considers *tzedakah* a step higher than *tzedek*, but writes that *we* are the ones performing the *tzedakah* mentioned in this verse. There are two levels of serving Hashem, he writes. (a) All beings are obligated to serve Hashem out of fear, because we are all His servants and a servant fears his master. The need to perform this basic level of service is mentioned in the Torah in the verse, "What does Hashem, your God, ask of you? Only to fear Hashem, your God" (*Devarim* 10:12). (b) A more exalted level is to serve Him out of love. A servant is not required to love his master; as long as he serves his master properly, the master owes him sustenance. The "servant" who *loves* Hashem is therefore on a higher level.

The Torah's response to the wise son's question, in the Book of *Devarim,* discusses both levels of service. First the Torah states, "Hashem commanded us to perform all these decrees, *to fear Hashem,* our God, for our good all the days, to give us life." The Torah is saying that service out of fear is for our good, and it will bring us our basic need — life itself — just as any master will provide the basic needs of servants who serve him out of fear.

The Torah then moves on to the next level, stating that, "*It will be a merit for us* if we are careful to perform this entire commandment before Hashem our God, as He commanded us." When we serve Hashem not out of fear but because He has commanded us to do so — emulating King David's feeling, "To fulfill Your will, my God, do I desire" (*Tehillim* 40:9) — we serve Him out of love, because our souls yearn to be close to Him and to please Him. This level is considered a *merit for us*, because it is more than we are minimally required to do, and Hashem will reward those who show Him that extra level of devotion. In truth,

When we serve Hashem not out of fear but because He has commanded us to do so, we serve Him out of love, because our souls yearn to be close to Him and to please Him.

concludes *Ohr HaChaim*, we should pay Hashem for allowing us to taste the sweetness of His service, but He allows us to enjoy His service *and* be rewarded for it.

When we serve Hashem out of love, we are serving with tzedakah, and Hashem repays us in proportion.

Thus *Ohr HaChaim* teaches that we are repaid for serving Hashem out of fear with *tzedek,* in exact fairness, just as in any master-servant relationship, but when we serve Hashem out of love, we are serving with *tzedakah*, and Hashem repays us in proportion. *Ohr HaChaim's* definition of *tzedakah* is in line with the definition of *Ramban* and *HaK'sav VehaKabbalah,* that *tzedakah* goes beyond the minimum requirement.

III. Elul — Days of Love and Favor

*O*HR HACHAIM'S EXPLANATION OF THE NAME VERSE EXPLAINS how *tzedakah* relates to the month of Elul, the month of *teshuvah,* but first let us understand the uniqueness of the month.

After the Jewish people sinned by serving the Golden Calf on the seventeenth of Tammuz, Moshe spent forty days praying that they not be wiped out. Hashem agreed to forgive them, but that forgiveness did not atone for the sin — it only spared them from punishment. Moshe then spent another forty days, from Rosh Chodesh Elul through Yom Kippur,[7] praying for their complete atonement. Hashem acquiesced, renewing His bond of love toward Israel and once again resting His Presence upon the nation.

Elul is an auspicious time for teshuvah because it is the month when Hashem expressed great love for His people, and when there was a reborn closeness between Him and Israel.

Consequently, Elul is an auspicious time for *teshuvah* because it is the month when Hashem expressed great love for His people, and when there was a reborn closeness between Him and Israel. Moshe's efforts instilled a strong feeling of penance into this month, and Hashem is more disposed to accept *teshuvah* in the month when the bond between Him and Israel was renewed. This also explains why repentance in Elul is more propitious than in other months.

[The comparison to the relationship between a master and servant is apropos here as well. At first there is fear, but gradually they come to know and love one another, and their relationship becomes transformed. After the sin of the Golden Calf, the people's service of God was infused with fear, but as they repented Moshe prayed first for their survival and then for a renewal of the former relationship of mutual love. And this newborn relationship characterizes Elul to this day.

---

7. This timetable is based on *Pirkei D'Rabbi Eliezer*, Ch. 46.

THE CONCEPT OF *TESHUVAH* IS SO ABOVE HUMAN COMPREHENSION that only Hashem Himself — in His infinite Kindness — was able to

Teshuvah: Exalted and Incomprehensible

bring it into existence. *Talmud Yerushalmi*[8] states, "They asked wisdom, 'What is a sinner's punishment?' [Wisdom] answered, "Evil pursues sinners" (*Mishlei* 13:21). They asked prophecy, 'What is a sinner's punishment?' [Prophecy] answered, "The soul that sins — it shall die" (*Yechezkel* 18:4). They asked Hashem, 'What is a sinner's punishment?' Hashem answered, 'Let him repent, and he will receive atonement.' As King David wrote, "Therefore He guides sinners on the way" (*Tehillim* 25:8) i.e., He guides sinners toward the path of repentance.

In other places, *Chazal* spoke of *teshuvah* as a deep, supernatural concept — even stating that it is one of seven things that were created before the world, meaning that the opportunity to repent was a necessary prerequisite of Creation,[9] because without it, man could not survive.

They also spoke at length about the great power of *teshuvah*,[10] stating that it:

- Brings healing to the world.
- Reaches the Throne of Glory.
- Hastens the redemption.
- Lengthens a person's life.

Baal HaTurim[11] notes that the Torah states, "When you listen to the voice of Hashem, your God, to observe His commandments and His decrees ... when you shall return to Hashem, your God, with all your heart and all your soul" (*Devarim* 30:10). The implication of the verse is that *teshuvah* is equal to all other mitzvos in the Torah!

IF WE DELVE MORE DEEPLY INTO SEVERAL POINTS RAISED ABOVE, we can come to a more satisfactory understanding of *why teshuvah*

Elul — Repenting out of Love

is accepted more readily in Elul. We have seen that Elul is a month in which Hashem's love for His people was revealed. That extra measure of love inspires us to repent out of

We have seen that Elul is a month in which Hashem's love for His people was revealed.

---

8. *Makkos* 2:6.
9. *Nedarim* 55a.
10. *Yoma* 86a-b.
11. *Devarim* 30:10.

love during Elul. Given that *teshuvah* is supernatural, we can accept the seemingly illogical fact that it more readily accepted during one time of the year than another. That time is the one when God revealed His love for Israel

King Shlomo wrote, "One who has found a wife has found goodness, and has brought forth favor from Hashem" (*Mishlei* 18:22). *Bnei Yissaschar* comments that although this verse should certainly be taken in a literal sense, the "favor" referred to in this verse is also a homiletical allusion to Elul, the month in which Moshe ascended to the Heavens to pray for the Jewish people, eventually to descend with the Second *Luchos* (Tablets), which represented Hashem's renewed love. From that time on, the days of Elul, more than any other time, are days in which we are naturally drawn to repent, and when Hashem's hand is outstretched, as it were, to accept repentance.

The days of Elul are days in which we are naturally drawn to repent, and when Hashem's hand is outstretched, as it were, to accept repentance.

Ever since Adam sinned by eating from the Tree of Knowledge, continues *Bnei Yissaschar*, there is a mixture of good and evil in every person. Generally, the bad overpowers the good, to the extent that we even come to rationalize that the bad is essentially good. When Hashem inspires us to repent during Elul, however, we discover what is truly good. We feel guilty and repent for our bad deeds, and consequently "bring forth favor from Hashem," and He accepts our repentance.

Bnei Yissaschar is teaching that our natural predilection toward *teshuvah* during Elul is due to Hashem drawing us to Him, as He did when He forgave Israel for the sin of the Golden Calf, arousing us to repent wholeheartedly.

It follows that our service of Hashem during Elul — service out of love — is qualitatively different from that of the rest of the year. All year round, our hearts and minds are preoccupied with the trivialities that fill our lives. During Elul, however, our hearts are stirred to return to Hashem wholeheartedly, because His overwhelming love for us draws us to him. *Vilna Gaon* writes[12] that when we pursue something with all our heart and desire, we can attain lasting results, but if we do not put our heart into our efforts, the resulting achievement fades away. Since our hearts are sincerely devoted toward repentance during Elul, our *teshuvah* is more meaningful, and, therefore, more readily accepted, and also more likely to be long-lasting.

During Elul, our hearts are stirred to return to Hashem wholeheartedly, because His overwhelming love for us draws us to him.

---

12. To *Mishlei* 23:12.

IV. Teshuvah: Tzedek, Tzedakah, and Heartfelt Love

NOW IT WILL BECOME CLEAR THAT ALL THE ABOVE ELEMENTS and the Name Combination — וּצְדָקָה תִּהְיֶה לָנוּ כִּי, *it will be a merit for us* — correspond to the essence of Elul, the month of *teshuvah* motivated by love. As noted above, the commentators explain that the word *tzedakah* has two definitions: it can refer to justice and fairness — the "*tzedek*" aspect of *tzedakah* — and it can refer to a more generous way of dealing with people, a manner that goes beyond the scope of basic fairness, which is called *tzedakah*.

THE OPPORTUNITY TO REPENT DURING ELUL CONTAINS BOTH ASPECTS of the word *tzedakah*. On the one hand, when a person sincerely

Both Aspects

repents and returns to Hashem, and — in *Rambam's* words — changes himself, he is no longer the same person he was when he sinned. Since Hashem has, in His mercy, incorporated *teshuvah* into the fabric of Creation, it is only fair and just that He should forgive the person for his sins. This is *tzedek*. However, the fact that Hashem takes the initiative and draws us to Himself and awakens our desire to do *teshuvah* is not mandated by justice and fairness. This is *tzedakah*. Elul is, therefore, the embodiment of the verse וּצְדָקָה תִּהְיֶה לָנוּ כִּי, in both senses of the word: *tzedek* and *tzedakah*.

We can also explain the rest of the verse in the same light. The verse reads וּצְדָקָה תִּהְיֶה לָנוּ כִּי נִשְׁמֹר לַעֲשׂוֹת, *It will be a merit for us if we are careful to perform this entire commandment before Hashem, our God, as He commanded us. Ksav Sofer* interprets the word נִשְׁמֹר not as being careful, but in the sense of וְאָבִיו שָׁמַר אֶת הַדָּבָר, *but his father kept the matter in mind (Bereishis* 37:11). Thus the efficacy of *teshuvah* depends on a person's sincere desire to repent and change. When can we hope for the וּצְדָקָה תִּהְיֶה לָנוּ, for the loving pull from Hashem toward Himself? Only if we keep our minds focused on repenting, and make that our single-minded desire.

It is told that the great Rav Chaim of Sanz was once sitting at his table, watching as the food was being passed around. When a very fine portion was being passed from hand to hand, R' Chaim turned to his son, the Rav of Shinova, and said, "You see that poor person sitting at the end of the table? He will receive that special portion, because he has *mazal*."

The fact that Hashem takes the initiative and draws us to Himself and awakens our desire to do teshuvah is not mandated by justice and fairness. This is tzedakah.

"If he has *mazal*," asked the Shinova Rav, "Then why is he a pauper, relegated to the far end of the table?"

"His problem is that all he desires in life is to receive a special portion of food," explained R' Chaim. "Whatever he sets his mind upon, he will receive, because he has good *mazal*. If only he would set his mind on greater things!"

This is the essence of Elul, that we can merit special love and guidance from Heaven to repent — *tzedakah* — but only if we sincerely desire to repent.

We can merit special love and guidance from Heaven to repent only if we sincerely desire to repent.

The Response to the Wise Son

WE WONDERED WHY THE HAGGADAH DID NOT QUOTE THE TORAH'S response to the wise son's question, which speaks of the Exodus and includes the Name Combination quoted above. Instead the Haggadah says, אֵין מַפְטִירִין אַחַר הַפֶּסַח אֲפִיקוֹמָן, *One may not eat dessert after the final taste of the Pesach offering [afikoman]*, which not only ignores the Torah's own response, but seems not to respond to the wise son's question.

We suggest that the response found in the Torah and that of the Haggadah are actually one and same. The true objective of the Pesach offering and the *afikoman* is to bring us to love Hashem, by discussing and appreciating the miracles that He performed for us when he took us out of Egypt, and reinforcing our faith in him. A person who finds a need to eat after the Pesach offering shows that he has missed the point. Had he focused on the correct ideals, he would never consider delving into so mundane an act as eating after completing the lofty service of the Pesach offering. The sacred service of eating the Pesach offering would have given him supreme gratification, and he would have not given even a thought to what dessert was available to him.

The true objective of the Pesach offering and the afikoman is to bring us to love Hashem.

The response found in the Haggadah is therefore the essence of the Pesach offering, a wholehearted love of Hashem and dedication to Him. As noted above, particularly in the light of *Ksav Sofer*'s comment, the Torah's answer to the wise son is based on the principle that single-minded devotion to God is the key to observance of the commandments. Thus the Torah says that the Jew has a strong desire to fulfill Hashem's will, to be נִשְׁמֹר לַעֲשׂוֹת, to come to serve Hashem through love and devotion. In essence, this is the message of not eating after the *afikoman*.

FINALLY, WE CAN RETURN TO OUR QUESTION OF WHY THE *RAMBAM* stresses the need for a *baal teshuvah* to engage in *tzedakah* more than any other mitzvah in the Torah.

Tzedakah — A Means to Sincere Teshuvah

Maharal[13] states that when a person gives charity or lends money to another person, he should do so not only to fulfill the commandment of the King. The primary fulfillment of these mitzvos is the generosity with which the donor or lender does so. As we have seen, sincerity and wholeheartedness are the key ingredients of both charity and repentance.

There is a well-known homily that the Hebrew word אַהֲבָה, *love,* is an acronym of אֵין דָּבָר הָעוֹמֵד בִּפְנֵי הָרָצוֹן, *Nothing stands in the way of desire.* The reason *Rambam* stresses the need to engage in *tzedakah* is because no mitzvah better places a person on the road to the purpose of Elul: the trait of love that leads to perfect repentance. The end of this road is a complete transformation of a person, as *Rambam* puts it: Among the ways of teshuvah is that the penitent should cry out constantly before Hashem … perform tzedakah according to his full capacity, and **change his name, *i.e., I am now someone else; I am not the same person [who sinned].***

Sincerity and whole-heartedness are the key ingredients of both charity and repentance.

---

13. *Gur Aryeh, Shemos* 20:22.

Appendix

The Power of the Hebrew Letters and the Name Combinations of Hashem's Name

THE VERY EXISTENCE OF EVERY CREATURE FROM ANGELS TO PEBBLES IS dependent on the spiritual content with which it was created. This concept is not as esoteric as it seems. Though no one has seen a soul, we all know that the human body ceases to live when its soul leaves it. On the cosmic level, the Sages have taught that Torah study is the "soul" of creation, and that the entire universe would come to an end if no Torah were being studied anywhere, even for an instant. Thus, a lonely scholar in a forlorn corner may well be responsible for the survival of billions of people and trillions of stars.

In teaching that the universe was created with ten Godly utterances (*Avos* 5:1), the Sages have provided an insight into the process of creation. *Maharal* explains that the term מַאֲמָרוֹת, which we translate *utterances*, is different from the virtually synonymous דִבּוּר. The word מַאֲמַר alludes primarily to the intent, the forethought, the motive of the One Who spoke, while דִבּוּר connotes the external, physical process of speech. By telling us that God created the universe בַּעֲשָׂרָה מַאֲמָרוֹת, *with ten utterances,* the Sages wish us to understand that the building blocks of creation were the spiritual motives behind the speech. God had a purpose and the world came into being in order to fulfill it.

Before creation there was nothing physical. There was but God's desire; the universe came into being in order that the tools would exist for His will to be fulfilled. He wanted children to honor parents, so He created a world in which man and woman join to bear and raise children. In other words, man exists to carry out God's will as expressed in the Torah, the universe exists to provide the conditions for man to do so; nothing could exist if Creation were to be devoid of purpose — if it were not the physical translation of the Divine will being God's "utterances."

לְעוֹלָם ה' דְּבָרְךָ נִצָּב בַּשָּׁמָיִם, *FOREVER, HASHEM, YOUR WORD STANDS FIRM IN HEAVEN* (*Tehillim* 119:89).

The Letters Are Eternal

The *Baal Shem Tov* explained that the "word" of God in this verse refers to His utterance יְהִי רָקִיעַ, *let there be a firmament* (*Bereishis* 1:6). With these words, the heaven came into existence at that primeval instant — but what prevents the heaven from aging, decaying, crumbling? Why shouldn't the heaven grow stale like yesterday's loaf of bread or crumble like the last century's highways? Why are some parts of the universe eternal, while others last for only a brief season?

The Psalmist answered these questions when he said: *Forever, HASHEM, Your word stands firm in heaven.* The word of God that brought the heaven into being remains within it. The heaven continues to exist because not an instant goes by without God continuing to say, in effect, *Let there be a firmament* — otherwise it would return to the status that prevailed before God's will was uttered. So it is with every aspect of Creation. God's original Ten Utterances are repeated constantly in the sense that the Divine will of the original six days remains in force. Otherwise, everything would revert to the nothingness of before Creation.

Just as the "word of God" gave being to the heaven, so it is His word that gives being to everything. Let us try to understand further what is meant by God's "word." And how do the specific, limited utterances of Creation account for the infinite number of species and objects in the universe?

Rabbi DovBer, the Maggid of Mezeritch, writes: It is known in Kabbalistic literature that the letters of the *Aleph Beis* were created first of all. Thereafter, by use of the letters, the Holy One, Blessed is He, created all of the worlds. This is the hidden meaning of the first phrase in the Torah, "*In the beginning God created* אֵת" — that is, God's first act was to create the letters from א to ת (*Ohr Torah;* see p. 35).

R' TZADDOK HAKOHEN (*MACHSHEVOS CHARUTZ*, CH. 11 AND 12) ELABORATES ON THIS concept. The twenty-two sacred letters are profound, primal, spiritual forces. They

The Letters as Spiritual Forces

are, in effect, the raw material of Creation. When God combined them into words, phrases, commands, they brought about Creation, translating His will into reality, as it were. There is a Divine Science in the Hebrew alphabet. *Sefer Yetzirah* [*The Book of Creation*] the early Kabbalistic work ascribed to the Patriarch Abraham, describes how Hashem used the sacred letters as the agency of Creation. The work speaks of the letters as "stones," or "building blocks," that were assembled to create the structure of Creation as we see it. These "building blocks" can be ordered in countless combinations, by changing their order within words and interchanging letters according to the rules of various Kabbalistic letter-systems. Each rearrangement of the same letters results in a new blend of the cosmic spiritual forces represented by the letters. An analogy can be found in the physical sciences. One combination of hydrogen and oxygen produces water, while another produces hydrogen peroxide. So it is with all the elements and the infinite number of possible combinations.

God's utterance that created heaven also created everything associated with it. The Sages and the literature of Kabbalah teach that there are seven heavens representing distinct spiritual levels. Each has its functions and beings that enable it to perform its mission. And each of those, in ways unknown to us, is a product of the combinations of spiritual forces represented by the letters — in their various arrangements — of the words יְהִי רָקִיעַ בְּתוֹךְ הַמָּיִם וִיהִי מַבְדִּיל בֵּין מַיִם לָמָיִם, *Let there be a firmament in the midst of the waters, and let it separate between water and water* (*Genesis* 1:6).

THIS EXPLAINS WHY MAN'S FIRST EXERCISE OF MASTERY AND DEMONSTRATION OF greatness came when God asked Adam to give names to all the creatures of the new

Adam's Insight

universe. God brought the birds and animals to him לִרְאוֹת מַה יִּקְרָא לוֹ, *to see what he would call each one* (*Genesis* 2:19). וְכָל אֲשֶׁר יִקְרָא לוֹ הָאָדָם נֶפֶשׁ חַיָּה הוּא שְׁמוֹ, *and whatever man called each living creature, that remained its name* — as if there is something eternally significant in the combination of consonants and vowels that are assigned to this or that creature.

Once we have achieved a rudimentary understanding of the spiritual content of the Hebrew letters, Adam's task takes on major dimensions. The man whom God created *"in Our image, in Our likeness"* (*Bereishis* 1:26), was being asked by God to demonstrate a spiritual insight that was profound beyond our imagination. When Adam said that a bull should be called שׁוֹר and an eagle should be called נֶשֶׁר, he was saying that the spiritual forces expressed by those letters, in the formula signified by those unique arrangements of letters and vowels, were translated by God into the nerve, sinew, skin, size, shape, strength, and ability that we see when a sturdy bull pulls a plow or a soaring eagle excites our imagination. The same spiritual forces that God translated into a שׁוֹר at the dawn of creation remain the essence of a bull for all time.

Having arrived this far, we must acknowledge that the *Aleph-Beis* is not a commonly accepted convention like all other alphabets.

THIS CONCEPT WAS EXPRESSED BY THE GREAT KABBALIST RABBI MOSHE CORDEVERO:

The Aleph Beis of Torah

Many have assumed that the letters were conventions, that is, that scholars agreed to assign identifying names to the various vocal sounds. For example, they agreed that the sounds formed by the lips, which are ב, ו, מ, פ should be represented by the written forms of those letters. If that were so, there is no difference between the letters of the *Aleph Beis* and the language symbols of other peoples in their various lands and national groups .... In consonance with this view, there emerges a consensus in which the particular written symbols have no independent validity other than revealing the intent of the speaker or writer. It is like a doctor who sets forth his knowledge in a medical book. There is no intention that the book *itself* is a medicine of any sort; rather the author's intention is that he wishes to share his knowledge through the book .... When the reader thoroughly understands and assimilates the knowledge contained in the book, it has no further utility for him. Conversely, if someone were to study the book for several years, but does not understand its contents, it does him no good .... This is the opinion of some people regarding the Torah [that once someone knows it — or if someone finds it impossibly difficult — the book has no further value] ....

Such a view is an impossible absurdity. For surely the words of the Torah restore the soul (*Tehillim* 19:8). The proof of this is that we are required to repeat the weekly Torah portion twice in the original text and once in its *Targum* [or other translation or commentary], even such words as עֲטָרוֹת וְדִיבֹן (*Bamidbar* 32:3) [which are simple place names with no translation and to which the repetition would seem to add nothing]. This is an indication of the perfection of the Torah, and that it contains an inner meaning, hidden mysteries, spirituality, and vitality (*Sefer HaPardes, Shaar* 27).

WHEN APPLIED TO GOD, THE TERM "LETTERS" AND "UTTERANCES" ARE FIGURATIVE, like such terms as God's "mouth," "arm," and so on, with which we describe God's

The Power of the Letters

deeds in human terms in order to make them more understandable to us.

Degel Machneh Ephraim teaches that man has the power to affect the sacred letters with which God created heaven and earth. When he sins, he cheapens and sullies the Divine powers allotted him. But when he acts properly, he enables the powers within the *Aleph Beis* to achieve their purpose and reflect their full holiness. He can elevate not only his personal universe, but that of everyone around him.

אָמַר רָבָא, אִי בָּעוּ צַדִּיקֵי בָּרוּ עַלְמָא שֶׁנֶּאֱמַר כִּי אִם עֲוֹנֹתֵיכֶם הָיוּ מַבְדִּלִים בֵּינֵיכֶם [הָא אִם לֹא הָיוּ בָהֶם עֲוֹנוֹת אֵין כָּאן הַבְדָּלָה לְבֵין אֱלֹקֵיכֶם (רש"י)].

Rava said: If the righteous wanted to, they could create a universe — as is written (Yeshayah 59:2): But your sins would separate between you and your God (Sanhedrin 65b). However, if they had had no sins, there would not have been a separation (Rashi).

The term צֵירוּפֵי אוֹתִיּוֹת is commonly translated as *combinations of letters*, a rendering that is quite accurate, for it refers to the various combinations of spiritual forces that God used in creation. *Degel Machneh Ephraim* adds a deeper meaning, however. He relates צִידוּפֵי to the term מְצָרֵף כֶּסֶף, *purifying silver,* by purging it of its impurities. The most precious metals must be purified in order to attain their maximum beauty and value.

This is why Rava says that truly righteous people could create a world, if sins did not separate them from the Godly powers available to them. Let them free themselves from sin and they could realize the full potential of the twenty-two sacred letters contained in their own "miniature" worlds. Rava demonstrated what could be accomplished in this manner. According to the Talmud (*Sanhedrin* 65b), he created a person, and *Rashi* explains that he did so by means of *Sefer Yetzirah,* which contains the formulas for using the letters of the *Aleph Beis* to effect Creation. Rava was able to utilize the full capability of the sacred letters because he had never erected barriers between himself and the holiness of the letters. Man was meant to utilize awesome powers — provided he had the knowledge and had not corroded his bond with God.

The *Aleph Beis* is the brick and mortar and soul of the universe, as it is of individuals with their personal capacities. The letters that brought the world into existence remain with us every instant, for God's utterances are eternal. Though we have great powers as individuals, when we unite into the unit of Israel we are even mightier.

Of all the words and letters that were building blocks of Creation, the most important was the Four-letter Name of Hashem, not only the Name but also the twelve possible ways its letters can be arranged and how those combinations of the letters correspond to, and affect, the twelve months of the year. This concept was first found in *Tikkunei Zohar,* and is also discussed in many other classic works, among them *Shelah Hakadosh, Mishnas Chassidim, Bnei Yissaschar* and *Machshevos Charutz.*

THIS WORK, *THE WISDOM IN THE HEBREW MONTHS,* DRAWS HEAVILY ON THE FORMULAtions of *Bnei Yissaschar (Maamar Kiddush Hachodesh 1:4).* He writes:

The Letter Combinations

The word חֹדֶשׁ, *month,* has the numerical value of 312. Now there are 12 possible arrangements of the letters of the Four-letter Name י-ה-ו-ה, and each month is illuminated by one of the Name Combinations, so that there are twelve months and twelve Name Combinations. The twelve Name Combinations multiplied by the twelve months equals 312, the same as the sum of the letters of חֹדֶשׁ, the word for month. The word חֹדֶשׁ also means *renewal,* because each new month brings with a new kind of mission. According to the change of the order of letters in the Name Combination, there is a new existence.

[This implies that the character of each individual month is predetermined by its Name Combination and is, therefore, unchanging but this is not so.] The Torah states הַחֹדֶשׁ הַזֶּה לָכֶם, *This new month shall* be **yours** (*Shemos* 12:1), because it is in the power of the Jewish people to change the [nature of the] times by following the ways of the Torah and Divine service, and we can change the Name Combinations from harsh judgment to mercy.

This was taught by the Maggid of Mezeritch, R' DovBer, based on the verse זֹאת עוֹלַת חֹדֶשׁ בְּחָדְשׁוֹ, *this is the burnt-offering of the month on its month* (*Bamidbar* 28:14). [The Maggid notes the double use of the word "month."] There are two forms of Divine conduct of the universe. One is based on the law of nature, as formulated in the seven days of Creation. This is reflected in the order of the twelve Name Combinations and the signs of the Zodiac that apply to the respective months, according to the nature assigned to each month through the power of Hashem, blessed is He. This particular aspect of Divine conduct is represented by the letter *zayin*, which has the numerical value of *seven,* and alludes to the seven days of Creation.

However, there is also a higher form of Divine conduct. This second form is that which is controlled by [Israel's] observance of the Torah, by means of which Israel can bring about a renewal of the times for good and for life. That higher form of conduct is represented by the word אֶת, which alludes to the *Alef Beis*, the twenty-two letters of the Hebrew alphabet, with which the Torah is written. [Consequently, the observance of the Torah, by means of which Israel can change history and overturn the ostensibly inviolable control of the monthly Name Combination, is symbolized by the alphabet from *alef* to *tav*.].

The above first and second modes of control are jointly symbolized by the word זֹאת, which has both the letter *zayin* and the letters *alef* and *tav.* Consequently when the above-cited verse uses the word "month" two times, it means to imply that even though every month has its own quality as ordained by nature and its Name Combination, it also has the alternate potential of being fashioned by the observance of the Torah, which is written with the twenty-two letters of the *Alef Beis* (this ends the words of the *Maggid*) ....

In my opinion, this is the secret of the sanctification of the new months, which the Torah assigns to Israel. It is they who sanctify the months according to their judgment ... as the Midrash teaches. If on Rosh Hashanah, the chairs of the Divine Court were prepared for the Day of Judgment — and then the Jewish court decided to add a day to the month of Elul and thereby to put off Rosh Hashanah for a day, the Heavenly Court removes its preparations for judgment, for everything [regarding the calendar] depends on the Jewish people ....

BNEI YISSASCHAR (IBID. 1:11) CITES A SEEMINGLY STRANGE MIDRASH (MIDRASH Tehillim 91) that the reason Jews' prayers are not answered is because they do not

Knowing the Name

know how to pray using God's Name, as the verse states: אֲשַׂגְּבֵהוּ כִּי־יָדַע שְׁמִי. יִקְרָאֵנִי וְאֶעֱנֵהוּ, *I will elevate him because he knows My Name. He will call upon Me and I will answer him (Tehillim 91:14-15). How can this be? How can the Sages say that Jews do not know the Name of Hashem, something that is common knowledge and that is constantly used in our prayers?

Bnei Yissaschar explains that the Sages are not referring to the universally known Four-letter Name — that is something that everyone knows. The "unknown Name" is the Name Combination of each individual month. When someone prays for God to reverse his bad fortune or to increase his good fortune, it is wise to know the Divine influence that rests upon the month. Since each month is associated with its own Name Combination, an efficacious prayer should be based on knowledge of that Name.

For this reason, several sacred works write that when reciting the middle blessing of the *Mussaf* of Rosh Chodesh, one should have in mind the Name Combination and the relevant Scriptural verse of the Name for that particular month. Many *siddurim* include these Name Combinations with the text of the Rosh Chodesh *Mussaf*. For the convenience of the reader, we include that table and the relevant verses at the end of this Appendix.

Reb Zvi Ryzman's explanation of the relationship between the respective months, their Name Combinations, and the verses that allude to these combinations is unprecedented. To the best of our knowledge, a work of this kind has never before existed. We are confident that the readers of his treatments will be enlightened and gratified and we hope that this essay will assist the reader in understanding the background of Reb Zvika's expositions.

Rabbi Nosson Scherman

צירופי שמות לי"ב חדשי השנה מבוארים בספר משנת חסידים					
לכוון מדי חודש בחדשו בברכת ברוך אתה **יהוה** מקדש ישראל וראשי חדשים.					
יוצא מפסוק ונקודותיו	צירוף	חודש	יוצא מפסוק ונקודותיו	צירוף	חודש
וַיִּרְאוּ אוֹתָהּ שָׂרֵי פַרְעֹה	וַהְיָהַ יַהָאָה	תשרי	יִשְׂמְחוּ הַשָּׁמַיִם וְתָגֵל הָאָרֶץ	יְהֹוָה אֶהְיֶה	ניסן
וּדְבַשׁ הַיּוֹם הַזֶּה יְהוֹה	וּהְהֵי יְהַהָא	חשון	יִתְהַלֵּל הַמִּתְהַלֵּל הַשְׂכֵּל וְיָדֹעַ	יֶהֱהָן אֶהְהַי	אייר
וַיֵּרָא יוֹשֵׁב הָאָרֶץ הַכְּנַעֲנִי	וַיָהָה יַאֲהָה	כסלו	יְדוֹתִיו וּלְצַלְעוֹת הַמִּשְׁכָּן הַשֵּׁנִית	יֶוּהָה אִיהָה	סיון
לַיהוֹה אֹתִי וּנְרוֹמְמָה שְׁמוֹ	הַיֶהֹן הַאֵהִי	טבת	זֶה אֵינֶנּוּ שׁוֶֹה לִי	הֲוִיהֵי הֶיַהָא	תמוז
הָמֵר יְמִירֶנּוּ וְהָיָה הוּא	הָיֶוֶה הָאִיֶה	שבט	הַסְכֵּת וּשְׁמַע יִשְׂרָאֵל הַיּוֹם	הֹוִיֶה הַיַאָה	אב
עִירֹה וְלַשֹּׂרֵקָה בְּנִי אֲתֹנוֹ	הֶהֱיֶן הַהְאַי	אדר	וּצְדָקָה תִהְיֶה לָּנוּ כִּי	הֶהֱנֵי הֶהֱיָא	אלול
ובאדר שני יכוון בכללות כולם יחד כל י"ב צירופי הוי"ה ואהיה					

Glossary

GLOSSARY

A

achlamah — a translucent reddish gemstone, one of the stones on the Kohen Gadol's Breastplate

ad d'lo yada — until one cannot differentiate

adanim — sockets (of the Tabernacle)

admorim — Chassidic leaders

adnus — Hashem's Lordship

afikoman — the Pesach offering

Akeidas Yitzchak — the Binding of Isaac

Al Hamichyah — the three-faceted blessing said after eating certain foods

Aleph Beis — the Hebrew alphabet

amah, amos — a cubit unit of measure

Amidah — lit., standing prayer; the *Shemoneh Esrei*

amud — the lectern of the prayer-leader

arayos — illicit relationships

Asarah b'Teves — the 10th of Teves, a public fast day

Aseres Yemei Teshushah — the Ten Days of Repentance from Rosh Hashanah through Yom Kippur

av — a father

Avodah — Service, esp. the service of Hashem

ayin ra'ah — an "evil" eye

ayin tovah — a "good" eye

ayir — a type of donkey

B

baal teshuvah — a penitent; one who returns to mitzvah observance

becher, bechor — firstborn

bechorah — rights of the firstborn

bein adam l'chaveiro — between man and his fellow

bein adam l'Makom — between man and God

Bein HaMetzarim — the three-week period of mourning from the 17th of Tammuz through the 9th of Av

Beis Din — rabbinical court

Beis HaMikdash (pl. Batei Mikdash) — the Holy Temple(s)

ben sorer u'moreh — a wayward and rebellious son

berachah, berachos — blessing(s)

beraisa, beraisos — Rabbinic teaching(s) and exposition(s) complied at the time of Mishnah, but not included in the Mishnayos

besulah — a virgin

Bikkurim — first fruits presented to a Kohen in the *Beis HaMikdash*

binyan av — a general principle

Bircas HaChodesh — a prayer heralding the arrival of a new month

Bircas HaMazon — Grace After Meals

bri'ach hatichon — the center bar running through the walls of the Tabernacle

Bris Bein HaBesarim — the Covenant between the Parts, made between God and Abraham

Bris Milah — circumcision

C

chamor — a type of donkey

chas v'Shalom — Heaven forbid

chashiver Yid — a prestigious Jew

Chazal — the Sages, of blessed memory

chazzan — a cantor

chelek Elokim miMa'al — A Divine element

chessed — kindness

Chiddushei Torah — novel Torah thoughts and explanations

chodesh — month

chomer — earthiness; physicality

Choshen — Breastplate worn by the Kohen Gadol

chukim — decrees (unexplained Torah commandments); Midrashic teachings derived from the Torah

churban — destruction; (cap.) destruction of the Holy Temple

D

d'vash — honey

davar shelo ba le'olam — something that has not yet come into existence

derech hamemutzah — "the middle road"

devarim — lit., words; teachings that are explicitly written in the Torah; (cap.) Deuteronomy, the fifth book of the Torah

dever — an epidemic causing the sudden death of animals

din — strict justice; law

Dor Haflagah — Generation of the Dispersion

dudaim — a type of flower

E-F

eglah arufah — an axed heifer, brought by the elders of a city when a person was killed on the outskirts of the city

eidos — testimonials; mitvos which commemorate a specific event or concept

ein mazal l'Yisrael — the concept that *mazal* (the constellations) do not exert control over the Jewish nation *emes* — truth

Eretz Yisrael — the Land of Israel

eruv, eruvin — lit., to combine; to mix together; usually refers to a the halachic procedures allowing one to carry between domains on the Sabbath, to prepare for the Sabbath on a Festival, or to walk beyond the 2,000-cubit limit generally applied on the Sabbath

G

gedi — a kid; a young goat

gefen — a grape vine

gematria — numerical value

Gemilus Chassadim — acts of loving-kindness

Geonim — post-Tamudic sages;

gevurah — strength

gid hanasheh — sinew of the hip socket

gilah — joy

h

haftarah — the selection from the Prophets read following the Torah reading on the Sabbath, Festivals, and fast days

HaKadosh Baruch Hu — the Holy One, blessed be He; Hashem

Halachah L'Moshe MiSinai — specific laws taught to Moses at Mt. Sinai and transmitted orally

halachah — Torah law and practice

Hallel — a thanksgiving prayer comprised of selected Psalms, recited on Rosh Chodesh and most festivals

hilchos — the laws of ...

I-J

Ikvesa D'Meshicha — the period leading to Mashiach's arrival

iro — a type of donkey

k

kaballah — (literally) to take; the Torah's esoteric teachings

kavannah, pl. *kavannos* — intention(s), esp. when reciting a prayer or performing a mitzvah

kedeishah — a woman of ill repute

Kedushah — holiness

keresh, kerashim — board(s) of the Tabernacle

Kerias Yam Suf — the Splitting of the Sea of Reeds

kesher, kesharim — connection(s); bond(s)

keshes — a rainbow

kesones passim — a fine woolen tunic

Kiddush Hashem — sanctifying Hashem's Name

Kiddush Levanah — Sanctification of the Moon
kila'im — forbidden mixtures of crops or fabrics; using different animals together
Kinnos — elegies read on the Ninth of Av
Klal Yisrael — the Jewish nation
Kohen Gadol — High Priest
Kohen, Kohanim — a priest; members of the priestly caste
Korban Pesach — the Passover Offering
korban, korbanos — sacrificial offering(s)
Krias HaTorah — the Torah Reading

L

Lashon HaKodesh — lit., the holy language; the Hebrew of the Bible
Leil Shimurim — a night of watching or anticipation (the eve of the 15th of Nissan)
Luchos — The Tablets of the Ten Commandments

M

Ma'asei Avos Siman L'Banim — all events that occurred to the forefathers are portents for their descendants
Maariv — the evening prayer service
Mabul — the Biblical Flood at the time of Noach
machatzis hashekel — a half-shekel
machshavah — thought
Malchiyos — Kingship; the section of the Rosh HaShahnah *Mussaf* service that speaks of God's Kingship over the universe
mar — bitter
maror — bitter herbs used at the Passover Seder
Mashiach — the Messiah
Mattan Torah — the Giving of the Torah at Sinai
mazal, mazalos — constellation(s); also, fortune
Me'ein Olam Haba — a semblance of the World to Come (the Sabbath)
mekabel — to accept; to be the beneficiary
melachah — labor, esp. one of the labors prohibited on the Sabbath
Meor HaTorah — the light of the Torah
meraglim — spies; (cap.) the Spies who were sent into Israel by Moshe Rabbeinu
mes mitzvah — a corpse that has no one to tend to its burial (also used colloquially to refer to a topic of study which is often ignored or a law whose observance has been largely abandoned)
mesirus nefesh — selfless devotion, to the extent that one is willing to give his or her life to sanctify Hashem's Name
mikveh — a ritual bath
Minchah — a meal-offering; the afternoon prayer service
Mishkan — the Tabernacle
Mishneh Torah — repetition (Review) of the Torah; Sefer Devarim (Deuteronomy); Maimonides' halachic code

mishpatim — ordinances; the laws of the Torah that are also logical

mitzvah, mitzos — commandment(s)

mo'ed — a festival

moser nefesh — self-sacrificing

Mussaf(im) — sacrificial offering(s) for the Sabbath, Rosh Chodesh and festivals; a special prayer recited on those days

mussar — reprimand; ethical teachings

N

navi — prophet

nes, nissim — miracle(s)

neshamah — the soul

nesinah — to give; a gift

netilas yadayim — washing the hands; the rule that one must wash hands following certain activities, and before eating bread or touching sanctified foods

niftar — to pass away; a person who has passed away

Nissuch Hamayim — the water libation during the Succos festival

noseh ba'ol im chaveiro — sharing the burden of others

O

odem — a red gemstone, one of the stones on the Kohen Gadol's Breastplate

olah — an offering that is completely burned on the Altar

Olam HaBa — the World to Come

Olam HaZeh — the physical, lower world

olim — people called to the Torah during prayer services

P

Parah Adumah — Red Calf, used as part of the process of purifying those who contracted impurity from a corpse

parashah, parashiyos — Torah portion(s); parchment inscribed with prayers and inserted into tefillin

pitda — a green gemstone; one of the stones on the Kohen Gadol's Breastplate

piyyut — liturgical poem

R

rachamim — mercy

re'iyah — seeing; the offering brought when one visited the Temple for the three Pilgrimage Festivals

Rosh Chodesh — the start of the new month. When Rosh Chodesh has two days, the first day is actually the last day of the preceding month.

ruach — spirit

Ruach HaKodesh — Divine inspiration; Divine Spirit

S

sa'ir — a mature he-goat

sapir — sapphire, one of the stones on the Kohen Gadol's Breastplate

Sefer HaYetzirah — the Book of Creation

Sefiras Ha'omer — Counting of the Omer

Sefiros — emanations of God's holiness

Shalheves Kah — "the flame of God"

shaliach tzibbur — prayer leader

Shechinah — God's Presence

shefer — beauty

sheker — falsehood

Shema Yisrael, Hashem Elokeinu Hashem Echad — Hear, O Israel, the Lord Our God is the One and Only (primary expression of faith)

shemiyah — hearing

Shemoneh Esrei — lit. "eighteen"; the *Amidah*, the core prayer.

shevet, shevatim — tribe(s)

shevo — a grayish, dark-blue gemstone, one of the stones on the Kohen Gadol's Breastplate

shirayim — food of which a righteous person has partaken

shittim — acacia trees

shiurim — lectures, classes; measurements

shofaros — shofar blasts;

shofet, shoftim — a judge; (cap.) the Biblical Book of Judges

simchah — happiness, joy; a joyous occasion

soreika — a type of grapevine

T

talmid(ei) chacham(im) — an accomplished Torah scholar(s)

techeiles — a unique blue dye; wool dyed with this dye; the blue thread of *tzitzis*

tefillah — prayer

Tefillas — lit., prayer of; the text of a specific prayer service

temarim — dates

temurah — lit. exchange; a animal declared to be a substitute for a consecrated animal. Both the original animal and the substitute are considered sanctified

teshuvah — repentance

Tiferes Yisrael — the Splendor of Israel; the Shechinah; a commentary on the Mishnah

tiferes — splendor

Tochachah — Admonishment

Torah Sheb'al Peh — the Oral Torah

Torah Shebichsav — the Written Torah

tumah — spiritual impurity

Tzaddik Yesod Olam — the Righteous One Who is the foundation of the universe

tzedakah — charity

tzedek — justice

Tzidduk Hadin — Acceptance of (Divine) Judgment

Tzirufei Shemios — letter configurations of the Divine Name

U

Unesaneh Tokef — a prayer recited on the Days of Awe, vividly describing God's judgement on these days

Urim v'Tumim — the slip with the Ineffable Name of God inscribed on it, which was inserted into the Kohen Gadol's Breastplate

V-W-X

Vayehi Bachatzi Haleiylah — It happened at Midnight (liturgical poem recited at the Passover seder)

Y

Ya'aleh Veyavo — a supplicatory paragraph inserted into the Amidah and Grace After Meals on Rosh Chodesh and most festivals

yahalom — a diamond, one of the stones on the Kohen Gadol's Breastplate

yahrzeit — anniversary of a death

yahsfeh — a multicolored stone, one of the stones in the Kohen Gadol's Breastplate

yedid, yedidim — beloved

yedidus — the act of cherishing

yemei hara'ah — the bad days

yerios — the fabric coverings of the Tabernacle

yetzer hara — evil inclination

Yichud Hashem — recognition of Hashem's sole control of the world

yirah — awe of Hashem

yom echad — the first day of Creation; "the day of the One and Only"

Yom HaZikaron — Day of Remembrance; Rosh Hashanah

Yom Kippur Kattan — a "miniature" Day of Atonement

yom sh'lishi — the third day

yom sheini — the second day

Yovel — the Jubilee year

Z

zechus — merit

zechusim gedolim — great merits

zichronos — remembrance; memories; the section of the Rosh Hashahnah *Mussaf* service that speaks of God's remembering people and events

zivah — forms of bodily emission that effect ritual impurity